Subordination and Defeat

An Evolutionary Approach to Mood Disorders and Their Therapy

Subordination and Defeat

An Evolutionary Approach to Mood Disorders and Their Therapy

Edited by

Leon Sloman
Centre for Drug Addiction and Mental Health, Toronto

Paul Gilbert
Kingsway Hospital, Derby, UK

LAWRENCE ERLBAUM ASSOCIATES, PUBLISHERS
2000 Mahwah, New Jersey London

Lawrence Erlbaum Associates, Inc., Publishers
10 Industrial Avenue
Mahwah, NJ 07430

Cover design by Gary Hasey

Library of Congress Cataloging-in-Publication Data

Subordination and defeat : an evolutionary approach to mood disorders and their therapy / edited by Leon Sloman, Paul Gilbert.
p. cm.
Includes bibliographical references and index.
ISBN 0-8058-3298-X
1. Affective disorders. 2. Depression, Mental. I. Sloman, Leon. II. Gilbert, Paul.
RC537 .S89 2000
616.85'27—dc21 99-046620
CIP

Books published by Lawrence Erlbaum Associates are printed on acid-free paper, and their bindings are chosen for strength and durability.

Printed in the United States of America
10 9 8 7 6 5 4 3 2 1

Contents

Preface vii

Introduction ix

Part I: Subordination Strategies and Depression

1 Varieties of Submissive Behavior as Forms of Social Defense: Their Evolution and Role in Depression 3
Paul Gilbert

2 How the Involuntary Defeat Strategy Relates to Depression 47
Leon Sloman

Part II: Biological Correlates of Subordination and Depression

3 Dysthymic Disorder, Regulation–Dysregulation Theory, CNS Blood Flow, and CNS Metabolism 71
Michael McGuire, Fawzy Fawzy, James Spar, and Alfonso Troisi

4 Major Depression and the Involuntary Defeat Strategy: Biological Correlates 95
Robert D. Levitan, Gary Hasey, and Leon Sloman

Part III: Psychosocial Dimensions of the Involuntary Defeat Strategy

5 The Involuntary Defeat Strategy and Discrete Emotions Theory 121
Glenn E. Weisfeld and Craig A. Wendorf

6 Social Comparison Processes Among Depressed Individuals: Evidence for the Evolutionary Perspective on Involuntary Subordinate Strategies? 147
Bram P. Buunk and Veerle Brenninkmeyer

7 Subordination, Self-Esteem, and Depression 165
John Price

Part IV: Psychotherapeutic Approaches

8 A Cognitive Behavioral Perspective on the Involuntary Defeat Strategy 181
Stephen R. Swallow

9 Social Competition and Attachment 199
Leon Sloman and Leslie Atkinson

10 Concluding Comments 215
Leon Sloman and Paul Gilbert

Author Index 219

Subject Index 235

Preface

Most people now accept that huan beings are the product of millions of years of mammalian evolution and, more recently, primate evolution. This book explores the implications of our evolutionary history for theories and therapies of depression. In particular, the focus is on how social conflict has shaped various behavioral and psychophysiological systems. Special attention is given to the evolved mechanisms for dealing with social defeat and subordination in both animals and humans. By linking human depression to the activation of ancient psychobiological progaras for deling with social conflict, we are able to understand the function of depression within groups, family systems, and between individuals and begin to distinguish depressions that may have adaptive functions from those that are the result of maladaptive feedback systems. We hope this book will help illuminate old problems in new ways, link a common disabling condition to evolved mental mechanisms, and point to potential new approaches to prevention and intervention.

ACKNOWLEDGMENTS

In an endeavor such as this one, we have obviously been aided by those close to us. We thank our wives, Valerie (for Leon) and Jean (for Paul), for providing invaluable support, understanding, and feedback. Daniel (Leon's son) deserves special attention for his much-appreciated help with figures and diagrams, and Gary Hasey for his imaginative cover design. We would also like to thank various friends and colleagues who have listened, supported, criticized, and inspired us through the ups and downs of manuscript preparation. Of course, no book such as this would even be possible without the insights and sharing that numerous patients have offered, and it is in the spirit that these kinds of theoretical developments may help to shed light on new therapies that we offer this book. Finally, we thank our contributors for their extraordinary patience and preparedness to make frequent changes. To each and all we offer our heartfelt thanks.

Introduction

EVOLUTIONARY PERSPECTIVES

Evolutionary and ethological approaches to the study of human psychology begin with the premise that humans evolved from primates, which in turn evolved from earlier mammals and reptiles. This journey has taken place over many millions of years of phylogenetic adaptation and change. The sculptress of change has been a continuing process of selection— the driving force of evolution. Animals that have traits that offer advantage in the struggle for survival and reproduction pass their genes for those traits on to their offspring. It is now commonly agreed that a salient arena of selection takes places in the context of conspecific competition. Be it for food, territory access to breeding partners or (as in humans) prestige and social approval, when these resources are in short supply or limited, those who are able to outmaneuver, overpower, or entice resources from others, will do better than those who cannot do these things. To put this another way, as human psychology evolved, various strategies developed that provided the means to recognize and cope with conflicts of interest between conspecifics.

This book explores the implications of this historical approach. Because in any conflict situation there will often be a winner and a loser, a central question arises: Which strategies have evolved to enable the one who is losing to decide when to try harder and when to accept the inevitability of defeat and adjust one's behavior accordingly? Generally, fighting or struggling on, when the odds against one are overwhelming, is maladaptive. This is because the loser wastes energy in a fruitless struggle and may even risk serious injury. Sometimes it is better to run away and fight another day; sometimes it is better to turn one's potential competitor into an ally. The contributors this volume all address this salient issue and explore how the various strategies for dealing with losing and failing can become a source for psychopathology, especially mood disorders.

DOMAINS OF CONFLICT

Although dominance and subordination are often considered to be related to formal social hierarchies, this is too narrow a focus. A social hierarchy grows out of the results of past conflicts and submissive and dominant enactments. Indeed, social hierarchies are reflections of outcomes of conflicts: Those at the top have usually escalated and won, whereas those at the bottom have usually been outmaneuvered, overwhelmed, lost, and have had to de-escalate. Moreover, we suggest that the strategies for escalation (trying harder) and de-escalation (submitting, giving up) can be activated to a greater or lesser degree in a variety of different types of relationships. Indeed, evolution, working over many millions of years, has given rise to a vast array of different types of relationships; for example, alliance formation (friends and in-groups), care of offspring (attachment and parental investment), same-sex rivalries, sibling alliances and rivalries, and so forth. Conflicts of interest, which can fuel various negative feelings and behaviors, can arise in any of these social relationships. Indeed, it is now recognized that the most common conflicts occur over status and rank (Archer, 1988; Barkow, 1989; Caryl, 1988; Daly & Wilson, 1994; Gilbert, 1992; Price & Sloman, 1987); the amount and availability of care and affection bestowed on offspring (Trivers, 1985); defection of allies and nonreciprocation (de Waal, 1989; Trivers, 1985); defection of, and cheating by, sexual partners (Wilson & Daly, 1992); exclusion and ostracism from groups (Baumeister & Leary, 1995); and conflicts with other groups (Barkow, 1989; van der Dennen, 1986).

Hence, conflicts of interest between individuals operate in a variety of domains. Sometimes an individual's efforts to raise his or her status (control over others and resources) may or may not be successful: An individual many want more help, support, or approval from allies, friends, or lovers than others are willing to offer; a child may want more care or freedom than a parent is willing to give. The domain specificity of the conflict will obviously have a bearing on how the individual perceives the costs of losing and copes with losing the conflict. For example, children in conflict with parents may come to accept that they cannot have their own way and thus "submit" to the parents' authority; or they may submit but feel deeply resentful and continually try to win by having tantrums, attempting to induce guilt, and so forth. Indeed, throughout this book various authors explore how the domain of conflict, whether it is in the context of attachment, friends, or with strangers, has a bearing on how losing is managed and becomes expressed. A common theme that many authors take up is the issue of acceptance of losing, without either having strong, perhaps unexpressed, wishes to retaliate on the one hand, or seeing oneself as having fallen in status—an inferior loser—on the other.

INVOLUNTARY SUBORDINATE STRATEGIES

Clearly, in many human contexts people may choose to be submissive; they realize that it is advantageous to comply with others and not contest the allocation of resources. The benefits outweigh the costs. Such submissive behavior need not be associated with a lack of confidence. However, in many cases of psychopathology this is not the case. People can have strong desires to obtain more status, sex, care, love, and support than they are currently receiving, but they are losing in the battle to bring such things about. In this context, involuntary subordinate strategies can be activated. In other cases, they might have an excellent chance of obtaining what they want if they are able to assert themselves, but are prevented from doing so by overly strong subordinate strategies, often mediated by social anxiety, which contribute to their submissive behavior.

The term *involuntary* is used by many authors in this volume. This refers to a biologically based strategy that is automatically triggered in specific situations. For example, if a lover suddenly defects to another person, this loss may produce major changes in the loser's state of mind, making the person jealous, anxious, and depressed. Clearly, the person has no wish to be jealous, anxious, or depressed; rather he or she may find there is little control over this state of mind. Similarly in shame, a person may not wish to blush, or drop their gaze, or to feel impelled to run away and hide, but these responses seem to be triggered automatically. To give one more example, losing at a competitive sport might lead to anger, dysphoria, and fatigue even though the person may wish to stay in a confident and energetic state of mind and wish he or she was not so badly affected by the loss. Hence, when a state of mind, with its accompanying affects, cognitions, and behaviors, is triggered automatically, even against a person's conscious wishes, we suggest that this is an involuntary change in state triggered by the activation of evolved strategies.

So in general, we see the evolution of strategies to cope with losing as salient components of human psychology. These strategies are especially prominent in states of psychopathology. The various contributors in this volume address these issues and highlight how those strategies that evolved to cope with losing can intensify and interact with various other strategies such as those for affiliation and attachment.

OVERVIEW

This volume is divided into four parts. Part I, Subordinate Strategies and Depression, covers basic theory. In chapter 1, Gilbert outlines the varieties of submissive behavior and their evolved functions. Special attention is given to the increasing complexity of these strategies in primates. The menu of such strategies can include flight, arrested flight, defensive aggression, reverted escape, and infantile appeals. In chapter 2, Sloman explores how the involuntary defeat strategy (IDS) is involved in various forms of psychopathology. The chapter explores how the involuntary subordinate strategies have impacts on cognitions, such as self-perceptions of inferiority, worthlessness, and inadequacy; emotions, such as feelings of hopelessness, anxiety, and anger; behavior, such as social withdrawal and body postures; and physical states such as fatigue and sleep disturbance.

Part II, Biological Correlates of Subordination and Depression, explores the role of brain neurotransmitters. In chapter 3, McGuire, Fawzy, Spar, and Troisi present research findings from studies of adult male vervet monkeys and patients with depressive illness, in particular a group with dysthymic disorder. In chapter 4, Levitan, Hasey and Sloman examine the biological changes in depression and consider how these changes could originally have been the mediators for adaptation to agonistic encounters. The biological mediators of the IDS are considered.

Part III, Psychosocial Dimensions of the Involuntary Defeat Strategy, begins with chapter 5, in which Weisfeld and Wendorf consider the mechanisms of dominance and subordination in relation to human behavior with special reference to shame and pride and the affective components of gains and involuntary losses of status. In chapter 6, Buunk and Brenninkmeyer note the central importance of social comparison as a regulator of subordinate behavior and its links with psychopathology, especially depression. In chapter 7, Price responds to questions posed by Wright (1994), who said "There is much talk about boosting 'self-esteem', but little understanding of what self-esteem is, what it's for, or what it does" (p. 83). Price addresses these issues by focusing on the evolutionary function of variations in self-esteem.

Part IV, Psychotherapeutic Approaches, explores what the evolutionary model means for treatment. In chapter 8, Swallow gives consideration to how techniques developed from cognitive therapy approaches can be used to moderate the effects of maladaptive subordinate strategies. In chapter 9, Sloman and Atkinson consider how involuntary subordination can be understood as one of an indeterminate number of behavioral-motivational control systems in human beings, comparable to the attachment system as described in Bowlby's comprehensive model of ethological-evolutionary control systems. They also explore the interaction between mechanisms for the de-escalation of conflicts and attachment and affiliative behavior.

The study of the biopsychosocial interactions of conflict coping strategies is in its infancy. This volume is designed to introduce the reader to what is currently known, what is not known and what urgently needs to be researched. There is little doubt that losing conflicts can be biologically powerful and disregulating. Moreover, many of the biological differences between those who suffer mental health problems and those who do not may be related to the fact that people with mental health problems have been subject to a variety of conflicts from which they were unable to escape or were unable to control. We believe that the contextualization of mental disorder in general and depression in particular in an evolutionary framework opens up the possibility of new insights and more adequate theories and points toward promising research avenues in the effort to understand these common, distressing states of mind.

REFERENCES

Archer, J. (1988). *The behavioral biology of aggression*. Cambridge, UK: Cambridge University Press.

Barkow, J. H. (1989). *Darwin, sex and status: Biological approaches to mind and culture*. Toronto: University of Toronto Press.

Baumeister, R. F., & Leary, M. R. (1995). The need to belong: Desire for interpersonal attachments as a fundamental human motivation. *Psychological Bulletin*, *117*, 497–29.

Caryl, P. G. (1988). Escalated fighting and the war of nerves: Games theory and animal combat. In P. H. Bateson & P. H. Klopfer (Eds.), *Perspectives in ethology: Advantages of diversity* (Vol. 4, pp. 199–224). New York: Plenum Press.

Daly, M., & Wilson, M. (1994). Evolutionary psychology of male violence. In J. Archer (Ed.), *Male violence* (pp. 253–288). London: Routledge.

de Waal, F. M. B. (1989). *Peacemaking among primates*. Harmondsworth: Penguin.

Gilbert, P. (1992). *Depression: The evolution of powerlessness*. Hove: Lawrence Erlbaum Associates.

Price, J. S., & Sloman, L. (1987). Depression as yielding behavior: An animal model based on Schjelderupp-Ebbe's pecking order. *Ethology and Sociobiology*, *8*, 85S–98S.

Trivers, R. (1985). *Social evolution*. Menlo Park, CA: Benjamin/Cummings.

van der Dennen, J. M. G. (1986). Ethnocentricism and in-group/out-group differentiation. A review and interpretation of the literature. In V. Reynolds, V. Falger, & I. Vine (Eds.), *The sociobiology of ethnocentricism: Evolutionary dimensions of xenophobia, discrimination, racism and nationalism* (pp. 1–47). London: Croom Helm.

Wilson, M., & Daly, M. (1992). The man who mistook his wife for a chattel. In J. H. Barkow, L. Cosmides, & J. Tooby (Eds.), *The adapted mind: Evolutionary psychology and the generation of culture* (pp. 289–322). New York: Oxford University Press.

Wright, R. (1994). *The moral animal: Why we are the way we are*. London: Little, Brown & Co.

PART I

Subordination Strategies and Depression

CHAPTER ONE

Varieties of Submissive Behavior as Forms of Social Defense: Their Evolution and Role in Depression

PAUL GILBERT
Kingsway Hospital, Derby, UK

The origins of submissive behaviors can be traced back to the reptiles (MacLean, 1990) and all social animals are capable of expressing them, including humans (Buss & Craik, 1986). However, there are many varieties of submissive behavior, some of which are affiliative, whereas others are not. Given the variety and complexity of submissive behavior, this chapter (a) explores the evolved functions of submissive behavior; (b) places submissive behavior in the context of social defensive strategies; (c) outlines variations of submissive behavior in terms of flight, arrested flight, defeat, reverted escape, infantile appeals, and affiliative submission; and (d) explores the role of submissive behaviors in psychopathology with a special focus on depression.

Within sociology, anthropology (e.g., Clark, 1990; Kemper, 1990; Scott, 1990), and gender studies (Radtke & Stam, 1994), issues of social power, social control, and submissiveness have been central areas of study. These social dynamics have been shown to affect self-identities, values, and social behaviors. In the field of psychopathology, problems in being able to act assertively, standing up for one's rights, making demands on others, or behaving overly submissively have long been associated with a variety of psychological problems, especially depression and social anxiety (e.g., Arrindell et al., 1990; Birtchnell, 1993; Gilbert, 1992; Horowitz & Vitkus, 1986; Kiesler, 1983; Wagner, Kiesler & Schmidt, 1995). However, the variety and complexity of submissive behavior has rarely been studied. In this chapter, I suggest that insight into the pathogenic aspects of social power and submissive behavior can be gleaned from an evolutionary analysis of the functions of submissive behaviors and their social contexts. I argue that although some submissive behaviors are related to psychopathology, others are not.

In fact, the origins of submissive behavior go back hundreds of millions of years. Indeed, many of the earliest forms of social behavior such as courting, sexual advertising, mating, threatening, harassing, territorial defense, ritual threat displays, and submission are to be found in the modern-day descendants of our early ancestors, the reptiles (MacLean, 1990). Submissive behaviors evolved as fundamental social behaviors that facilitated control over aggression and social cohesion. As MacLean (1990) pointed out,

> Ethologists have made it popularly known . . . that a passive response (a submissive display) to an aggressive display may make it possible under most circumstances to avoid unnecessary, and sometimes mortal, conflict. Hence it could be argued that the *submissive display is the most important of all displays* because without it numerous individuals might not survive. (italics added, p. 235).

Submissive behaviors and de-escalating of conflict strategies can also aid in the formation and maintenance of alliances (de Waal, 1996). Indeed, so important are submissive behaviors that over millions of years there has been a gradually increasing complexity to their form, expression, and use.

SOCIAL THREATS AND DE-ESCALATING BEHAVIORS

Submissive behaviors can be viewed as stable strategies that can be expressed in a variety of ways, but their original purpose was as defenses against conspecific aggression. In most mammals, reproductive success depends on social success in pursuing various social goals and roles. These include outcompeting others, attracting mates, caring for offspring, and forming helpful alliances[1] (Buss, 1991, 1995; Gilbert, 1989, 1995). The most common threats to these goals are from conspecifics (Bailey, 1987; Gardner, 1988; Gilbert, 1989, 1993; MacLean, 1990; Trivers, 1985). Such threats involve direct down-hierarchy attacks (Archer, 1988; Caryl, 1988; Price, 1972, 1988; Price & Sloman, 1987), loss of status and social

---

[1] It is, of course, not necessary for individuals to know they are pursuing biosocial goals to try to maximize their fitness. In the past, fitness would have followed if animals felt sufficiently rewarded by their acquisitions and pained by their loss. Today, the pursuit of fitness-maximizing resources may not be translated into fitness as such (e.g., in pursuing careers people limit the size of their families or have none at all). Fitness was never a motivated reward in itself—only the things that led to it were. And as noted later, the rewards were often in the form of social signals (e.g., signals of status, help from allies, and, in humans, love and affection). Indeed, many of our emotions seem set up to help us along paths toward goals that in the past increased fitness. Thus, we feel good when we are loved, respected, wanted, and chosen; we feel bad when we are rejected, marginalized, lose status, and are not chosen. In other words, the rewards of social success are the motivators, not fitness (Nesse, 1990).

standing (Barkow, 1980, 1989; Daly & Wilson, 1994; Gilbert, 1992; Gilbert & McGuire, 1998), disruptions of attachment and separation from attachment objects (Bowlby, 1969, 1973), defection of allies and deception (de Waal, 1989; Trivers, 1985), losing access to sexual partners including defection of and cheating by sexual partners (Buss & Malamuth, 1996; Wilson & Daly, 1992), exclusion from groups and ostracism (Baumeister & Leary, 1995), and threats from other groups (Barkow, 1989; van der Dennen, 1986).

So, in pursuing any biosocial goal and gaining access to resources (e.g., territories, sexual opportunities, or making alliances), an animal will encounter others who will be pursing the same goals and must deal with competitors. In many contexts animals need to work out whether it is worth fighting or threatening others (or increasing efforts) to secure goals or whether it is better to give up, submit, escape, and generally decrease efforts and avoid escalating conflicts or effort. Evolution theorists have used game theory to explore the question of possible strategies relating to conflict escalation and de-escalation. The most basic strategies for conflict negotiation have been labeled *hawk or dove* (Caryl, 1988; Cronin, 1991; Krebs & Davies, 1993; Maynard Smith, 1982). Hawks contest all resources to the death but risk serious injury, whereas doves display but do not fight and risk injury. Generally, dove strategies are expressed as submissive *de-escalation strategies.* A dove's first priority is to avoid serious injury by, for example, running away, breaking contact, backing down, and so on, and not escalating the conflict. Such behaviors act to limit fighting and risk of harm.

Without an innate preparedness for weaker animals to inhibit their fighting behavior in conflict situations, fighting would be constant. This would be damaging, wasteful, and with risks of injury (Archer, 1988; Caryl, 1988; Trivers, 1985) and loss of alliances (de Waal, 1996). Therefore, the most stable (competitive) strategies turn out to be a mixture of both hawk and dove (Caryl, 1988; Cronin, 1991; Krebs & Davies, 1993) such that any one individual must (a) have the potential to escalate or de-escalate as conditions change, and (b) have internal assessment mechanisms for working out when to do which. Such strategies evolved to be sensitive to social contexts. In other words, each individual will fight harder (hawk) in some contexts, but submit or run away in others (dove). Some key questions therefore include: What triggers the activation of hawk (escalating) or dove (de-escalating) strategies? Once triggered, how do they present and show themselves in behavior? How might social rank and de-escalation relate to depression and other psychopathologies and the degree of individual variation within populations (i.e., personality differences in the preparedness to attack or submit)?

Mind Games

Before moving on to consider these questions, one further point should be made about social strategies. Social strategies work by affecting the psychobiological state (and behavior) of both the actor and the one(s) to whom it is directed. So dove strategies can only work if they either remove the animal from the danger or if that is not possible, they (a) influence the state of mind of the (potential) submitter to make him or her try to reduce conflict and adopt submissive postures, and (b) these postures cause some changes in the state of mind of the potential attackers and competitors so that they limit their attacks to relatively nondamaging threats (Keltner & Harker, 1998). Submissive strategies are therefore useless in avoiding predators. In mammals, the most primitive forms of dove strategies are probably fear motivated, meaning we should label them as a *fear dove* strategy.

TRIGGERS OF SUBMISSIVE BEHAVIOR

Social Comparison

In the natural environment, hawk–dove strategies require abilities to (a) evaluate the value of a resource (and increase fighting as resource value increases), and (b) evaluate the chances of winning, that is, whether one is weaker or stronger than the opponent. This is *social comparison,* one of the oldest social evaluative competencies (Buunk & Brenninkmeyer, chap. 6, this volume; Gilbert, Price, & Allan, 1995). Without an ability to judge if one is stronger or weaker than a potential opponent, an animal could take on fights with superior opponents, lose, and be seriously injured. It might also fail to challenge for resources in situations where it could win (Parker, 1974). There is now evidence from human research that these types of judgments (e.g., is this person a threat to me or not? Is he or she superior or weaker than self?) are made very rapidly (Kalma, 1991). Interestingly, nonhuman primate juveniles who are impulsive and do not control their agonism (possibly due to low serotonin, 5-HT) tend to pick fights with more powerful others and have a high mortality rate (Higley et al., 1996). So in general the one who sees itself as weaker is oriented to avoid initiating fights with more powerful others and to de-escalate actual conflict or attack by sending nonaggressive signals; that is, use a fear dove strategy (Archer, 1988; Caryl, 1988). Hence, a trigger for fear-based submissive strategies depends on certain kinds of evaluation (e.g., unfavorable social comparison).

Of course, in socially complex animals there are many other constraints on both aggression and submitting (e.g., fight harder if there is a probability of allies coming to one's aid, de-escalate if there is a possibility of forming an alliance with the more powerful other, or reduce aggression if there is concern not to damage the individual one is in conflict with; de Waal, 1996). In humans social comparisons can be used in a complex array of social contexts (e.g., between siblings, enemies, friends, and groups; Buunk & Brenninkmeyer, this volume; Gilbert et al., 1995; Sloman, chap. 2, this volume; Swallow, chap. 8, this volume).

However, for the moment I explore the simplified case of contest-competitive strategies involving either (a) *escalating*—challenging, attacking, or threatening—that increases the chances of gaining or maintaining control over resources but risks injury (hawk), or (b) *de-escalating*—retreating, avoiding, or backing down from challenges—that reduces the risk of injury but also reduces the control over resources (dove).

Dominance or Subordinate Hierarchies?

Submissive behaviors are of central importance in social groups where the potential threat from conspecifics needs to be known and established. This working out of who can threaten whom and who submits to whom gives rise to social hierarchies, the type of which depends on the species. Those who are territorial have territorial hierarchies in which losers simply leave the territory, thus ending contact between loser and winner. However, there are disadvantages to this strategy (e.g., giving up resources, predator pressure, and lack of opportunities for breeding). Group living solves both problems. Subordinates are offered some protection from predators and although a position among the most subordinate in a group may offer fewer reproductive chances than a dominant position, their chances are greater than they would be in isolation (Dunbar, 1988; Trivers, 1985). Once in a group, the relative control over and access to resources is related to social rank. However, dominance or high rank is not a goal in itself; only the things (e.g., access to resources) that go with it are, together with the affective states associated with dominance or winning (M. McGuire, personal communication, May 1996). Moreover, dominance and subordination describe relationships rather than individuals. When psychologists talk about a dominant personality or dominant style there is no guarantee that these actually translate into dominance (i.e., increased access to resources), and they might, for example, result in rejection. It may be more accurate therefore to speak of types of competitiveness (Gilbert, 1989). Second, although we often talk about dominance hierarchies, it might be more revealing and accurate to speak of subordinate hierarchies. In fact, it is not only aggression that determines a dominance hierarchy, but also the subordinate behaviors that are elicited. Bernstein (1980) put it this way:

> A dominance relationship between two individuals is inferred not because one or both "assert" their dominance but because one readily submits. If, and only if, the subordinate recognizes the relationship, or "predicts" the outcome of an agonistic encounter by immediately showing submission, can we assume that a dominance relationship exists. . . . It is . . . the timing and sequencing of submissive signals in an interaction that allows us to infer the existence of a dominance relationship between two individuals.
>
> It is only the submission of subordinates that allows us to argue that dominance may function to partition resources or reduce fighting. (pp. 80–81)

Chance and Jolly (1970) and Chance (1984, 1988) also noted that it is in the attention structure (the attention subordinates pay to certain individuals) that a rank hierarchy can be observed. For these reasons it is useful to focus on the many strategies subordinates can use to cope with having to live with threatening or more powerful or competent others. These strategies range from straightforward escape to making them friends and allies.

VARIETIES OF SUBMISSIVE STRATEGIES

The term *strategies* can have two meanings (Krebs & Davies, 1993). The first refers to typical species behaviors; for example, the breeding strategies of turtles are different than those of primates, or the breeding strategies of high-ranking animals are different than those of low-ranking animals (Dunbar, 1988). A second meaning refers to internal psychobiological response patterns that are typically aroused to specific stimuli. So, for example, *defensive strategies* refer to psychobiological response patterns that are triggered by certain threat signals and their interpretation, (Gilbert, 1984, 1992). Strategies follow an "If A do B" rule (Krebs & Davies, 1993; Trivers, 1985) and are part of a menu of innate potential responses (e.g., fight–flight; Gilbert, 1993; Marks, 1987). For example, to a specific signal the strategies might be: if stimuli indicate a large predator, run; if a possible mate, engage courting; if a dominant threat, submit; if a subordinate challenger, threaten it. Each of these strategies varies in its patterns of psychobiological activation. Strategies reflect various options that are coded in gene-neural pathways. An activated defensive strategy often has the power to override conscious wishes. For example, although someone may deeply wish to stand up to a bully at work and may plan what to say, when in the presence of the bully they find themselves anxious, their mind blank, and experiencing great urges to run away. This is not to say that personal experiences of strategies are inflexible and cannot be affected by development, cultural rules, or therapy. It is just to make the point that defensive strategies operate by generating powerful psychobiological responses that often impel actions (e.g., fight / flight / submit) and can be difficult to consciously control. In this sense they are often *involuntary* (Sloman, chap. 2, this volume)

In general, defensive submissive strategies orient an individual to adopt certain behaviors that include primarily: (a) vigilance to social threats (from social dominants), (b) moderate or curtail approach to resources (e.g., sex or food), to avoid eliciting dominant attacks, and (c) avoidance of escalating conflicts into injurious fights by submitting quickly. However, different species have evolved a variety of such submissive strategies. For example, whereas some species (e.g., primates) have very elaborate ways of coping with social conflicts and threats, the strategies of others (e.g., birds and rodents) are less complex. The degree of elaboration of submissive behavior depends on whether a species is group living or territorial and its social ecology (Krebs & Davies, 1993).

TABLE 1.1
Varieties of Social Defensive (Submissive) Strategies

Name	*Function*
1. Escape	Remove self from the vicinity of the threat. When away there are no visual or other cues activating the defense system.
2. Ambivalent	Remain sensitive and open to possibility of switching from one strategy (e.g., flight) to another (e.g., fight).
3. Arrested flight	When escape is not possible, demobilize, engage in cutoff from the environment (to reduce arousal), attempt to hide (e.g., in corners and reduce outputs) and signal no threat to possible dominant(s) or threatening others.
4. Arrested fight	Suppress aggression to higher ranks and avoid instigating or escalating attacks. However, may remain in aggressive states of mind.
5. Loss of control	Demobilize, engage in cutoff from the environment (to reduce arousal). Switch to passive coping strategies. Attempts to hide?
6. Defeat	Leave territory or situation, disengage, and try again elsewhere. If trapped, then (as in arrested flight and arrested fight) behaviorally demobilize, engage in cutoff from the environment (to reduce arousal) and attempt to hide (e.g., in corners) and signal no threat to possible dominants. Need to acclimate to new lower status.
7. Enclosed avoidance	Keep distance from, but remain aware of, source of threat (e.g., dominant).Take what opportunities arise. Do not demobilize but remain aroused and vigilant to possible attacks.
Strategies that involve affiliative elements	
8. Reverted escape	Return to dominant and calm himself or herself down by giving submission signals—elicit reassurance. Allow tension to relax and attention to be directed to other things apart from avoiding attacks from dominant.
9. Infantile	Signal no threat and elicit help and support from others. Reduce risks of fighting and openly contesting.
10. Affiliative	No need to signal any kind of weakness or inability, but can signal strength and ability that is put at the disposal of others (e.g., group or dominant). Benefits include sharing in resources and raising status via the approval given by others.

The following sections explore various options of submissive strategies. An overview of these are given in Table 1.1.

Escape and Flight Strategies

Faced with an aggressive dominant, the most basic and simplest defensive strategy for a loser or less powerful animal is escape behavior, or flight. Escape behavior has been well studied in a variety of species (Marks, 1987), and there are many studies of its neurophysiology (e.g., Gray, 1982, 1987). I do not review this literature here except to say that escape or flight behavior is one of the most primitive defensive behaviors, is used to avoid many types of threat including predators, and is often involved in more complex submissive responses to threats. Gray (1982, 1987) pointed out that stimuli that signal punishment, nonreward, and novelty operate through a behavioral inhibition system that causes an animal to stop, look, and listen and increase arousal. According to the way in which such information is processed and the type of threat encountered, a variety of evolved responses are then possible (e.g., fight or flight, passive avoidance, help seeking; Gilbert, 1989).

Escape behavior need not involve much in the way of social communication because the animal simply removes itself from the threat. In fact, all flight is the antithesis of approach (A. K. Dixon, 1998; A. K. Dixon, Fisch, & McAllister, 1990), although as Gray (1987) pointed out, when flight is toward safety, what the animal flees to has positive rewarding properties. In other words, flight can also be seen as approach behavior to safety stimuli. An example might be a child fleeing back to his or her mother for protection and reassurance after being threatened by a conspecific. In general however, the focus here is flight from rather than flight to.

Once flight has taken place and an animal is no longer within the orbit of a potential dominant or threatening other, it can relax its attention and psychobiology. It has removed itself from the signal(s) that trigger flight and returned to signals (presence of supportive others) that signal safety. This is entirely different from the situation of enclosed avoidance (discussed later). The disadvantage with flight is that the animal has to give up the resource it was pursuing. So although it avoids certain harms, it loses possible control and access to resources. Also, in group living, animals' flight beyond the boundaries of the group may increase predatory threat and, if distance is maintained, may reduce opportunities for mating and alliance formation.

Ambivalent Defensive Strategies

As noted earlier, a flexible strategy of submitting to the stronger and challenging the weaker (Hinde, 1982) is more evolutionarily stable than a rigid one of always attacking or always submitting. However, the flexibility of evolved strategies comes with the cost of conflicts between strategies. This leads to ambivalence, where more than one option is possible and primed. Buck (1988) and A. K. Dixon (1998; A. K. Dixon et al., 1990) noted that some defensive behaviors are highly ambivalent in that the animal can shift between attack–threaten defensive aggression, and flight behaviors—or express elements of each. Moreover, even though some animals may socially withdraw and appear socially avoidant, they can be aggressive to others who approach them. Subordinate animals can be defensively aggressive, attack others lower in the hierarchy if they have been attacked from above, and, as noted in the reverted escape situation (see later), can have tantrums if they are not reassured by a dominant. As Sloman (chap. 2, this volume) points out, some depressed patients oscillate between aggressive and highly avoidant submissive behaviors in a kind of win–lose, either–or way, rather than seeking a compromise or acting assertively.

In fact, some states of psychopathology suggest rapid shifts in attack–threaten and back down–retreat behavior, and in higher primates reassurance seeking. Gilbert (1984) pointed out that defensive behaviors vary as to their strength of activation, but under high arousal they could be analyzed using catastrophe theory. This allows for the exploration of factors that cause rapid switching in behavior (e.g., from attack to flight). (For a review of such models see Barton, 1994.) Even if an individual behaves submissively, he or she can harbor strong attack or revenge fantasies and ideas. Their expression may be inhibited because the person is too fearful of an overpowering escalation or would feel too guilty to actually act on them (Allan & Gilbert, 1997). Hence, in many conflict situations the subordinate must suppress its fight behaviors, and it is appropriate to label this as *arrested* or *blocked fight* (A. K. Dixon, 1998).

Blocked Escape

What happens if escape is blocked or prevented? The main social defensive strategies in territorial species are fight and flight (Hinde, 1982). Birds, for example, often have skirmishes at the boundaries of their territory. If losers are free to fly away there is no need for any further communication between loser and winner and no need for any other defensive strategy. However, in limited territory or where escape (ability to move away) is not possible (called *blocked escape*), a major change in the bird's state has been noted following serious defeat. Schjelderup-Ebbe, who coined the term *pecking order* in the 1930s, described the consequences of losing dominance in farmyard fowl, where escape to a new territory was not possible. Following defeat, the bird's

> behavior becomes entirely changed. Deeply depressed in spirit, humble with dropping wings and head in the dust, it is—at any rate, directly upon being vanquished —overcome with paralysis, although one cannot detect any physical injury. The bird's resistance now seems broken, and in some cases the effects of the psychological condition are so strong that the bird will sooner or later come to grief. (cited in Price & Sloman, 1987, p. 87)

This coming to grief is the result of the animal's change of state, not physical injury. MacLean (1985, 1990) also noted that reptiles who lose rank often lose their bright colors and may die shortly afterward. Von Holst (1986) found that defeated tree shrews could suffer the same fate. Defeat is explored shortly, but the important point is that defeat may not be too much of a problem provided the animal can escape. It is only when escape is blocked that the serious changes of state occur (A. K. Dixon, 1998). Because this state of defeat often follows loss of rank and serious conflicts, Price and Sloman (1987) called it the yielding subroutine of ritual agonistic behavior. The caveat to Price and Sloman's view is that there are probably a number of different yielding subroutines, each of which evolved to cope with different contexts; for example, submissive flight and submissive postures or displays. Another is arrested flight.

Arrested Flight Strategies

A. K. Dixon, Fisch, Huber, and Walser (1989) suggested that blocked escape gives rise to a special type of social defensive behavior called *arrested flight.* In many animals, flight behaviors are commonly activated in subordinates and intruders by threat and attacks by dominant animals. When challenged by more dominant animals (who are aggressive and chase) subordinates are defensively aggressive and flee. Successful flight for the subordinate

> means that the flight-evoking features of the dominant animal are no longer in sight and so its own propensity to flee subsides. This facilitates the resumption of social activities. When escape is prevented, e.g., by lack of an escape route, static or arrested forms of flight appear. The lack of movement serves to reduce the output of signals which would provoke attacks by the opponents, i.e., these elements of blocked escape have low signal output. . . . Furthermore, since the animal cannot reduce the input of flight-evoking signals by escaping, it resorts to cut-off and postures . . . which have the same function. The simplest cut off is to turn the head away from the attacker or cover the eyes and ears. A more subtle form of cut-off is seen in primates, including humans, in that gaze is averted, while the head remains orientated in the general direction of the partner. Such cut-offs are very common in our own behavior and . . . , are very common in the mentally ill. Cut-offs serve to reduce the input of disturbing stimuli usually conducive to flight. (p. 46)

A. K. Dixon et al. (1989) noted that escape behavior is controlled by social status, territorial context, distance from the source of threat, previous experience, and possible escape routes. If an individual cannot get away, reducing inputs (cutoffs) helps to control arousal and sends no-threat signals to conspecifics. In other words, it is important that the animal does not send ambivalent signals to the dominant, but clearly indicates it is not in a state where a fight (a counterattack or resource-acquiring behavior) might be possible. Blocked escape can thus give rise to a behavioral profile of arrested flight (A. K. Dixon, 1998). This involves suppression of explorative behavior (especially approach), submissive or static postures (to reduce outputs), and cutoff (to reduce inputs). Arrested flight in the loser seems to result in the dominant (attacker) losing interest in continuing to attack (and later to stay away and not bother with the loser) by reducing social outputs, social interaction, and signaling "out of action." In enclosed spaces, such animals usually huddle in the corners and rarely venture out (A. K. Dixon, personal communication, June 1994). As MacLean (1990) noted, once an animal goes into these types of states it tends to stay in them for some time.

Arrested Fight Strategies

Almost by definition, a de-escalation strategy should involve aggression suppression. It is generally accepted that on the whole aggression tends to flow down the rank order rather than up it, and it is only when a subordinate judges that it has a chance of winning that it will attack a higher ranking animal. A de-escalating strategy need not mean that the desire to fight is quelled (unless perhaps there is serious demobilization). Rather, submission may be highly ambivalent (Gilbert, 1992). People may recognize that they have to behave submissively (make apologies, give in) to reduce the tension or threats between themselves and a more dominant and powerful other, and feel relief when they succeed, but they may still harbor desires for later revenge. Thus, in some situations subordinate behavior can involve the inhibition of aggression expression but not reduce the motive or desire to attack, challenge, or dominate. Indeed, Allan and Gilbert (1997) found that submissive behavior in depression was significantly associated with angry thoughts and feelings but not aggressive behaviors. In these contexts it might be appropriate to refer to this as *arrested fight*. As noted later (and see Sloman, chap. 2, this volume) arrested fight appears quite common in depression. By keeping aggression primed but not expressed, the subordinate may stay vigilant to opportunities to make a comeback or counterattack. It should also be noted that subordinates are not necessarily nonaggressive, as they can launch attacks on or threaten those even more subordinate than themselves.

Loss of Control Strategies

A research paradigm that is very similar to arrested flight is *learned helplessness* (Peterson, Maier, & Seligman, 1993; Seligman, 1975). This research paradigm has led to the study of the psychobiological effects of lack of control over (e.g., inability to escape from) aversive conditions. Seligman (1975) argued that:

> When a traumatic event first occurs, it causes a heightened state of emotionality that can loosely be called fear. This state continues until one of two things happen; if the subject learns that he can control the trauma, fear is reduced and may disappear altogether; or if the subject finally learns he cannot control the trauma, fear will decrease and be replaced by depression. (pp. 53–54)

Seligman (1975) suggested that the generalized inhibition of behavior following inescapable shock was due to learning. Although it may be true that animals did learn, they had no control in aversive situations, this research also demonstrated the psychobiological consequences of blocked escape and arrested fight.

The state of helplessness has serious effects on escape behavior in that it causes increased immobility, a switch to passive forms of coping, and makes active avoidance learning and behavior almost impossible (e.g., Anisman, Pizzino, & Sklar, 1980; Peterson et al., 1993; Toates, 1995). Seligman (1975) described how, even when animals were dragged to the safe, no-shock areas, they struggled to learn the escape response. However, some researchers such as Weiss and his colleagues (Weiss, Glazer, & Pohorecky, 1976; Weiss, Glazer, Pohorecky, Bailey, & Schneider, 1979; Weiss & Simson, 1985) suggested an alternative theory called the motor activation deficit hypothesis. In Weiss's theory, the stress of lack of control produces central biological changes that inhibit animals from executing escape behavior. Looked at from an evolved strategy point of view, psychomotor deactivation may be part of an innate strategy (operative in a variety of species) for coping with blocked escape in aversive situations.

There is clear evidence that control (and history of control) over important social and nonsocial resources significantly contributes to psychopathology (Chorpita & Barlow, 1998). In some contexts lack of control over aversive situations can produce behavioral demobilization in rodents, primates, and humans (Toates, 1995; Willner, 1993a, 1993b). However, from an evolutionary point of view there are two other aspects of note. The first concerns the degree to which the *demobilization* (motor activation deficits) of learned helplessness serves any social communicative functions and orients the animal to adopt certain social roles (e.g., send signals of subordinate, defeated, out of action). Such out-of-action signals are powerful communications to potential attackers of "I'm defeated so there is no need to injure me further" (Keltner & Harker, 1998; Price, 1988; Price & Sloman, 1987) and changes the attacker's behaviors. The second concerns the extent to which the psychobiological profile (strategies) of learned helplessness evolved in the context of evolving social behavior. It would seem reasonable to argue that the most common source of repeated aversive stimulation in social animals will be from other conspecifics. An interaction between shock-induced helplessness and submissive behavior was found by Williams and Lierle (1986; see also Toates, 1995). Inescapable shock increases submissive behavior. In other words, the stress of lack of control in aversive situations changes the biological state of animals, which in turn primes a greater readiness to adopt submissive behavior to conspecific challenges.

Blocked escape and arrested flight may be central to both learned helplessness and severe defeat states. Anisman (1978) pointed out that as stress increases and control decreases there are various central biological changes, including a reduction in central monoamine stores as utilization outstrips synthesis, increased reuptake, changes in MAO and COMT, and release of stress hormones. More recent work has also shown major changes in other neurochemical systems such as GABA (Peterson et al., 1993). Stimuli associated with uncontrollable stress may come to elicit these biological effects (Anisman & Sklar, 1979; Peterson et al., 1993). Such changes in central biological processes are so common and observable in most species studied that it is unlikely these are biological errors or dysfunctions as such, but rather they represent evolutionary strategies. In other words, this is what the brain is designed to do under conditions of high stress and low control. I suggest that what is being studied here is the biological mediators of a strategy for demobilization.

As Chorpita and Barlow (1998), Sapolsky (1994), and Toates (1995) pointed out, the salient dimensions of control and predictability operate in all stress situations be they social or nonsocial. Hence, even if the psychobiological profile of learned helplessness was originally not specifically social (and can now be activated by inescapable shock) it is possible that it evolved to become readily incorporated into a social behavioral repertoire to have communicative functions and be activated by social signals. This may explain why arrested flight behaviors have such powerful social signaling components readable in body displays (e.g., head down, lowered body posture, gaze avoidance; A. K. Dixon, 1998). In such a social context an animal needs to signal that its internal inhibitory mechanisms are activated, it will shut down explorative and acquisitive behavior, and it will be a passive nonchallenger.

Social Defeat Strategies

Various threats that produce effective escape behavior are mediated through the sympathetic nervous system. Prolonged aversive stimulation from which escape is not possible produces patterns of behavior that are often referred to as *defeat* (Henry, 1982). Defeat involves the parasympathetic nervous system along the hypothalamic–pituitary–adrenal–cortical axis (see Gilbert, 1989; Henry, 1982; Toates, 1995) and many other physiological changes (see Levitan, Sloman, & Hasey, chap. 4, this volume, for a review). Activation of these mechanisms seems to be associated with major inhibitions on inputs and outputs (e.g., reduced explorative behavior and reduced social affiliation). Defeats have major effects on baseline hormonal states (Leshner, 1978; Toates, 1995). Laboratory studies on rodents show that repeated defeat experiences reliably result in physiological and behavioral consequences including a decrease in offensive aggression (Lagerspetz & Sandnabba, 1982), an increase in defensive responses (Frischknecht, Siegfried, & Waser, 1982; Kulling, Frischknecht, Pasi, Waser, & Siegfried, 1987), decreases in subsequent exploratory behavior and increases in freezing (Raab et al., 1986), weight loss (Adams & Boice, 1983; Raab et al., 1986), reduction of appetitive behaviors (van de Poll, Smeets, van Oyen, & van de Zwan, 1982), and disruption of escape learning (Williams & Lierle, 1988). Meerlo, de Boer, Koolhaas, Daan, and Van den Hoofdakker (1996) found that a single episode of social defeat in rats could have measurable affects on biological rhythms and eating and social behavior in an open field up to 7 days later. Sapolsky (1994) found that blood pressure in subordinate baboons remained higher for much longer after a conflict than it did in dominant animals. Defeats seem to be associated with animals losing interest in their environments and in resource acquisition (Willner, 1993a, 1993b). This may be (or have been) adaptive to the extent that loss of interest means one is not motivated to pursue resources in a social environment where doing so might elicit injurious down-rank attacks.

Research by Von Holst (1986) suggests that within a species there may be different strategies for dealing with defeat. He placed tree shrews in a confined territory, resulting in fighting. The victor became dominant and showed a slight increase in body weight and relative stress response. The defeated losers, however, adopted two different strategies. Some animals (called *subdominants*) adopted typical submissive patterns. They continued with activities but in a rather timid and cautious way. They showed an elevated stress response, especially of an adrenal medullary response and elevated tyrosine hydroxylase activity. However, other defeated animals (called *submissives*) were quite different. These animals became seriously demobilized, with greatly elevated cortisol and corticosterone responses and reductions in tyrosine hydroxylase. They died within 14 days of the confrontation. Even separating victor and loser with wire mesh placed between them did not save these animals. The presence of the dominant was enough to have a major biological impact.

The biological consequences of defeat are many and affect stress hormones, central neurotransmitter pathways, and immune functions (Henry, 1982; Levitan et al., chap. 4, this volume; Toates, 1995). Although Von Holst's (1986) work shows there is more than one strategy for coping with defeat (see Toates, 1995, for further examples), insofar as defeats seem to reliably produce characteristic physiological changes, it may be useful to consider the possible existence of an *involuntary defeat strategy* (IDS) as a subroutine of a submissive strategy set. This strategy is especially likely to be triggered in situations of (a) subordinate status, (b) high conflict or aversive stimulation, and (c) blocked escape (unable to disengage). Sloman (chap. 2, this volume) offers further discussion of the IDS and how the inability to disengage from a conflict may be crucial for its maintenance.

Enclosed Avoidance Strategies

The subdominants in Von Holst's (1986) study were not seriously demobilized, but used what I call *enclosed avoidance strategies.* These are different from blocked escape strategies in a number of ways. First, the subordinate animal does not actually (try to) escape from the dominant in the sense that it moves to a new territory where the dominant can no longer reach it and is thus not receiving any signals from the dominant. Rather, dominant and subordinate remain in sufficient proximity to each other so that conflicts and fights could break out at fairly short notice. The subordinate controls this by keeping its distance (Chance & Jolly, 1970). However, to do this, the subordinate must remain vigilant to the whereabouts of the dominant, remain mobile, and be able to coordinate its avoidant behavior to that of the dominant(s). The loss of mobility that can occur in severe states of defeat and helplessness (motor activation deficits) would not be adaptive. Rather, such animals remain in states of high arousal (braced readiness) and they are ready to give up resources if challenged and de-escalate attacks coming from above. This braking on behavior may be controlled via septo-hippocampal systems (see Gilbert, 1984, pp. 109–110).

Second, the subordinate does have some control over social encounters but mostly those of avoiding or responding quickly to social threats. In these contexts it would be adaptive to inhibit its ambitions (e.g., for sex, or making claims on other resources) to avoid eliciting attacks from more dominant individuals. Enclosed avoidance therefore requires a controlled (de)mobilization in which an animal is not so knocked out that it becomes retarded and immobile, but is sufficiently mobilized that it (a) remains vigilant, (b) does not make claims on resources that would reignite attacks, and (c) adopts submissive behaviors quickly if challenged. This is possibly a common situation for many primates who live in groups (Chance & Jolly, 1970; Sapolsky, 1989). It is also the typical behavior associated with the lack of assertiveness problems associated with psychopathology (Allan & Gilbert, 1997; Arrindell et al., 1990; Gilbert & Allan, 1994).

The stress of having to be constantly vigilant to potential dominant threats is known to be pathogenic (Sapolsky, 1994). It is not difficult to extrapolate from such observations and note enclosed avoidance in work situations in which a subordinate is constantly tense and waiting for the next attack from the boss (Wilkinson, 1996) and in families. Allan and Gilbert (1997) found that coping with interpersonal conflicts by efforts to avoid others was significantly correlated with depression and other psychopathological symptoms.

SUBMISSIVE DISPLAY STRATEGIES

In many species submissive strategies also involve communicative displays designed to impact on the receiver or target of the display and thus reduce the need to become seriously behaviorally demobilized or distant. Hence, there are forms of submissive display behavior that evolved to cope with social threats and attacks, but do not involve quite such drastic (demobilization) changes in state as occurs in, for example, some defeats. Insofar as the most typical evolved contexts of high stress and low control are likely to be social, then the social behavior emitted in such states requires consideration.

Although it can be in the interests of dominants to keep their subordinates somewhat demobilized, stressed, lacking in confidence, and submissive (and this may be the strategy used by bullies), there are various contexts in which it is adaptive for both subordinate and dominant animals to avoid the extremes of flight, demobilization, and serious aggression. In group-living animals it is not necessarily advantageous for a dominant to induce escape or demobilization in all subordinates, for both may at times be dependent on each other (e.g., for grooming, predator defense, cooperation in child care or hunting, or as allies against others). A deferential relationship of subordinate to dominant allows the dominant some control over the subordinate but also opens opportunities to form alliances (de Waal, 1996).

Ohman (1986) noted that in humans a submissive fear response could be activated by facial signals (e.g., the aggressive face). Submissive behavior in humans can also be triggered by threats or actual criticism or rejection. In nonhuman primates also, a stare or aggressive grimace from a dominant may be enough to trigger a submissive display. Submissive displays, which form the basis of deference, are purely social and only ever activated by and expressed towards conspecifics. Primate submissive displays involve salient nonverbal signals. These include eye gaze avoidance, turning the head away, angling the head to the side, dropping the shoulders, shifting weight and positioning to flee, fear grinning, crouching, lowering the hind quarters, and screaming (A. K. Dixon et al., 1989; Gilbert & McGuire, 1998; Harper, 1985; Hinde, 1982; McGuire, personal communication, May 1996). In many primates, dominant–subordinate interactions are common throughout the day, but such threaten–submit encounters are short lived (over in seconds—unless there is a struggle for rank) and they rarely involve physical contact (M. McGuire, personal communication, May 1996). Submissive display behavior balances flight and fight, allows groups to form, and assists in group cohesion, making it a uniquely social mechanism. Submissive displays can be preemptive as signs of deference or respect as well as reactive to threats from dominants. Sending and responding to social threats are significantly mediated by 5-HT (Gilbert & McGuire, 1998).

Like other social defensive responses, submissive displays can also be ambivalent and conflict with other potential responses—showing that both aggressive and fearful displays can be primed at the same time. Consider, for example an observation by Chenery, Seyfarth, and Smuts (1986):

> In a captive group of chimpanzees two adult males Nicki and Luit were engaged in a prolonged struggle for dominance. During one fight Nicki was driven into a tree. As Luit sat at the bottom of the tree, he nervously "fear grinned." He then turned away from Nicki, put a hand over his mouth and pressed his lips together to hide a sign of submission. Only after the third attempt when Luit succeeded in wiping the grin from his face did he once again turn to face Nicki. (p. 1364)

Luit seems to have some awareness that he should conceal certain kinds of social signals (the submissive fear grin) he was emitting involuntarily to advance his dominance chances. In humans, too, coping with and controlling (involuntarily) activated display signals is often paramount to social success (M. R. Leary & Kowalski, 1990). Such behaviors may well be noted in our efforts to inhibit the revelation of negative information about the self and to conceal signals or behaviors that might elicit negative responses from others (Ekman, 1991); that is, they are tactics of deception. The key point is that the processes controlling certain affects and behavior, including nonverbal social communication, can at times be activated independently of each other, and indeed independent of an individual's conscious wishes. Some activated strategies and defensive responses may even be in considerable conflict, and at odds with, those wishes.

The Reverted Escape Strategy

As noted earlier, enclosed avoidance is likely to be tense and stressful for subordinates. Interestingly some primates, especially chimpanzees, have evolved novel ways of relaxing this tension through processes of reconciliation (de Waal, 1989, 1996). One such strategy is called *reverted escape.* This subordinate strategy involves a particular sequence of interactions that seem to depend on both fear (avoidance) and attraction (approach). It was first noted by the ethologist Chance (1984, 1988) in his studies of nonhuman primates. In some primates, if a subordinate has been attacked by a dominant, the first response is to flee, but subsequently the subordinate seems motivated to return to the dominant—the very source of the threat (A. K. Dixon, 1998). It is as if the dominant now has some attraction to the subordinate. Often, Chance observed, there can be a cautious and tense return, in which approach and avoidance seem to compete. Gradually, moving forward and expressing highly submissive behaviors, the subordinate comes nearer and nearer to the dominant until they are close. Then, not uncommonly, the dominant will often pat, stroke, or even embrace the subordinate. These behaviors have a calming effect on both the dominant and subordinate. The subordinate has, as it were, lessened the threat, by eliciting acceptance of itself from the dominant, via ensuring that its submission is accepted. It has changed the state of mind of the dominant from anger to reassurance. This has been called reverted escape, meaning that coping with a threat from a dominant actually involves returning to it and calming it down.

Goodall (1975) observed such behavior in chimpanzees, which she felt is related to a need for contact (although the need to calm the dominant is also probably, if not more, important). She gave a good example of reverted escape:

> Perhaps the most dramatic illustration of the chimpanzee's need for physical contact is after he has been threatened or attacked by a superior, particularly when a young adolescent male has been victimised by a high-ranking adult male. Once Figan, aged about 10 years, was badly pounded by the alpha male (Goliath at the time). Screaming and tense, Figan began cautiously approaching his aggressor who sat with his hair still bristling. Every so often, the desire to flee seemed almost to overcome the adolescent's desire for contact and he turned, as though to retreat. But each time he went on again until eventually he was crouched, flat on the ground in front of Goliath. And there he stayed, still screaming, until Goliath, *in response to his submission,* began to pat him gently on the back, on and on until the screaming gradually subsided and Figan sat up and moved away quite calmly. Such incidents are common and almost always the aggressor responds to the

> submissive gestures of the subordinate with a touch, a pat or even an embrace. Occasionally, if a young male is not reassured in this way in response to his submission, he may actually fly into a tantrum, hitting the ground and screaming so intensely that he almost chokes. (italics added, p. 144)

Reverted escape is a tension diffuser and reducer. This ability to modulate arousal and allow social closeness has been seen as important to the evolution of intelligence (Chance, 1988; Chance & Jolly, 1970). In some species (e.g, bonobos) sex can be used as a tension diffuser, stopping conflicts before they begin (de Waal, 1996), and bonobos have the most affiliative nonhuman primate organization of all the primates. It is unknown how far, in conflict situations, reverted escape or the use of sex operate in humans as tension reducers because this form of submissive behavior has rarely been studied. Anecdotal evidence for behaviors such as seeking redemption, (religious) confessions, and making apologies aimed to engage and calm a dominant and stop them from attacking or rejecting the subordinate might be examples (Gilbert, 1989). Presumably when these work they have a salient effect on the mental state of both the subordinate and dominant. Similarly, some people may use sex (or gift giving) as a tension reducer, to calm their partners, or at least to stop them from continuing in a hostile frame of mind.

These types of submissive behavior cannot be understood as simply an inverse of assertiveness. Attempts to calm a potentially powerful dominant by expressing submissive behaviors implies that it is the subordinate who is attempting to exert some control over the interaction; and indeed not only elicit reassurance signals that will calm itself but also change the dominant's state of mind (e.g., reduce the attack or punishment motivation of the dominant; Keltner & Harker, 1998). Although reassurance seeking following an attack (Goodall, 1990) and reconciliation after conflict (de Waal, 1989) have evolved in some primates to be very powerful ways of controlling stressful conflict interactions, a subordinate might still harbor desires for revenge; that is, their fight is arrested and suppressed but still internally activated.

Infantile and Illness Strategies

Another type of submissive display signal seems to be derived from more infantile (child–parent) behavior. For example, Eibl-Eibesfeldt (1990) noted:

> In many mammals, infantile appeals are used to diminish a partner's fear and buffer aggression. When a male hamster follows a female during courtship, he utters the call by which a baby alerts its mother to distress. A wolf approaches a high-ranking individual of its pack by pushing with its snout against the corners of the mouth of the high ranking individual. Wolf-pups perform this behavior when they beg for food. In submission, a wolf rolls onto its back, offering its belly to the opponent in the way pups do when they offer themselves for cleaning to their mothers. Often, the lower ranking wolf urinates, which releases licking by the dominant one. Thus, a hostile relation can be turned into a friendly one. (p. 156).

Eibl-Eibesfeldt (1990) pointed out that some submissive behaviors also convey affiliative signals. In humans, crying, especially in conflict situations, is sometimes seen as a submissive behavior (Buss & Craik, 1986) designed to terminate aggression. The use of care-eliciting signals (signaling childlike vulnerability) to both control potential agonistic encounters and elicit caring behavior from a dominant, have been linked to dependency and depression (e.g., see Price & Gardner, 1995). And the *Diagnostic and Statistical Manual of Mental Disorders* (4th ed. [DSM-IV]; American Psychiatric Association, 1994) criteria for dependent personality disorder are mostly made up of submissive behaviors.

In humans, dependent submissive strategies serve a number of functions. For example, they do not risk open fighting and contesting for resources, but seek to gain a share in those gained by (more dominant) others. Thus these types of social signals can be used not only as aggression-controlling submissive signals, but also to try to elicit help, support, and other resources from others (Bornstein, 1995). Interestingly, as Bornstein (1995) observed, dependent individuals, who may use this strategy, can become angry and aggressive if help is not forthcoming. As with reverted escape, if care-eliciting strategies do not work, individuals may switch to more coercive attempts. Price and Gardner (1995) noted that a similar case can be made for signaling sickness; that is, this signal is not only one of out of action (no threat or challenge), but also a call for help.

Love–Dove Strategies: The Role of Affiliative Submissive Behavior

Apart from controlling threats, there have evolved a host of submissive behaviors that serve affiliative ends. When it comes to conflicts with kin relations and allies, alliances often depend on de-escalation strategies that are affiliative (contact seeking or maintaining) rather than fearful passivity or withdrawing and avoidant (de Waal, 1996). Indeed, as Hartup (1989) noted, friends are far more affiliative, forgiving, and reconciling over conflicts than are strangers. Therefore, conflicts may follow different rules between kin, friends, and strangers. Indeed, there are many contexts in which submitting also carries significant benefits. I suggest that when submissive behavior is perceived to be voluntary—that is, when people do not wish to contest their rank, position, and possible constraints or requests placed on them—submissive behavior is often associated with cooperation and affiliation.

Submissive behaviors can often be used to gain allies and (paradoxically) gain status and rank. There is increasing evidence that in many nonhuman primates, rank (and the benefits it offers) depends on alliances (de Waal, 1989, 1996). This is especially true for females (Kevles, 1986). Alliance building is related to rank. Chapais (1992) reviewed the evidence that shows that in female primates, high-born compared to low-born females have more allies, more active and powerful allies, and more support from allies. Male primates, who will become dominant, often have strong affiliations with certain other males and females. These behaviors are mediated through increases in approach behavior, social grooming, reciprocal exchanges of help, and reduced aggressiveness. These might be called *love–dove*, or *affiliative–dove* strategies.

Raleigh, McGuire, Brammer, Pollack, and Yuwiler (1991) reviewed the evidence for the role of affiliative behavior in status acquisition and maintenance and the role of serotonergic mechanisms in status enhancement. Selected male vervet monkeys were given drugs that augment serotonergic activity (tryptophan and fluoxetine) or drugs that disrupt serotonergic activity (fenfluramine and cyproheptadine). It was found that in each case animals treated with tryptophan and fluoxetine gained dominance and did so with significant increases in approach, grooming, proximity to others, and decreased aggressive behavior. Those animals treated with fenfluramine and cyproheptadine, however, significantly increased their aggressive behavior but reduced their affiliative behaviors of approach, proximity, and grooming. Increased aggressiveness was not associated with status enhancement, but rather its reduction was.

As Raleigh et al. (1991) pointed out, such findings contribute to the growing awareness that aggressiveness and rank need to be separated and attention needs to be focused more on alliance formation. Indeed, Barkow (1980, 1989) and Gilbert (1989, 1992, 1997a) suggested that a salient dimension of social rank in humans is *social attractiveness*. In this model, although rank can be gained and maintained through threat and displays of fighting ability (called *resource-holding power* [RHP]; Parker, 1974), it can also be gained and maintained via social displays and communications that others find attractive and bestow rank on (e.g., sexual beauty, intellectual talents, friendliness, athletic skill, etc.). The technical term used to describe this aspect is *social attention-holding potential* (SAHP), which contrasts it with RHP (see Gilbert et al., 1995, and Gilbert, 1997a, for a review). SAHP allows for culturally derived qualities (athletic skill and courage, research abilities, playing the guitar) to gain or lose rank and status in human groups.

Friendly and Hostile Submission

T. Leary (1957) outlined a model of social behavior that suggested two central dimensions of human social behavior: dominance–submission and love–hate. Various patterns of social behavior and internal psychological states could be viewed as the products of various combinations of these two dimensions. Both dominance and submissiveness could be either affiliative and friendly or hostile and aggressive. There have since been various modifications to this model (Birtchnell, 1993; Kiesler, 1983; Wagner et al., 1995). Birtchnell (1993) pointed to subordinate behaviors that can be used to seek close affiliations with others. As he suggested, subordinate behavior can have many benefits, such as the safeness of acceptance by parents, a peer group, and its leaders (Baumeister & Leary, 1995). Support and approval of higher ranking members, contingent on one's loyal subordination, may raise one's own status within a group. Signals of being valued by one's group and leaders (in contrast to being devalued and rejected) may be biologically potent. Indeed, positive social affiliations may boost endorphins (Dunbar, 1996). There are also some social contexts in which individuals may actually deceive themselves into believing they are more subordinate than in fact they are (Hartung, 1987). However, such subordinate behaviors increase attractiveness to others rather than reduce it. Presumably what makes submissive behavior attractive to others is that it signals a preparedness to be a willing and capable ally and not contest rank (i.e., a nonrival).

As Coyne (1976) noted, however, the reassurance seeking of depressed people can often be unattractive and aversive to others (Segrin & Abramson, 1994). This may be because potential helpers do not anticipate any increase in status from helping, association with a depressed person may reduce rather than increase status, the depressed person may be seen as too weak to make a useful or capable ally, and the depressed person cannot reciprocate in mutually affiliative interactions (McGuire & Troisi, 1998). Interactions with depressed people are unlikely to boost endorphins and are usually seen as depressing.

Group Defense

When a group is under threat, there is increased submission to the group's goals and its leaders. When individuals in groups seek to expand or defend their self-interests and control (be this for territory, economic resources, professional boundaries, or exporting values—as in religion) there can be a collective change in the psychology of individual members. Van der Dennen (1986) gave a concise summary of these:

> Within the groups members close ranks; there is an increase in group cohesiveness and solidarity; the own group is considered superior to the other group; each group becomes hierarchically organised; there is a greater willingness to accept centralised leadership; deviating opinions are barely tolerated; the group demands more loyalty and conformity from its members. Between groups negative stereotypes tend to develop; communication between groups decreases, preventing the correction of negative stereotypes; during intergroup negotiations, members pay more attention to points of disagreement than they do to agreement; distrust and hostility towards the other group rises, sometimes erupting in open aggression; tactics and strategy for winning are emphasised at the expense of concern about the merits of the problem negotiated. (p. 36)

Thus, the evidence suggests that to external threats there are increases in within-group voluntary submissive behavior and compliance to group norms and leaders (Beahrs, 1996). As N. Dixon (1976) noted, in contexts of low threat, subordinates prefer democratic-type leaders, but in contexts of high external threat they prefer strong leaders who will take charge and tell them what to do. Hence, voluntary subordinate tendencies are controlled via the social context (e.g., perceived external threat).

Groups often seek to dominate other groups, defend their own interests, attempt to limit subordinate groups' access to resources, and at times attack them. Pratto, Sidanius, Stallworth, and Malle (1994) called this *social dominance orientation,* and explored how people take their self-identities from their own group and set about subordinating other groups. Hence, even between groups, subordinate positions can be aversive. Again whether a subordinate group resists or accepts their position as their lot determines how subordinates act toward the ruling groups. Subordination, by class, caste, or gender, if supported by various historical or religious values, can lead to acceptance and readiness to play the submissive role. However, as these values dissolve—for example, as subordinate groups question the fairness or legitimacy of ruling groups—passive and aggressive forms of resistance can ensue (Scott, 1990). The behaviors of subordinate group resistance can, however, be difficult to detect, for as Scott (1990) made clear, they are designed not to be detected; that is, they are hidden. On the other hand, desires for revenge by subordinated or humiliated groups, who are no longer held in check by religious or social values, can lead to serious violence once a group thinks it can win or the fight is worth it (Scheff, 1994).

INVOLUNTARY SUBMISSIVE STRATEGIES: TOWARD A MODEL OF DEPRESSION

Having outlined the complex forms of defensive behavior and (subordinate) strategies that have evolved for social living, it is now possible to explore how these may operate in psychopathology, especially depression. Basically the depressed person is caught in what can be called involuntary submissive and defeat strategies. In the following, I outline how this shows up in depressive perceptions of subordinate status and defeat together with notable expressions of arrested fight and flight.

The term *involuntary* has two meanings. The first refers to external constraints or coercion. Many states labeled as psychopathological are associated with interpersonal conflict, desires to resist others, an inability to control social adversity, or an inability to obtain desired social outcomes. Conflicts of interest can be between siblings, parents, children, lovers, friends, work colleagues, competitors, or enemies. Depressed people usually feel they are losing in conflict or competitive situations. This may be because they see themselves as being subordinated and exploited in some way, they are failing to raise or maintain their status and reach goals, or they are receiving insufficient boosting signals (of praise and approval; SAHP) from others (Gilbert, 1992). Depressed people may feel they are either already subordinate and losers or are at risk of becoming so. The person is in (or sees himself or herself as in) a social position or social role he or she does not want to be in. The importance of perceived control is salient here (Chorpita & Barlow, 1998).

A second aspect of *involuntary* is related to internal states; to unwanted negative emotions over which the person feels he or she has no control. McGuire and Troisi (1987, 1998) called such states *dysregulated states,* meaning that persons are unable to control inner aversive thoughts and feelings. When people find themselves subject to involuntarily aggressive, fearful, or depressed feelings or subject to unpleasant ruminations or images, they may engage in many self-control strategies (Parkinson, Totterdell, Brinder, & Reynolds, 1996) including turning to drugs and therapy. Uncontrollable internal states can also activate strong flight or escape motives—and anger—in the form of frustration in being unable to control painful feelings and thoughts (Gilbert & Allan, 1998).

Defeat

Activation of involuntary subordinate strategies (involving, e.g., loss of confidence and depression) are most likely under conditions of social adversity and lack of control (Chorpita & Barlow, 1998; Peterson et al., 1993). Defeat arises from the loss of control over goals and interpersonal conflicts. It is focused on a sense of a failed struggle. Indeed, many theories of depression capture the essence of a failed struggle in depression onset. In attachment theory, despair follows protest (Bowlby, 1980); in learned helplessness theory, the animal first makes invigorated attempts to escape but becomes demobilized when it fails to escape (Seligman, 1975); and in incentive disengagement theory, the individual is first invigorated to secure the incentive but then becomes demobilized when these efforts fail (Klinger, 1975). Anger is often a first affective response to having a path to a goal blocked.

Social rank theory tends to focus on interpersonal conflicts but one may feel defeated in the pursuit of biosocial goals in the absence of conflict (e.g., on becoming infertile; M. McGuire, personal communication, May 1996; McGuire & Troisi, 1998). And many human defeats are not aggressive (e.g., failure at a beauty contest or an exam). Thus, in humans the notion of a failed struggle for a valued resource can apply across a wide variety of domains (see Sloman, chap. 2, this volume). Table 1.2 sets out a variety of areas and predispositions that might end up as a failed struggle.

There are many domains that involve defeat. In the ongoing environmental domain, Brown, Adler, and Bifulco (1988) and Brown, Bifulco, and Harris (1987) found that it is only life events that have long-term negative consequences that are related to depression. Such events include:

1. Direct attacks and setbacks that force a person to lower his or her standard of living (e.g., Ganzini, McFarland, & Cutler, 1990).
2. Direct attacks on self-esteem that are shaming and humiliating (criticism and general putting down in salient relationships; e.g, Belsher & Costello, 1988; Brown, Harris, & Hepworth, 1995; Hooley & Teasdale, 1989).

TABLE 1.2
Sources of Defeat and Subordination

Low or loss of resources

1. Struggling and failing to achieve highly valued goals, especially if others are successful.
2. Failing to maintain (hang onto) or losing highly valued resources.
3. Overwhelmed by responsibilities and demands.
4. Stuck in low resource and non socially cooperative environment (e.g., rundown estates).

External attack and social put down

5. Being subjected to (and trapped in) hostile (abusive, or high expressed emotion) environments where one is labeled inferior, shamed, humiliated, and subordinated. Losing the "conflicts of interest" battles.
6. Being neglected and marginalized so that in effect one experiences few boosts to one's self-esteem or sense of status or worth. One is treated as subordinate or irrelevant by omission.
7. Loss of major roles that have shaped one's identity such that with their passing or loss one feels subordinate, useless, and unwanted—loss of identity-boosting signals.

Internal sources of attack

8. Internal (superego) cognitions that are self-attacking and give rise to judgments of personal worthlessness, badness, and failure—the undesired self
9. Unfavorable social comparisons that give rise to unwanted feelings of inferiority or undesirability.
10. Having ambitions that outstrip ability; feeling disappointed with failure. Depression is most likely when the person cannot live up to their standards and aspirations and becomes self-attacking. This includes such attitudes as perfectionism and the fear of failure.

Note. Some of these items may be objectively true, whereas others may be personal perceptions of being true.

3. Loss of (control over) core roles that are important for a person's sense of self and offered a sense of status, value, or prestige (e.g., Champion & Power, 1995; Gilbert, 1992; Rooke & Birchwood, 1998).
4. Indirect attacks such as being ignored, marginalized, and lacking support or a confidante (Brown & Harris, 1978).
5. Blocked escape where a person cannot get away from an aversive situation (e.g., an abusive or neglectful marriage, run down estate, or work bully; Brown et al., 1995; Gilbert, 1992).

Defeat pertains to the situation in which no matter how hard you struggle you cannot win or change the situation. Defeat states can be activated by conflict-ridden relationships. Spouse criticism has been found to be a predictor of relapse in depression (Belsher & Costello, 1988; Hooley & Teasdale, 1989). There is increasing evidence that high expressed emotion is centrally related to mental illness (e.g., Jenkins & Karno, 1992), with a salient dimension being criticism. Vinokur and van Ryn (1993) found that social undermining (defined as social hindrance, negative social support, and social conflict) had a stronger, although more volatile, impact on mental health than social support over two time periods. Family therapists target the high rates of denigrating, criticizing, blaming, and threats or use of violence behaviors that can be prevalent in some marriages (Beach, Sandeen, & O'Leary, 1990). Indeed, Beach et al. (1990) highlighted how these status-attacking behaviors are positively associated with depression whereas self-esteem boosting and supportive behavior from spouses are associated with reduced depression.

A sense of defeat can also arise from feeling that one cannot meet the demands and responsibilities placed on one. For example, Hobfoll (1989) developed a model of stress that focuses on feelings that demands on the self outstrip one's resources to meet those demands. A typical example here might be a young mother struggling to meet the competing demands of young children, marriage, and work. James (1997) reviewed the evidence that depression (especially in women) was associated with role strain, resulting from too many competing demands and responsibilities that lead to a sense of failure in the adequate performance of a role—often associated with ideas that one was "not up to it."

A MODEL

Figure 1.1 outlines the beginnings of a model outlining the interactions of defeat and arrested defensive strategies (fight/flight) that are part of depression. It begins with some experience(s) of being thwarted and losing (control over) important social biosocial goals and resources—that is, there is a high degree of social adversity and/or thwarting in the environment and the person perceives that his or her efforts will not succeed in altering this. As noted earlier, there is much evidence that depressives are often in aversive social environments. The first option in such contexts is to fight or try harder. If this succeeds in regaining control, depression is self-limiting. Another option is to move on, escape, or take flight and find new resources and opportunities elsewhere (Nesse, 1998). If this is successful there may be some mourning for what has been given up, but escape is often experienced as a relief (Gray, 1982) and depression is self-limiting. If one cannot fight harder (and win) or escape, one might simply accept the situation, or in the case of acknowledging someone has more power than oneself, develop an affiliative, friendly, subordinate relationship and agree to the limitations placed on one in return for benefits such as protection, care, or shared resources (love–dove).

Aversive social environments will impact internal psychobiological processes. These may include psychobiological states as operate in subordinates (e.g., low 5-HT and high cortisol; Levitan et al., chap. 4, this volume; Sapolsky, 1989, 1990a, 1990b) that predispose them to subordinate defenses (e.g., fearful avoidance, submission) in the face of social challenges. In humans, aversive social environments will impact internal models of self–other relationships. Specifically

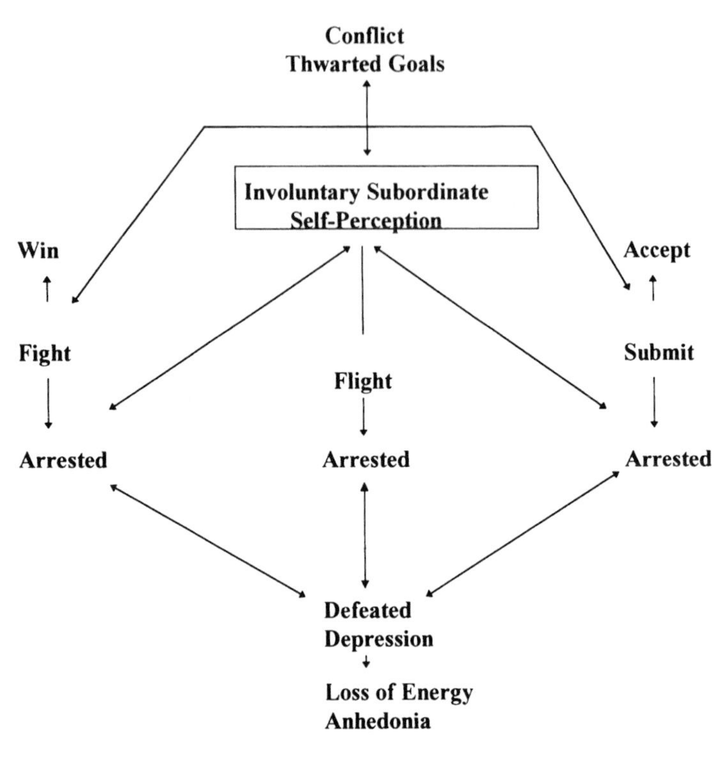

Non Depression	*Depression*
Assertion, anger results in a win	**Want to fight harder but expects to lose or be heavily put-down or shamed**
Take flight and feel relived at escaping	**Blocked from escape - or feel guilt/fear and more subordinate (inferior, bad) for leaving**
Accepts compromises or giving in, affiliative subordinate.	**Feels weak, inferior, blocked and trapped in having to give in and submit.**

FIG 1.1. Relation of arrested flight-fight and submission to depression.

it will impact on what I have called *involuntary subordinate self-perception* (Gilbert, 1992). There are a number of sources for this.

Development

Being in, or having grown up in, environments that are hostile or abusive and where a person is or was subject to continual conflicts and social put-downs (loss of status, treated in a highly subordinate manner) is common to many depressed people, especially those with chronic disorders (Andrews, 1998). It is now recognized that adverse rearing experiences (including emotional neglect, affectionless control, physical and sexual abuse) can significantly affect psychobiological maturation and functioning (Hart, Gunnar, & Cicchetti, 1996; Rosenblum et al., 1994; Schore, 1994). The psychological domain of these aversive rearing experiences sensitizes people to have low self-esteem (low status perceptions), to have poor self-efficacy and shame, and to be highly emotionally responsive to attacks on their status—desirability or lovability (Bifulco & Moran, 1998; Gilbert, 1992). Further, they have considerable difficulty moderating fight or flight emotions (see Sloman, chap. 2, this volume).

Social Comparisons and Social Rank

Depressed and socially anxious people make unfavorable judgments about their relative rank, in terms of their attractiveness, talents, competencies, desirability to others, or power (Allan & Gilbert, 1995; Beck, Emery, & Greenberg, 1985; Buunk & Brenninkmeyer, chap. 6, this volume; Swallow & Kuiper, 1988). Allan and Gilbert (1997) and Gilbert and Allan (1998) found that in depressed people, submissive behavior, strength of escape motivation, and sense of defeat are all highly correlated with unfavorable social comparisons. Moreover, these negative social comparisons relate to both feeling inferior to others, and feeling less attractive and different to others or as an outsider. Social comparisons also impact general confidence (Gilbert, Allan, Ball, & Bradshaw, 1996). It would seem, then, that those who see themselves as subordinate cannot afford to risk overconfidence (Scott, 1990). In social rank terms, low self-esteem, which is associated with unfavorable social comparisons, and is well known to be associated with depression, can be seen as involuntary subordinate self-perception (Gilbert, 1992; Price, chap. 7, this volume). It is probably the social comparison elements of low self-esteem that prime submissive behavior and increase dispositions for escape behavior and arrested fight in conflict situations.

Shame

Kaufman (1989) called shame the affect of inferiority (and see Weisfeld & Wendorf, chap. 5, this volume). Gilbert, Pehl, and Allan (1994) found that shame was associated with heightened self-consciousness, feelings of helplessness, anger at self, and a heightened sense of personal inferiority. Shame proneness was also found to be associated with submissive behavior, now regarded as one of the typical markers of shame. A shame (submissive) display may serve to limit attacks from others (Keltner & Harker, 1998). Hence, the shamed person may adopt all the body postures of a submissive strategy: head down, slumped postures, eye gaze avoidance, and cutoff (A. K. Dixon, Gilbert, Huber, Gilbert, & van Hoek, 1997; Gilbert & McGuire, 1998; Keltner, 1995). Self-consciousness seems to be a heightened vigilance to the signals one is sending others to avoid sending signals that might result in loss of status or rejection. Desires to escape from social situations and social scrutiny are noted in difficulties such as social phobia, avoidant personality disorder, and shame. Many researchers believe that shame usually primes escape or desires to run away, hide, and conceal the self (Lewis, 1986; Tangney, Burggraf, & Wagner, 1995). Shame seriously disrupts social behavior, especially social affiliation and moral behavior (Tangney, 1995). Sarnoff and Zimbardo (1961) found that inducing shame in college students could lead to a reduced desire for social interaction and greater social avoidance. To be shamed is to be seen as weak, inadequate, bad, and of low rank (Gilbert, 1998; Gilbert & McGuire, 1998). Mental illnesses are associated with feelings of shame, loss of social standing, and unattractiveness to others. Such shame may motivate avoidance and wariness of others. A sense of shame and failure may also arise from feeling unable to meet competing demands and responsibilities, especially if one believes that one should be able to cope and others seem able to cope with such demands.

The Internalization of Put-Down Signals

An important aspect of human depression (and the maintenance of involuntary subordinate self-perceptions and sense of defeat) is that many of the signals that activate a sense of defeat and being subordinate are internalized. This dimension is often a focus for psychotherapy (Gilbert, 1997b). There is now increasing evidence that self-punishment (Rehm, 1988), self-criticism (Blatt, Quinlan, Chevron, McDonald, & Zuroff, 1982; Driscoll, 1988; Zuroff & Mongrain, 1987), or what might be called internalized hostile dominant–subordinate self-relationships, are associated with psychopathology. This view has some similarities to psychoanalytic views, especially those that articulate differences between ego and superego functions or internal self–object relationships (J. R. Greenberg & Mitchell, 1983). However, I suggest that self-criticism and self-punishment can have the effect of activating internal strategies that evolved to coordinate submissive (and defeat) behavior. For example, just as fantasizing on sexual images can lead to sexual arousal even in the absence of an external sexual object, so self-attacking may activate subordinate states in the self (Gilbert, in press).

The power of self-attacking to activate submissive behavior can be seen from use of the two-chair therapy technique (Gilbert, in press; L. S. Greenberg, 1979;

L. S. Greenberg, Rice, & Elliott, 1993). In one chair (the accusing chair) a person voices evaluations of himself or herself (e.g., you are useless, no good, worthless, you don't try hard enough, etc.). After this the person is invited to sit in a facing chair (the feeling chair) and reflect on how he or she feels when listening to these critical messages. Two things often happen in depression. First, the person usually agrees that the messages of the critic (from the accusing chair) are accurate; the individual is useless. Second, when sitting in the feeling chair the person often takes up a lowered posture, often hunched, with eyes cast down. The person may become tearful and feel as if he or she is getting smaller. In effect these people take up a highly submissive posture to their own attacks. L. S. Greenberg, Elliott, and Foerster (1990) did not focus on submissive behavior, but they also pointed out that it is how a person responds to his or her own self-criticisms that is often crucial to whether depressed affect occurs—it is when people cannot defend themselves against attacks that depression takes hold. They argued:

> Depression is much more likely if a person's weak/bad, hopeless, self-organisation is triggered, than if the critical self and negative cognitions alone are activated. It is much more the person's response to the negative cognitions and their inability to cope with the self-criticisms, than the cognitions and criticisms alone, that lead to depression. People are unable to counter or combat the negative cognitions when the weak/bad helpless state has been evoked. This is when depressed affect emerges. (p. 170)

These between-chair dialogues can be used to affect psychological change (Gilbert, in press; L. S. Greenberg et al., 1993). Although cognitive therapists (e.g., Beck et al., 1985) have made clear how thoughts can activate and maintain feelings, there are very few data on how fight–flight and submissive strategies are activated by internal aversive self-evaluations. Nor are there many data on the fact that, insofar as people cannot control painful states of mind, they are in a sense in a blocked escape situation. It remains an intriguing but untested proposition that chronic activation of painful states of mind that one cannot control or escape from can lead to the arrested flight and demobilization. Indeed, Gilbert and Allan (1998) developed a measure of internal entrapment (e.g., cannot get away from painful thoughts and feelings) and found that, like external entrapment, it was highly correlated with depression. It is not uncommon for depressed and chronically anxious people to say that they long for sleep, because this is the only time they experience any peace from their own thoughts and feelings.

Powerlessness and Involuntary Subordination

Although in the majority of cases patients do feel themselves to be worthless and failures in a personal sense, this is not always necessary. As noted earlier, loss of control over important resources may be sufficient in some cases. For example, a patient became depressed following a redundancy. There was a chance that he might lose his house. Another loss was of his "old self." Whereas before he had felt others could depend on him, now he felt guilty for his increased irritability and the fact that his family would suffer from his loss of income. The point is that powerlessness can be a source of involuntary subordinate self-perception (Gilbert, 1992). He did not blame himself, nor was he self-attacking (he blamed the firm). In an area of high unemployment, and given his age, he felt totally trapped and that trying harder to obtain another job was pointless.

ARRESTED FIGHT AND FLIGHT: A KEY TO DEPRESSED DEMOBLIZATION?

In all of the domains outlined in Table 1.2, people have to accommodate themselves to failure or loss. As noted elsewhere (Gilbert, 1984; Sloman, chap. 2, this volume) it may be when individuals are defeated but cannot give up and move on or change their goals and aspirations that serious depression is more likely. More specifically, acceptance and accommodation to defeats, failures, and setbacks require the turning off of fight–flight strategies (Sloman, chap. 2, this volume). An inability to moderate strong fight or flight motives in a losing context switches to the third evolved option of demobilization.

Subordinates are more likely than dominants to have serious blocks to their fight–flight options and indeed the arrest of fight and flight is often part of the subordinate strategy (i.e, subordinates are more restrained in being able to escape or fight harder). If an individual can accept the defeat and move on, depression may be mild and relatively short lived (Sloman, chap. 2, this volume). It is when a mild demobilization of defeat does not deactivate fight–flight, but at the same time they are blocked and arrested, that defeat states may turn to more serious depression. There is now some evidence that feeling defeated (forced into a subordinate position) is highly correlated with desires to escape but feeling trapped, and this combination is highly depressogenic (Brown et al., 1995; Gilbert & Allan, 1998).

Arrested Fight in Depression

There is much evidence in the animal and human literature that social rank plays an important role in the expression of aggressive behavior (Ray & Sapolsky, 1992; Sapolsky, 1989, 1990a, 1990b); that is, in general, aggressive attacks and threats flow down the social rank (from dominant to subordinate) and rarely up it (Archer, 1988; Toates, 1995). There is also considerable evidence that depressed people often feel heightened levels of anger that are not expressed (Riley, Treiber, & Woods, 1989). Although excessive anger expression is associated with poorer health and poorer social relationships than mild to moderate expression (Broman & Johnson, 1988), it has also been found that anger inhibition (Riley et al., 1989), submissive behavior (Allan & Gilbert, 1997) and poor assertiveness, especially emotional distress at expressing assertive behaviors (Arrindell et al., 1990) have been linked with many forms of psychopathology, especially depression.

Cochrane and Neilson (1977) found that inhibited aggression was especially marked in endogenous depression. Pilowsky and Spence (1975) found that hostility was rarely expressed in the presence of vegetative symptoms, and Riley et al. (1989) found depressed patients suppressed anger more than normal controls or a posttraumatic stress group. G. A. Fava et al. (1986) found there were differences in hostility in patients who had experienced losses compared to those who had not. Depression can also be associated with anger and rage attacks (M. Fava, Anderson, & Rosenbaum, 1990). Weissman, Klerman, and Paykel (1971) found depressed women had greater hostility toward those with whom they shared a close relationship.

The evidence seems clear that many depressed patients experience forms of arrested fight; that is heightened anger that is not expressed. This anger is probably aroused by frustration and loss of control over important goals and interpersonal interactions or conflicts (see Sloman, chap. 2, this volume). Table 1.3 outlines some of the reasons patients have offered in therapy as to why their anger may not be expressed.

The failure to be able to use anger or act assertively to get one's own way (or agree on some compromise) not only confirms one to be in a subordinate, powerless position, but also increases the desire to escape. Ongoing research in our department has shown that anger suppression is significantly correlated with feelings of entrapment and wish for escape.

The fight strategy can, however, be directed toward the self. As noted earlier, negative self-evaluations, often imbued with hostility, are typical of depressed cognitions. In other words, the self becomes the subordinate object for attack. This increases the put-down signals impinging on affect systems and may increase the sense of defeat, or of not being up to it, not being good enough, and so on (Gilbert, in press).

TABLE 1.3
Some Typical Sources of Arrested Fight and Anger Suppression

1. Fear of an overpowering counterattack.
2. Dependence on the object of one's anger (e.g., one's ally or spouse could leave, defect, or withdraw support; a boss could fire one).
3. Shame of one's anger (feel like a bad person for feeling or acting aggressively).
4. Fear of losing control (e.g., my anger would damage all around me).
5. Fear of making a fool of oneself—being easily put down, shamed, or humiliated.
6. Fear of harming others (guilt) or damaging a relationship.
7. Fear of loss of love—being rejected.
8. Fear of the feelings of anger themselves.

Entrapment, Arrested Flight, Depression and Suicide

A. K. Dixon et al. (1989) and A. K. Dixon (1998) were the first to draw attention to the profiles of arrested flight in depressed states. Gilbert (1992) suggested that entrapment in unrewarding (few signals of being valued) environments, or not being able to escape from hostile or abusive others, may be particularly depressogenic—and more so than losses (Hammen, 1988). Brown et al. (1995) investigated this possibility by measuring life events associated with both humiliation and entrapment. They found that these events were associated with a greater risk of depression than loss or danger events alone without humiliation or entrapment implications. Gilbert and Allan (1998) found that feeling defeated by life, perceptions of entrapment, and escape motivation are all significantly associated with depression.[2] Rooke and Birchwood (1998) found that loss of status, sense of defeat, and entrapment were also powerfully related to depression in people suffering from schizophrenia. What evidence there is supports the view that many depressed people suffer arrested flight.

Baumeister (1990) developed a theory of suicide based on there being strong desires to escape that are blocked. Desired escape may be from external aversive situations such as critical others or work overload, but it can also be internal (e.g., thoughts of failure, hopelessness and general painful states of mind, illnesses, or damaged, deformed bodies). When all other escape routes seem shut off and others do not seem able to help (lack of supportive allies), suicide may result. Central to these ideas is that it is not just the controllability of a stressor that motivates suicide, but the strength of (blocked) escape motivation. Indeed, it is clinically well known that people can become so depressed they feel unable to carry out any behavior, but as they regain the power to act, underlying escape motivation may be translated into suicide.

Not only is entrapment a powerful external event in depression, but the theme of entrapment is common in depressive imagery. For example, patients may describe their depressions as being stuck in a dark hole or pit and unable to climb out.

Social Distancing and Enclosed Avoidance

As noted earlier, when escape is not possible, animals (and humans) may be forced into distancing maneuvers where they try to keep their distance from

---

[2]In the modern world people can be trapped on rundown estates or in unrewarding jobs or marriages. These set socially constructed domains of confinement. Although learning to cope in these situations can be helpful, so can a simple ability to leave. Not surprisingly dreams of winning a lottery are common. In a recent British television program it was revealed that on average the poor spend a greater percentage of their income on lotteries than the moderately well off, even to the point of getting into debt. Preoccupation with a strong desire to escape may reduce positive affect and interest in exploring opportunities in the current environment. Many health indexes are related to social rank with the poor sections of society being most at risk (Adler et al., 1994; Wilkinson, 1996).

those they are in conflict with. In humans this may vary from avoiding certain topics of conversation known to ignite conflicts to physical distancing and social avoidance. There is evidence from various studies of nonverbal communication that social distancing is common in depression. For example, severely depressed people are often socially withdrawn, rarely initiate social interactions, receive less social behavior directed at them, have lower speech outputs, are retarded in posture, and express eye gaze avoidance. Changes in social distancing behaviors, in particular becoming more socially engaged and responsive, are predictors of recovery (Schelde, 1998a, 1998b). Using a self-report scale especially designed to measure how people cope with interpersonal conflict, it was found that keeping one's distance was significantly associated with depression (Allan & Gilbert, 1997).

Ambivalent Escape—Reasons for Entrapment

As Gilbert (1992) and Nesse (1998) noted, escape behavior in humans may be compromised, arrested, and blocked for many reasons and it is useful for clinicians to have some overview of these. Table 1.4 builds on those suggested elsewhere (Gilbert, 1992; Nesse, 1998).

TABLE 1.4
Some Typical Sources of Arrested Flight and Entrapment

External

1. Lack of resources—resources or supports are so low that moving on is not possible because there is nowhere to go.
2. Loss of resources (seems) too high (e.g., stay in an unhappy marriage because one cannot afford to settle; child cannot escape an abusive parent).
3. Lack of alternatives—person cannot conceptualize alternatives or in reality there are none.
4. Getting away may be associated with the fear of pursuit (e.g., spouse threatens to kill or harm partner or escapee).
5. Others demand compliance (e.g., cults, autocratic families).

Internal fears and concerns

6. Ashamed to ask for help to leave or ashamed of what others will think (e.g., a quitter, cannot cope).
7. Shame to acknowledge defeat, give up, and move on.
8. Fear that any new place or situation would only be worse.
9. Fear that one will not be able to cope alone (abandonment anxiety or cultlike dependency).
10. Fear of the new (e.g., social anxiety of meeting new people, starting again).
11. Guilt and moral concerns with hurting others (e.g., giving up caring role or harming children via divorce).
12. Beliefs that "it is my fault things are bad here, so there is no point in moving on."
13. Beliefs that one has to prove oneself (or this is God's will; or I deserve punishment; working out one's karma).
14. Beliefs that things "can change if I just hang in here."
15. High ambivalence in current situation—strong motives to stay and to go.
16. Depression itself—simply too tired or exhausted to get going to move on.

As Table 1.4 notes, therefore, human escape behavior may be compromised for many reasons (e.g., conflicts over alternatives, lack of resources, low self-esteem, reduced confidence, or guilt). Even if people are strongly motivated and have the resources to escape, they may still refrain from doing so. For example, they may feel others (e.g., a child or dementing relative) are dependent on them. Knowing that others are dependent on them may stop suicide (Beck, Rush, Shaw, & Emery, 1979) but not reduce depression. Whatever it is that traps people in the current domain, having strong desires to escape but feeling unable to is likely to be depressogenic. My clinical impression is that highly flight-motivated people are also less likely to be able to focus on the positive qualities in their current domain and to improve their current situation. Recent work in our department suggests the entrapment and sense of defeat are highly associated with anhedonia (Gilbert, Allan, & Brough, in preparation). Be it in a marriage, work situation, or living area, flight motivation often makes working to help people improve their current situation more difficult. The therapeutic dilemma is then how to work with patients' goals for escape, yet also to help them focus on how they can improve their current situation so that their flight motivation reduces.

Finally, as already noted, internal stimuli can also activate evolved strategies. Hence strong flight motivation, aroused to one's own thoughts or feelings, or psychotic voices (or hating a part of oneself), feeling imprisoned in a sick or damaged body—a kind of "flight from the self" (as measured by internal entrapment; Baumeister, 1990; Gilbert & Allan, 1998)—can be depressogenic. Basically, in all these domains people experience themselves in an arrested flight situation. The suggestion is that the stronger the flight motivation, and the greater the experience of being trapped and blocked in the ability to escape, the greater the depression and demoblization is likely to be (A. K. Dixon, 1998). More research is needed on these internal processes, but by placing the notions of defeat, arrested fight, and escape as central to depression, we may gain new insights in addition to those already gained from the study of control (Chorpita & Barlow, 1998).

Overview

Evolutionary theory does not suggest that the extremes of psychopathology (e.g., of depression, paranoia, or panic attacks) are adaptive in the modern context (see Lilienfeld & Marino, 1995; and McGuire & Troisi, 1998, for a discussion of these issues). Rather it suggests that there are old, previously adaptive mechanisms and strategies that evolved in prehuman (and preprimate) times that underlie many states we label as psychopathological (Bailey, 1987; MacLean, 1990). Seasonal affective disorder, for example, is probably dependent on ancient and certainly preprimate psychobiological mechanisms. Some states of psychopathology may represent the activation of old mechanisms of defensive behavior (e.g., from reptilian brain) clashing with more recent adaptations (e.g., neocortex) and contextual requirements. The extreme form of demobilization, seen following defeat, blocked escape, and helplessness, is usually not adaptive to humans today but a variety of species exhibit this potential response (MacLean, 1990; Peterson et al., 1993; Toates, 1995) and it is likely it has been conserved in humans. When triggered it can give rise to serious psychopathology.

A central adaptation for humans is the internalization of signal, in which our own thoughts and fantasies can activate internal psychobiological response patterns (e.g., sexual). This allows for highly maladaptive feedback loops of thought (and internal models of self, other, and future) to maintain negative moods. This recent (possible) maladaption has come from a trade-off between the properties and advantages of the neocortex, with the ability for self-awareness, self-evaluation, planning, and foresight, against the disadvantages of positive feedback loops between negative self-evaluation and mood control. As can be seen from Tables 1.3 and 1.4 there are now many complications to the smooth operation of fight and flight in human affairs.

CONCLUSION

Each member of a species has to have strategies for coping with social threats and conflicts (loss of control over punishments and rewards) and be capable of behaving in ways that do not escalate attacks they could not win, able or escape or terminate attacks if they occur, and curtail efforts in the face of nonreward. Controllability is therefore a salient aspect to this discussion (Chorpita & Barlow, 1998). However, control varies greatly according to the rank of an animal. In regard to subordinate submissive strategies there are a variety of potential options. In many species, subordinates are generally more tense and defensive than dominant animals. They show reduced explorative behavior and social confidence, have higher levels of stress hormones, such as cortisol, and lower 5-HT. To a specific down-rank threat they can flee, adopt submissive postures and displays, or engage reverted escape. In limited territory where escape is blocked and harassment takes place, their flight is arrested and they may enter a state of demoblization. These behaviors can be seen as strategic devices mediated by neurobehavioral systems and activated by the appropriate signals. In humans these signals can also be supplied by internal images and thoughts (e.g., perhaps neocortically).

Social defensive behaviors are often not "either–or" but rather various potentials (attack, retreat, demobilize, seek reassurance) vary in strength and can conflict with each other. As A. K. Dixon et al. (1990) noted, these are forms of ambivalent defense. In situations of high arousal, defensive behavior can be modeled using catastrophe theory (Gilbert, 1984) in which dramatic switches can occur in defensive behavior and states of mind (e.g., shifts from attack to flight, sudden freeze states, or tantrums following failed approach in eliciting reassurance). In the study of depression we can start to explore how these submissive and defeat strategies operate and especially what happens when fight and flight are highly aroused but blocked and arrested. In these contexts there can be a switch to a depressive demobilization.

I have not focused too much on the actual goals that people feel they are defeated over. For one person it might be elicitation of signals of love, care, and support; for another it might be related to ambition. It may turn out that the actual goals that people feel defeated and thwarted over are less important than the value they place on them and the degree to which they find themselves failing and in an arrested fight or flight situation. Exploring psychopathology from the point of view of activated submissive strategies may offer new insights into the variety and forms of psychopathology.

ACKNOWLEDGMENTS

I would like to acknowledge the help of Professor M. McGuire and Dr. J. Price and S. Allan during the writing of earlier versions of this chapter.

REFERENCES

Adams, N., & Boice, R. (1983). A longitudinal study of dominance in an outdoor colony of domestic rats. *Journal of Comparative Psychology, 97*, 24–33.

Adler, N. E., Boyce, T., Chesney, M. A., Cohen, S., Folkman, S., Kahn, R. L., & Syme, S. L. (1994). Socioeconomic status and health. *American Psychologist, 49*, 15–24.

Allan, S., & Gilbert, P. (1995). A social comparison scale: Psychometric properties and relationship to psychopathology. *Personality and Individual Differences, 19*, 293–299.

Allan, S., & Gilbert, P. (1997). Submissive behaviour and psychopathology. *British Journal of Clinical Psychology, 36*, 467–488.

American Psychiatic Association. (1994). *Diagnostic and statistical manual of mental disorders* (4th ed.). Washington, DC: Author.

Andrews, B. (1998). Shame and childhood abuse. In P. Gilbert & B. Andrews (Eds.), *Shame: Interpersonal behavior, psychopathology and culture* (pp. 176–190). New York: Oxford University Press.

Anisman, H. (1978). Neurochemical changes elicited by stress: Behavioral correlates. In H. Anisman & G. Bignami (Eds.), *Psychopharmacology of aversively motivated behavior* (pp. 119–172). New York: Plenum.

Anisman, H., Pizzino, A., & Sklar, L. S. (1980). Coping with stress, norepinephrine depletion and escape performance. *Brain Research, 191*, 583–588.

Anisman, H., & Sklar, L. S. (1979). Catecholamine depletion in mice upon re-exposure to stress: Mediation of the escape deficits produced by inescapable shock. *Journal of Comparative and Physiological Psychology, 93*, 610–625.

Archer, J. (1988). *The behavioural biology of aggression*. Cambridge, UK: Cambridge University Press.

Arrindell, W. A., Sanderman, R., Hageman, W. J. J. M., Pickersgill, M. J., Kwee, M. G. T., Van der Molen, H. T., & Lingsma, M. M. (1990). Correlates of assertiveness in normal and clinical samples: A multidimensional approach. *Advances in Behaviour Theory and Research, 12*, 153–282.

Bailey, K. (1987). *Human paleopsychology: Applications to aggression and pathological processes.* Hillsdale, NJ: Lawrence Erlbaum Associates.
Barkow, J. H. (1980). Prestige and self-esteem: A bioscocial interpretation. In D. R. Omark, F. F. Strayer, & D. G. Freedman, (Eds.), *Dominance relations: An ethological view of conflict and social interaction* (pp. 319–332). New York: Garland.
Barkow, J. H. (1989). *Darwin, sex and status: Biological approaches to mind and culture.* Toronto: University of Toronto Press.
Barton, S. (1994). Chaos, self-organization, and psychology. *American Psychologist, 49,* 3–14.
Baumeister, R. F. (1990). Suicide as escape from self. *Psychological Review, 97,* 90–133.
Baumeister, R. F., & Leary, M. R. (1995). The need to belong: Desire for interpersonal attachments as a fundamental human motivation. *Psychological Bulletin, 117,* 497–529.
Beach, S. R. H., Sandeen, E. E., & O'Leary, K. D. (1990). *Depression in marriage.* New York: Guilford.
Beahrs, J. O. (1996). Ritual deception: A window to the hidden determinants of human politics. *Politics and The Life Sciences, 15,* 3–12
Beck, A. T., Emery, G., & Greenberg, R. L. (1985). *Anxiety disorders and phobias: A cognitive approach.* New York: Basic Books.
Beck, A. T., Rush, A. J., Shaw, B. F., & Emery, G. (1979). *Cognitive therapy of depression.* New York: Wiley.
Belsher, G., & Costello, C. G. (1988). Relapse after recovery from unipolar depression: A critical review. *Psychological Bulletin, 104,* 84–86.
Bernstein, I. S. (1980). Dominance: A theoretical perspective for ethologists. In D. R. Omark, F. F. Strayer, & D. G. Freedman (Eds.), *Dominance relations: An ethological view of conflict and social interaction* (pp. 71–84). New York: Garland.
Bifulco, A., & Moran, P. (1998). *Wednesday's child: Research into women's experiences of neglect and abuse in childhood, and adult depression.* London: Routledge.
Birtchnell, J. (1993). *How humans relate: A new interpersonal theory.* Westport, CT: Praeger.
Blatt, S. J., Quinlan, D. M., Chevron, E. S., McDonald, C., & Zuroff, D. (1982). Dependency and self criticism: Psychological dimensions of depression. *Journal of Consulting and Clinical Psychology, 50,* 113–124.
Bornstein, R. F. (1995). Active dependency. *Journal of Nervous and Mental Disease, 182,* 64–77.
Bowlby, J. (1969). *Attachment: Attachment and loss* (Vol. 1). London: Hogarth.
Bowlby, J. (1973). *Separation, anxiety and anger: Attachment and loss* (Vol. 2). London: Hogarth.
Bowlby, J. (1980). *Loss: sadness and depression: Attachment and loss* (Vol. 3). London: Hogarth.
Broman, C. L., & Johnson, E. H. (1988). Anger expression and life stress among Blacks: Their role in physical health. *Journal of the National Medical Association, 80,* 1329–1334.
Brown, G. W., Adler, W. Z., & Bifulco, A. (1988). Life events, difficulties and recovery from chronic depression. *British Journal of Psychiatry, 152,* 487–498.
Brown, G. W., Bifulco, A., & Harris, T. O. (1987). Life events, vulnerability and onset of depression: Some refinements. *British Journal of Psychiatry, 150,* 30–42.
Brown, G. W., & Harris, T. O. (1978). *The social origins of depression.* London: Tavistock.
Brown, G. W., Harris, T. O., & Hepworth, C. (1995). Loss, humiliation and entrapment among women developing depression: A patient and non-patient comparison. *Psychological Medicine, 25,* 7–21.
Buck, R. (1988). *Human motivation and emotion.* New York: Wiley.
Buss, D. M. (1991). Evolutionary personality psychology. In M. R. Rosenzweig & L. W. Porter (Eds.), *Annual review of psychology* (Vol. 45, pp. 459–491). Palo Alto, CA: Annual Reviews.
Buss, D. M. (1995). Evolutionary psychology: A new paradigm for psychological science. *Psychological Inquiry, 6,* 1–87.
Buss, D. M., & Craik, K. H. (1986). Acts, dispositions and clinical assessment: The psychopathology of everyday conduct. *Clinical Psychology Review, 6,* 387–406.
Buss, D. M., & Malamuth, N. M. (1996). *Sex, power, conflict: Evolutionary and feminist perspectives.* New York: Oxford University Press.

Caryl, P. G. (1988). Escalated fighting and the war of nerves: Games theory and animal combat. In P. H. Bateson & P. H. Klopfer (Eds.), *Perspectives in ethology: Advantages of diversity* (Vol. 4, pp. 199–224). New York: Plenum.

Champion, L. A., & Power, M. J. (1995). Social and cognitive approaches to depression. *British Journal of Clinical Psychology, 34,* 485–503.

Chance, M. R. A. (1984). Biological systems synthesis of mentality and the nature of the two modes of mental operation: Hedonic and agonic. *Man–Environment Systems, 14,* 143–157.

Chance, M. R. A. (1988). Introduction. In M. R. A. Chance (Ed.), *Social fabrics of the mind* (pp. 1–35). Hove, UK: Lawrence Erlbaum Associates.

Chance, M. R. A., & Jolly, C. (1970). *Social groups of monkeys, apes and men.* London: J. Cape.

Chapais, B. (1992). The role of alliances in social inheritance of rank among female primates. In A. H. Harcourt & F. B. M. de Waal (Eds.), *Coalitions and alliances in humans and primates* (pp. 29–59). New York: Oxford University Press.

Chenery, D., Seyfarth, R., & Smuts, B. (1986). Social relationships and social cognition in nonhuman primates. *Science, 234,* 1361–1365.

Chorpita, B. F., & Barlow, D. (1998). The development of anxiety: The role of control in the early environment. *Psychological Bulletin, 124,* 3–21.

Clark, C. (1990). Emotions and micropolitics in everyday life: Some patterns and paradoxes of "place." In T. D. Kemper (Ed.), *Research agendas in the sociology of emotions.* New York: State University of New York Press.

Cochrane, N., & Neilson, M. (1977). Depressive illness: The role of aggressiveness further considered. *Psychological Medicine, 7,* 282–288.

Coyne, J. C. (1976). Towards an interactional description of depression. *Psychiatry, 39,* 28–40.

Cronin, H. (1991). *The ant and the peacock.* New York: Cambridge University Press.

Daly, M., & Wilson, M. (1994). Evolutionary psychology of male violence. In J. Archer (Ed.), *Male violence* (pp. 253–288). London: Routledge.

de Waal, F. M. B. (1989). *Peacemaking Among Primates.* New York: Penguin.

de Waal, F. M. B. (1996). *Good natured: The origins of right and wrong in humans and other animals.* Cambridge, MA: Harvard University Press.

Dixon, A. K. (1998). Ethological strategies for defence in animals and humans: Their role in some psychiatric disorders. *British Journal of Medical Psychology, 71,* 417–445.

Dixon, A. K., Fisch, H. U., Huber, C., & Walser, A. (1989). Ethological studies in animals and man: Their use in psychiatry. *Pharmacopsychiatry, 22,* 44–50.

Dixon A. K., Fisch, H. U., & McAllister, K. H. (1990). Ethopharmacology: A biological approach to the study of drug-induced changes in behavior. In P. J. B. Slater. J. S. Rosenblatt, & C. Beer (Eds.), *Advances in the study of behavior* (Vol. 16, pp. 171–204). New York: Academic Press.

Dixon, A. K., Gilbert, P., Huber, L., Gilbert, J., & van Hoek, G. (1997). *An ethological analysis of non-verbal behavior in a neutral and shame interview.* Unpublished manscript.

Dixon, N. F. (1976). *On the psychology of military incompetence.* London: Cape.

Driscoll, R. (1988). Self-condemnation: A conceptual framework for assessment and treatment. *Psychotherapy, 26,* 104–111.

Dunbar, R. I. M. (1988). *Primate social systems.* London: Croom Helm.

Dunbar, R. I. M. (1996). *Grooming, gossip, and the evolution of language.* London: Faber & Faber.

Eibl-Eibesfeldt, I. (1990). Dominance, submission and love: Sexual pathologies from the perspective of ethology. In J. R Feierman (Ed.), *Pedophilia: Biosocial dimensions* (pp 150–175). New York: Springer.

Ekman, P. (1991). *Telling lies: Clues to deceit in the marketplace, politics and marriage.* New York: Norton.

Fava, G. A., Kellner, R., Lisansky, J., Park, S., Perini, G. I., & Zielenzny, K. (1986). Hostility and recovery from melancholia. *Journal of Nervous and Mental Disease, 174,* 414–417.

Fava, M., Anderson, K., & Rosenbaum, J. F. (1990). "Anger attacks": Possible variants of panic in major depressive disorders. *American Journal of Psychiatry, 147,* 867–870.

Frischknecht, H. R., Siegfried, B., & Waser, P. G. (1982). Learning of submissive behaviour in mice: A new model. *Behavioural Processes, 7,* 235–245.
Ganzini, L., McFarland, B. H., & Cutler, D. (1990). Prevalence of mental disorder after a catastrophic financial loss. *Journal of Nervous and Mental Disease, 178,* 680–685.
Gardner, R. (1988). Psychiatric infrastructures for intraspecific communication. In M. R. A., Chance (Ed.), *Social fabrics of the mind* (pp. 197–226). Hove: Lawrence Erlbaum Associates.
Gilbert, P. (1984). *Depression: From psychology to brain state.* London: Lawrence Erlbaum Associates.
Gilbert, P. (1989). *Human nature and suffering.* Hove, UK: Lawrence Erlbaum Associates.
Gilbert, P. (1992). *Depression: The evolution of powerlessness.* Hove: Lawrence Erlbaum Associates, and New York: Guilford.
Gilbert, P. (1993). Defense and safety: Their function in social behaviour and psychopathology. *British Journal of Clinical Psychology, 32,* 131–154.
Gilbert, P. (1995). Biopsychosocial approaches and evolutionary theory as aids to integration in clinical psychology and psychotherapy. *Clinical Psychology and Psychotherapy, 2,* 135–156.
Gilbert, P. (1997a). The evolution of social attractiveness and its role in shame, humiliation, guilt and therapy. *British Journal of Medical Psychology, 70,* 113–147.
Gilbert, P. (1997b). *Overcoming depression: A self-guide using cognitive behavioural techniques.* London: Robinsons.
Gilbert, P. (1998). What is shame? Some core issues and controversies. In P. Gilbert & B. Andrews (Eds.), *Shame: Interpersonal behavior, psychopathology and culture* (pp. 3–38). New York: Oxford University Press.
Gilbert, P. (in press). The evolved social self: Internal conflict and the role of inner warmth and compassion in cognitive therapy. In P. Gilbert & K. Bailey (Eds.), *Genes on the couch: Explorations in evolutionary psychotherapy.* Hove, UK: The Psychology Press.
Gilbert, P., & Allan, S. (1994). Assertiveness, submissive behaviour and social comparison. *British Journal of Clinical Psychology, 33,* 295–306.
Gilbert, P. & Allan, S. (1998). The role of defeat and entrapment (arrested flight) in depression: An exploration of an evolutionary view. *Psychological Medicine, 28,* 584–597.
Gilbert, P., Allan, S., Ball, L., & Bradshaw, Z. (1996). Overconfidence: An exploration based on social rank. *British Journal of Medical Psychology, 69,* 59–68.
Gilbert, P., Allan, S., & Brough, S. (in preparation). Anhedonia and positive affect: An exploration of an evolutionary model.
Gilbert, P., & McGuire, M. (1998). Shame, social roles and status: The psychobiological continuum from monkey to human. In P. Gilbert & B. Andrews (Eds.), *Shame: Interpersonal behavior, psychopathology and culture* (pp. 99–125). New York: Oxford University Press.
Gilbert, P., Pehl, J., & Allan, S. (1994). The phenomenology of shame and guilt: An empirical investigation. *British Journal of Medical Psychology, 67,* 23–36.
Gilbert, P., Price, J. S., & Allan, S. (1995). Social comparison, social attractiveness and evolution: How might they be related? *New Ideas in Psychology, 13,* 149–165.
Goodall, J. (1975). The chimpanzee. In J. V. Goodall (Ed.), *The quest for man.* London: Phaidon.
Goodall, J. (1990). *Through a window: Thirty years with the chimpanzees of Gombe.* New York: Penguin.
Gray, J. A. (1982). *The neuropsychology of anxiety.* Oxford, UK: Oxford University Press.
Gray, J. A. (1987). *The psychology of fear and stress* (2nd ed.). Cambridge, UK: Cambridge University Press.
Greenberg, J. R., & Mitchell, S. A. (1983). *Object relations in psychoanalytic theory.* Cambridge, MA: Harvard University Press.
Greenberg, L. S. (1979). Resolving splits: Use of the two-chair technique. *Psychotherapy, Theory, Research and Practice, 16,* 316–324.
Greenberg, L. S., Elliott, R. K., & Foerster, F. S. (1990). Experiential processes in the psychotherapeutic treatment of depression. In C. D. McCann & N. S. Endler (Eds.), *Depression: New directions in theory, research and practice* (pp. 157–185). Toronto: Wall & Emerson.

Greenberg, L. S., Rice, L. N., & Elliott, R. (1993). *Facilitating emotional change: The moment-by-moment process.* New York: Guilford.

Hammen, C. (1988). Depression and cognitions about personal stressful life events. In L. B. Alloy (Ed.), *Cognitive processes in depression* (pp. 77–108). New York: Guilford.

Harper, R. C. (1985). Power, dominance and nonverbal behavior: An overview. In S. L. Ellyson & J. F. Dovidio (Eds.), *Power, dominance and nonverbal behavior* (pp. 29–48). New York: Springer-Verlag.

Hart, J., Gunnar, M., & Cicchetti, D. (1996). Altered neuroendocrine activity in maltreated children related to symptoms of depression. *Development and Psychopathology, 8,* 201–214.

Hartung, J. (1987). Deceiving down: Conjectures on the management of subordinate status. In J. Lockard & D. Pulhus (Eds.), *Self-deceit: An adaptive strategy* (pp. 170–185). Englewood Cliffs, NJ: Prentice-Hall.

Hartup, W. (1989). Social relationships and their developmental significance. *American Psychologist, 44,* 120–126.

Henry, J. P. (1982). The relation of social to biological process in disease. *Social Science Medicine, 16,* 369–380.

Higley, J. D., Mehlman, P. T., Higley, S., Fremald, B., Vickers, J., Lindell, S. G., Taub, D. M., Suomi, S. J., & Linnoila, M. (1996). Excessive mortality in young free-ranging male nonhuman primates with low cerebrospinal fluid 5-hydroxyindoleacetic acid concentrations. *Archives of General Psychiatry, 53,* 537–543.

Hinde, R. A. (1982). *Ethology.* London: Fontana.

Hobfoll, S. E. (1989). Conservation of resources: A new attempt at conceptualizing stress. *American Psychologist, 44,* 513–524.

Hooley, J. M., & Teasdale, J. D. (1989). Predictors of relapse in unipolar depressives: Expressed emotion, marital distress and perceived criticism. *Journal of Abnormal Psychology, 98,* 229–235.

Horowitz, L. M., & Vitkus, J. (1986). The interpersonal basis of psychiatric symptoms. *Clinical Psychology Review, 6,* 443–470.

James, O. (1997). *Britain on the couch: Why we're unhappier than we were in the 1950's—Despite being richer.* London: Century.

Jenkins, J. H., & Karno, M. (1992). The meaning of expressed emotion: Theoretical issues raised by cross-cultural research. *American Journal of Psychiatry, 149,* 9–21.

Kalma, A. (1991). Hierarchisation and dominance assessment at first glance. *European Journal of Social Psychology, 21,* 165–181.

Kaufman, G. (1989). *The psychology of shame: Theory and treatment of shame-based syndromes.* New York: Springer-Verlag.

Keltner, D. (1995). Signs of appeasement: Evidence for the distinct displays of embarrassment, amusement and shame. *Journal of Personality and Social Psychology, 68,* 441–454.

Keltner, D., & Harker, L. A. (1998). The forms and functions of the nonverbal signal of shame. In P. Gilbert & B. Andrews (Eds.), *Shame: Interpersonal behavior, psychopathology and culture* (pp. 78–98). New York: Oxford University Press.

Kemper, T. D. (1990). *Social structure and testosterone: Explorations of the socio-bio-social chain.* New Brunswick, NJ: Rutgers University Press.

Kevles, B. (1986). *Females of the species: Sex and survival in the animal kingdom.* Cambridge, MA: Harvard University Press.

Kiesler, D. J. (1983). The 1982 interpersonal circle: A taxonomy for complementarity in human transactions. *Psychological Review, 90,* 185–214.

Klinger, E. (1975). Consequences and commitment to aid disengagement from incentives. *Psychological Review, 82,* 1–24.

Krebs, J. R., & Davies, N. B. (1993). *An introduction to behavioral ecology* (3rd ed.). Oxford, UK: Blackwell Scientific.

Kulling, P., Frischknecht, H. R., Pasi, A., Waser, P. G., & Siegfried, B. (1987). Effects of repeated as compared to single aggressive confrontation on nociception and defense behaviour in C57BL/6 and DBA/2 mice. *Physiology & Behaviour, 39,* 599–605.

Lagerspetz, K. M. J., & Sandnabba, K. (1982). The decline of aggressiveness in male mice during group caging as determined by punishment delivered by the cage mates. *Aggressive Behaviour, 8,* 319–328.

Leary, M. R., & Kowalski, R. M. (1990). Impression management: A literature review and two-component model. *Psychological Bulletin, 107,* 34–47.

Leary, T. (1957). *The interpersonal diagnosis of personality.* New York: Ronald.

Leshner, A. I. (1978). *Introduction to behavioral endocrinology.* New York: Oxford University Press.

Lewis, H. B. (1986). The role of shame in depression. In M. Rutter, C. E. Izard, & P. B. Read (Eds.), *Depression in young people: Developmental and clinical perspectives* (pp. 325–339). New York: Guilford.

Lilienfeld, S. O., & Marino, L. (1995). Mental disorder as a roschian concept: A critique of Wakefield's "harmful dysfunction" analysis. *Journal of Abnormal Psychology, 104,* 411–420.

MacLean, P. (1985). Brain evolution relating to family, play and the separation call. *Archives of General Psychiatry, 42,* 405–417.

MacLean, P. D. (1990). *The triune brain in evolution.* New York: Plenum.

Marks, I. M. (1987). *Fears, phobias, and rituals: Panic, anxiety and their disorders.* Oxford, UK: Oxford University Press.

Maynard Smith, J. (1982). *Evolution and the theory of games.* Cambridge, UK: Cambridge University Press.

McGuire, M. T., & Troisi, A. (1987). Physiological regulation-disregulation and psychiatric disorders. *Ethology and Sociobiology, 8,* 9S–12S.

McGuire, M. T., & Troisi, A. (1998). *Darwinian psychiatry.* New York: Oxford University Press.

Meerlo, P., de Boer, S. F., Koolhaas, J. M., Daan, S., & Van den Hoofdakker, R. H. (1996). Changes in daily rhythms of body temperature and activity after a single social defeat in rats. *Physiology and Behaviour, 59,* 735–739.

Nesse, R. M. (1990). Evolutionary explanations of emotions. *Human Nature, 1,* 261–289.

Nesse, R. (1998). Emotional disorders in evolutionary perspective. *British Journal of Medical Psychology, 71,* 397–415.

Ohman, A. (1986). Fear the beast and fear the face: Animal and social fears as prototypes for evolutionary analyses of emotion. *Psychophysiology, 23,* 123–145.

Parker, G. A. (1974). Assessment strategy and the evolution of fighting behaviour. *Journal of Theoretical Biology, 47,* 223–243.

Parkinson, B., Totterdell, P., Brinder, R. B., & Reynolds, S. (1996). *Changing moods: The psychology of mood & mood regulation.* London: Longman.

Peterson, C., Maier, S. F., & Seligman, M. E. P. (1993). *Learned helplessness: A theory for the age of personal control.* New York: Oxford University Press.

Pilowsky, I., & Spence, N. D. (1975). Hostility and depressive illness. *Archives of General Psychiatry, 32,* 1154–1157.

Pratto, F., Sidanius, J., Stallworth, L. M., & Malle, B. (1994). Social dominance orientation: A personality variable predicting social and political attitudes. *Journal of Personality and Social Psychology, 67,* 741–763.

Price, J. S. (1972). Genetic and phylogenetic aspects of mood variations. *International Journal of Mental Health, 1,* 124–144.

Price, J. S. (1988). Alternative channels for negotiating asymmetry in social relationships. In M. R. A. Chance (Ed.), *Social fabrics of the mind* (pp. 157–195). Hove, UK: Lawrence Erlbaum Associates.

Price, J. S., & Gardner, R. (1995). The paradoxical power of the depressed patient: A problem for the ranking theory of depression. *British Journal of Medical Psychology, 68,* 193–206.

Price J. S., & Sloman, L. (1987). Depression as yielding behaviour: An animal model based on Schjelderup-Ebb's pecking order. *Ethology and Sociobiology, 8* (Suppl.), 85–98.

Raab, A., Dantzer, R., Michaud, B., Mormede, P., Taghzouti, K., Simon, H., & LeMoal, M. (1986). Behavioural, physiological and immunological consequences of social status and aggression in chronically co-existing resident–intruder dyads of male rats. *Physiology and Behaviour, 36,* 223–228.

Radtke, H. L., & Stam, H. J. (Eds.). (1994). *Power/gender: Social relations in theory and practice.* London: Sage.

Raleigh, M. J., McGuire, M. T., Brammer, G. L., Pollack, D. B., & Yuwiler, A. (1991). Serotonergic mechanisms promote dominance acquisition in adult male vervet monkeys. *Brain Research, 559,* 181–190.

Ray, J. C., & Sapolsky, R. M. (1992). Styles of social behavior and their endocrine correlates among high-ranking wild baboons. *American Journal of Primatology, 28,* 231–250.

Rehm, L. P. (1988). Self-management and cognitive processes in depression. In L. B. Alloy (Ed.), *Cognitive processes in depression* (pp. 143–176). New York: Guilford.

Riley, W. T., Treiber, F. A., & Woods, M. G. (1989). Anger and hostility in depression. *Journal of Nervous and Mental Disease, 177,* 668–674.

Rooke, O., & Birchwood, M. (1998). Loss, humiliation and entrapment as appraisals of schizophrenic illness: A prospective study of depressed and non-depressed patients. *British Journal of Clinical Psychology, 37,* 259–268.

Rosenblum, L. A., Coplan, J. D., Friedman, S., Bassoff, T., Gorman, J. M., & Andrews, M. W. (1994). Adverse early experiences affect noradrenergic and serotonergic functioning in adult primates. *Biological Psychiatry, 35,* 221–227.

Sarnoff, I., & Zimbardo, P. G. (1961). Anxiety, fear and social affiliation. *Journal of Abnormal and Social Psychology, 62,* 356–363.

Sapolsky, R. M. (1989). Hypercortisolism among socially subordinate wild baboons originates at the CNS level. *Archives of General Psychiatry, 46,* 1047–1051.

Sapolsky, R. M. (1990a). Adrenocortical function, social rank and personality among wild baboons. *Biological Psychiatry, 28,* 862–878.

Sapolsky, R. M. (1990b). Stress in the wild. *Scientific American,* pp. 106–113.

Sapolsky, R. M. (1994). Individual differences and the stress response. *Seminars in the Neurosciences, 6,* 261–269.

Scheff, T. J. (1994). *Bloody revenge: Emotions, nationalism and war.* Boulder, CO: Westview.

Scheld, J. T. M. (1998a). Major depression: Behavioral markers of depression and recovery. *Journal of Mental and Nervous Disease, 186,* 133–140.

Scheld, J. T. M. (1998b). Major depression: Behavioral parameters of depression and recovery. *Journal of Mental and Nervous Disease, 186,* 141–149.

Schore, A. N. (1994). *Affect regulation and the origin of the self: The neurobiology of emotional development.* Hillsdale, NJ: Lawrence Erlbaum Associates.

Scott, J. C. (1990). *Domination and the arts of resistance.* New Haven, CT: Yale University Press.

Segrin, C., & Abramson, L. Y. (1994). Negative reactions to depressive behaviours: A communication theories analysis. *Journal of Abnormal Psychology, 103,* 655–668.

Seligman, M. E. P. (1975). *Helplessness: On depression development and death.* San Francisco: Freeman.

Swallow, S. R., & Kuiper, N. A. (1988). Social comparison and negative self evaluation: An application to depression. *Clinical Psychology Review, 8,* 55–76.

Tangney, J. P. (1995). Shame and guilt in interpersonal relationships. In J. P Tangney & K. W. Fischer (Eds.), *Self-conscious emotions: The psychology of shame, guilt, embarrassment and pride* (pp. 114–139). New York: Guilford.

Tangney, J. P., Burggraf, S. A., & Wagner, P. E. (1995). Shame-proneness, guilt-proneness, and psychological symptoms. In J. P Tangney & K. W. Fischer (Eds.), *Self-conscious emotions: The psychology of shame, guilt, embarrassment and pride* (pp 343–367). New York: Guilford.

Toates, F. (1995). *Stress: Conceptual and biological aspects.* Chichester, UK: Wiley.

Trivers, R. (1985). *Social evolution.* Menlo Park, CA: Benjamin/Cummings.

van de Poll, N. E., Smeets, J., van Oyen, H. G., & van de Zwan, S. M. (1982). Behavioural consequences of agonistic experiences in rats: Sex differences and effects of testosterone. *Journal of Comparative and Physiological Psychology, 96,* 893–903.

van der Dennen, J. M. G. (1986). Ethnocentrism and in-group/out-group differentiation: A review and interpretation of the literature. In V. Reynolds, V. Falger, & I. Vine (Eds.), *The sociobiology of ethnocentrism: Evolutionary dimensions of xenophobia, discrimination, racism and nationalism* (pp. 1–47). London: Croom Helm.

Vinokur, A. D., & van Ryn, M. (1993). Social undermining: Their independent effects on the mental health of unemployed persons. *Journal of Personality and Social Psychology, 65,* 350–359.

Von Holst, D. (1986). Vegetative and somatic components of tree shrews' behaviour. *Journal of the Autonomic Nervous System,* (suppl.), 657–670.

Wagner, C. C., Kiesler, D. J., & Schmidt, J. A. (1995). Assessing the interpersonal transaction cycle: Convergence of action and the reaction interpersonal circumplex measures. *Journal of Personality and Social Psychology, 69,* 938–949.

Weiss, J. M., Glazer, H. I., & Pohorecky, L. A. (1976). Coping behavior and neurochemical changes. An alternative explanation for the original "learned helplessness" experiments. In G. Serban & A. Kling (Eds.), *Animal models in human psychobiology* (pp. 141–173). New York: Plenum.

Weiss, J. M., Glazer, H. I., Pohorecky, L. A., Bailey, W. H., & Schneider, L. H. (1979). Coping behavior and stress-induced behavioral depression: Studies of the role of brain catecholamines. In R. A. Depue (Ed.), *The Psychobiology of the depressive disorders.* New York: Academic Press.

Weiss, J. M., & Simson, P. G. (1985). Neurochemical mechanisms underlying stress-induced depression. In T. M. Field, P. M. McCabe, & N. Schneiderman (Eds.), *Stress and coping* (pp. 93–116). London: Lawrence Erlbaum Associates.

Weissman, M. M., Klerman, G. L., & Paykel, E. S. (1971). Clinical evaluation of hostility in depression. *American Journal of Psychiatry, 128,* 261–266.

Wilkinson, R. G. (1996). *Unhealthy societies: The affiliations of inequality.* London: Routledge.

Williams, J. L., & Lierle, D. M. (1986). Effects of stress controllability, immunization, and therapy on the subsequent defeat of colony intruders. *Animal Learning and Behavior, 14,* 305–314.

Williams, J. L., & Lierle, D. M. (1988). Effects of repeated defeat by a dominant conspecific on subsequent pain sensitivity, open-field activity, and escape learning. *Animal Learning and Behavior, 16,* 477–485.

Willner, P. (1993a). Anhedonia. In C. G. Costello (Ed.), *Symptoms of depression* (pp. 63–84). New York: Wiley.

Willner, P. (1993b). Animal models of stress: An overview. In C. Stanford & P. Salmon (Eds.), *Stress: From synapse to syndrome* (pp. 145–165). London: Academic Press.

Wilson, M., & Daly, M. (1992). The man who mistook his wife for a chattel. In J. H. Barkow, L. Cosmides, and J. Tooby (Eds.), *The adapted mind: Evolutionary psychology and the generation of culture* (pp. 289–322). New York: Oxford University Press.

Zuroff, D. C., & Mongrain, M. (1987). Dependency and self criticism: Vulnerability factors for depressive affective states. *Journal of Abnormal Psychology, 96,* 14–22.

CHAPTER TWO

How the Involuntary Defeat Strategy Relates to Depression

Leon Sloman
Centre for Addiction and Mental Health, Toronto, Ontario

Whereas the psychotherapist often formulates the client's depressive disorder in psychodynamic terms, the biologically oriented North American psychiatrist conceptualizes the client's depression in terms of the *Diagnostic and Statistical Manual of Mental Disorders* (4th ed., American Psychiatric Association, 1994) and brain neurotransmitter changes. In contrast, the family therapist attributes the depressive symptoms to interpersonal transactions. The thoughtful practitioner, however, considers all these perspectives in formulating the case. The etiology of depression within these frameworks includes adverse developmental environments, intrapsychic conflicts, previous losses, genetic factors, and brain neurotransmitter changes. Although comprising different perspectives, all conceptualize depression in terms of specific aspects of the interaction between the individual's biology and life experience.

Evolutionary explanations deal with the impact of evolution by natural selection. When applied to psychological phenomena, they incorporate biological goals, trait heritability, and trait variation. The origins of behavioral mechanisms may antedate our primate ancestors, going back even further to our reptilian ancestors. Using this evolutionary approach, I explore how some features of depression (but not depression itself) may have arisen from their improving the overall chances of success of the individual's genes surviving in the gene pool. The evolutionary theorist faces the challenge of having to explain why mood disorders, which are often maladaptive for the individual, have not been weeded out by natural selection and, moreover, continue to have a high prevalence. An understanding of the role of depression requires a consideration of the evolutionary function of the mechanisms involved and a differentiation between when they function effectively and when they do not.

In this chapter I show how psychodynamic, interpsychic, and biological mechanisms operate synergistically to help the individual cope with competitive loss. I argue that a better understanding of how in-built strategies facilitate adaptation to defeat in competitive encounters will, in turn, clarify the etiology and phenomenology of some forms of depression. I demonstrate the pivotal role of a normally adaptive strategy—the involuntary defeat strategy (IDS)—in the etiology of depression. The role of the IDS in avoiding and rapidly terminating conflict is described, as well as situations that render the IDS ineffective. This is followed by a demonstration of how ineffective functioning of the IDS can contribute to depressive disorders and other forms of psychopathology. Clinical examples are provided to illustrate these themes.

EVOLUTIONARY EXPLANATIONS OF DEPRESSION

According to the conservation-withdrawal theory of depression (Schmale, 1973), some forms of depressive illness facilitate the restoration of depleted resources by causing the individual to withdraw and "lay low." However, because depressive illness in adults is typically associated with biological hyperarousal (Levitan, Hasey, & Sloman, chap. 4, this volume), it would deplete rather than conserve resources. This suggests that the conservation-withdrawal hypothesis would be more relevant to infants than to older people.

According to attachment theory (Bowlby, 1980), the infant's response to separation occurs in stages. In the initial protest stage, the infant is agitated and frantic and emits distress vocalizations. In the following despair stage, the infant becomes inactive, withdrawn, and silent. The protest behavior is thought to increase the probability that the mother will find the infant. If the mother fails to find the infant, continued protest would deplete the infant's physiological resources and would attract predators. The despair response conserves energy and protects the infant from predators. This scenario, in which both the protest and despair reactions are causally related to separation from mother and to each other, suggests that the separation response could be positively selected in an evolutionary sense (Kaufman, 1977).

Klinger (1977) claimed that depression acts as a disengagement process because of a loss of incentive resulting from failure to achieve a goal. Klinger distinguished four phases in an incentive-disengagement cycle provoked by loss or goal nonattainment: (a) increased activity or invigoration; (b) aggression; (c) grief, apathy, or depression; and (d) detachment or recovery. These stages have been observed in people and animals. The first stage is adaptive in that it incites the individual to try harder to succeed. The second phase involves an increased effort to exert control in an unfavorable situation; that is, the individual protests, and seeks out the lost attachment object, or fights. It may be seen as a last-resort effort to direct maximum effort to achieve an important incentive. If this fails, the individual may try to escape. The third (depressive) stage is viewed as a shut-off mechanism evolved to reduce activity; when the costs of pursuing something become too large compared to the probable gains, the organism stops. Klinger's stages are relevant to social competition, as I illustrate in what follows.

Nesse (1991) suggested that mood regulates resource allocation, which refers to animals' decisions about what to do next—sleep, forage, find a mate, dig a den, and so on. High mood encourages the individual to allocate time and energy to the activities most likely to result in success. Low mood causes him or her to withdraw from wasted enterprises. Nesse saw the social competition model as a subset of his model, and his notion that mood variation leads to a more productive allocation of resources has an elegant simplicity. He did not, however, delineate the specific strategies that contribute to the switching from less to more productive activities.

THE IDS AND THE SOCIAL COMPETITION MODEL OF DEPRESSION

Our model has been labeled the *social competition hypothesis of depression* (Price, Sloman, Gardner, Gilbert, & Rhode, 1994) and was initially advanced by Price (1967). Drawing on observations of long-tailed macaques (Zuckerman, 1932), Price noted the similarity between depressed patients and animals who lose in hierarchical encounters and are pressed into a subordinate social role. He proposed that "states of depression, anxiety, and irritability are the emotional concomitants of behavior patterns which are necessary for the maintenance of dominance hierarchies in social groups" (Price, 1967, p. 244). According to Price (1967), the main prediction from the hypothesis was that "factors which increase or reduce dominance behavior will have malignant or beneficial effects on mental illness" (p. 243). He went on to say, "it is difficult to think of a behavior pattern more likely to result in adjustment to lower level in the hierarchy than the sort of behavior and symptoms we observe in depressed patients" (p. 244). His premise was that ideas of inferiority and unworthiness, withdrawal, loss of self-esteem, loss of libido, and other characteristic features of depression were specifically designed to discourage the individual from continuing the competitive struggle or attempting to regain his or her former status.

Price (1969) proposed that depression, anxiety, and feelings of inferiority evolved as the "yielding component of ritual agonistic encounters" (p. 1107). Yielding may bring the agonistic encounter to an end if the adversary accepts his or her submission. This reduces the chances of injury or death and can, in some instances, turn a competitive encounter into an affiliative one.

Schjelderup-Ebbe (1935) introduced the concept of *pecking order* and described, albeit somewhat anthropomorphically, how an alpha-bird reacts to losing a fight by taking refuge in flight:

> Deeply depressed in spirit, humble, with drooping wings and head in the dust, it is—at any rate directly on being vanquished—overcome with paralysis, although one cannot detect any physical injury. The bird's resistance now seems broken, and in some cases the effects of the psychological condition are so strong that the bird sooner or later comes to grief.

Price and Sloman (1987) used Schjelderup-Ebbe's observations to link the "yielding subroutine of ritual agonistic behavior" (p. 85S) with depression.

Price et al. (1994) renamed the yielding subroutine the *involuntary subordinate strategy* (ISS) in their social competition hypothesis of depression. They postulated that "the depressive state evolved in relation to social competition as an unconscious involuntary losing strategy enabling the individual to accept defeat in ritual agonistic encounters and to accommodate to what would otherwise be unacceptably low social rank" (p. 309). In this book, we replace ISS with IDS, as it is more specific. Gilbert (1992) pointed out that depression often follows an unsuccessful struggle to achieve goals, following which people describe their position as one of defeat (Gilbert & Allan, 1998). This perspective is congruent with that of Klinger (1977).

The IDS is a genetically preprogrammed strategy, triggered by an individual's recognition that defeat in social competition is inevitable. This strategy reduces the risk of injury or death to both combatants, first by convincing the loser of the futility of further struggle and triggering either flight or submission and promoting subjective acceptance of the new status quo. In addition, it conveys to the winner that his or her opponent is no longer a threat, because the battle is more or less over. This may convince the winner to accept the opponent's submission and end the struggle. The IDS is *involuntary* because it is triggered automatically by the recognition that one has lost the competitive encounter or that defeat is inevitable. The term *defeat* refers to the fact that it is triggered by defeat and also to its role in promoting accommodation to subordinate status. The term *strategy* reflects its genetic preprogramming to fulfill an adaptive function.

According to Levitan et al. (chap. 4, this volume), the IDS can be thought of as a preprogrammed neural circuit linking the limbic system, prefrontal cortex, and striatum, which mediate the emotional, cognitive, and behavioral components, respectively, of the IDS.

HAWK-DOVE STRATEGIES

When the tide is turning against one in a conflict, one faces the choice of escalating, which causes one to try harder or use more hardball tactics, or de-escalating, which involves going for damage limitation, backing off, retreating, or giving up. Maynard Smith (1982) and Gilbert (chap. 1, this volume) referred to these options as *hawk and dove strategies.* When pursuing a meaningful resource such as food, territory, or sexual opportunity, the animal may have to deal with competitors. When the animal is evaluating his chances of success prior to engaging in a competitive struggle, or during the course of a struggle, he has to evaluate the relative merits of a hawk versus dove strategy. A dove strategy enables one to avoid getting into, or prolonging a struggle one will lose, whereas a hawk strategy facilitates better access to resources. The decision to employ a dove or hawk strategy can be complex, and making the right decision can have far-reaching consequences. If the individual has, because of earlier experiences, been programmed to be overly submissive or overly challenging, he or she may, as a result, make decisions that are not in his or her best interests. This may become an important issue in psychotherapy.

FUNCTIONS OF THE IDS

The mild forms of IDS play a crucial role in the individual's accommodation to a subordinate social role and assist in the modification of unrealistic goals and aspirations. The IDS has three functions:

1. An executive function that inhibits aggressive or escalating competitive or acquisitive behavior to rivals and superiors. This creates a subjective sense of incapacity so that the individual loses his or her motivation to continue the fight or struggle on.
2. A signaling function to signal "no threat" to rivals and "out of action" to any kin or supporters who might wish to press the individual back into the fray.
3. A facilitative function that puts the individual into a "giving up" state of mind. This may trigger escape or submission, thus promoting fading of resentment and facilitating psychological acceptance of the outcome of competition or the inability to achieve goals. Acceptance serves to switch off the IDS and frees the individual to relate to his or her successful opponent in a more affiliative way and redirect his or her efforts into other endeavors.

SUBMISSIVE BEHAVIOR, THE IDS AND PSYCHOPATHOLOGY

Gilbert and Allan (1994) found that submissiveness, or low assertiveness, was associated with depression, social anxiety, and personality factors such as neuroticism and introversion. I attribute submissiveness to early automatic triggering of the IDS so that Gilbert and Allan's findings support the proposed link -

between the IDS and depression. Furthermore, Gilbert (chap. 1, this volume) and Allan and Gilbert (1997) again reported that some forms of submissive behavior, particularly those associated with passive withdrawal and inhibition, are associated with a wide variety of psychological problems, especially depression.

In humans, subordinates with psychological problems usually lack confidence in social domains of relating, fearing either rejection, criticism, or attacks (Allan & Gilbert, 1997). Although different labels might be required, the same kind of link appears to apply to nonhumans. For example, Sapolsky (1994) commented that subordinate animals are often tense, hypervigilant to attack, flight motivated, nonexplorative. They also often occupy peripheral positions in groups. Submissive behavior is probably indicative of quick triggering of the IDS. The origins of the link between submissiveness and premature triggering of the IDS are discussed later in this chapter in the section on Factors Affecting Effectiveness of the IDS. I now discuss the link between defeat and depression.

RELATION BETWEEN BIOLOGICAL CHANGES IN DEFEAT AND DEPRESSION

Another way to link the IDS with depression is to demonstrate the similarity between the biological changes associated with defeat and with depression. Animal studies have found a significant relation between the biological changes in animals experiencing defeat in hierarchical contests and those associated with human depression (Gilbert, chap. 1, this volume; Levitan et al., chap. 4, this volume; and McGuire, Fawzy, Spar, & Troisi, chap. 3, this volume). The function of the IDS is to de-escalate conflict, but if the IDS is ineffective, de-escalation does not occur and the physiological activation associated with conflict persists. The changes observed in human depression can be attributed to a failure of demobilization; the individual remains primed for combat though he or she recognizes that he or she cannot win (Levitan et al., chap. 4, this volume).

THE ROLE OF DEFEAT AND ENTRAPMENT IN DEPRESSION

Gilbert (chap. 1, this volume) and Gilbert and Allan (1998) showed that being defeated and having to stay or being trapped in the arena of conflict is highly associated with depression, more so than hopelessness. One example would be Schjelderup-Ebbe's (1935) defeated chicken, which cannot escape from the scene. Another example is learned helplessness (Peterson, Maier, & Seligman, 1993), in which the animal first makes vigorous attempts to escape but becomes immobilized when it fails to escape.

Gilbert and Allan (1998) developed new measures of entrapment and defeat and found that these measures correlated significantly with depression. Entrapment and defeat added substantially to the explained variance of depression after controlling for the other social rank variables such as submissive behavior and social comparison. The apparent reason for defeat and entrapment leading to depression is that, if the defeated individual escapes from the scene or if the individual's submission is accepted by the opponent, the individual accepts defeat and moves on to more productive activities. Acceptance of disappointment and defeat serves to switch off the IDS, which enables the individual to feel less depressed. In the case of defeat and entrapment, the individual feels caught so that his or her IDS is not switched off, resulting in a persistent IDS and increasing frustration, a recipe for depression.

SHAME

Gilbert and McGuire (1998) defined shame as "an aversive experience related to feeling demeaned, reduced, disgraced, or diminished which people are highly motivated to avoid" (p. 99). They argued that shame evolved from phylogenetically older mechanisms that originally evolved to regulate social rank and status behavior. Gilbert and McGuire suggested that, in its potentially adaptive role, shame functions "to alert actors to the fact that certain social signals they are sending . . . will elicit negative (devaluation) signals from others. Hence a loss of status or diminishment in the role is a likely consequence of sending . . . certain inappropriate signals" (p. 104). They commented that shame signals (e.g., head down, gaze avoidance, and hiding) are generally regarded as appeasement displays, designed to de-escalate or escape from conflicts. They viewed shame as a damage limitation strategy adopted when continuing in a shameless, nonsubmissive way might provoke very serious attacks or rejection by others. They concluded, "Thus an experience of shame can be seen as an involuntary submissive response, typically triggered by social threat, the function of which is to de-escalate conflict" (p. 102).

Gilbert and McGuire (1998) said that "human social status and acceptance in groups have evolved to be highly reliant on signals of being attractive, valued, wanted and approved by others" (p. 99). Gilbert (1997) concluded that competition by attraction has largely replaced competition by intimidation and is the main form of competition seen in primitive tribes by anthropologists. Gilbert and McGuire's description of the function of shame corresponds to that of the IDS. However, the role of shame appears to be specifically associated with competition by attraction. Competition by attraction is less applicable to the sports arena, but may be applicable to most other arenas. This would suggest that shame is sometimes associated with the IDS so that the features of the IDS would vary depending on the nature of the conflict. In fact, one commonly observes various admixtures of shame with other features of depression.

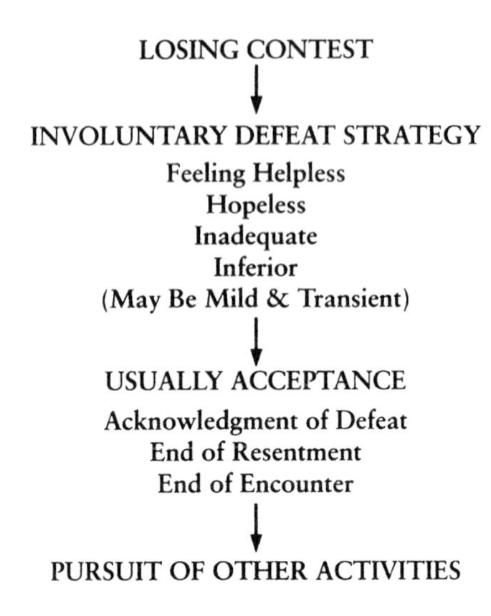

FIG. 2.1. Involuntary defeat strategy and acceptance.

THE EFFECTIVE IDS

The effective IDS reduces motivation to continue the struggle, adjusts aspirations, and increases readiness to flee or submit while engaged or considering engagement in a confrontation. A mild IDS may be characterized as disappointment; a more powerful IDS may be associated with feelings of depression.

Figure 2.1 illustrates stages of competitive interaction associated with an effective IDS. The IDS is triggered by defeat, and then itself triggers escape or submission and acceptance. This flexible responsiveness to the changed situation is associated with an effective IDS and a strong sense of self. The behavior of the winner may have a substantial impact on the loser's IDS. For example, the winner may show magnanimity by saying "you put up a good fight" or saying "that was a great game, you played very well." The winner may also share the spoils of the fight or, in other species, accept grooming from the defeated rival. Such friendliness and positive acknowledgment of the loser's prowess make it easier to accept defeat. Receiving support from someone to whom he or she is securely attached or a secure attachment to the agonistic adversary lowers the individual's level of arousal, causing resentment to fade and promoting acceptance. Acceptance is associated with termination of the IDS.

THE COMPETITIVE STRATEGY SET

The competitive strategy set is comprised of three stages, the first of which is the escalating strategy. The escalating strategy is geared to enhance the likelihood of success by putting more effort into winning the competitive encounter. There is a triggering of the fight response at the start of conflict associated with arousal and escalation as the individual goes all out to win. An optimistic orientation and the arousal of anger may make one try harder to win.

The second stage is the IDS. The optimistic attitude of the previous stage is now replaced by a pessimistic appraisal of the outcome of the encounter. The individual now feels incompetent, weak, inadequate, and hopeless about the chances of winning and there is an inhibition of aggressive behavior. The function of the IDS is to de-escalate the conflict as exemplified by the attitude that there is no point in continuing a struggle one cannot win.

The third stage is the stage of acceptance. Its function is to facilitate reconciliation after the conflict has passed. One now treats the opponent as stronger than oneself and the fading of resentment enables one to accept defeat and the new status quo. As a result one can either resume an affiliative relationship with the opponent, look for another territory, or pursue new alternatives. Achievement of the stage of acceptance reflects termination of the IDS.

THE INEFFECTIVE IDS

Whereas effective functioning of the IDS reduces the risk of psychopathology, ineffective functioning of the IDS often contributes to clinical depression and other forms of psychopathology. An overly persistent IDS is usually indicative of ineffectiveness and this may manifest as extreme submissiveness. This would account for the link between submissiveness, the IDS, and psychopathology (described earlier in this chapter).

We have seen how defeat can lead to a triggering of the IDS followed by submission or acceptance. Combatants' anger or need to win, after the initial defeat, may compel them to continue the struggle with three possible outcomes, shown in Fig. 2.2. First, there is the possibility that, as a result of their increased efforts, the tide will turn in their favor. Second, if they continue to lose, this may quickly convince them that further struggle is hopeless, causing them to flee or to accept defeat, submit, and bring the struggle to an end. A more negative outcome occurs when their IDS has been triggered, but they are prevented from giving up the struggle by strong feelings of resentment, or by the refusal of the opponent to accept their submission. This can cause negative affect and cognitions associated with the IDS to intensify as they see their efforts are to no avail. Accordingly, they feel increasingly disempowered and become more and more depressed. In these situations, the IDS continues to operate and the features that are geared to bring an end to the struggle (i.e., to de-escalate) have failed to achieve their purpose and instead cause an intensification at the intrapsychic level and possibly at the interpsychic level. At the intrapsychic level, feelings of helplessness and hopelessness, which have the function of triggering submission

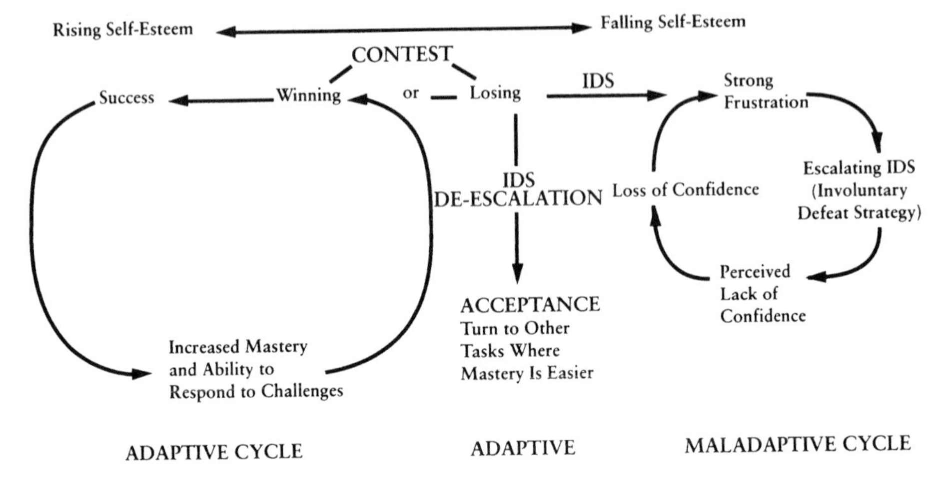

FIG. 2.2. Adaptive and maladaptive cycles in response to success and failure.

or flight, are no longer effective. As a result, they become more intense and manifest as a depressive disorder. At the interpsychic level, the intensification may manifest as power struggles (Sloman, 1981), put-downs or "double-bind" communications (Bateson, Jackson, Haley, & Weakland, 1956). The presence of the persistent IDS may prevent the individual from engaging in open conflict, but the conflict continues in a covert fashion.

Another explanation of the cause of a persistent IDS is the notion of *kindling* (Post & Weiss, 1998; Segal, Williams, Teasdale, & Gemar, 1996). Kindling means that, when the IDS has been overstimulated at an earlier point in time, a smaller amount of stimulation is subsequently required to produce the same strength of reaction. The notion of kindling purports to explain why the first depressive illness may be precipitated by a major loss, whereas subsequent relapses are triggered by much smaller losses.

FACTORS AFFECTING EFFECTIVENESS OF THE IDS

The effectiveness of the IDS, that is, the readiness to give up the struggle, may be influenced by a number of factors. These include (a) resource value, (b) group interaction variables, (c) entrapment, and (d) personality and psychodynamic factors. Many factors may contribute to how an individual deals with competitive loss.

Resource Value

The resource value is the value that the individual attaches to the resource that is the object of the struggle. In many conflicts of interest, defeat may be painful, but the practical consequences are minor. This makes it easier to accept defeat. Even if one has to leave the arena permanently, there may be other arenas in which one can experience success. In such an instance the setback is only temporary. However, at times, submission to the opponent entails giving up a great deal so that the options of submitting or continuing the struggle are both unacceptable. This is exemplified by the case of Cindy outlined later.

Group Interaction Variables

An extreme and long-standing resentment between the competitors may make it too painful for the loser to submit and for the winner to accept the submission. In this situation the triggering of the loser's IDS fails to trigger acceptance by either or both parties. If the adversary refuses to accept submission and continues to behave competitively by using put-downs, this is likely to result in anger and resentment. If the adversary appears more powerful, this resentment may trigger a persistent IDS, which can culminate in depression or an escalating power struggle. This pattern is often observed in contentious divorces. Another factor that makes it harder to accept defeat is group pressure from other members of the same group, who, for their own reasons, want the struggle to continue. Examples of what they might say include, "Don't let him get away with that," or "Don't let him make a fool of you," or "Don't let us down."

Support from other members of the group can also make it easier to accept defeat. For example, statements like "You did very well" or "We were proud of you" serve to soften resentment and make it easier to accept defeat, thus freeing one to engage in more productive activities.

Entrapment

Gilbert (chap. 1, this volume) noted that in many cases defeat may be less pathogenic if the loser can escape the arena, move away, leave the territory, and so on. When escape is blocked (flight is not possible), defeatlike states seem especially prolonged and severe. Gilbert and Allan (1998) found that entrapment perceptions, (e.g., inability to get out of a relationship), were highly correlated with depression. Individuals became trapped for many reasons (e.g., lack of resources to leave, fear of moving on, external pressure to stay, etc.). Whatever the reason, the individual is highly motivated for flight or escape, but is stuck. Acceptance of defeat and accommodation to the new situation of defeat cannot proceed when the person is flight motivated.

Personality and Psychodynamic Factors

The individual's sense of self or self-esteem will have consequences for the response to competitive loss. Kohut and Wolfe (1978) said:

> a strong sense of self allows us to tolerate even wide swings in self-esteem in response to victory or defeat, success or failure. . . . If our self is firmly established we shall neither be afraid of the dejection that may follow a failure or of the expansive fantasies that may follow a success—reactions that would endanger those with a more precariously established self. (pp. 414–415)

Premature triggering of the IDS may be attributed to a history of having autocratic and punitive parents, physical abuse, or sexual abuse. This may result in the subsequent automatic triggering of the IDS in every conflict or potential conflict. Sometimes, however, siblings react differently to the same parent, so that one is overly submissive and the other is openly rebellious. A weak passive parent may also contribute to a child becoming submissive, because the child feels the parent cannot tolerate the child's aggression. This is exemplified by the unassertive client, who said, "My loyalty to my father has prevented me from being more assertive than he was."

An overly persistent IDS is associated with a rigidity in the pattern of responsiveness. These individuals find it difficult to end the agonistic encounter and accept defeat and they are often quick to anger, which can manifest as a quickness to take offense. If the individuals perceive, in the course of escalating conflict, that defeat is inevitable, there is a further triggering of the IDS, which causes them to feel more subordinate. They therefore become more sensitive to criticism or rejection, which generates a spiraling cycle characterized by an increasing intensity of anger or resentment that makes them feel unfairly treated or victimized. This is described as *rejection sensitivity* (Downey & Feldman, 1996; Klein, 1971; Sloman, 2000). The quick arousal of their anger and the quick triggering of their IDS generates a spiraling cycle that makes these individuals prone to a persistent IDS that manifests as depression.

RELATION BETWEEN DESIGN AND FUNCTION OF IDS

The component features of an effectively functioning IDS are listed in Table 2.1. The table illustrates behaviors, emotions, cognitions, self-perceptions, and perceptions of others. These different aspects of the IDS are exquisitely designed for coping with the varying situations associated with loss in competition. Because people differ in how they handle competitive encounters and respond to defeat, no two competitive encounters are alike, so one is unlikely to find all the listed features of the IDS in a single individual.

TIMING OF SUBMISSION

Effective functioning of the IDS causes loss of motivation to continue the adversarial encounter, which prompts the decision that further struggle would be

TABLE 2.1
How the IDS Influences Perceptions of Self and Others

Loser's Perception of		
Self		*Other*
Inferior Weaker Incompetent Loss of Confidence	Cognitions	Superior More Powerful Competent Gain in Confidence
Fear Disappointment Hopelessness Shame Resentful Helplessness	Emotions	Anger Indignation Punitiveness
Inhibition of Aggressive Behavior	Behavior	
Non-threatening Behavior		

useless. This is followed by adjustment to the new situation, acceptance of the subordinate role, and termination of the IDS. The outcome of such encounters may leave people with a more realistic appraisal of their own and others' strengths and abilities and also leave them free to move on to face new challenges. However, in the instance of escape, the IDS may be terminated without acceptance, as they may be generating resources for renewed attack. However, some are reluctant to submit, even though they feel there is no chance of winning, because losing has serious consequences for them. They may continue to have difficulty submitting in spite of a persistent IDS. Finally, they only submit because of severe depression.

Because it is more functional to accept subordinate status than to persist in a self-defeating strategy, why are we not more programmed to show acceptance? One answer probably has to do with fighting strategies. To win, we must maintain our belief that victory will come our way. If we react to every minor setback, we might betray this information to our adversary. This would give him or her more heart and thus bring about our own defeat. It seems likely that one reason the IDS evolved was to counteract this implacable resolve to win at all costs. Social life would not be possible with a Titan mentality.

To summarize, when the IDS functions effectively, it helps avoid unnecessary conflict or brings conflict to an end. Termination of the conflict leads to escape, submission, or acceptance. When the submission has been accepted and the need to submit subsides, the IDS is switched off. Similarly, if one escapes and feels free, the IDS is no longer required. However, if they cannot relinquish their unattainable goals and the IDS persists, individuals may become depressed or abusive to others, or lock into unproductive power struggles (Sloman, 1981) that lead to dysfunctional interactions in both family and other social domains.

ACCEPTANCE AND SUBMISSION

Acceptance of defeat is a part of normal social interaction. It may simply be a matter of saying "You were right and I was wrong." However, continued anger about the loss makes it difficult to accept the loss and concede defeat. In some cases, one privately recognizes defeat, but avoids conceding defeat. Alternatively, one may submit without accepting the loss. For example, a client said sometimes after he submits, he ends up being mad with himself for doing so. It was not that he thought he could have won, but rather that, for him, submitting is a sign of weakness. As noted earlier, support from others can facilitate acceptance by lowering one's level of arousal, which, in turn, reduces feelings of resentment.

VOLUNTARY SUBMISSION AND THE IDS

Sloman and Price (1987) distinguished between the IDS and voluntary submission. Price (1998) saw the IDS as analogous to the shivering response. Both are automatically triggered and voluntary submission is analogous to switching on the central heating or putting on warm clothing. Similarly, one can submit voluntarily, before the IDS has been triggered, thereby avoiding the discomfort of the IDS. This distinction highlights the advantage of rational objective evaluation before engaging in conflict. This is illustrated by the case of Betty later in this chapter. It could be argued that so-called voluntary submission is in fact triggered by a mild feeling of discomfort, associated with a weak IDS that the person is hardly aware of. Therefore, instead of distinguishing between voluntary submission and the IDS, one could distinguish between a mild and more powerful IDS. For example, a very intense competitive encounter requires a powerful IDS to bring the conflict to an end, whereas a mild difference of opinion can be readily resolved.

CLINICAL EXAMPLES OF THE IDS

The clinical relevance of the IDS is illustrated through the following case histories.

Elizabeth

Elizabeth was a 29-year-old woman who came to see me because her 6-year-old son was having trouble adjusting to her separation, 1 year earlier, and her depressive illness. Prior to the separation, there had been many fights with much anger and shouting. Things escalated to the point that she threw things at her husband and walked out on him. She had made a number of suicide attempts, apparently triggered by conflicts with her husband. She recalled a very oppressive childhood with two alcoholic parents and a mother who was domineering and controlling. However, she and her sister were constantly vying for her mother's attention. As a child, she was submissive and did not dare challenge her parents. She said, "I heard from my mother all the time that I was stupid and incompetent and would never amount to anything," and "As an adult I had to win, because I could never win as a child." She added, "I persevere for a while—then I give up." As to her husband, she said, "A core of my anger is a strong sense of injustice and I feel I have to fight to correct that. Then, because my sense of injustice has not been righted—because I feel that he is not going to believe me, I throw up my hands and get depressed." Her husband recalled an unhappy childhood related to having a tyrannical father. Although observation of Elizabeth and her husband fighting might have given the impression that they were being assertive, closer inspection made it apparent that their fights had a fixed, repetitive pattern; were unresolvable; were fueled by low self-esteem; and, in turn, contributed to a further lowering of each others' self-esteem. The fights were, by her admission, designed to compensate for the loss of self-esteem associated with her submissive relationship with her mother. One might conclude that Elizabeth and her husband were both exhibiting a premature triggering of their IDS, attributable to the abuse they experienced as children, so that both felt one-down and hard done by. This perception fed their anger, which, because they both felt one-down, triggered a more powerful IDS in both, contributing to an intensification of the conflict and making resolution of the conflict more difficult.

The abuse and neglect Elizabeth suffered as a child contributed to the development of an insecure attachment and premature triggering of her IDS. This premature triggering presently manifests as low self-esteem and is the basis for her feeling that she has to fight to correct "the strong sense of injustice." Elizabeth's anxious-ambivalent attachment led her to make constant demands on her husband for soothing. His failure to respond led to an activation of her dominance–subordinate system (Hilburn-Cobb, 1998) in an effort to regulate discomfort. Her subordinate behavior led to an escalation of her clinging, but was associated with shame that accentuated her feeling of victimization. This feeling of discomfort and frustration arising from her husband's failure to provide adequate soothing aroused her rage, resulting in conflict between herself and her husband, which then triggered her IDS. Both her neediness and lack of self-assertion contributed to her anger at being victimized. Her newfound awareness of these dynamics was a breakthrough for her, as revealed by the statement, "If I was self-confident, I wouldn't have that fear of failure and it wouldn't be so important for me to win."

Sylvia

The presence of the IDS may be heralded by only one of its features. For example, Sylvia, a bright, attractive, 17-year-old girl, came to see me complaining of feelings of inferiority. Her mother was an anxious, controlling woman and Sylvia's sister had already been treated for school phobia, related to the mother's difficulty in separating from her. It turned out that Sylvia felt a lot of anger toward her mother, which perpetuated a mental set of struggle rather than acceptance. She did not express this anger because of fear of challenging her mother. Her feelings of inferiority were attributed to a persistent IDS. She was informed that her feelings of inferiority were the price she paid for her decision to be a dutiful daughter and to avoid fighting with her mother. She subsequently decided that she would like to give up her feelings of inferiority and learn how to be more assertive with her mother, feeling that this would help her become more assertive in other areas of her life.

When clients complain of symptoms of mild to moderate depression, it may be helpful to first look for signs of underlying rage or resentment that may prevent realistic acceptance or withdrawal and prevent effective problem solving to mount a better challenge. If anger is present, one can then explore against whom this rage is directed, whether this relationship is a competitive one, and whether the IDS appears to play a role. In some cases, the rage may initially appear not to be directed at anyone in particular, but further inquiry may reveal that it is.

Diana

Diana was a 30-year-old woman with dysthymic disorder. She had childhood memories of a weak submissive mother who failed to protect her from an unpredictable and violent father. Her two sisters rebelled against the father, and Diana was the good child who tried to play a mediating role. She remembers feeling that she should not allow herself to surpass her mother because of her fear that her father would prefer her, which might cause him to leave her mother. One therapeutic goal was to teach her how to avoid triggering her IDS. This enabled her to become more self-assertive, which in turn helped her become less depressed. She initiated the last interview by apologizing for not doing the assignment I had given her, saying it had been a bad week and she was feeling quite discouraged. She then spoke of her need to justify herself to her friends and her husband. She said, "I see myself as the little kid who has to report to my mommy and daddy." I then discussed the fact that she had started the session by apologizing and I wondered what the significance of that might be. She acknowledged that she was reacting to me as a subordinate child. She later said, "My adult side says I don't have to explain anything to anyone—unless I want to give them an explanation." She then continued, "I must say this is quite liberating. What is liberating is my getting permission not to have to report to people. I feel this physical relief. As I had these thoughts, I envisaged myself as much taller."

Because of her "clinginess," I saw her as having an anxious-ambivalent attachment to me and her efforts to regulate her distress had activated her subordinate system as a way of getting additional soothing. My exploration of why she needed to apologize for not doing her assignment led her to also examine why she had to justify herself to other people. She then came to the decision that she did not have to take a subordinate stance with any of these people. Her feeling of power was triggered by her realization that she no longer needed to behave like a child. This enabled her to recognize that she could challenge others without triggering her IDS. My acceptance of her aggressiveness facilitated her empowerment by providing her with a secure base. Our previous focus on how she could avoid triggering her IDS made it easier for her to take this further step. In the last session, she described how she had always been doing things for other people without giving any thought to what she herself wanted. She went on to express concern that paying more attention to her own needs might make her into a more selfish person. I commented that paying more attention to her own needs did not necessarily imply that she would become more selfish. On the contrary, she could find herself having a warmer relationship with those she helped.

Sally

Sally is a 55-year-old married woman with dysthymic disorder, whom I had been seeing in weekly psychotherapy over the last 2 years. Sally's mother died when Sally was a teenager. In the final days of her life, her mother spent more time with her stepfather than with her. Sally reacted with "an incredible rage and a deep pain" that she never expressed to her mother. Sally had made good progress and was functioning fairly well but still had some unresolved issues. She commenced the interview by speaking of a friend, Betty, who had died 3 days earlier. She said, "I have not cried. There is a sense of artificiality," by which she meant she was putting up a false front by being "nice" to Betty's family. She said, "I don't like myself for resenting the family's demands." Referring to the previous interview, she said, "It seemed that you were not there for me. It seemed that there had been a death. I shut off. I didn't think of you at all. If I hadn't shut off, there would have been a confrontation." She felt that the week before "there had been too much closeness" and "both the thought of confrontation and the closeness were frightening." She then continued, "As my mother was dying there was so much I wanted to deal with and neither of us did." She had not been able to express her anger with her stepfather because she perceived him as being too powerful, and she had not been able to express her anger with her mother because she was dying. Her anger had triggered feelings of helplessness and inadequacy (the IDS) that contributed toward the feeling of unreality and her feeling of depression. She was also unable to express her anger with me for not being there for her, because of her fear that, if she challenged me, "my fear is that confrontation would lead me or you to close the door." In response to my next query, she said, "I felt that you had decided not to handle the intimacy, because what you found out was not what you liked."

A couple of sessions later, just prior to her leaving on vacation, she made a big issue of the fact that I refused to discuss my recent visit to that resort. She accused me of being stubborn and controlling, but, after a while, she said, "I guess I am the one that is being controlling of you." She continued, "There was a moment of trying to get your approval and, when I didn't get, I got mad and then took a one-down position." She saw this as contributing to her stubbornness, saying, "I feel stubborn, because I feel threatened and I understand that I have taken a one-down position."

This illustrates how frustration of Sally's need for approval led to anger that triggered her IDS, which, in turn, contributed to the power struggle between us. Sally appeared to have a preoccupied attachment toward me. She would constantly try to obtain a positive response from me. Although she was leaving me, she felt it was I that was abandoning her, and she was trying to assuage the negative affect associated with our separation by getting my approval. When she failed to obtain relief through her attachment system, she related to me through the dominance–submissive mode, but, because of her inability to challenge me directly, this was also ineffective. As a result, she found herself involved in a power struggle she felt she could not win. The presence of a secure attachment facilitates the normal expression of anger, because there is little fear of negative consequences. Sally's anxious insecure attachment was related to her difficulty in challenging me, which led to a struggle for control between us.

Joan

Joan, a 51-year-old woman, was a regular churchgoer who had become very depressed and stopped going to church after losing her child in a tragic accident. When the therapist asked Joan whether she might be angry with God, she gave an equivocal response. This prompted the therapist to ask whether she might feel afraid to express her anger with God because of her fear of how God would react. This time Joan responded with great intensity saying that, because she had already witnessed God's awful power, she was trying her best to avoid provoking God to prevent his doing more harm to her family. It appeared that her anger over her child's death was being directed at God. Because she saw God as being much more powerful than herself, this anger triggered the IDS. The therapist felt that, before trying to assist her in letting go of her anger, it would be expedient to help her become more accepting of her anger by assisting her to switch off the IDS. His strategy was to say that God could accept her anger and God would prefer to face her anger rather than her withdrawal. He encouraged Joan to discuss the issue with the parish priest, who supported the therapist's stance.

Betty

Betty was a 55-year-old woman who requested immediate psychiatric admission, because she was "going crazy." She was an executive in a large corporation. After a recent change in administration, she had been given notice. She said that she would fight to the bitter end to keep her job. I did not consider her psychotic but thought of her as having a high anxiety level. However, in discussing her situation, it appeared that her fight to keep her job was a lost cause. I advised her to confine her struggle to obtaining better severance pay.

Because Betty felt victimized, she felt she had to right the wrong that had been done to her so that she was now engaged in a struggle she herself felt she could not possibly win. This triggered her IDS and made her feel she was going crazy. When she accepted my advice and fought instead to get a better severance package, she did have some success and her symptoms disappeared.

CONCLUSION

The role of the IDS in conflict resolution has been examined and it has been shown that, when the IDS is ineffective in terminating aggression, it can contribute to the development of depressive illness. This is more likely to occur in those who are insecurely attached. If it becomes apparent that the IDS has been inappropriately triggered in that the client has the ability to win the adversarial encounter, the therapist can teach the client how to avoid prematurely triggering the IDS, which is also a way of teaching self-assertion. If the IDS has been triggered, because of recognition that the adversary is more powerful, the therapeutic task might be to help the client develop more realistic goals. One crucial issue in psychotherapy is to help clients evaluate how realistic their goals are.

The interrelation between attachment theory and social competition theory has been described. It has been shown that the presence of insecure attachment may undermine efforts to soothe tension so that the dominant or subordinate systems are activated to reduce distress. Conversely, the person with ineffective dominant behavior may turn to the attachment system to regulate tension (see the case of Cindy; Sloman & Atkinson, chap. 9, this volume). Both attachment and social competition theory have their roots in ethology and both—in particular, attachment theory—have been well studied. Attachment theory has also provided a framework for studying the development of psychopathology (Atkinson & Zucker, 1997). When these two models are combined, they provide a useful model for the formulation of both intrapsychic dynamics and interpersonal processes. This biologically based model of psychotherapy can be readily integrated with brain neurotransmitter models.

REFERENCES

Allan, S., & Gilbert, P. (1997). Submissive behavior and psychopathology. *British Journal of Clinical Psychology, 36,* 467–488.

American Psychiatric Association. (1994). *Diagnostic and statistical manual of Mental Disorders* (4th ed.). Washington, DC: Author.

Atkinson, L., & Zucker, K. J. (Eds.). (1997). *Attachment and psychopathology.* New York: Guilford.

Bateson, G., Jackson, D. D., Haley, J., and Weakland, J. (1956). Toward a theory of schizophrenia. *Behavioral Science, 1,* 251–264.

Bowlby, J. (1980). *Attachment and loss: Sadness and depression.* New York: Basic Books.

Downey, G., & Feldman, S. I. (1996). Implications of rejection sensitivity for intimate relationships. *Journal of Personality and Social Psychology, 70,* 1327–1343.

Gilbert, P. (1992). *Depression: The evolution of powerlessness.* Hove, UK: Lawrence Erlbaum Associates.

Gilbert, P. (1997). The evolution of social attractiveness and its role in shame, guilt, humiliation and therapy. *British Journal of Medical Psychology, 70,* 113–147.

Gilbert, P., & Allan, S. (1994). Assertiveness, submissive behaviour and social comparison. *British Journal of Clinical Psychology, 33,* 295–306.

Gilbert, P., & Allan, S. A. (1998). The role of defeat and entrapment (arrested flight) in depression: An exploration of an evolutionary view. *Psychological Medicine, 28,* 585–598.

Gilbert, P., & McGuire, T. (1998). Shame, social roles and status: The psychobiological continuum from monkey to human. In P. Gilbert & B. Andrews (Eds.), *Shame; Interpersonal behavior, psychopathology and culture* (pp. 99–125). New York: Oxford University Press.

Hilburn-Cobb, C. (1998, Oct. 2–3). *Adolescent disorganization of attachment and its relation to psychopathology.* Paper presented at the Second International Conference on Attachment and Psychopathology, Toronto, Canada.

Kaufman, I. C. (1977). Developmental considerations of anxiety and depression. Psychological studies in monkeys. In T. Shapiro (Ed.), *Psychoanalysis and contemporary science* (Vol. V, pp. 317–363). International Universities Press.

Klein, D. F. (1971). Approaches to measuring the efficacy of treatment of personality disorders: Analysis and program. In J. Levine, B. C. Schiele, & L. Bouthiler (Eds.), *Principles and problems in establishing the efficacy of psychotropic agents* (pp. 187–20F). (Public Health Service No. 2138). Washington, DC: U.S. Department of Health, Education, and Welfare.

Klinger, E. (1977). *Meaning and void.* Minneapolis: University of Minnesota Press.

Kohut, H., & Wolfe, E. (1978). The disorders of the self and their treatment: An outline. *International Journal of Psycho Analysis, 59,* 413–425.

Maynard Smith, J. (1982). *Evolution and the theory of games.* Cambridge, UK: Cambridge University Press.

Nesse, R. (1991, November–December). What good is feeling bad? The evolutionary benefits of psychic pain. *The Sciences,* pp. 30–37.

Peterson, C., Maier, S. F., Seligman, M. E. P. (1993). *Learned helplessness.* New York: Oxford University Press.

Post, R. M., & Weiss, S. R B. (1998). Sensitization and kindling phenomena mood, anxiety and obsessive-compulsive disorders: The role of serotonergic mechanisms in illness progression. *Biological Psychiatry, 44,* 193–206.
Price, J. S. (1967). Hypothesis: The dominance hierarchy and the evolution of mental illness. *Lancet, 2,* 243–246.
Price, J. S. (1969). Ethology and behaviour. *Proceedings of the Royal Society of Medicine, 62,* 1110.
Price, J. S. (1998). The adaptive function of mood change. *British Journal of Medical Psychology, 71,* 469.
Price, J. S., & Sloman, L. (1987). Depression as yielding behavior: An animal model based on Schelderup-Ebbe's pecking order. *Ethology and Sociobiology, 8,* 85S–98S.
Price, J. S., Sloman, L., Gardner, R., Gilbert, P., & Rhode, P. (1994). The social competition model of depression. *British Journal of Psychiatry, 164,* 309–315.
Sapolsky, R. M. (1994). Individual differences and the stress response. *Seminars in the Neurosciences, 6,* 261–269.
Schjelderup-Ebbe, T. (1935). Social behavior of birds. In C. Murchison (Ed.), *Handbook of social psychology* (pp. 947–972). Worcester, MA: Clark University Press.
Schmale, A. (1973). The adaptive role of depression in health and disease. In J. P. Scott & F. C. Senay (Eds.), *Separation and depression* (p. 187). Baltimore: King.
Segal, Z. V., Williams, J. M., Teasdale, J. D., & Gemar, M. A. (1996). Cognitive science perspective on kindling and episode sensitization in recurrent affective disorder. *Psychological Medicine, 26,* 371–380.
Sloman, L. (1981). Intrafamilial struggles for power: An ethological perspective. *International Journal of Family Therapy, 2,* 13–33.
Sloman, L., & Price, J. S. (1987). Losing behavior (yielding subroutine) and human depression: Proximate and selective mechanisms. *Ethology and Sociobiology, 8,* 99S–109S.
Sloman, L. (2000). Evolutionary principles in psychotherapy: The syndrome of rejection sensitivity. In P. Gilbert & K. Bailey (Eds.), *Genes on the couch: Explorations in evolutionary psychotherapy.* London, UK: Routledge.
Zuckerman, S. (1932). *The social life of monkeys and apes.* London: K. Paul, Trench, Trubner.

PART II

Biological Correlates of Subordination and Depression

CHAPTER THREE

Dysthymic Disorder, Regulation–Dysregulation Theory, CNS Blood Flow, and CNS Metabolism

Michael McGuire
Fawzy Fawzy
James Spar
University of California, Los Angeles

Alfonso Troisi
Universita Tor Vergata, Rome, Italy

According to the most recent version of the *Diagnostic and Statistical Manual of Mental Disorders* (4th ed. [*DSM–IV*]; American Psychiatric Association, 1994), the essence of dysthymic disorder (DD) is chronic depressed mood of greater than 2 years' duration. Regulation–dysregulation theory (RDT) models the effects of others' signals (communications) on receivers' physiological and psychological states. Positron emission tomography (PET) facilitates the study of regional central nervous system (CNS) blood flow and glucose metabolism. This chapter uses data from studies of the neurotransmitter serotonin and social-status interactions among nonhuman primates and humans, RDT, PET, and related clinical and research reports to model symptom changes among persons with DD who were studied over an 18-month period. The key hypotheses of the chapter are: (a) individuals with DD have suboptimal information processing and signaling capacities that contribute to inefficient problem solving and a failure to elicit others' signals that are essential for regulation; (b) individuals with DD have an excessive number of dysphoric thoughts that result in specific types of regional CNS blood flow and metabolism; (c) individuals with DD are physiologically atypical; and (d) the absence of positive signals from others and specific types of CNS blood flow and metabolism explain in part the symptoms and dysfunctional capacities characteristic of individuals with DD.

RDT—A REVIEW

The term *regulation* references a state in which physiological and psychological systems function optimally. The term is synonymous with homeostasis as it is used in the medical literature: a state of equilibrium or balance between opposing pressures in the body with respect to functions and to the chemical compositions of fluids and tissues (Steadman's Medical Dictionary, 1990). One feels well, has the energy to do what one wants to do, thinks clearly, and is asymptomatic. For many reasons (e.g., disorder predisposition or disorder vulnerability), individuals differ not only in their physiological and psychological states relative to ideal states, but also in their capacities to tolerate physiological and psychological change without experiencing symptoms (McGuire & Troisi, 1987a, 1987b). The term *dysregulation* refers to atypical physiological and psychological states associated with symptoms (e.g., depression, anxiety, anger, boredom) and reduced capacities to act efficiently.

RDT attempts to integrate the following findings: (a) humans are social animals strongly predisposed to live in close proximity and to interact; (b) individuals are highly sensitive to others' signals; (c) others' signals influence receivers' physiological and psychological states; (d) specific signals by others are essential for maintaining regulation; (e) dysregulation is associated with unpleasant feelings and thoughts, an increased probability of disorders among persons at risk for disorders, and the emergence of symptoms and signs among individuals with disorders; and (f) individuals seek out social environments that facilitate regulation (McGuire, 1988; McGuire, Raleigh, & Pollack, 1994; McGuire & Troisi, 1987a, 1987b).

The idea that social interactions have physiological and psychological consequences undoubtedly extends back beyond antiquity, but it had to await the investigations of Freud and Bowlby (1969, 1973) in this century before becoming a cornerstone of psychiatric thinking. For these and numerous other investigators, normal and atypical development, as well as daily functioning, are contingent on social interaction type and frequency during development. Infants require holding, touching, and vocal input. Without such interactions, they become psychologically distraught and physiologically dysregulated (Hofer, 1984). Extended social deprivation results in the failure to thrive and, eventually, in death (Spitz, 1945). Analogous observations apply to nonhuman primates, where studies have repeatedly documented that specific types of social interactions are essential for optimal maturation (Harlow & Harlow, 1962; Kraemer & Clarke, 1991; Reite, Short, Seiler, & Pauley, 1981). A review of many of the physiological systems that are affected by social interactions can be found elsewhere (McGuire, 1988; McGuire & Troisi, 1998).

Similar points apply to adult humans, although they sometimes assume otherwise. Adults need to talk, touch, and receive others' recognition; otherwise undesirable physiological and psychological changes occur (e.g., the unpleasant feelings associated with social isolation). The near total elimination of auditory and visual stimuli that occurred during the 1960s in studies of sensory deprivation using normal adult participants led to such a high prevalence of adverse psychological responses that the studies were discontinued (Schultz, 1965). Well-controlled studies have shown significant increases in the frequency of depression, psychosis, and attempted suicide among persons in penal institutions who are placed in solitary confinement (Volkart, Dittrich, Rothenfluh, & Werner, 1983). In addition, there is a vast body of literature documenting the positive psychological effects of psychotherapy.

There are, of course, both individual and situational differences. For example, some individuals are often oriented to defensive behavior such as fight, flight, and submission in the presence of negative signals from others, whereas other individuals fail to respond to such signals. Dominant individuals are more likely to aggress toward the threats of subordinate individuals than vice versa, and subordinate individuals are more likely to flee or submit to a threat by a dominant individual than vice versa. Sex differences are also observed. Male–male, female–female, and male–female interactions have different signaling profiles.

Such differences notwithstanding, the key point is that humans, like other primates, live in a world of conspecifics with whom they interact, a world of social noise, visual stimuli, physical contact, and the exchange of thoughts and feelings. It is not surprising that humans seek out persons with whom they experience pleasurable feelings, or that they avoid persons who have the opposite effects. It is also not surprising that persons who, for whatever reasons, are not adept at interpreting, managing, and exchanging information or eliciting others' positive responses are at risk for dysregulation and symptoms.

SEROTONIN MEASURES AND SOCIAL STATUS

Nonhuman Primate Studies

Experimental data consistent with RDT can be found in reports of investigators studying a variety of nonhuman primate species (e.g., Kravitz, 1988; Reite et al., 1981; Rosenblum et al., 1994; Sapolsky, 1989, 1990). For the moment, we focus on interactions between social status and peripheral and CNS serotonin (5-HT) measures in adult male vervet monkeys (*Cercopithecus aethiops sabaeus*). Details of studies reviewed here can be found elsewhere (McGuire, Raleigh, & Johnson, 1983; McGuire et al., 1994; Raleigh, Brammer, McGuire, & Yuwiler, 1985; Raleigh & McGuire, 1989, 1993; Raleigh, McGuire, Brammer, Oikkacjm, & Yuwiler, 1991; Raleigh, McGuire, Brammer, & Yuwiler, 1984).

Among adult male vervets, there are strong positive correlations between peripheral 5-HT levels, CNS 5-HT responsivity, and social status. (CNS 5-HT responsivity is inferred from the magnitude of behavioral or peripheral physiological change following physiological or social challenges to the CNS 5-HT system.) High-status or dominant adult males have peripheral 5-HT levels averaging between 1.5 and 2.0 times the levels of low-status or subordinate males. In addition, dominant males show proportionally greater behavioral responses to substances such as tryptophan and fluoxetine that influence CNS 5-HT concentrations and function. The greater the response to such substances, the greater the CNS 5-HT responsivity. When CNS 5-HT responsivity is high, the frequency of initiated aggressive behavior is low; animals are more relaxed socially, minimally vigilant of other group members, and more tolerant of the behavior of other animals. They also more frequently initiate and respond to affiliative gestures. Essentially opposite findings apply to animals with low CNS 5-HT responsivity: Animals initiate and receive fewer affiliative behaviors, receive and initiate more threats, and devote a high percentage of their time to interanimal vigilance.

Adult male vervets compete for high social status because high status is associated with priority access to females, food, and perches, but findings also permit the hypothesis that they compete because of the physiological and psychological effects associated with elevated CNS 5-HT responsivity; for example, an increase in the frequency of received affiliative behaviors compared to lower status animals. Such behavior is analogous to humans competing for specific social roles (high status) because such roles are assumed or known to be associated with desired psychological and physiological states.

Figure 3.1 illustrates the preceding points through an analysis of agonistic interactions between dominant and subordinate males and peripheral 5-HT levels.

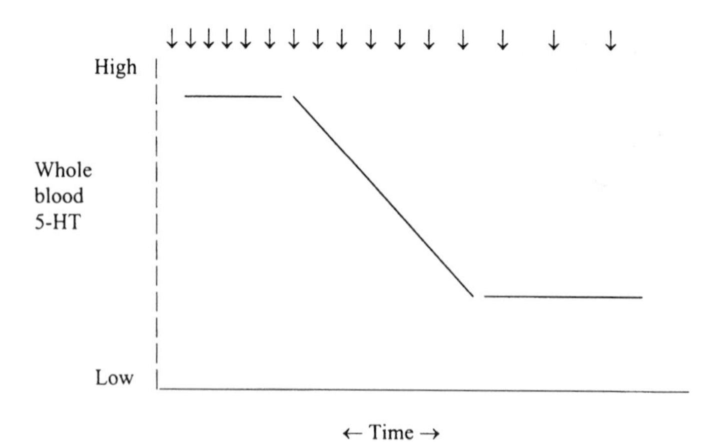

FIG. 3.1. Changes in peripheral 5-HT levels among dominant male vervet monkeys as a function of the frequency of submissive displays by subordinate males. Adapted from Raleigh et al. (1984) and McGuire and Troisi (1987a).

The vertical axis in Fig. 3.1 depicts peripheral blood 5-HT levels in a socially dominant male; the horizontal axis measures time. At the top of the figure, the downward pointing arrows depict both the frequency per unit time of dominance displays by a dominant male directed toward a subordinate male and the frequency of submissive displays by a subordinate male that are directed toward the dominant male. Among vervets, dominant males initiate dominance displays toward subordinate males approximately 30 times per day, although this number will vary for reasons discussed later. Further, subordinate males seldom engage in submissive displays unless dominant males first initiate dominance displays. In the majority of instances (more than 80%), subordinate males respond submissively to dominance displays by lowering their hind-quarters, backing off, shifting their weight, angling their head to the side, and positioning themselves to flee. On occasion, subordinate males threaten dominant males. Dominant males are tolerant of such behavior provided it is infrequent and not intense. However, if subordinate males threaten excessively, dominant males will respond aggressively. Physical contact rarely occurs in these interactions. Rather, they are ritualized and serve to confirm and perpetuate hierarchical relationships.

If the frequency of submissive displays by subordinate males declines, peripheral 5-HT levels decline among dominant males. This effect is illustrated in the righthand half of the figure. The effect can be demonstrated experimentally by manipulating the frequency of submissive displays received by dominant males; for example, temporarily separating dominant and subordinate males, or placing dominant males behind one-way mirrors where they can observe and threaten subordinate males but where they do not receive submissive displays in return. One-way mirror studies are used to determine if a reduction in dominance displays by dominant males, which occurs when dominant and subordinate males are physically and visually separated but not when dominant males are behind one-way mirrors, is a factor contributing to the decline in peripheral 5-HT levels. Because one-way mirror studies show the same rate of decline in peripheral 5-HT levels as is seen when dominant animals are socially isolated, the observation of submissive displays by subordinate animals appears to be essential for maintaining high peripheral 5-HT levels and elevated CNS 5-HT responsivity among dominant males.

In both natural and captive settings, the behavior of high-status males can be characterized in terms of their moving back and forth along the top of Fig. 3.1, where the following behavior–physiological events are postulated to occur:

1. Dominant males with high CNS 5-HT responsivity and high levels of peripheral 5-HT (a regulated state).
2. Increased tolerance toward subordinate males and reduced frequency of dominance displays by dominant males.
3. Reduced frequency of submissive displays by subordinate males.

4. Decline in CNS 5-HT responsivity and peripheral 5-HT levels in dominant males (a moderately dysregulated state).
5. Increased frequency of dominance displays by dominant males.
6. Increased frequency of submissive displays by subordinate males.
7. Increased CNS 5-HT responsivity and peripheral 5-HT levels among dominant males (a regulated state).

In this model, subordinate males are moderately dysregulated physiologically, whereas dominant males move back and forth from regulated to moderately dysregulated states. Should a subordinate male become dominant, or a dominant male become subordinate, their behavior and physiological measures change to those characteristic of their new social status. In the RDT model, physiological and psychological regulation and dysregulation are not permanent states; rather, they are contingent states, changing in response to social information type and frequency, of which social behavior, peripheral 5-HT levels, and CNS 5-HT responsivity serve as measures.

The 5-HT system is, of course, far more complex than the preceding discussion suggests. For example, there are at least 13 subtypes of 5-HT receptors, many of which have different functions. And, contrary to the generally held views that 5-HT is primarily a modulator of the actions of other neurotransmitters, and that the 5-HT system has diffuse and largely nonspecific projections throughout functionally diverse regions of the forebrain, recent studies show region-specific patterns of 5-HT forebrain axon termination, differential distribution of 5-HT receptor subtypes in forebrain termination fields, and region-specific release of 5-HT in response to specific environmental stressors (Waterhouse, 1996).

Recent findings from nonhuman primate studies add to the complexity. For example, Clarke et al. (1995) reported that cerebrospinal fluid (CSF) measures of a major 5-HT metabolite, 5-hydroxyindoleacetic acid (5-HIAA), are influenced by pedigree. Higley et al. (1996) showed that the rate of aggressive behavior seen among animals with low CSF 5-HIAA increases when CSF testosterone concentrations are high. Mehlman et al. (1998) showed that high CSF 5-HIAA levels positively correlate with affiliative sociality and low levels correlate with reduced social competence. Similar findings were reported by Botchin, Kaplan, Manuck, and Mann (1993) using techniques that challenge CNS 5-HT responsivity. Shively, Laber-Laird, and Anton (1997) established that subordinate females are differentially responsive to hypothalamic–pituitary–adrenal dysfunction and engage in a greater frequency of behavioral depression compared to dominant females.

Human Studies

Positive correlations between social status and peripheral 5-HT levels are known among human males (Madsen, 1985, 1986; Madsen & McGuire, 1984). These and related studies point to at least a four-way relation among status, personality, genetic information, and 5-HT measures. For example, in male college students, peripheral 5-HT levels and high status positively correlate among socially interactive competitors (sometimes called *Machiavellians*). For more deferent (less socially interactive), high-status individuals (sometimes called *moralists*), the relation is strongly negative (Madsen, 1986). The ratio of Machiavellians to moralists is 7:1 among the samples studied thus far (D. Madsen, personal communication, 1998). Studies of personality and personality disorders suggest that different ratios of the neurotransmitters 5-HT, norepinephrine, and dopamine are associated with distinct personality types, and different ratios positively correlate with behavior patterns, such as harm avoidance and sensation seeking (Cloninger, 1986; Cloninger, Svracik, & Przybeck, 1993). To the degree that personality disorders are genetically influenced, and data suggest they are (Coryell, 1980; Guze, Goodwin, & Crane, 1970), different baseline levels of peripheral and CNS 5-HT responsivity are likely.

Again, other factors require consideration. For example, the mean rate of 5-HT synthesis in normal men is reported to be 52% higher than among normal women (Nishizawa et al., 1997), a finding that may explain in part the reported lower frequency of depression in men. There are also age factors in that 5-HT responsivity is reported to decline with age (McBride, Tierney, DeMeo, Chen, & Mann, 1990). This finding may partially explain the increased incidence of depression among the elderly.

Taken together, these findings suggest that baseline CNS 5-HT availability, responsivity, and metabolism differ across individuals. Social status, therefore, is likely to be only one of the contributing factors influencing CNS 5-HT responsivity, although most likely a far from inconsequential factor. Internal models are also important. Individuals form models of their status that are likely to influence 5-HT mechanisms. Thus, both internal and external information is implicated in CNS 5-HT availability, responsivity, and metabolism.

PET STUDIES

Although neither PET methodology nor the interpretation of PET findings are free of ambiguities, a substantial number of reports and independent replications document interactions between mood states, local cerebral glucose metabolism, regional cerebral blood flow, and cognitive processes. These studies allow for interesting inferences about the effects of both external and internally generated information on brain function.

For example, compared to controls, individuals with unipolar depression have significantly lower rates of glucose metabolism in the caudate nucleus, the frontal dorsolateral areas, and the parietal cortex, but higher metabolism in the orbital frontal lobe (Baxter et al., 1985; Biver et al., 1994). Significant left–right prefrontal metabolism asymmetry has been observed among some depressed persons before, but not after, successful treatment. However, among other persons, diminished hypofrontal and whole-cortex hypometabolism is observed following successful treatment (Martinot et al., 1990). Thus, glucose metabolism abnormalities characteristic of depression may not always be state dependent. Studies of regional cerebral blood flow show decreased flow in the left anterior cingulate and left dorsolateral prefrontal cortex of depressed patients. When depressed individuals with and without cognitive impairment are compared, the impaired group demonstrates significant decreases in regional blood flow in the left medial frontal gyrus accompanied by increased flow in the cerebellar vermis. These findings suggest an anatomical dissociation between the effects of depressed mood and depression-related cognitive impairment (Bench et al., 1992). Other studies designed to measure the activity and regionality of labeled 5-hydroxytroptophan (5-HTP) and dihydroxyphenylalanine (L-DOPA) show decreased uptake of 5-HTP and L-DOPA across the blood–brain barrier in depressed individuals compared to normal controls, as well as an increased utilization of 5-HTP, but not L-DOPA, in the lower medial prefrontal cortex of depressed individuals, primarily on the left side (Agren & Reibring, 1994). George, Ketter, and Post (1993) summarized these findings as follows: "Frontal lobe hypometabolism is emerging as a common final pathway for most types of primary and secondary depression, regardless of original cause" (p. 6; see Wiesel, 1992, for a similar interpretation).

Regional cerebral blood flow studies in normal individuals demonstrate that dysphoric thoughts lead to bilateral inferior and orbitofrontal activation in women, whereas men display predominantly left-sided activation in these areas (Pardo, Pardo, & Raichle, 1993). Other investigations of normal participants have found that transient sadness significantly activates bilateral limbic and paralimbic structures (cingulate, medial prefrontal, and mesial temporal cortex), as well as parts of the brain stem, thalamus, and caudate/putamen (George et al., 1995). Many of these areas are activated during depression (e.g., George et al., 1993). In contrast, transient, experimentally induced pleasant thoughts not only reveal no areas of significantly increased blood flow activity, but they are also associated with significant and widespread reductions in cortical regional blood flow, especially in the right prefrontal and bilateral temporal-parietal regions (George et al., 1995).

Yet other PET findings are likely to contribute to our understanding of specific features of depression. For example, sustained attention studies in healthy individuals show increased blood flow in the prefrontal and superior parietal cortex, primarily in the right hemisphere (Pardo, Fox, & Raichle, 1991). During anticipatory anxiety, there are significant blood flow increases in both temporal poles (Reiman, Fusselman, Fox, & Raichle, 1989). Different word tasks, such as listening to pairs of real active words versus nonwords, have different blood flow effects for the superior temporal gyri; and during verb generation there is activation of the left premotor and prefrontal cortex (Wise et al., 1991). Clinically, the reduced ability to sustain attention, increased anticipatory anxiety, and atypical responses to others' verbal communications are observed among depressed individuals and may reflect disorder-typical changes in cerebral blood flow and metabolism.

Findings linking CNS blood flow and depression invite the following questions: Is CNS blood flow reduced and are cognitive capacities constrained among either chronically subordinate or transiently subordinate individuals? Although we know of no studies that directly address this question, clinical data suggest a positive answer to the preceding question. For example, among both chronically and transiently subordinate individuals, cognitive constraints (e.g., lack of responsiveness to novel ideas) are often apparent. Further, when individuals who are transiently subordinate are no longer subordinate, they often are noticably more receptive to novel information. This relation raises the possibility that analogous blood flow events occur in depression and subordination.

IMPLICATIONS FOR A PSYCHOBIOLOGICAL MODEL OF SOCIAL INTERACTIONS

As noted, implications of many PET findings remain to be worked out. For example, increased regional blood flow is usually associated with learning or new experiences, and the degree of blood flow diminishes when information becomes familiar. On the other hand, glucose metabolism is believed to reflect the energy needed to maintain sodium–potassium gradients and thus may reflect long-term synaptic function and regional CNS activity. Further, under basal conditions glucose metabolism may be high when blood flow is low. Despite the complex interactions between blood flow and metabolism, a number of tentative interpretations addressing the psychobiological nature of social interactions are possible: (a) There are identifiable differences in regional blood flow and glucose metabolism among depressed and nondepressed individuals; (b) depression-characteristic blood flow and glucose metabolism measures normalize among a percentage of depressed persons following successful treatment, but normalization fails to occur among other depressed individuals; (c) regionally specific increased blood flow in specific parts of the brain is initiated by dysphoric thoughts; and (d) different types of environmental stimuli lead to alterations in regional blood flow. For this chapter, these inferences have at least three potentially important implications:

1. The observation that both external (e.g., words) and internal information (e.g., dysphoric thoughts) can lead to different regional blood flow profiles is consistent with the hypothesis that external information and dysphoric thoughts (including fantasies) have region-specific influences on CNS physiology.

2. The finding that some depressed persons who are successfully treated (as assessed by clinical criteria and self-report) continue to show frontal lobe and whole-cortex hypometabolism is consistent with the hypothesis that persons with DD may be chronically dysregulated and have enduring compromised cognitive function. The latter inference is also consistent with findings showing that a percentage of persons in postdepression periods reveal expressive hypofunctionality (Gaebel & Wolwer, 1992; McGuire & Essock-Vitale, 1982). When these possibilities are combined with findings from normal individuals that show region-specific patterns of 5-HT forebrain axon termination, as well as the differential distribution of 5-HT receptor subtypes in forebrain termination fields (Waterhouse, 1996), the possibility that depression is in part mediated by both adverse external information and excessive dysphoric thoughts via their effects on blood flow and metabolism in regions with specific 5-HT axon termination and receptor profiles becomes both an attractive and testable hypothesis.

3. Dominant–subordinate interactions and relationships enter the discussion in the following way. Dominance behavior by Person A is likely to trigger changes in CNS regional blood flow and glucose metabolism among persons (or animals) who are recipients of such signals. In turn, internal negative signals may decrease CNS 5-HT activity, constrain cognition, limit behavior options, and initiate the use of dominant–subordinate behavioral strategies.

DD AND SYMPTOMS

The following discussion of DD refers to findings reported in part elsewhere (Essock-Vitale & McGuire, 1990; McGuire & Troisi, 1998) involving a study of 42 dysthymic disorder participants (DDPs) and 22 control participants (CPs).

DD—Clinical Description

According to *DSM–IV* (American Psychiatric Association, 1994), the diagnostic criteria for DD are:

1. Depressed mood for most of the day, more days than not, for at least 2 years.
2. At least two of the following symptoms: poor appetite or overeating, insomnia or hypersomnia, low energy or fatigue, low self-esteem, poor concentration or difficulty making decisions, and feelings of hopelessness.
3. During a 2-year period, never without the preceding symptoms for more than 2 months at a time.
4. No major depressive episode during the first 2 years of the disturbance.

5. No history of a manic or hypomanic episode and criteria have never been met for cyclothymic disorder.
6. Signs and symptoms are not superimposed on a chronic psychotic disorder.
7. The symptoms are not due to the direct physiological effects of a substance.
8. The symptoms cause clinically significant distress or impairment in social, occupational, or other important areas of functioning.

Criteria from the Diagnostic and Statistical Manual of Mental Disorders (3rd ed. [*DSM–III*]; American Psychiatric Association, 1980) for DD, which differ minimally from *DSM-IV* criteria, were used in the study.

Participant Selection

All DDPs were women between the ages of 22 and 45; they were English speaking, met *DSM–III* diagnostic criteria for DD, and were without evidence of a personality disorder. Prior to becoming participants, 37 of 42 DDPs had received treatment for psychological distress, including medication, counseling, or psychotherapy. At best, treatments were effective for only brief periods. None of the treatments satisfactorily ameliorated the patients' signs and symptoms. CPs were between the ages of 20 and 45, English speaking, and without evidence of a mental disorder. Prior to the study, 3 of the CPs had received treatment for psychological distress. None had been diagnosed as suffering from a mental disorder. No DDPs or CPs used psychotropic medications during the study. Intelligence, class, and education did not differ among the DDPs and CPs (Essock-Vitale & McGuire, 1990; Marsh & Marsh, 1991).

Selected findings from structured interviews are presented here. Percentages for both participant groups ($n = 42$ for DDPs; $n = 22$ for CPs) are rounded to the nearest whole number.

Pedigree Influences. Thirty-six percent of the DDPs reported that their mothers, fathers, or siblings had symptoms similar to their own. Nine percent of the CPs reported that first-degree relatives had symptoms similar to those of DD.

Developmental Disruptions. Forty percent of the DDPs reported that they were physically or emotionally abused as children. Only 4 (9%) reported that the abuse was both intense and repetitive. One CP reported that she was physically and emotionally abused as a child. The abuse was not intense or repetitive.

Social Functional Capacities. Eighty-one percent of the DDPs reported difficulties adjusting to school, developing satisfactory or peer-comparable social support networks, or holding jobs. Fourteen percent of the CPs reported similar difficulties.

Responses to Minor Undesirable Events. Seventy-four percent of the DDPs reported that minor frustrating events (e.g., a friend arriving 30 minutes late for a social engagement, failing to find a desired item at the grocery store) positively correlated with either the onset of symptoms, often including anger, or an increase in the intensity of already present symptoms. CPs reported that similar events often caused frustration, but they did not result in symptoms.

Reading Others' Behavior Rules (Assessing How Others Think and Feel). DDPs expressed strikingly limited views of others' behavior rules. Statements such as "She screws everyone she can," "All she does is look out for herself," and "All he wants is sex" were typical of the ways DDPs portrayed others. In contrast, CPs offered far more complex views of others' motivations and behavior rules, (e.g., "She wants to help her brother and his wife but she thinks that her offer will be misinterpreted," and "She loves her kids even though her son gives her a lot of trouble"). Among CPs, others' behavior rules were more often viewed as socially positive than negative, whereas the opposite was true among DDPs.

Causal Modeling. DDPs developed models of events and attributed causes to others' behavior using minimal information. They seldom changed their models or attributions despite new (model-disconfirming) information. CPs also developed causal models and attributed causes using minimal information. Unlike DDPs, the majority of CPs changed their models in response to new information.

Novel Behavior Strategies. DDPs frequently repeated the same behavior strategy (e.g., communicating to kin or friends that they were ill and struggling financially) although strategies were often ineffective in achieving desired ends (e.g., eliciting empathy and acquiring financial support). In contrast, CPs seldom used the same strategy twice if it was ineffective; none reported that they presented themselves to others as ill.

Self-Monitoring. DDPs were aware that many of their social strategies were ineffective in achieving desired goals. On this assessment, they did not differ from CPs who were also aware when their strategies failed to work as planned. However, more than 85% of DDPs failed to use their knowledge of ineffective strategies to develop novel behavior strategies, compared to only 9% of CPs.

Explanation of Symptoms. Half of the DDPs viewed the behavior of others or external events as the primary cause of their symptoms, as well as the primary reason for the difficulties they experienced in social relationships and at work (if applicable). One fourth saw themselves as suffering from a disorder over which they had no control. One fourth saw their own behavior as a contributing factor to their distress. Blaming others or external events for their frustrations and difficulties occurred among 9% of the CPs. The remaining 91% of the CPs saw their own behavior as a contributing factor to the difficulties they experienced in social relationships and at work.

Others' Response to Participants' Distress. The majority of DDPs reported that others sometimes responded during periods of distress, although many persons who had previously done so no longer did. However, DDPs were hesitant in responding to other's requests for assistance, often feeling that others were "better off" and "didn't need" help. CPs reported that others responded when they experienced distress and vice versa.

Participants' Social Environment. CPs actively interacted with kin and nonkin, with members of both sexes, and with persons of different ages. Their likes and dislikes of others were based primarily on personal experiences. DDPs interacted primarily with women of the same age and selected kin. When possible, DDPs avoided social and work environments associated with increased symptoms, although none was fully successful at doing so. Nonkin men generally were viewed as insensitive, exploitative, and persons to be avoided. Compared to CPs, DDPs reported a threefold greater frequency of being "deceived by males" with whom they had interacted sexually. The majority of DDPs reported that prior to entering the study they suffered frequent competitive losses (e.g., loss of friends, jobs, kin support) and declines in social status (e.g., reduction in income and social influence).

Self-Esteem. Although the majority of CPs respected themselves, the majority also acknowledged that there were ways in which they could improve their self-esteem (e.g., by being more sensitive to others). A different picture emerged among DDPs. One fourth of the DDPs viewed themselves as superior to others, particularly close kin or former friends, whereas one half of the DDPs disliked themselves. The remaining one fourth of the DDPs did not differ from CPs. Three fourths of the DDPs reported that they were rarely free of dysphoric thoughts.

A particularly interesting finding emerged from tests designed to assess novel behavior strategy capacities. DDPs not only failed to adjust their strategies to novel situations, but they also reported an increase in symptoms (particularly anxiety) in situations requiring strategy adjustments. These outcomes suggest that DDPs had both limited capacities to conceptualize and manage their task-related activities and limited flexibility in their behavioral repertories. Over the 18 months of the study, DDPs changed minimally in their task-related capacities, a finding that is consistent with chronic frontal lobe dysfunctionality. These findings are consistent with recent reports showing significant disturbances in neurophysiological processes subserved by prefrontal cortex and the cerebellar vermis (e.g., response suppression, memory impairment) among depressed individuals (Sweeney, Stojwas, Mann, & Thase, 1998).

Symptom profiles of DDPs did change, however. Table 3.1 presents findings from symptom assessments of the first 20 DDPs entering the study (the only DDPs tested for symptom changes) at Months 1, 6, 12, and 18 of the study. In reviewing Table 3.1, the following points should be kept in mind. The study did not include formal treatment (e.g., psychotherapy, drugs). However, DDPs were the recipients of frequent positive social signals each time they came to the research laboratory.

When participants entered the study, they identified themselves as symptom-afflicted, low-status individuals. Over the course of the study they spent more than 150 hours interacting with investigators and participating in a variety of research assessments. DDPs had a special room with coffee and donuts where they could socialize. They were aware of their importance to the study. Research schedules were posted several days in advance and were altered to meet the extraresearch needs and responsibilities of DDPs. Each of the research protocols was explained in detail prior to testing. Soon after the study began, DDPs began socializing among themselves, both at the research site and elsewhere. Thus, in total, DDPs spent more than 300 hours in study-associated activities in which their lives differed significantly compared to the prestudy period. In effect, DDPs entered a social environment that was supportive, appreciative of their participation, socially rewarding, nonjudgmental (only 1 DDP dropped out of the study over the 18-month period), and in which they were high-status individuals. Such environments positively correlate with changes in the direction of psychological regulation and a reduction of symptoms.

To collect the data for Table 3.1, each of the 40 symptoms listed in the table was printed on a card along with a common language description. The cards were shuffled and DDPs were asked to select those cards that described their symptoms. To qualify for selection, a symptom had to be present each day for the 14 days prior to the assessment, and it had to result in a change in a participant's living routine (e.g., cancellation of an appointment). Investigators then reviewed the cards that were selected and verbally verified the 14-day and alteration-of-living-routine requirements. An independent (blind) assessment of symptoms (using a structured interview designed for the study) was conducted by two investigators. This assessment resulted in essentially the same symptom profile and findings shown in the table.

The numbers in the table listed under each of the four assessments refer to the number of DDPs who, during each assessment, reported the presence of each symptom listed in the lefthand column. The symptoms are listed from the most to the least frequent when scores for all four sampling periods are totaled (row totals).

A comparison of the Assessment 1 (Month 1) with the Assessment 4 (Month 18) column of the table shows that the frequency of symptoms declined for all

TABLE 3.1
Changes in Symptom Frequency Among DDPs

Symptoms	Assessments 1 (1) ↓	2 (6) ↓	3 (12) ↓	4 (18) ↓
(Months) →				
1. Fatigue	17	19	15	13
2. Specific worries	19	15	14	10
3. Feelings of inadequacy	18	16	10	10
4. Decreased effectiveness	17	13	9	10
5. Pessimistic	16	13	9	9
6. Avoid situations	13	12	13	8
7. Feeling slowed down	13	14	10	6
8. Insomnia/hypersomnnia	9	12	14	6
9. On edge, irritable	14	9	13	5
10. Generalized worries	15	12	7	6
11. Difficulty concentrating	11	9	8	8
12. Poor memory	11	9	8	8
13. Less talkative	12	10	10	4
14. Tearfulness, crying	14	11	5	5
15. Obsessions	12	9	7	5
16. Guilt	12	7	5	7
17. Diminished interest	13	9	7	2
18. Social withdrawal	10	9	6	6
19. Decreased pleasure	12	8	6	4
20. Pain in back, joints	9	8	5	5
21. Decreased interest in sex	8	6	6	6
22. Urinary frequency	9	5	4	5
23. Diarrhea, constipation	4	7	5	5
24. Paresthesia	7	6	2	4
25. Palpitations	9	7	1	1
26. Dizziness, vertigo	6	5	2	3
27. Feelings of unreality	3	6	4	1
28. Chest pain, discomfort	7	3	1	2
29. Feeling can't accomplish	6	3	3	1
30. Trembling, shaking	5	4	3	1
31. Hyperalertness	4	1	4	3
32. Fear of dying	7	2	1	1
33. Choking, smothering	3	3	2	1
34. Sweating	4	2	2	0
35. Shortness of breath	2	2	3	0
36. Poor recall	2	2	3	0
37. Self-mutilation	2	3	0	1
38. Recurrent dreams	2	2	1	1
39. Faintness	1	3	2	0
40. Hot and cold flashes	2	1	0	0
Column totals	360	287	230	173

40 symptoms over the course of the study. A comparable symptom assessment for CPs revealed only an occasional symptom. Note that the symptoms were not confined to those usually associated with depression, but extend over a wide range. Also, recall that prior to entering the study the majority of DDPs had received treatment that had been minimally effective in reducing their symptoms, and that DDPs did not take psychotropic medications over the course of the study.

A closer look at Table 3.1 suggests the possibility that symptoms may change at different rates. For example, the symptoms of avoiding situations (Symptom 6), being less talkative (Symptom 13), and diminished interest (Symptom 17) decline most dramatically during the 12– to 18-month period. Generalized worries (Symptom 10) and tearfullness and crying (Symptom 14) decline most dramatically during the 6- to 12-month period. Guilt (Symptom 16) and decreased pleasure (Symptom 19) decline most dramatically during the 1- to 6-month period. Such differences suggest several possibilities, including the idea that clusters of symptoms with different causes may track at different rates and some symptoms may be more closely tied to physiological states, whereas others are more closely tied to psychological states.

AN INTERPRETATION OF FINDINGS FROM THE DD STUDY USING RDT, PET, AND PHYSIOLOGICAL DATA

The decline in symptoms shown in Table 3.1 is consistent with predictions from RDT. Although other investigators have reported that nonspecific psychosocial interventions tend to produce clinical improvement (e.g., Wolpe, 1988), what is usually absent in such reports is an explanation of the mechanisms that account for symptom reduction. RTD provides a partial explanation of such reductions.

Although DDPs improved, their symptoms did not entirely disappear, as indicated by the column entries for Assessment 4 in Table 3.1. Findings from structured interviews of DDPs and PET may explain this finding. Compared to CPs, DDPs frequently misinterpreted others' social signals, they had limited capacities to accurately model social events or their own behavior, and they experienced difficulty utilizing self-monitoring information to develop novel strategies. These characteristics, which existed prior to the study and changed minimally over the course of the study, may be regarded as risk factors for the development of dysregulation and, eventually, DD. As a result, DDPs were less likely to interact socially. When they did, they were less likely to be attractive to others (McGuire & Essock-Vitale, 1982). Compared to CPs, DDPs had smaller social support networks and interacted with both kin and nonkin significantly less often (Essock-Vitale & McGuire, 1990). Further, the majority of DDPs frequently experienced dysphoric thoughts, which implicates specialized regional CNS activation and metabolism. When the preceding points are coupled with the finding

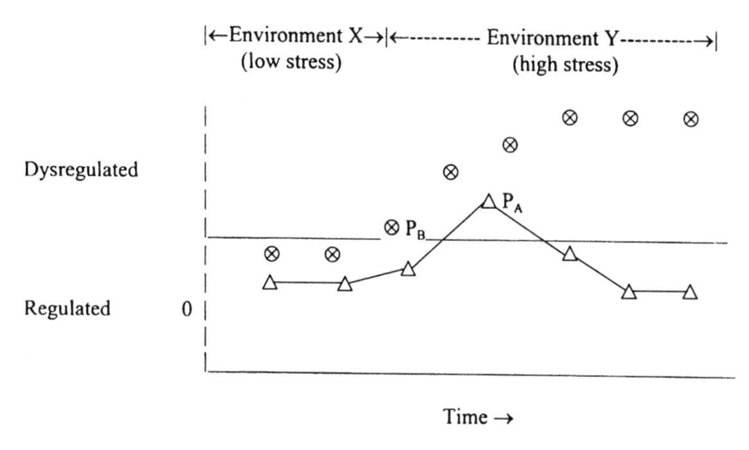

FIG. 3.2. Relations between physiological dysregulation, two social environments, and the probability of symptoms.

of whole-cortex hypometabolism affecting areas responsible for memory, word processing, and so on, the possibility that DD is associated with both internally and externally induced chronic physiological and psychological dysregulation increases.

Physiological findings are also relevant here. Some authors have suggested that alterations in 5-HT_{1A} receptors in response to stress contribute both to the onset and the duration of depression (Lopez, Chalmers, Little, & Watson, 1998). Omega-3 fatty acids in red blood cell membranes have been found to be depleted in depressed persons relative to nondepressed controls (Peet, 1998). Further, recovery from major depression does not appear to normalize CNS 5-HT function (Flory, Mann, Manuck, & Muldoon, 1998). This is a potentially important finding because it suggests that the 5-HT system may be atypical among a percentage of persons with depression (see also Clarke et al., 1995; Mehlman, et al., 1998).

Figure 3.2 extends the points developed in the previous paragraph and ideas developed in association with Fig. 3.1 in ways that are consistent with findings from the DD study. Figure 3.2 shows a model of changing physiological and psychological states for Persons A and B in social Environments X and Y. The horizontal axis depicts time. The vertical axis shows areas depicting regulated and dysregulated states. Zero on the horizontal axis references optimal physiological regulation. In Environment X, others are supportive, minimally competitive, and minimally demanding, and there are numerous social options. Environment X is a "low-stress" environment in which social interactions are rewarding and regulating. In Environment Y, others are not supportive, but are competitive and socially demanding, and there are fewer social options. Environment Y is a "high-stress" environment; that is, one that can easily contribute to dysregulation. Person A has optimal capacities to change his or her behavior; Person B has suboptimal capacities.

In Environment X, Persons A and B are maximally regulated physiologically and psychologically (not suffering from symptoms), although Person B is less regulated than Person A. Person A is not symptomatic, and Person B, which in this discussion can be taken to represent a modal DDP, is moderately symptomatic. When Persons A and B are in Environment Y, they become dysregulated and symptomatic (e.g., tense, anxious, depressed, preoccupied, bored, angry). This change develops because of characteristics specific to Environment X (e.g., increased competition) that fail to facilitate regulation.

Critical differences in Person A's and Person B's responses to Environment Y occur at times P_A and P_B, the points at which Persons A and B first experience symptoms. Person B becomes dysregulated and symptomatic sooner (point P_B) than Person A. At point P_A, Person A has two options to avoid further dysregulation: He or she can change behavior strategies and engage persons in Environment Y in ways that lead to regulation (e.g., become dominant, increase social support networks), or he or she may leave Environment Y and return to Environment X, where less competitive and stressful social interactions will facilitate regulation. The first alternative is shown in the figure: Person A changes behavior strategies and reregulates. In principle, the same options are available to Person B. However, Person B lacks capacities to change behavior to the degree required for regulation in Environment Y. Should Person B remain in Environment Y for an extended period—dysregulation does not occur instantly—dysphoric thoughts are likely to increase, he or she will become increasingly dysregulated, symptom number and intensity will increase, and a disorder may be triggered. Person B could regulate by returning to Environment X, but clinical experience suggests that a large percentage of persons with suboptimal capacities either fail to locate themselves in environments that are optimal for regulation, or such environments are not readily available to them.

Figure 3.2 depicts only a subset of the factors influencing symptom number and intensity. For example, defensive- and safety-mediated behavior (Gilbert, 1993), assertiveness (Gilbert & Allan, 1994), maturation in response to dealing with depressed mood (Gut, 1989), and individual differences (unrelated to disorders) in response to environmental stimuli (e.g., Berger et al., 1987) are likely contributing factors. A more detailed analysis of DD would incorporate such findings. Sex differences might also be added to this list. The lifetime prevalence rates for DD among women is 8%, whereas for men it is 4.8% (Kessler et al., 1994). This sex difference may in part be linked to the male–female differences in cerebral blood flow mentioned earlier.

DISCUSSION

The findings from the DD study can be used to evaluate other explanations of depression, such as the social competitive hypothesis discussed by Price, Sloman, Gardner, Gilbert, and Rohde (1994). This hypothesis, which postulates that "the depressive state evolved in relation to social competition, as an unconscious, involuntary losing strategy, enabling the individual to accept defeat in ritual agonistic encounters and to accommodate to what would otherwise be unacceptably low social rank" (p. 309), may explain increases in already existing symptoms among DDPs who were involved in unsatisfactory relationships. Prior to entering the study, the vast majority of DDPs reported that they had repeatedly suffered social competitive losses (e.g., loss of friends, jobs, family support), and that their social status was diminished (e.g., declines in income, social importance, social influence). Once in the study, DDS encountered a supportive environment in which they were important and they had a clearly defined social status. In addition, over the course of the study they extended the size of their social support networks through relationships developed with other DDPs. During the 18-month study period the potential advantages of using an involuntary losing strategy declined. As the study progressed, participants less and less frequently identified themselves to others as ill. CNS functional alterations are likely to accompany these changes. That DDPs did not completely recover can be attributed to the physiological, psychological, and functional consequences of enduring suboptimal capacities such as suboptimal social competence, as well as atypical 5-HT systems (Essock-Vitale & McGuire, 1990; Grant, 1968).

An alternative explanation relates the chronicity of DDPs to the broader phenotype of autism (Bailey, Phillips, & Rutter, 1996; LeCouteur et al., 1996). The broader phenotype concept builds from a number of findings, the most salient of which is that in a percentage of monozygotic twins, when the probands have autism and the other twins do not meet criteria for pervasive developmental disorder, the other twins have specific cognitive deficits, including the atypical processing of social cues. Future research may support the broader concept characterization. However, from an evolutionary perspective, it will be critical to determine if atypical processing of social cues is best thought of as a mild form of disorder or a reflection of species-typical variation in processing capacities.

The findings may also inform our understanding of the effects of drugs, such as fluoxetine (Prozac), that influence the 5-HT system (Beasley, Masica, & Potvin, 1992; Wong, Bymaster, & Engleman, 1995). As noted, fluoxetine has similar directional effects on subordinate and dominant vervet monkeys. Specifically, it increases interanimal tolerance, reduces interanimal distance, and increases the frequency of initiated and received affiliative behavior. These effects are proportionally greater in dominant compared to subordinate males. In nondepressed humans, an increase in affiliative behavior is reported to occur in response to drug-mediated increases in CNS 5-HT function (Knutson et al., 1997). Among persons who are depressed without associated suboptimal information processing and functional capacities, fluoxetine can be expected to increase CNS 5-HT activity and contribute to behavior that elicits signals from others that favor physiological and psychological regulation. (Ongoing studies of vervet monkeys by McGuire suggest that one effect of fluoxetine is to reduce the importance attributed to and response to other animals' agonistic signals.) In contrast, only partial symptomatic improvement would be predicted among persons with suboptimal physiological and social competence capacities. This interpretation is consistent with clinical findings: In typical studies, only about 70% of participants sustain significant remission of symptoms with fluoxetine treatment. For the occasional patient who reports that his or her life has changed significantly following the use of fluoxetine, improved social status, the social rewards associated with status improvement, and their further regulating effects are implicated.

ACKNOWLEDGMENTS

We thank the Giles and Elise Mead Foundation, the Harry Frank Guggenheim Foundation, the University of California at Los Angeles, the Veterans Administration, Paul Gilbert, and Leon Sloman for their support.

REFERENCES

Agren, H., & Reibring, L. (1994). PET studies of presynaptic monamine metabolism in depressed patients and healthy volunteers. *Pharmacopsychiatry, 27,* 2–6.

American Psychiatric Association. (1980). *Diagnostic and statistical manual of mental disorders* (3rd ed.). Washington DC: Author.

American Psychiatric Association. (1994). *Diagnostic and statistical manual of mental disorders* (4th ed.). Washington DC: Author.

Bailey, A., Phillips, W., & Rutter, M. (1996). Autism: Towards an integration of clinical, genetic, neuropsychological, and neurobiological perspectives. *Journal of Child Psychology and Psychiatry, 37,* 89–126.

Baxter, L. R., Phelps, M. E., Mazziotta, J. C., Schwartz, J. M., Gerner, R. H., Selin, C. E., & Sumida, R. M. (1985). Cerebral metabolic rates for glucose in mood disorders. *Archives of General Psychiatry, 42,* 441–447.

Beasley, C. M., Masica, D. N., & Potvin, J. H. (1992). Fluoxetine: A review of receptor and functional effects and their clinical implications. *Psychopharmacology, 107,* 1–10.

Bench, C. J., Friston, K. J., Brown, R. G., Scott, L. C., Frackowiak, R. S. J., & Dolan, R. J. (1992). The anatomy of melancholia—Focal abnormalities of cerebral blood flow in major depression. *Psychological Medicine, 22,* 607–615.

Berger, M., Bossert, S., Krieg, J.-C., Dirlich, G., Ettmeier, W., Schreiber, W., & von Zerssen, D. (1987). Interindividual differences in the susceptibility of the cortisol system: An important factor for the degree of hypercortisolism in stress situations. *Biological Psychiatry, 22,* 1327–1339.

Biver, F., Goldman, S., Delvenne, V., Luxen, A., DeMaertelaer, V., Hubain, P., Mendlewicz, J., & Lotstra, F. (1994). Frontal and parietal metabolic disturbances in unipolar depression. *Biological Psychiatry, 36,* 381–388.

Botchin, M. B., Kaplan, J. R., Manuck, S. B., & Mann, J. J. (1993). Low versus high prolactin responders to fenfluramine challenge: Marker of behavioral differences in adult male *Cynomolgus Macaques. Neuropsychopharmacology, 9,* 93–99.

Bowlby, J. (1969). *Attachment and loss: Vol. I. Attachment.* London: Hogarth.

Bowlby, J. (1973). *Attachment and loss: Vol. II. Separation: Anxiety and anger.* London: Hogarth.

Clarke, A. S., Kammerer, C. M., George, K. P., Kupfer, D. J., McKinney, W. T., Spence, M. A., & Kraemer, G. W. (1995). Evidence for heritability of biogenic amine levels in the cerebrospinal fluid of rhesus monkeys. *Biological Psychiatry, 38,* 572–577.

Cloninger, C. R. (1986). A unified biosocial theory of personality and its role in the development of anxiety states. *Psychiatric Developments, 3,* 167–226.

Cloninger, C. R., Svrakic, D. M., & Przybeck, T. R. (1993). A psychobiological model of temperament and character. *Archives of General Psychiatry, 50,* 975–990.

Coryell, W. A. (1980). A blind family history study of Briquet's syndrome: Further validation of the diagnosis. *Archives of General Psychiatry, 37,* 1266–1269.

Essock-Vitale, S. M., & McGuire, M. T. (1990). Social and reproductive histories of depressed and anxious women. In R. W. Bell & N. J. Bell (Eds.), *Sociobiology and the social sciences* (pp. 105–118). Lubbock, TX: Texas Technical University Press.

Flory, J. D., Mann, J. J., Manuck, S. B., & Muldoon, M. F. (1998). Recovery from major depression is not associated with normalization of serotonergic function. *Biological Psychiatry, 43,* 320–326.

Gaebel, W., & Wolwer, W. (1992). Facial expression and meotional face recognition in schizophrenia and depression. *European Archives of Psychiatry and Clinical Neuroscience, 242,* 46–52.

George, M. S., Ketter, T. A., Parekh, P. I., Horwitz, B., Herscovitch, P., & Post, R. M. (1995). Brain activity during transient sadness and happiness in healthy women. *American Journal of Psychiatry, 152,* 341–351.

George, M. S., Ketter, R. A., & Post, R. M. (1993). SPECT and PET imaging in mood disorders. *Journal of Clinical Psychiatry, 54*(Suppl), 6–13.

Gilbert, P. (1993). Defence and safety: Their function in social behaviour and psychopathology. *British Journal of Clinical Psychology, 32,* 131–153.

Gilbert, P., & Allan, S. (1994). Assertiveness, submissive behaviour and social comparison. *British Journal of Clinical Psychology, 33,* 295–306.

Grant, E. C. (1968). An ethological description of non-verbal behaviour during interviews. *British Journal Medical Psychology, 41,* 177–182.

Gut, E. (1989). *Productive and unproductive depression.* New York: Basic Books.

Guze, S. B., Goodwin, D. W., & Crane, J. B. (1970). A psychiatric study of the wives of convicted felons: An example of assortative mating. *American Journal of Psychiatry, 126,* 1773–1776.

Harlow, H. F., & Harlow, M. K. (1962). Social deprivation in monkeys. *Scientific American, 207,* 136–146.

Higley, J. D., Mehlman, P. T., Poland, R. E., Taub, D. M., Vickers, J., Suomi, S. J., & Linnoila, M. (1996). CSF testosterone and 5-HIAA correlate with different types of aggressive behavior. *Biological Psychiatry, 40,* 1067–1082.

Hofer, M. A. (1984). Relationships as regulators: A psychobiologic perspective on bereavement. *Psychosomatic Medicine, 46,* 183–197.

Kessler, R.C., McGonagle, K. A., Zhao, S., Nelson, C. B., Hughes, M., Eshelman, S., Wittchen, H.-U., & Kendler, K. S. (1994). Lifetime and 12-month prevalence of DSM–III–R psychiatric disorders in the United States. *Archives of General Psychiattry, 51,* 8–19.

Knutson, B., Wolkowitz, O. M., Cole, S. W., Chan, T., Moore, E. A., Johnson, R. C., Terpstra, J., Turner, R. A., & Reus, V. I. (1997). Serotonergic intervention alters a major dimension of normal personality. *American Journal of Psychiatry, 155*(3), 373–379.

Kraemer, G. W., & Clarke, A. S. (1991). The behavioral neurobiology of self-injurious behavior in rhesus monkeys. *Progress in Neuropsychopharmacology, Biology, and Psychiatry, 14,* S141–S168.

Kravitz, E. A. (1988). Hormonal control of behavior: Amines and the biasing of behavioral output in lobsters. *Science, 241,* 1775–1781.

LeCouteur, A., Bailey, A., Goode, S., Pickles, A., Robertson, S., Gottesman, I., & Rutter, M. (1996). A broader phenotype of autism: The clinical spectrum in twins. *Journal of Child Psychology and Psychiatry, 37,* 785–801.

Lopez, J. F., Chalmers, D. T., Little, K. Y., & Watson, S. J. (1998). Regulation of serotonin$_{1A}$, glucocorticoid, and mineralocorticoid receptor in rat and human hippocampus: Implications for the neurobiology of depression. *Biological Psychiatry, 43,* 547–573.

Madsen, D. (1985). A biochemical property relating to power seeking in humans. *American Political Science Review, 79,* 448–457.

Madsen, D. (1986). Power seekers are biochemically different: Further biochemical evidence. *American Political Science Review, 80,* 261–269.

Madsen, D., & McGuire, M. T. (1984). Whole blood 5-HT and the Type A behavior pattern. *Psychosomatic Medicine, 46,* 546–548.

Marsh, J., & Marsh, G. (1991). *Neuropsychological studies of dysthymia.* Unpublished manuscript.

Martinot, J.-L., Hardy, P., Feline, A., Huret, J-D., Mazoyer, B., Attar-Levy, D., Pappata, S., & Syrota, A. (1990). Left prefrontal glucose hypometabolism in the depressed state: A confirmation. *American Journal of Psychiatry, 147,* 1313–1317.

McBride, P. A., Tierney, H., DeMeo, M., Chen, J. & Mann, J. J. (1990). Effects of age and gender on CNS serotonergic responsivity in normal adults. *Biological Psychiatry, 27,* 1143–1155.

McGuire, M. T. (1988). On the possibility of ethological explanations of psychiatric disorders. *Acta Psychiatrica Scandinavica, 77*(Suppl), 7–22.

McGuire, M. T., & Essock-Vitale, S. M. (1982). Psychiatric disorders in the context of evolutionary biology: The impairment of adaptive behaviors during the exacerbation and remission of psychiatric illnesses. *Journal of Nervous and Mental Disease, 170,* 9–20.

McGuire, M. T., Raleigh, M. J., & Johnson, C. (1983). Social dominance in adult male vervet monkeys: General considerations. *Social Science Information, 22,* 106–117.

McGuire, M. T., Raleigh, M. J., & Pollack, D. B. (1994). Personality features in vervet monkeys: The effects of sex, age, social status, and group composition. *American Journal of Primatology, 33,* 1–13.

McGuire, M. T., & Troisi, A. (1987a). Physiological regulation-dysregulation and psychiatric disorders. *Ethology and Sociobiology, 8,* 9S–12S.

McGuire, M. T., & Troisi, A. (1987b). Unrealistic wishes and physiological change. *Psychotherapy and Psychosomatics, 47,* 82–94.

McGuire, M. T., & Troisi, A. *Darwinian psychiatry.* (1998). New York: Oxford University Press.

Mehlman, P. T., Higley, J. D., Faucher, I., Lilly, A. A., Taub, D. M., Vickers, J., Suomi, S. J., & Linnoila, M. (1998). Correlation of CSF 5-HIAA concentration with sociality and the timing of emigration in free-ranging primates. *American Journal of Psychiatry, 152,* 907–913.

Nishizawa, S., Benkelfat, C., Young, S. N., Leyton, M., Mzengeza, S., de Montigny, C., Blier, P., & Diksic, M. (1997). Differences between males and females in rates of serotonin synthesis in human brain. *Proceedings of the National Academy of Science, 94,* 5308–5313.

Pardo, J. V., Fox, P. T., & Raichle, M. E. (1991). Localization of a human system for sustained attention by positron emission tomography. *Nature, 349,* 61–64.

Pardo, J. V., Pardo, P. J., & Raichle, M. E. (1993). Neural correlates of self-induced dysphoria. *American Journal Psychiatry, 150,* 713–719.

Peet, M., Murphy, B., Shay, J., & Horrobin, D. (1998). Depletion of Omega-3 fatty acid levels in red blood cell membranes of depressive patients. *Biological Psychiatry, 43,* 315–319.

Price, J. S., Sloman, L., Gardner, R., Gilbert, P., & Rohde, P. (1994). The social competition hypothesis of depression. *British Journal of Psychiatry, 164,* 309–315

Raleigh, M. J., Brammer, G. L., McGuire, M. T., & Yuwiler, A. (1985). Dominant social status facilitates the behavioral effects of serotonergic agonists. *Brain Research, 348,* 274–282.

Raleigh, M. J., & McGuire, M. T. (1989). Female influences on male dominance acquisition in captive vervet monkeys, *Cercopithecus aethiops sabaeus. Animal Behavior, 38,* 59–67.

Raleigh, M. J., & McGuire, M. T. (1993). Environmental constraints, serotonin, aggression, and violence in vervet monkeys. In R. Masters & M. McGuire (Eds.), *The neurotransmitter revolution* (pp. 129–145). Carbondale, IL: Southern Illinois University Press.

Raleigh, M. J., McGuire, M. T., Brammer, G. L., Oikkacjm D. B., & Yuwiler, A. (1991). Serotonergic mechanisms promote dominance acquisition in adult male vervet monkeys. *Brain Research, 559,* 181–190.

Raleigh, M. J., McGuire, M. T., Brammer, G. L., & Yuwiler, A. (1984). Social and environmental influences on blood 5-HT concentrations in monkeys. *Archives of General Psychiatry, 41,* 405–410.

Reiman, E. M., Fusselman, M. J., Fox, P. T., & Raichle, M. E. (1989). Neuroanatomical correlates of anticipatory anxiety. *Science, 243,* 1071–1074.

Reite, M., Short, R., Seiler, C., & Pauley, J. D. (1981). Attachment, loss, and depression. *Journal of Child Psychology and Psychiatry, 22,* 221–227.

Rosenblum, L. A., Coplan, J. D., Friedman, S., Bassoff, T., Gorman, J. M., & Andrews, M. W. (1994). Adverse early experiences affect noradrenergic and serotonergic functioning in adult primates. *Biological Psychiatry, 35,* 221–227.

Sapolsky, R. M. (1989). Hypercortisolism among socially subordinate wild baboons originates at the CNS level. *Archives of General Psychiatry, 46,* 1047–1051.

Sapolsky, R. M. (1990). Adrenocortical function, social rank, and personality among wild baboons. *Biological Psychiatry, 28,* 862–878.

Schultz, D. P (1965). *Sensory restriction.* New York: Academic Press.

Shively, C. A., Laber-Laird, K., & Anton, R. F. (1997). Behavior and physiology of social stress and depression in female *Cynomolgus* monkeys. *Biological Psychiatry, 41,* 871–882.

Spitz, R. (1945). Hospitalism. In A. Freud, H. Hartman, & E. Kris (Eds.), *The psychoanalytic study of the child* (Vol 1, pp. 53–74). New York: International Universities Press.

Steadman's Medical Dictionary (25th ed.). (1990). Baltimore: Williams & Wilkins.

Sweeney, J. A., Stojwas, M. H., Mann, J. J., & Thase, M. E. (1998). Prefrontal and cerebellar abnormalities in major depression: Evidence from oculomotor studies. *Biological Psychiatry, 43,* 584–594.

Volkart, R., Dittrich, A., Rothenfluh, T., & Werner, P. (1983). Eine kontrollierte untersuchung uber psychopathologische effekte der einzelhaft [A controlled study about the psychopathological effect of solitary confinement]. In H. Huber (Ed.), *Revue Suisse de Psychologie Pure et Appliquee* (pp. 1–24). Bern, Switzerland: Verlag.

Waterhouse, B. (1996, January). *Neurobiology of the dorsal raphe nucleus: New evidence for functional specificity within a broadly projecting brainstem monaminergic pathway.* Paper presented at the Twenty-Ninth Annual Winter Conference on Brain Research, Snowmass Village, CO.

Wiesel, F.-A. (1992). Glucose metabolism in psychiatric disorders: How can we facilitate comparisons among studies? *Journal of Neural Transmission, 37*(Suppl), 1–18.

Wise, R., Chollet, F., Hadar, U., Friston, K., Hoffner, E., & Frackowiak, R. (1991). Distribution of cortical neural networks involved in word comprehension and word retrival. *Brain, 114,* 1803–1817.

Wolpe, J. (1988). The renascence of neurotic depression: Its varied dynamics and implications. *Journal of Nervous and Mental Diseases, 176,* 607–613.

Wong, D. T., Bymaster, F. P., & Engleman, E. A. (1995). Prozac (fluoxetine, Lilly 110140), the first selective serotonin uptake inhibitor and an antidepressant drug: Twenty years since its first publication. *Life Sciences, 57,* 411–441.

CHAPTER FOUR

Major Depression and the Involuntary Defeat Strategy: Biological Correlates

Robert D. Levitan
Centre for Addiction and Mental Health, Toronto, Ontario

Gary Hasey
Hamilton Psychiatric Hospital
McMaster University, Hamilton, Ontario

Leon Sloman
Centre for Addiction and Mental Health, Toronto, Ontario

Major depression is a common, poorly understood set of disorders characterized by dysfunction in a variety of fundamental homeostatic processes. Depressed patients can exhibit marked changes in neurovegetative functioning including eating behavior, sleep, psychomotor activity, and libido; cognitive changes including reduced confidence, low self-esteem, and suicidal thoughts; changes in social functioning including social withdrawal, social anxiety, and impulsive behaviors; and basic changes in motivation and arousal. Patients with depression are often extremely vulnerable to stress, whether biological, cognitive, or psychosocial. Notwithstanding significant progress in recent decades, our basic understanding of the pathophysiological mechanisms underlying depression remains limited.

In earlier chapters, the pathophysiological features of depression have been conceptualized in terms of primate social hierarchy behavior, in particular as it relates to competitive loss. Many of the vegetative, motivational, and social behavioral changes seen in depression, and the biological processes underlying them, are highly analogous to phenomena observed in nonhuman primates who have experienced competitive loss. This suggests that the involuntary defeat strategy (IDS; see Sloman, chap. 2, this volume), the complex behavioral mechanism that limits the cost of competitive defeat, may be operative in all primates and play an integral role in mediating depressive symptomatology at many levels.

The possibility of involuntary defeat behavior and major depressive disorder being mechanistically linked was explored in the first two chapters, in which the concept of the IDS was delineated. If in fact the IDS is involved in the pathophysiology of depression, one would expect to find an overlap in the biological mechanisms relevant to competitive loss and involuntary defeat, and those relevant to major depression. The goal of this chapter is to explore possible biological links between involuntary defeat behavior and major depression, focusing primarily on the hypothalamic–pituitary–adrenal (HPA) axis and serotonin system. The neuroanatomical substrates of the IDS and the role of disrupted biological rhythms are also considered. We hypothesize that many of the biological changes found in major depression can be related to factors that render the IDS ineffective. For example, in response to a social challenge, both low-ranking primates and depressed humans frequently experience a state of chronic overarousal, which may result in a failure to turn off an otherwise adaptive fight or flight response, manifested hormonally as cortisol hypersecretion. In susceptible individuals, this state of hyperarousal may contribute significantly to the pathophysiological features of major depressive disorder, including changes in sleep, appetite, psychomotor activity, and cognition; circadian rhythmicity, and impulsivity. The role of decreased serotonin activity in primate social systems and major depression is also explored. We suggest that serotonergic dysfunction may link primate social behavior and human depressive disorders at many levels, promoting hostile or impulsive behavior and poor social affiliation, disrupting communication between key brain areas necessary for adaptive competitive defeat behavior, and also directly affecting mood-relevant brain mechanisms.

The next sections review the biology of primate social hierarchical behavior, highlighting important areas of overlap with biological research on major depression. Subsequently, we present an integrative theoretical model that attempts to link competitive loss, involuntary defeat behavior, and depression in terms of HPA-axis activity, serotonergic dysfunction, biological rhythms and neuroanatomical circuitry. Adaptation of the model to particular subtypes of depression and biological treatment issues are also discussed.

THE BIOLOGY OF PRIMATE SOCIAL HIERARCHICAL BEHAVIOR: OVERLAP WITH MAJOR DEPRESSION

The HPA Axis in Primate Social Behavior and Major Depression

The clearest overlap between the biology of competitive defeat and the biology of major depression relates to changes in stress hormone production.[1] Sapolsky and colleagues have been studying a population of wild baboons in East Africa since 1971. They found that basal HPA-axis activity in baboons is strongly associated with social rank, with lower rank and subordinance associated with increased cortisol levels and dexamethasone resistance (Sapolsky, 1982, 1983; Sapolsky, Alberts, & Altmann, 1997). Affiliation appears to play an important protective role in that social isolation in general is associated with hypercortisolism and/or dexamethasone nonsuppression, even in dominant males (Ray & Sapolsky, 1992; Sapolsky, 1983; Sapolsky et al., 1997). Low interaction with females and infants has also been associated with increased circulating cortisol levels in this population (Sapolsky & Ray, 1989). Sapolsky et al. suggested that dexamethasone resistance in these animals may be due to downregulation of hippocampal glucocorticoid (GC) receptors that play an important role in the negative feedback regulation of cortisol release. The linkage between social behavior and HPA overactivity may be mediated by the GC receptors as, in macaque monkeys, a link has been found between loss of hippocampal GC receptors, dexamethasone resistance, and social instability (Brooke, de Haas-Johnson, Kaplan, Manuck, & Sapolsky, 1994).

The emerging pattern of overactivity of the HPA axis in low-ranking primates is highly congruent with findings in individuals with major depression. CRF, a 41 amino acid peptide synthesized primarily in the hypothalamus, plays a key role in modulating various components of the stress response. Depressed individuals exhibit elevated levels of CRF (Arato, Banki, Bissette, & Nemeroff, 1989; Banki et al., 1992; Nemeroff et al., 1984; Risch et al., 1992) and blunted adrenocorticotropic hormone (ACTH) responses to CRF (Amsterdam, Marinelli, Arger, & Winokur, 1987; Gold et al., 1986; Holsboer et al., 1984; E. A. Young et al., 1990), consistent with an elevated HPA activity originating at the level of the central nervous system. Several anatomical changes in depressed individuals, including pituitary gland enlargement (Krishnan et al., 1991) and adrenal gland enlargement (Nemeroff et al., 1992), may indicate pathology at these levels, but are also consistent with a generalized, centrally driven overactivity of the HPA axis.

---

[1]Cortisol is the primary stress hormone released by activation of the HPA axis, however corticotropin-releasing factor (CRF), which may be released in the brain in response to stress, also has important effects on arousal and behavior. The stress response thus includes activity of both of these hormones.

About half of patients with major depression, particularly those with melancholic or psychotic features, show hypercortisolemia and a loss of suppression following dexamethasone challenge (Carroll, 1982). This could be accounted for by blunted negative feedback mediated through changes involving GC receptors. In support of this, it has been noted that suicide victims with a history of major depression exhibit downregulation of the hippocampal GC receptors that mediate negative feedback regulation of cortisol release (Lopez, Chalmers, Little, & Watson, 1998). The fact that antidepressant treatment can normalize cortisol levels and restore cortisol suppression by dexamethasone suggests that impaired negative feedback is largely state dependent in depressed individuals (Barden, Reul, & Holsboer, 1995).

In summary, several lines of evidence point to dysfunction at one or more levels of the HPA axis in both low-ranking or defeated primates and individuals with major depression. In both cases, the changes are consistent with failure to turn off these otherwise adaptive fight or flight mechanisms. If humans who react to competitive defeat in a particularly maladaptive way also experience these fundamental changes in HPA-axis activity, this might render them more vulnerable to subsequent major depressive disorder.

Serotonergic Mechanisms in Primate Social Behavior and Major Depression

Although differences in techniques of measurement limit direct comparison of human and animal work, the overall pattern of findings points to several potential areas of overlap in serotonergic functioning between defeated or low-ranking primates and individuals with major depression.

Sloman (chap. 2, this volume) argues that the IDS plays a crucial role in stabilizing primate hierarchies by de-escalating competitive behavior. There is a large body of work suggesting that serotonergic mechanisms may play a key role in this process at many levels. In nonhuman primates, maladaptive aggression and risk taking most often occurs in impulsive low-ranking subjects with low cerebrospinal fluid (CSF) 5-hydroxyindoleacetic acid (5-HIAA) concentrations (Mehlman et al., 1994; Raleigh & McGuire, 1994). 5-HIAA is the major metabolite of serotonin, with low levels likely (but not necessarily) reflecting decreased serotonin turnover. Female rhesus monkeys with low CSF 5-HIAA exhibit higher rates of spontaneous aggressive wounding and are more likely to be expelled from their social groups (Higley et al., 1996). In this same study, females with above-average CSF 5-HIAA were able to attain and maintain a high social dominance within their social group. This led Higley et al. to conclude that serotonin plays a crucial role in social affiliation and de-escalation by controlling impulses that regulate aggression and promote competent social behavior. Several other studies have found that nonhuman primates with high CSF 5-HIAA concentrations are more likely to engage and spend time in positive social interactions

(Higley, Linnoila, & Suomi, 1994; Mehlman et al., 1995; Raleigh, Brammer, & McGuire, 1983; Raleigh & McGuire, 1994).

The relation between social rank and serotonergic function may be bidirectional. Pharmacological intervention that increases brain serotonin can increase the frequency of positive social interaction and improve social rank, and the opposite is true when serotonin activity is pharmacologically reduced (Raleigh et al., 1986; Raleigh, McGuire, Brammer, Pollack, & Yuwiler, 1991). Conversely, changes in social rank may secondarily affect serotonin functioning (McGuire, Fawzy, Spar, & Troisi, chap. 3, this volume); that is, dominant males experimentally deprived of submissive gestures from lower ranking males exhibited marked drops in whole-blood serotonin activity and decreased social rank.

Human findings are consistent with those in nonhuman primates; serotonergic dysfunction and low CSF 5-HIAA have been associated with deficient impulse control (Soubrie, 1986), violence (Brown, Ballenger, Minchiello, & Goodwin, 1979; Linnoila et al., 1983; Virkkunen, Nuutila, Goodwin, & Linnoila, 1987), and personality disorders characterized by impulsivity and poor social affiliation (Coccaro & Kavoussi, 1996; Hollander et al., 1994; Siever & Trestman, 1993). Bulimia nervosa, an eating disorder often characterized by a variety of impulsive behaviors and depression, has also been associated with marked serotonergic dysfunction (Kaye et al., 1984; Levitan, Kaplan, Joffe, Levitt, & Brown, 1997). Manipulation of the serotonin system may have important effects on impulsivity and hostile mood both in humans and in nonhuman primates. For example, experimental depletion of the serotonin precursor tryptophan can promote hostile affect and behavior in normal males (Cleare & Bond, 1995; Moeller et al., 1996), whereas the selective serotonin reuptake inhibitor (SSRI) paroxetine reduces hostility and enhances affiliative behavior in normals (Knutson et al., 1998). Similar improvements following SSRI treatment have been found in psychiatric populations with impulsive or hostile characteristics (reviewed by Fuller, 1996), including personality disorders (Coccaro, Astill, Herbert, & Schut, 1990; Kavoussi, Liu, & Coccaro, 1994; Salzman et al., 1995), mental retardation with high aggression (Markowitz, 1992), bulimia nervosa (FBNC Study Group, 1992), and depression characterized by anger attacks (Fava et al., 1991).

Many different approaches have been used to study serotonergic functioning in depression. Prior to the arrival of modern neuroimaging and genetics, most research in this area was based on the hypothesis that serotonergic activity is generally decreased in depression. As our understanding of the complexities of the serotonin system has improved, models of dysregulation have largely replaced this simple dichotomous approach.

In the early 1980s, most research in this area was limited to indirect peripheral measures, allowing at least some direct comparisons to findings in nonhuman primates. For example, as is the case in low-ranking primates, low CSF 5-HIAA has been found in several studies of drug-free depressed patients (Agren, 1980; Asberg et al., 1984; Asberg, Traskman, & Thoren, 1976). Clinical correlates of low CSF 5-HIAA have generally been inconsistent, although the finding of an inverse relation between CSF 5-HIAA and a history of suicide attempts in unipolar depressed patients is relatively robust (Traskman-Bendz, Asberg, Nordstrom, & Stanley, 1989). Low CSF 5-HIAA has also been found in suicide attempters with diagnoses other than depression, suggesting that it may not be specific to this disorder (Brown et al., 1982). New evidence indicates that a particular polymorphism of the tryptophan hydroxylase gene may be associated with low 5-HIAA and suicidality (Nielsen et al., 1994).

Neuroendocrine challenge tests in depressed patients have demonstrated abnormal neuroendocrine responses to l-tryptophan (Cowen & Charig, 1987; Heninger, Charney, & Sternberg, 1984; Price, Charney, Delgado, & Heninger, 1991) and the serotonin-releasing drug fenfluramine (O'Keane & Dinan, 1991; Siever, Murphy, Slater, de la Vega, & Lipper, 1984), but normal responses to the direct 5-HT1a agonist buspirone (Cowen, 1993) and the primarily 5-HT2c/2a receptor agonist metachlorophenylpiperazine (mCPP; Anand et al., 1994; Kahn et al., 1990). However, other indirect studies of serotonin in depression have provided few consistent findings (e.g., DeMyer, Shea, Hendrie, & Yoshimura, 1981; Meltzer et al., 1981; Moller, Kirk, & Henore, 1979; Perry, Marshall, Blessed, Tomlinson, & Perry, 1983).

As our ability to directly assess central nervous system serotonergic functioning in humans has improved, a clearer pattern of dysfunction has begun to emerge. Rapid depletion of tryptophan has been found to induce negative mood states in healthy men (S. N. Young, Smith, Pihl, & Ervin, 1985), particularly those at genetic risk for major depression (Benkelfat, Ellenbogen, Dean, Palmour, & Young, 1994). Delgado et al. (1990) found that tryptophan depletion produced a transient depressive relapse in 67% of successfully treated depressed patients, with the greatest effects in patients treated with primarily serotonergic medications. Bremner et al. (1997), using positron emission tomography (PET) imaging, found that in patients with relapse of depression induced by tryptophan depletion, there was decreased brain metabolism in the dorsolateral prefrontal cortex, thalamus, and orbitofrontal cortex. Furthermore, decreased brain metabolism in these areas correlated strongly with depressive symptoms (Bremner et al., 1997). Other authors (Drevets & Raichle, 1992; George, Ketter, & Post, 1994) have speculated that the prefrontal–limbic–striatal regions, including important serotonergic pathways, comprise a functional circuit that may be dysfunctional in depressed patients. The possible role of this circuit in the IDS is discussed later.

Taken as a whole, serotonin studies in depression have provided significant evidence of dysfunction in at least a significant subgroup of depressed patients and individuals at genetic risk for this disorder. Serotonin pathways in the brain are complex and diverse, making it likely that more than one pattern of dysfunction can establish increased vulnerability to depression. Although differing methodologies make comparisons to the animal literature difficult, serotonergic activity clearly plays a major role in both primate social hierarchical behavior and mood regulation in humans, establishing several areas of potential overlap in these two processes. A more detailed consideration of these overlaps is outlined in our model that follows.

Biological Rhythm Alterations in Defeated Animals and Depressed Humans

Biological rhythms play a fundamental role in homeostasis by optimizing the relation between an organism's internal state and the predictably changing physical environment (Moore-Ede, 1986). In patients with major depression, pathophysiological features such as early morning awakening, diurnal variation in mood, and altered 24-hour patterns of cortisol secretion have led to several chronobiological theories of mood disorders (Czeisler, Kronauer, Mooney, Anderson, & Allan, 1987; Ehlers, Frank, & Kupfer, 1988; Halberg, 1968; Healy, 1987; Siever & Davis, 1985; Wehr & Wirz-Justice, 1982). There is also preliminary evidence that animals undergoing competitive defeat have marked changes in their biological rhythms.This points to another potential biological overlap linking competitive loss with major depression.

In their work with rats, Tornatzky and Miczek (1993) found that brief intermittent social stress produced by intruders can decrease the amplitude of circadian rhythms for as long as several weeks. Similarly, Harper, Tornatzky, and Miczek (1996) demonstrated that socially defeated rats had marked disruption in several circadian and ultradian rhythms for up to 12 days. Tornatzky, Cole, and Miczek (1998) subsequently demonstrated that ultradian heart rate and temperature rhythms can be entrained to the timing of recurrent aggressive episodes; these authors suggested that this enables an organism to optimally prepare for the physiological demands of predictable aggressive encounters.

Several chronobiological disturbances have been documented in depressed humans. Similar to animals undergoing social stress, depressed individuals often exhibit a marked reduction in the amplitude of circadian rhythms (Beersma, Hoofdakker, & Berkestijn, 1983; Schulz & Lund, 1983; von Zerssen et al., 1985). Depressed mood can be induced in normal controls by artificially phase advancing circadian rhythms relative to the sleep period (David, MacLean, Knowles, & Coulter, 1991); similar findings with transmeridian travel are well documented (Jauhar & Weller, 1982). Conversely, in some depressed patients, a phase advance of the sleep–wake cycle can have temporary antidepressant effects (Wehr, Wirz-Justice, Goodwin, Duncan, & Gillin, 1979). These various findings suggest that acute changes in the timing of various biological rhythms may contribute to depression (Wehr & Wirz-Justice, 1982). Other authors, such as Ehlers et al. (1988) and Healy and Waterhouse (1995), suggest that the fundamental chronobiological disturbance in depression is related to a loss of normal zeitgebers or rhythm entraining events of a physical, chemical, or psychosocial nature.

Although specific mechanisms need to be worked out, important chronobiological changes have been found both in animals that have experienced competitive defeat and in humans suffering from major depression. Alterations in biological rhythms might thus constitute another important pathway by which competitive defeat can promote affective disturbance in vulnerable individuals.

INVOLUNTARY DEFEAT BEHAVIOR, SOCIAL HIERARCHY, AND DEPRESSION: AN INTEGRATIVE MODEL

The preceding sections of this chapter reviewed the role of serotonin, HPA-axis activity, and biological rhythms in primate social behavior and major depression. The evidence gathered to date suggests that defeated primates and humans with clinical depression share many common biological features. The biological changes associated with competitive loss may thus constitute an important vulnerability factor for depressive disorders. In the following paragraphs we present an integrative model that attempts to link competitive loss, involuntary defeat behavior, and depression in terms of HPA-axis functioning, serotonin, and circadian rhythmicity. Possible neuroanatomical substrates of the IDS and its relevance to depression are also considered. Our main focus is on these particular biological systems, but we acknowledge that multiple other mechanisms are likely involved.

Given the heterogeneity and complexity of depression on the one hand, and primate behavior on the other, it is unlikely that the model we propose holds true for all depressed patients. Notwithstanding that, we hope to demonstrate how shared biological mechanisms may link primate subordinate behavior with depressive disorders in a given individual.

The Biology of the Normal IDS

Figure 4.1 summarizes normal activity and biology relevant to the IDS as it might apply in a human or nonhuman primate. In response to a competitive encounter, the individual experiences increased arousal with a rise in plasma cortisol levels that mobilizes metabolic, cognitive, and behavioral resources. If it becomes clear that the encounter will be lost and that further arousal will be counterproductive, there is a triggering of the IDS that, if effective, serves to de-escalate behavior and restore normal HPA-axis functioning. There is successful escape or submission, acceptance of the loss and new social status, and the IDS itself is terminated. At this point the HPA axis returns to its baseline state and homeostasis is reestablished.

At a neuroanatomical level, the IDS can be thought of as a preprogrammed neural circuit linking the limbic system, prefrontal cortex, and striatum, which mediate the emotional, cognitive, and behavioral components of the IDS,

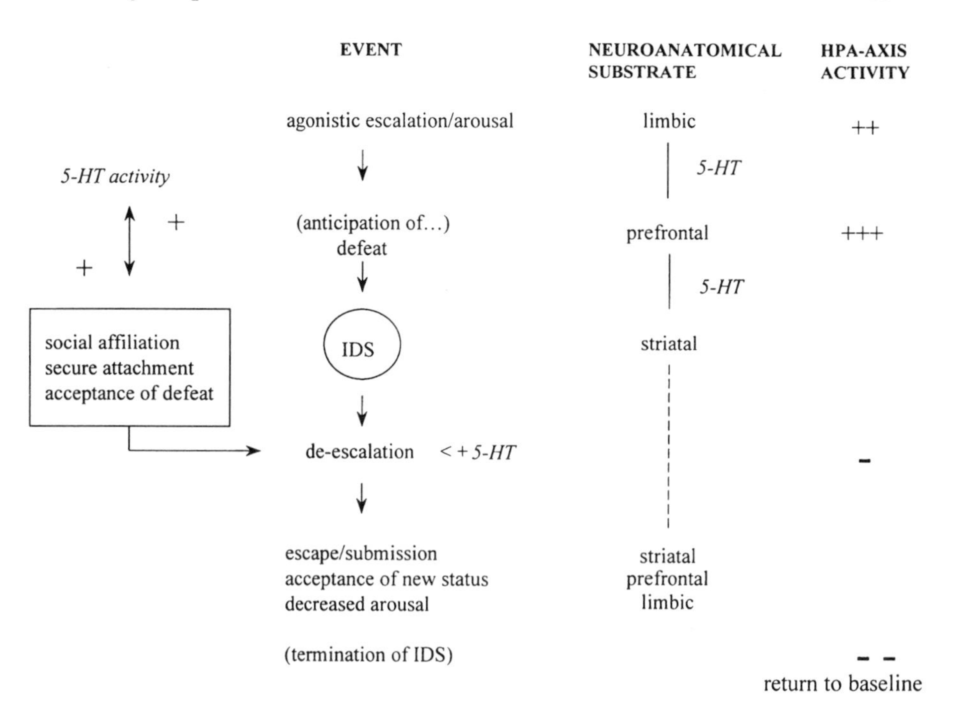

FIG 4.1. The biology of the normal IDS.

respectively. In response to a competitive threat, the limbic system would be activated with a concomitant increase in arousal and HPA-axis functioning. If competitive loss appears inevitable, the prefrontal cortex, responsible for higher order cognitive functions including anticipation and planning, would be activated and trigger cognitions related to anticipation of defeat. Activation of the striatum would trigger the appropriate behavioral/motor sequence (i.e., submissive gesturing or psychomotor inhibition, or possibly rapid flight from the encounter). If effective, the submissive IDS might involve further adaptive motor behaviors mediated by the striatum, a new cognitive set of acceptance mediated at the prefrontal cortex, and decreased arousal associated with lowered activity of the limbic system and HPA axis. These would all promote a successful return to a steady state.

Normal serotonergic functioning may play a modulatory role at many levels of this system. Serotonin may inhibit impulses that might be expressed as various forms of aggression, promoting de-escalation of behavior when competitive loss is inevitable. Serotonin may at the same time promote the competent social behavior that ensures a supportive social network, increasing the likelihood that the defeated individual will accept a new position in the social hierarchy. At a neuroanatomical level, serotonergic pathways link the limbic system, prefrontal cortex, and striatum (Bremner et al., 1997), and could play a major role in modulating the functional circuit of the IDS proposed earlier. In parallel to this, serotonergic activity would also modulate HPA-axis activity at both the hypothalamic (Liposits, Phelix, & Paull, 1987) and pituitary (Lewis & Sherman, 1984) levels, ensuring adaptive regulation of this system in response to the external threat.

The Biology of a Maladaptive IDS and Its Relation to Major Depression

Figure 4.2 illustrates how dysfunction in key biological systems might pròmote failure of the normal IDS and establish an important vulnerability factor for depressive illness.

In a competitive encounter, activation of the HPA axis produces a rise in plasma cortisol levels to mobilize necessary resources. If the HPA axis is not properly regulated or cannot be turned off (e.g., if there is a defect in the negative

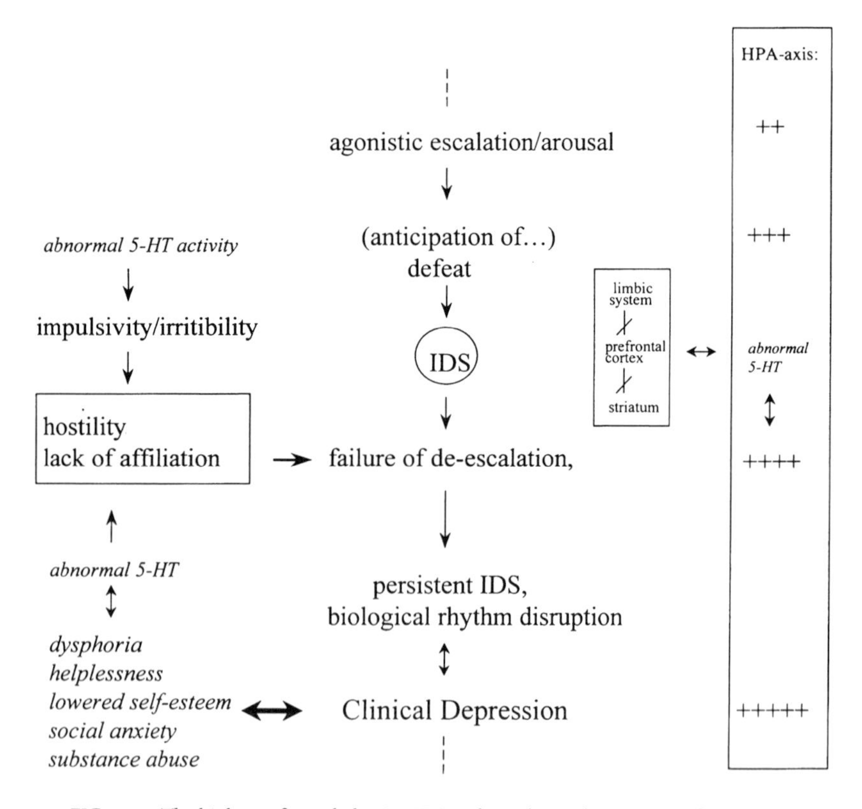

FIG. 4.2. The biology of a maladaptive IDS and its relationship to major depression.

feedback mechanism or chronic overdrive above the level of the hypothalamus), high cortisol levels are maintained, contributing to a failure of de-escalation, prolongation of the competitive encounter, and further experience of defeat as already described. In a clinical depression, the HPA axis is further activated, leading to a vicious cycle of increased arousal, repeated defeat, further maladaptive triggering of the IDS, and increasing helplessness and depression.

Low serotonergic activity promotes impulsive behavior and increases hostility, interfering with normal social affiliation and preventing de-escalation of behavior in general. In response to impending competitive loss, this lack of submission and acceptance prolongs the encounter and experience of defeat. This might in turn reactivate the pathways mediating the IDS, this time with greater intensity as the conflict escalates. Repeated and prolonged experiences of defeat might trigger the clinical syndrome of depression, with dysphoria, helplessness, lowered self-esteem, social anxiety and withdrawal. Substance abuse may be used as a means of decreasing arousal. Once the state of clinical depression is entrenched, a vicious cycle of hyperarousal and further failure of the IDS is established.

We might speculate that abnormal serotonergic modulation of the limbic–prefrontal–striatal circuits leads to chaotic, disorganized activity in this system, further preventing the normal unfolding of the IDS in a coordinated fashion. A failure of this circuit might lead to functional isolation of one or more of its components, leading to dysregulated, autonomous activation in some cases, and underactivity in others. Overactivity can be experienced subjectively as intense arousal or anxiety (limbic), obsessive rumination (prefrontal), and psychomotor agitation (striatal). Underactivity of these sites might be experienced as emotional blunting or apathy (limbic), paucity of thought and planning (prefrontal), and psychomotor retardation (striatal). Once serotonergic dysfunction interferes with normal communication in this functional loop, various combinations of these depressive symptoms might be produced in a given individual.

While serotonin dysfunction can be a causal factor in depression, serotonergic dysfunction may also be promoted by the depressed state. For example, the hypercortisolemia that accompanies depression may have disruptive effects on brain serotonergic pathways (DeKloet, Sybesma, & Reul, 1986; Joels, Hesen, & De Kloet, 1991).

The higher prevalence of depression among women suggests that sociocultural factors related to gender, or the sex hormones themselves, may directly or indirectly influence susceptibility to depression. Estrogen in particular has well documented effects on both the HPA axis (Gundlah, Pecins-Thompson, Schutzer, & Bethea, 1999; Rubinow, Schmidt, & Roca, 1998) and serotonin system (Komesaroff, Esler, Clarke, Fullerton, & Funder, 1998), each intrinsically important in our proposed model. Sex hormones may thus play a key role in linking competitive defeat with affective disorders. Mazur and Booth (1998) proposed that high or rising testosterone, by encouraging dominant behavior, induces men to compete for higher status. The experience of winning or successfully defending high rank boosts testosterone, which in turn promotes more dominant behavior. This constitutes a positive feedback loop linking testosterone with dominance, with each positively reinforcing the other. The functional implication of this system is that initial competitive success leads to more success.

The recurrent experience of defeat resulting from an ineffective IDS may also contribute to depression through disruption of biological rhythms. As discussed earlier, social defeat in animals has been linked to altered biological rhythms long after social challenges have been terminated (Harper et al., 1996), and several chronobiological disturbances have been found in individuals with major depression (e.g., Beersma et al., 1983; David et al., 1991).

Adaptation of the Model for Subtypes of Depression

As already stated, the heterogeneity and complexity of depressive disorders and the interaction of multiple biological systems makes it unlikely that one model would be applicable to all individuals. We consider in this section how the model might be adapted to various depressive subgroups.

The description of major depression as a state of chronic hyperarousal, with concommitant overactivity of the HPA axis, is most applicable to patients with so-called classic or melancholic features such as insomnia, decreased appetite, and weight loss (Gold et al., 1986). However, many depressed individuals present with the opposite pattern of hypersomnia, increased appetite, and weight gain, often with leaden paralysis (i.e., psychomotor retardation), prominent fatigue, and extreme sensitivity to interpersonal rejection. This atypical depressive presentation is more suggestive of a state of hypoarousal than of hyperarousal (Chrousos & Gold, 1992).

How might the model be relevant to atypical depression? In a large community study in Ontario, Levitan, Parikh, et al. (1998) found that depression with atypical features is associated with high rates of childhood physical and sexual abuse. It is possible that severe traumatic experiences in childhood would have profound and long-lasting effects on brain mechanisms relevent to competitive defeat. An efficient IDS would be highly adaptive for a defenseless child, de-escalating conflict in a potentially traumatic situation.This could include the promotion of a "freezing" response, a strategy often seen in animals to quickly terminate overwhelming encounters. If this type of de-escalation strategy is mediated by a particular brain circuit, and is activated repeatedly in childhood, it is likely that the threshold for activation would be progressively lowered over time. Later in life, activation of such a circuit might contribute to the experience of leaden paralysis with prominent fatigue and psychomotor slowing described by individuals with atypical depression. Increased sleep and food intake, as well as social withdrawal, may be other ways to decrease arousal and withdraw from conflictual situations. Rejection sensitivity is also a characteristic symptom, and may be conceptualized as the anticipation of defeat in response to even slight competitive escalation; this may again reflect the residual effects of early traumatic experiences.

In summary, it might be that melancholic depression is associated with chronic hyperarousal, with HPA-axis overactivity that renders the IDS ineffective by preventing de-escalation of competitive encounters. In atypical depression, the IDS may be highly developed and particularly effective in decreasing arousal, but at the cost of producing a depressive syndrome characterized by overly submissive behavior, psychomotor retardation, and a variety of avoidance strategies.

Seasonal affective disorder (SAD) is a recurrent form of depression that resembles atypical depression in many ways. In nonhuman primates, and in human societies prior to the modern era, fall and winter would have been a time of limited food supplies, increasing the competition for these limited resources. A highly activated IDS might be adaptive during such times, when competitive encounters would be particularly fierce, and ongoing energy utilization particularly costly. It is interesting to note that in the fall and winter months, individuals with SAD report marked fatigue, social withdrawal, increased eating, and increased sleep, similar to patients with atypical depression. This may be consistent with a state of low arousal, and may again reflect an exaggerated IDS. Serotonin activity is lowest in the fall and winter months (Brewerton, Berrettini, Nurnberger, & Linnoila, 1988), and there is significant evidence for serotonergic dysfunction in SAD (Lam et al., 1996; Schwartz et al., 1997; Levitan, Kaplan, et al., 1998). PET work has demonstrated altered metabolic rates in the prefrontal cortex and basal ganglia in patients with SAD (Cohen et al., 1992). Taken as a whole, these various lines of evidence suggest that anatomical circuits mediating the IDS might have different levels of activity across seasons, depending on the status of modulatory serotonergic input.

One theoretical challenge is explaining the mood swings associated with bipolar disorder. We have described how competitive defeat can trigger an overly persistent or recurring IDS, which can eventually culminate in depression. It is interesting to speculate whether an overly persistent dominant strategy might contribute to the pathophysiological features of manic states (Gardner, 1982). In many competitive situations there can be a rapid change in fortunes. In these circumstances, the ability to rapidly switch from a dominant strategy to a submissive strategy, or vice versa, would be highly adaptive. It therefore seems likely that the brain mechanisms mediating dominant and defeat strategies would share a common regulatory pathway, so that only one or the other strategy is active at a given time. Recent models of bipolar disorder have speculated on the existence of abnormal brain circuits in this disorder (Post, 1992). If one such circuit modulates the turning on and off of these two extremes of competitive behavior, bipolar disorder might reflect a defect that results in the autonomous, random activation of dominant or defeat strategies over time. Clinically, this would produce the cycles of over- and underarousal characteristic of this disorder. Mixed states, in which there is a combination of manic and depressive symptoms, might reflect the simultaneous activation of both dominant and defeat strategies.

BIOLOGICAL TREATMENTS AND THE IDS

The role of psychosocial treatments in normalizing the IDS and thereby reversing depression is considered in other chapters (see Swallow, chap. 8, this volume; Sloman & Atkinson, chap. 9, this volume). Antidepressant medications of the serotonin reuptake inhibitor class might work at several levels to optimize the IDS. As already described, increased serotonin activity decreases impulsive behavior and hostility, while enhancing social affiliation and status in primates (e.g., Higley et al., 1996; Raleigh et al., 1991). Recent work suggests that serotonergic drugs may also enhance affiliative behavior in humans (Knutson et al., 1998), while improving the symptoms of social anxiety (Stein et al., 1998). These various lines of research suggest that serotonergic drugs may directly effect brain mechanisms that mediate primate affiliative behavior that is so important in promoting the normal unfolding of the IDS de-escalation strategy as described earlier.

It has been suggested that serotonergic antidepressants work in part by normalizing the communication and relative activity of key brain areas including the prefrontal cortex, limbic system, and striatum (Bremner et al., 1997; Drevets & Raichle, 1992), which are likely to be involved in the circuitry of the IDS.

Antidepressants may also enhance de-escalation by normalizing activity of the HPA axis (Barden, 1999; Barden et al., 1995), preventing the chronic, exaggerated release of CRH and cortisol that would otherwise maintain a high level of arousal. Antidepressants also interfere with the development of learned helplessness (Geoffroy, Tvede, Christensen, & Schou, 1991), an important result of a failed IDS but also a potential contributor to the ongoing maintenance of a maladaptive IDS and depressed state.

FINAL CONCLUSIONS

The general goal of this chapter was to consider whether the various biological changes characteristic of depression can be understood in terms of primate social hierarchy behavior, in particular competitive loss. As already reviewed, there are striking biological similarities between primates reacting to competitive defeat and individuals with clinical depression. This suggests that abnormal or maladaptive functioning of the IDS may play an integral role in mediating depressive symptomatology at many levels.

Although this chapter focused on the role of HPA-axis activity, serotonin, and biological rhythms in primate defeat behavior and depression, much more work is needed to examine the possible role of other biological variables on these processes. Going forward in time, further integration of findings from basic primate and clinical research may be a highly rewarding strategy to unravel the complexities of human affective disturbances.

REFERENCES

Agren, H. (1980). Symptom patterns in unipolar and bipolar depression correlating with monoamine metabolites in the cerebrospinal fluid: General patterns. *Psychiatry Research, 3,* 211–224.

Amsterdam, J. D., Marinelli, D. L., Arger, P., & Winokur, A. (1987). Assessment of adrenal gland volume by computed tomography in depressed patients and healthy volunteers: A pilot study. *Psychiatry Research, 21,* 189–197.

Anand, A., Charney, D. S., Delgado, P. L., McDougle, C. J., Heninger, G. R., & Price, L. H. (1994). Neuroendocrine and behavioral responses to intravenous m-chlorophenylpiperazine (mCPP) in depressed patients and healthy comparison subjects. *American Journal of Psychiatry, 151,* 1626–1630.

Arato, M., Banki, C. M., Bissette, G., & Nemeroff, C. B. (1989). Elevated CSF CRF in suicide victims. *Biological Psychiatry, 25,* 355–359.

Asberg, M., Bertilisson, L., Martenssen, B., Scalia-Tomba, G. P., Thoren, P., & Traskman-Bendz, L. (1984). CSF monoamine metabolites in melancholia. *Acta Psychiatrica Scandinavia, 69,* 201–219.

Asberg, M., Traskman, L., & Thoren, P. (1976). 5-HIAA in the cerebrospinal fluid: A biochemical suicide predictor? *Archives of General Psychiatry, 33,* 1193–1197.

Banki, C. M., Karmacsi, L., Bissette, G., & Nemeroff, C. B. (1992). CSF corticotropin-releasing hormone and somatostatin in major depression: Response to antidepressant treatment and relapse. *European Neuropsychopharmacology, 2,* 107–113.

Barden, N. (1999). Regulation of corticosteroid receptor gene expression in depression and antidepressant action. *Journal of Psychiatry and Neuroscience, 24,* 25–39.

Barden, N., Reul, J. M. H. M., & Holsboer, F. (1995). Do antidepressants stabilize mood through actions on the hypothalamic-pituitary-adrenocortical system? *Trends in Neuroscience, 18,* 6–11.

Beersma, D. G. M., Hoofdakker, R. H., & Berkestijn, H. W. B. M. (1983). Circadian rhythms in affective disorders: Body temperature and sleep physiology in endogenous depressives. In J. Mendlewicz & H. M. Van Praag (Eds.), *Biological rhythms and behavior* (pp. 114–127). New York: S. A. Karger.

Benkelfat, C., Ellenbogen, M. A., Dean, P., Palmour, R. M., & Young, S. N. (1994). Mood-lowering effect of tryptophan depletion: Enhanced sensitivity in young men at genetic risk for major affective disorders. *Archives of General Psychiatry, 51,* 687–697.

Bremner, J. D., Innis, R. B., Salomon, R. M., Staib, L. H., Ng, X. C. K., Miller, H. M., Bronen, R. A., Krystal, J. H., Duncan, J., Rich, D., Price, L. H., Malison, R., Dey, H., Soufer, R., & Charney, D. S. (1997). Positron emission tomography measurement of cerebral metabolic correlates of tryptophan depletion-induced depressive relapse. *Archives of General Psychiatry, 54,* 364–374.

Brewerton, T. D., Berrettini, W. H., Nurnberger, J. I., Jr., & Linnoila, M. (1988). Analysis of seasonal fluctuations of CSF monoamine metabolitites and neuropeptides in normal controls. *Psychiatry Research, 23,* 257–265.

Brooke, S., de Haas-Johnson, A., Kaplan, J., Manuck, S., & Sapolsky, R. (1994). Dexamethasone resistance among nonhuman primates associated with a selective decrease in glucocorticoid receptors in the hippocampus and a history of social instability. *Neuroendocrinology, 60,* 134–140.

Brown, G. L., Ballenger, J. C., Minchiello, M. D., & Goodwin, F. K. (1979). Human aggression and its relationship to cerebrospinal fluid 5-hydroxy-indolacetic acid, 3-methoxy-4-hydroxyphenol-glycol and homovanillic acid. In M. Sandler (Ed.), *Psychopharmacology of Aggression* (pp. 31–148). New York: Raven.

Brown, G. L., Ebert, M. H., Goyer, P. F., Jimerson, P. C., Klein, W. J., Bunney, W. E. & Goodwin, F. K. (1982). Aggression, suicide and serotonin: Relationship to CSF amine metabolites. *American Journal of Psychiatry, 139,* 741–746.

Carroll, B. J. (1982). Use of the dexamethasone test in depression. *Journal of Clinical Psychiatry, 43,* 44–50.

Chrousos, G. P., & Gold, P. W. (1992). The concepts of stress and stress system disorders: Overview of physical and behavioral homeostasis. *Journal of the American Medical Association, 267,* 1244–1252.

Cleare, A. J., & Bond, A. J. (1995). The effect of tryptophan depletion and enhancement on subjective and behavioral aggression in normal male subjects. *Psychopharmacology (Berlin), 118,* 72–81.

Coccaro, E. F., Astill, J. L., Herbert, J. L., & Schut, A. G. (1990). Fluoxetine treatment of impulsive aggression in DSM–III personality disorder patients. *Journal of Clinical Psychopharmacology, 10,* 373–375.

Coccaro, E. F., & Kavoussi, R. J. (1996). Neurotransmitter correlates of impulsive aggression. In D. M. Stoff & R. B. Cairns (Eds.), *Aggression and violence: Genetic, neurobiological and biosocial perspectives* (pp. 67–85). Hillsdale, NJ: Lawrence Erlbaum Associates.

Cohen, R. M., Gross, M., Nordahl, T. E., Semple, W. E., Oren, D. A., & Rosenthal, N.E. (1992). Preliminary data on the metabolic brain pattern of patients with seasonal affective disorder. *Archives of General Psychiatry, 49,* 545–552.

Cowen, P. (1993). Serotonin receptor subtypes in depression: Evidence from studies in neuroendocrine regulation. *Clinical Neuropharmacology, 16*(Suppl. 3), S16–S18.

Cowen, P. J., & Charig, E. M. (1987). Neuroendocrine responses to intravenous tryptophan in major depression. *Archives of General Psychiatry, 44,* 958–966.

Czeisler, C. A., Kronauer, R. E., Mooney, J. J., Anderson, J. L. & Allan, J. S. (1987). Biological rhythm disorders, depression and phototherapy: A new hypothesis. *Psychiatric Clinics of North America, 10,* 687–709.

David, M. M., MacLean, A. W., Knowles, J. B., & Coulter, M. E. (1991). Rapid eye movement latency and mood following a delay of bedtime in healthy subjects: Do the effects mimic changes in depressive illness? *Acta Psychiatrica Scandinavica, 84,* 33–39.

De Kloet, E. R., Sybesma, H., & Reul, J. M. H. M., (1986). Selective control by corticosterone of serotonin-1 receptor capacity in raphe-hippocampal system. *Neuroendocrinology, 42,* 513–521.

Delgado, P. L., Charney, D. S., Price, L. H., Aghajanian, G. K., Landis, H., & Heninger, G. R. (1990). Serotonin function and the mechanism of anti-depressant action: Reversal of anti-depressant-induced remission by rapid depletion of plasma tryptophan. *Archives of General Psychiatry, 47,* 411–418.

DeMyer, M. K., Shea, P. A., Hendrie, H. C., & Yoshimura, N. N. (1981). Plasma tryptophan and five other amino acids in depressed and normal subjects. *Archives of General Psychiatry, 38,* 642–646.

Drevets, W. C., & Raichle, M. E. (1992). Neuroanatomical circuits in depression: Implications for treatment mechanisms. *Psychopharmacology Bulletin, 28,* 261–274.

Ehlers, C. L., Frank, E., & Kupfer, D. J. (1988). Social zeitgebers and biological rhythms: A unified approach to understanding the etiology of depression. *Archives of General Psychiatry, 45,* 945–952.

Fava, M., Rosenbaum, J., McCarthy, M., Pava, J., Steingard, R., & Bless, E. (1991). Anger attacks in depressed outpatients and their response to fluoxetine. *Psychopharmacology Bulletin, 27,* 275–279.

Fluoxetine Bulimia Nervosa Collaborative (FBNC) Study Group. (1992). Fluoxetine in the treatment of bulimia nervosa. *Archives of General Psychiatry, 49,* 139–147.

Fuller, R. W. (1996). The influence of fluoxetine on aggressive behavior. *Neuropsychopharmacology, 14,* 77–81.

Gardner, R. J. (1982). Mechanisms in major depressive disorder: An evolutionary model. *Archives of General Psychiatry, 39,* 1436–1441.

Geoffroy, M., Tvede, K., Christensen, A. V., & Schou, J. S. (1991). The effect of imipramine and lithium on "learned helplessness" and acetylcholinesterase in rat brain. *Pharmacology, Biochemistry, and Behavior, 38,* 93–97.

George, M. S., Ketter, T. A., & Post, R. M. (1994). Prefrontal cortex dysfunction in clinical depression. *Depression, 2,* 59–72.

Gold, P. W., Loriaux, D. L., Roy, A., Kling, M. A., Calabrese, J. R., Kellner, C. H., Nieman, L. K., Post, R. M., Pickar, D., & Gallucci, W. (1986). Response to corticotropin releasing hormone in the hypercortisolism of depression and Cushings disease: Pathophysiologic and diagnostic implications. *New England Journal of Medicine, 314,* 1329–1335.

Gundlah, C., Pecins-Thompson, M., Schutzer, W. E., & Bethea, C. L. (1999). Ovarian steroid effects on serotonin 1A, 2A and 2C receptor mRNA in macaque hypothalamus. *Brain Research, Molecular Brain Research, 63,* 325–339.

Halberg, F. (1968). Physiologic considerations underlying rhythmometry with special reference to emotional illness. In J. de Ajuriaguerra (Ed.), *Cycles biologique et psychiatrie* (pp. 73–126). Paris: Georg.

Harper, D. G., Tornatzky, W., & Miczek, K. A. (1996). Stress induced disorganization of circadian and ultradian rhythms: Comparisons of the effects of surgery and social stress. *Physiology and Behavior, 59,* 409–419.

Healy, D. (1987). Rhythms and blues: Neurochemical, neuropharmacological and neuropsychological implications of a hypothesis of circadian rhythm dysfunction in affective disorders. *Psychopharmacology, 93,* 271–285.

Healy, D., & Waterhouse, J. M. (1995). The circadian system and the therapeutics of the affective disorders. *Pharmacology and Therapeutics, 65,* 241–263.

Heninger, G. R., Charney, D. S., & Sternberg, D. E. (1984). Serotonergic function in depression. *Archives of General Psychiatry, 41,* 398–402.

Higley, J. D., King, S. T., Hasert M. F., Champoux, M., Suomi, S. J., & Linnoila, M. (1996). Stability of interindividual differences in serotonin function and its relationship to severe aggression and competent social behavior in rhesus macaque females. *Neuropsychopharmacology, 14,* 67–76.

Higley, J. D., Linnoila, M., & Suomi, S. J., (1994). Ethological contributions: Experimental and genetic contributions to the expression and inhibition of aggression in primates. In M. Hersen, R. T. Ammerman, & L. Sisson (Eds.), *Handbook of aggressive and destructive behavior in psychiatric patients* (pp. 17–32). New York: Plenum.

Hollander, E., Stein, D. J., Decaria, C. M., Cohen, L., Saoud, J. B., Skodol, A. E., Kellman, D., Rosnick, L., & Oldham, J. M. (1994). Serotonergic sensitivity in borderline personality disorder: Preliminary findings. *American Journal of Psychiatry, 151,* 277–280.

Holsboer, F., Von Bardeleben, U., Gerken, A., Stalla, G. K., & Muller, O. A. (1984). Blunted corticotropin and normal cortisol response to human corticotropin-releasing factor in depression [letter]. *New England Journal of Medicine, 311,* 1127.

Jauhar, P., & Weller, M. P. L. (1982). Psychiatric morbidity and time zone changes: A study of patients from Heathrow Airport. *British Journal of Psychiatry, 140,* 231–235.

Joels, M., Hesen, W., & De Kloet, E. R. (1991). Mineralocorticoid hormones suppress serotonin induced hyperpolarization of rat hippocampal CAI neurons. *Journal of Neuroscience, 11,* 2288–2294.

Kahn, R. S., Wetzler, S., Asnis, G. M., Kling, M. A., Suckow, R. F., & van Praag, H. M. (1990). Effects of m-chlorophenylpiperazine in normal subjects: A dose response study. *Psychopharmacology, 100,* 339–344.

Kavoussi, R. J., Liu, J., & Coccaro, E. F. (1994). An open trial of sertraline in personality disordered patients with impulsive aggression. *Journal of Clinical Psychiatry, 55,* 137–141.

Kaye, W. H., Ebert, M. H., Gwirtsman, H. E., & Weiss, S. R. (1984). Differences in brain serotonergic metabolism between nonbulimic and bulimic patients with anorexia nervosa. *American Journal of Psychiatry, 141,* 1598–1601.

Knutson, B., Wolkowitz, O. M., Cole, S. W., Chan, T., Moore, E. A., Johnson, R. C., Terpstra, J., Turner, R. A., & Reus, V. I. (1998). Selective alterations of personality and social behavior by serotonergic intervention. *American Journal of Psychiatry, 155*, 373–379.
Komesaroff, P. A., Esler, M., Clarke, I. J., Fullerton, M. J., & Funder, J. W. (1998). Effects of estrogen and estrous cycle on glucocorticoid and catecholamine responses to stress in sheep. *American Journal of Physiology, 275*, E671–E678.
Krishnan, K. R. R., Doraiswamy, P. M., Lurie, S. N., Figiel, G. S., Husain, M. M, Boyko, O. B., Ellinwood, E. H., & Nemeroff, C. B. (1991). Pituitary size in depression. *Journal of Clinical Endocrinology & Metabolism, 72*, 256–259.
Lam, R. W., Zis, A. P., Grewal, A., Delgado, P. L., Charney, D. S., & Krystal, J. H. (1996). Effects of rapid tryptophan depletion in patients with seasonal affective disorder in remission after light therapy. *Archives of General Psychiatry, 53*, 41–44.
Levitan, R. D., Kaplan, A. S., Brown, G. M., Vaccarino, F. J., Kennedy, S. H., Levitt, A. J., & Joffe, R. T. (1998). Hormonal and subjective responses to intravenous m-chlorophenylpiperazine in women with seasonal affective disorder. *Archives of General Psychiatry, 55*, 244–249.
Levitan, R. D., Kaplan, A. S., Joffe, R. T., Levitt A. J., & Brown, G. M. (1997). Hormonal and subjective responses to intravenous metachlorophenylpiperazine in bulimia nervosa. *Archives of General Psychiatry, 54*, 521–527.
Levitan, R. D., Parikh, S. V., Lesage, A. D., Hegadoren, K. M., Adams, M., Kennedy, S. H., & Goering, P. N. (1998). Major depression in individuals with a history of childhood physical or sexual abuse: Relationship to neurovegetative symptoms, mania, and gender. *American Journal of Psychiatry, 155*, 1746–1752.
Lewis, D. A., & Sherman, B. M. (1984). Serotonergic stimulation of adrenocorticotropin secretion in man. *Journal of Clinical Endocrinology and Metabolism, 58*, 458- 462.
Linnoila, M., Virkunnen, M., Scheinin, M., Nuutila, A., Rimon, R., & Goodwin, F. K. (1983). Low cerebrospinal fluid 5-hydroxy-indolacetic acid concentration differentiates impulsive from nonimpulsive violent behavior. *Life Sciences, 33*, 2609–2614.
Lipositis, Z., Phelix, C., & Paull, W. K. (1987). Synaptic interaction of serotonergic axons and corticotropin releasing factor (CRF) synthesizing neurons in the hypothalamic paraventricular nucleus of the rat. *Histochemistry, 86*, 541–549.
Lopez, J. F., Chalmers, D. T., Little, K. Y., & Watson, S. J. (1998). Regulation of serotonin 1A, glucocorticoid, and mineralocorticoid receptor in rat and human hippocampus: Implications for the neurobiology of depression. *Biological Psychiatry, 43*, 547–573.
Markowitz, P. I. (1992). Effects of fluoxetine on self-injurious behavior in the developmentally disabled: A preliminary study. *Journal of Clinical Psychopharmacology, 12*, 27–31.
Mazur, A., & Booth, A. (1998). Testosterone and dominance in men. *Behavioral and Brain Sciences, 21*, 353–363.
Mehlman, P. T., Higley, J. D., Faucher, I., Lilly, A. A., Taub, D. M., Vickers, J., Suomi, S. J., & Linnoila, M. (1994). Low CSF 5HIAA concentrations and severe aggression and impaired impulse control in nonhuman primates. *American Journal of Psychiatry, 151*, 1485–1491.
Mehlman, P. T., Higley, J. D., Faucher, I., Lilly, A. A., Taub, D. M., Vickers, J., Suomi, S., & Linnoila, M. (1995). Correlations of CSF 5HIAA concentrations with sociality and the timing of emigration in free-ranging primates. *American Journal of Psychiatry, 152*, 907–913.
Meltzer, H. Y., Aurora, R. C., Baber, R., & Tricou, B. J. (1981). Serotonin uptake in blood platelets of psychiatric patients. *Archives of General Psychiatry, 38*, 1322–1326.
Moeller, F. G., Dougherty, D. M., Swann, A. C., Collins, D., Davis, C. M., & Cherek, D. R. (1996). Tryptophan depletion and aggressive responding in healthy males. *Psychopharmacology, 126*, 97–103.
Moller, S. E., Kirk, L., & Honore, P. (1979). Free and total plasma tryptophan in endogenous depression. *Journal of Affective Disorders, 1*, 69–76.
Moore-Ede, M. C. (1986). Physiology of the circadian timing system: Predictive versus reactive homeostasis. *American Journal of Physiology, 250*, R735–R752.

Nemeroff, C. B., Krishnan, K. R. R., Reed, D., Leder, R., Beam, C., & Dunnick, N. R. (1992). Adrenal gland enlargement in major depression: A computed tomographic study. *Archives of General Psychiatry, 49,* 384–387.

Nemeroff, C. B., Widerlov, E., Bissette, G., Walleus, H., Karlsson, J., Eklund, K., Kilts, C. D., Loosen, P. T., & Vale, W. (1984). Elevated concentrations of corticotropin-releasing factor-like immunoreactivity in depressed patients. *Science, 226,* 1342–1344.

Nielsen, D. A., Goldman, D., Virkkunen, M., Tokola, R., Rawlings, R., & Linnoila, M. (1994). Suicidality and 5-hydroxyindoleacetic acid concentration associated with a tryptophan hydroxylase polymorphism. *Archives of General Psychiatry, 51,* 34–38.

O'Keane, V., & Dinan, T. G. (1991). Prolactin and cortisol responses to d-fenfluramine in major depression: Evidence for diminished responsivity of serotonergic function. *American Journal of Psychiatry, 148,* 1009–1015.

Perry, E. K., Marshall, E. F., Blessed, G., Tomlinson, B. E., & Perry, R. H. (1983). Decreased imipramine binding in the brains of patients with depressive illness. *British Journal of Psychiatry, 152,* 188–192.

Post, R. M. (1992). Transduction of psychosocial stress into the neurobiology of recurrent affective disorder. *American Journal of Psychiatry, 149,* 999–1010.

Price, L. H., Charney, D. S., Delgado, P. L., & Heninger, G. R. (1991). Serotonin function and depression: Neuroendocrine and mood responses to intravenous L-tryptophan in depressed patients and healthy comparison subjects. *American Journal of Psychiatry, 148,* 1515–1525.

Raleigh, M. J., Brammer, G. L., & McGuire, M. T. (1983). Male dominance, serotonergic systems, and the behavioral and physiologic effects of drugs in vervet monkeys (Circopithecus aethiops sabaeus). In K. A. Miczek (Ed.), *Ethopharmacology: Primate models of neuropsychiatric disorders* (pp. 185–197). New York: Liss.

Raleigh, M. J., Brammer, G. L., Ritvo, E. R., Geller, E., McGuire, M. T., & Yuwiler, A. (1986). Effects of chronic fenfluramine on blood serotonin, cerebrospinal fluid metabolites, and behavior in monkeys. *Psychopharmacology, 90,* 503–508.

Raleigh, M. J., & McGuire, M. T. (1994). Serotonin, aggression, and violence in vervet monkeys. In R. D. Masters & M. T. McGuire (Eds.), *The neurotransmitter revolution* (pp. 129–145). Carbondale, IL: Southern Illinois University Press.

Raleigh, M. J., McGuire, M. T., Brammer, G. L., Pollack, D. B., & Yuwiler, A. (1991). Serotonergic mechanisms promote dominance acquisition in adult male vervet monkeys. *Brain Research, 559,* 181–190.

Ray, J., & Sapolsky, R. M. (1992). Styles of male social behavior and their correlates among high ranking wild baboons. *American Journal of Primatology, 28,* 231–250.

Risch, S. C., Lewine, R. J., Kalin, N. H., Jewart, R. D., Risby, E. D., Caudle, J. M., Stipetic, M., Turner, J., Eccard, M. B., & Pollard, W. E. (1992). Limbic–hypothalamic–pituitary–adrenal axis activity and ventricular-to-brain ratio in affective illness and schizophrenia. *Neuropsychopharmacology, 6,* 95–100.

Rubinow, D. R., Schmidt, P. J., & Roca, C. A. (1998). Estrogen–serotonin interactions: Implications for affective regulation. *Biological Psychiatry, 44,* 839–850.

Salzman, C., Wolfson, A. N., Schatzberg, A., Looper, J., Henke, R., Albanese, M., Schwartz, J., & Miyawaki, E. (1995). Effect of fluoxetine on anger in symptomatic volunteers with borderline personality disorder. *Journal of Clinical Psychopharmacology, 15,* 23–29.

Sapolsky, R. (1982). The endocrine stress-response and social status in the wild baboon. *Hormones and Behavior, 15,* 279–284.

Sapolsky, R. (1983). Individual differences in cortisol secretory patterns in the wild baboon: Role of negative feedback sensitivity. *Endocrinology, 113,* 2263–2269.

Sapolsky, R. M., Alberts, S. C., & Altmann, J. (1997). Hypercortisolism associated with social subordinance or social isolation among wild baboons. *Archives of General Psychiatry, 54,* 1137–1143.

Sapolsky, R., & Ray, J. (1989). Styles of dominance and their endocrine correlates among wild olive baboons (Papio anubis). *American Journal of Primatology, 18,* 1–13.

Schulz, H., & Lund, R. (1983). Sleep onset REM episodes are associated with circadian paramaters of body temperature: A study in depressed patients and normal controls. *Biological Psychiatry, 18,* 1411–1426.

Schwartz, P. J., Murphy, D. L., Wehr, T. A., Garcia-Borreguero, D., Oren, D. A., Moul, D. E., Ozaki, N., Snelbaker, A. J., & Rosenthal, N. E. (1997). Effects of meta-chlorophenylpiperazine infusions in patients with seasonal affective disorder and healthy control subjects: Diurnal responses and nocturnal regulatory mechanisms. *Archives of General Psychiatry, 54,* 375–385.

Siever, L. J., & Davis, K. L. (1985). Overview: Toward a dysregulation hypothesis of depression. *American Journal of Psychiatry, 142,* 1017–1031.

Siever, L. J., Murphy, D. L., Slater, S., de la Vega, E., & Lipper, S. (1984). Plasma prolactin changes following fenfluramine in depressed patients compared to controls: An evaluation of central serotonergic responsivity in depression. *Life Sciences, 34,* 1029–1039.

Siever, L. J., & Trestman, R. I. (1993). The serotonin system and aggressive personality disorder. *International Clinical Psychopharmacology, 8*(Suppl. 2), 33–39.

Soubrie, P. (1986). Reconciling the role of central serotonin neurons in human and animal behavior. *Behavioral and Brain Sciences, 9,* 319–364.

Stein, M. B., Liebowitz, M. R., Lydiard, R. B., Pitts, C. D., Bushnell, W., & Gergel, I. (1998). Paroxetine treatment of generalized social phobia: A randomized controlled trial. *Journal of the American Medical Association, 280,* 708–713.

Tornatzky, W., Cole, J. C., & Miczek, K. A. (1998). Recurrent aggressive episodes entrain ultradian heart rate and core temperature rhythms. *Physiology and Behavior, 63,* 845–853.

Tornatzky, W., & Miczek, K. A. (1993). Long-term impairment of autonomic circadian rhythms after brief intermittent social stress. *Physiology and Behavior, 53,* 983–993.

Traskman-Bendz, L., Asberg, M., Nordstrom, P., & Stanley, M. (1989). Biochemical aspects of suicidal behavior. *Progress in Neuro-Psychopharmacology and Biological Psychiatry, 13*(suppl.), 535–544.

Virkkunen, M., Nuutila, A., Goodwin, F. K., & Linnoila, M. (1987). Cerebrospinal fluid monoamine metabolite levels in male arsonists. *Archives of General Psychiatry, 44,* 241–247.

von Zerssen, D., Barthelms, H., Dirlich, G., Doerr, P., Emrich, H. M., Lindern, L. V., Lund, R., & Pirke, K. M. (1985). Circadian rhythms in endogenous depression. *Psychiatry Research, 16,* 51–63.

Wehr, T. A., Wirz-Justice, A., Goodwin, F. K., Duncan, W. C., & Gillin, J. C. (1979). Phase advance of the the circadian sleep–wake cycle as an antidepressant. *Science, 206,* 710–713.

Wehr, T. A., & Wirz-Justice, A. (1982). Circadian rhythm mechanisms in affective illness and in antidepressant drug action. *Pharmacopsychiatrica, 15,* 31–39.

Young, E. A., Watson, S. J., Kotun, J., Haskett, R. F., Grunhaus, L., Murphy-Weinberg, V., Vale, W., Rivier, J., & Akil, H. (1990). Beta-lipotropin-beta-endorphin response to low-dose ovine corticotropin-releasing factor in endogenous depression. *Archives of General Psychiatry, 47,* 449–457.

Young, S. N., Smith, S. E., Pihl, R. O., & Ervin, F. R. (1985). Tryptophan depletion causes a rapid lowering of mood in normal males. *Psychopharmacology* (Berlin), *87,* 173–177.

Appendix

DISCUSSION WITH FOCUS ON PSYCHOMOTOR RETARDATION AND GAIT

In this chapter, the complex interaction between social behavior and depressed affect has been discussed from the neurochemical and neuroendocrine perspective. This discussion focuses on one aspect of the IDS (see Sloman, chap. 2, this volume) namely, psychomotor retardation. Darwin (1872/1965) pointed out that clinically depressed people may signal their distress through psychomotor change, observing that they "no longer wish for action, but remain motionless and passive" (p. 176). More recently, Widlocher (1983) postulated that psychomotor retardation in depressed patients is "an active and deliberate response" (p. 31) intended, at least, in part, to avoid confronting their own psychological pain. Alternatively, one might also hypothesize that certain physical behaviors, such as gait, posture, and facial expression are nonverbal signals of social status and, as such, can reflect the extremely negative self-assessment held by many depressed patients. The linkage between psychological self-perception and physical movement may in fact be crucial to the development and maintenance of the complex social structure that gives humans and other primates a competitive advantage over other species.

The cooperativity, division of labor, and organized distribution of scarce resources and commodities that are characteristic of primate communities are highly dependent on rules of precedence and social ranking that are easily understood by members of the group. Among humans, these rules are conveyed by both verbal and nonverbal means. Among lower primates, however, social dominance hierarchies are largely manifest as manneristic or stereotypical physical behaviors that can carry distinct meaning to others in the group. The baboon that crouches, displaying the buttocks and showing relative physical immobility, is signaling submission to the other member of a dyad. For the higher ranking animal, dominance or higher social rank is reinforced and maintained by the submissive displays of others (McGuire et al., chap. 3, this volume). The biological consequences of such display behavior, as previously discussed in the chapter, might include enhanced serotonergic activity in the more dominant animal, reduced potential for impulsive aggressive action, and greater social stability. One might speculate that the benefit of the greater order that is thus imposed is reallocation of the energy that might otherwise be expended in internecine conflict to more productive activity such as food gathering. The exquisite sensitivity to relative rank required to maintain social order in this way may result in psychological distress in some individuals of perceived low rank.

Some aspects of human depression, then, may represent an extension of the behavioral and psychological set that allowed our species to acquire competitively advantageous social structure over millions of years. That is to say the stereotypical motor behaviors, physical slowing, and passivity seen in some depressed patients may be an exaggeration of deeply rooted primate signals of low social status within a group, arising through unfavorable comparison of the self with others. Even though the acquisition of speech renders physical behavior much less important as a mode of communication for humans than for other primates, in human society posture, gestures, and gait may still reflect status or rank. As evidence for this, Schmitt and Atzwanger (1995) described a highly significant correlation between ratings of social standing and observed gait speed in a large group of randomly chosen pedestrians traversing a street in a busy Austrian city.

Others have reported a linkage between gait and affective state. Using highly sensitive force platform technology in a sample of 87 normal older participants, Sloman, Pierrynowski, Berridge, Tupling, and Flowers (1987) demonstrated that the magnitude of downward and backward propulsive forces during normal gait is inversely correlated with self-rated depression scores. As further evidence for a linkage between mood and movement, Cress et al. (1995) reported that depressed mood was a strong independent predictor of self-perceived physical capability in a group of elderly individuals. In fact gait may be more strongly determined by mood than by physical ability. Buchner et al. (1996) showed, in the elderly, that improvement of gait speed with exercise was more strongly correlated with change in depression score than with change in physical fitness. This is further supported by the observation that depression is much more prevalent among patients with Parkinson's disease presenting with bradykinesia and disturbed gait compared with those whose pathology manifests mainly as tremor (Cummings, 1992).

Among patients diagnosed with major depressive disorder, cinematographic gait analysis reveals strides that are significantly more "lifting" and significantly less "propelling" than those of healthy control participants (Sloman, Berridge, Homatidis, Hunter, & Duck, 1982). This motor abnormality may not be confined to the lower limbs. Wolff, Putnam, and Post (1985) studied depressed patients using wrist-mounted motion detectors and noted significant decreases in motor activity compared with normal individuals. The decrement in motor activity was significantly improved with recovery from depression, but even during euthymia, motor activity in the depressed patients was still significantly lower than that seen in healthy controls.

In our own pilot project (Hasey, Sloman, & Mancewicz, 1996) we examined the relation between ratings of social comparison, social interaction, depression, and gait in 10 inpatients with major depression and 11 healthy controls. We hypothesized that locomotor activity would be decreased in depressed compared with control participants. Furthermore, we predicted that locomotor activity would correlate negatively with depression scores and positively with social comparison ratings. At baseline assessment we found that, compared with healthy controls, depressed patients rated themselves as significantly more depressed, more anxious, less socially desirable, and more tense in social interactions, although equally likely to make social contact. When all participants were considered together, as predicted, social comparison rating scale scores (high score = high relative status) were negatively correlated with Beck depression scores ($r = -.7$, $df = 1,17$, $p = .004$). Tension during social interaction scores were positively correlated with Beck scores ($r = .65$, $df = 1,16$, $p = .003$). Gait analysis prior to antidepressant treatment revealed that depressed patients walked significantly more slowly ($p = .003$) and with shorter strides ($p = .02$) compared with control participants. As predicted, social comparison scores were positively correlated with walking speed ($r = .64$, $df = 1,18$, $p = .004$) and negatively correlated with Beck depression scores ($r = .68$, $df = 1,17$, $p = .002$). After 6 weeks of treatment, depression scores improved significantly in depressed participants, but social comparison scores and some gait measurements did not change and some of the correlations between social comparison score and gait measure were still evident.

It may be then, that the IDS, the regulatory mechanism governing mood and certain aspects of locomotor activity, is deeply rooted in the neurophysiological pathways that developed over eons in primates to facilitate communal life in a hazardous and highly competitive environment. In this conceptualization, certain types of motor withdrawal, apparent apathy, and helplessness signal subordinate status, submission, and tacit support of the existing social hierarchy, thereby enhancing social stability. However, if sensitivity to unequal status becomes exaggerated, an individual might develop an unfounded bias toward consistent and inappropriate negative comparison of the self with others resulting in clinical depression.

Although the importance of gait patterns as a criterion of status and attractiveness may be a phylogenetic remnant from a time in human development when nonverbal means of communication were much more important determinants of status, even today our carriage and gait may influence the responses of others. From a clinical perspective, gait measurements might have value as a simple and objective way to quantitatively evaluate depressive affect and response to treatment. Gait measures may also reflect the activity of neuroanatomical structures, such as the striatum, which may be important in the pathophysiological changes of mood disorder.

REFERENCES

Buchner, D. M., Cress, M. E., Esselman, P. C., Margherita, A. J., Lateur, B. J., Campbell, A. J., & Wagner, E. H. (1996). Factors associated with changes in gait speed in older adults. *Journals of Gerontology. Series A: Biological Sciences and Medical Sciences, 51,* M297–M302.

Cress, M. E., Schechtman, K. B., Mulrow, C. D., Fiatarone, M. A., Gerety, M. B., & Buchner, D. M. (1995). Relationship between physical performance and self-perceived physical function. *Journal of the American Geriatric Society, 43,* 93–101.

Cummings, J. L. (1992). Depression and Parkinson's disease: A review. *American Journal of Psychiatry, 149,* 443–454.

Darwin, C. (1965). *The expression of the emotions in man and in animals.* Chicago: University of Chicago Press. (Original work published 1872)

Hasey, G., Sloman, L., & Mancewicz, A. (1996). *A pilot study of the relationship between social rank, mood and gait in depressed and healthy subjects.* Unpublished manuscript.

Schmitt, A., & Atzwanger, K. (1995) Walking fast—ranking high: A sociobiological perspective on pace. *Ethology and Sociobiology, 16,* 451–462.

Sloman, L., Berridge, M., Homatidis, S., Hunter, D, & Duck, T. (1982). Gait patterns of depressed patients and normal subjects. *American Journal of Psychiatry, 139,* 94–97.

Sloman, L., Pierrynowski, M., Berridge, M., Tupling, S., & Flowers, J. (1987). Mood, depressive illness and gait patterns. *Canadian Journal of Psychiatry, 32,* 190–193.

Widlocher, D. J. (1983). Psychomotor retardation: Clinical, theoretical and psychometric aspects. *Psychiatric Clinics of North America, 6,* 27–40.

Wolff, E., Putnam, F., & Post, R. (1985). Motor activity and affective illness: The relationship of amplitude and temporal distribution to changes in affective state. *Archives of General Psychiatry, 42,* 88–294.

PART III

Psychosocial Dimensions of the Involuntary Defeat Strategy

CHAPTER FIVE

The Involuntary Defeat Strategy and Discrete Emotions Theory

Glenn E. Weisfeld
Craig A. Wendorf
Wayne State University

The dominance hierarchy model can be used to understand normal social competition in humans and, by extension, pathological competitive behavior including some examples of depression. In the first section of this chapter, we analyze pride and shame, arguing that these represent a single basic human emotion, the origin and expression of which is homologous to dominance behavior in other species. We then describe various adaptive features of dominance hierarchy behavior. Two adaptive features of relevance to the involuntary defeat strategy (IDS) are highlighted: social withdrawal after defeat, and variations in physiological demobilization during and after competition. The remainder of the chapter deals with pathology. Several examples of behavioral pathology associated with social competition are discussed, including the pathological alteration of withdrawal and demobilization in depression. This leads to the suggestion that depression arising from shame, or subordination, be distinguished from the depression associated with grief, or loneliness.

PRIDE AND SHAME: A SINGLE BASIC EMOTION

Modern evolutionists have argued that pathological conditions, such as depression, are best conceived of as aberrations from normal behavioral functioning. What are these normal behavioral processes? As a first approximation, normal behaviors may be taken to be those that are present in all cultures, that comprise the human ethogram, or inventory of behaviors. By analogy to the work of animal ethologists, these behaviors include flight, feeding, sexual behavior, and so on—the universal human motives (G. E. Weisfeld, 1997b).

Unfortunately, pride/shame is one of the more neglected of these universal emotions, especially as considered from a comparative perspective (Gilbert, 1997; G. E. Weisfeld, 1980, 1997a). Research has been conducted on various manifestations of this emotion—on self-esteem, self-confidence, social comparison (Swallow, chap. 8, this volume), achievement motivation, moral development, altruism, and so on—but seldom are these behaviors regarded as having a phylogenetic history stemming from dominance behavior in other species. Because pride/shame is often involved in depression, analyzing it ethologically may prove useful for conceptualizing the features of this clinical condition. Therefore, the basic nature and functional utility of pride and shame is described next.

Pride/shame is sometimes dismissed merely as a "learned motive." To be sure, we learn when and how it is appropriate to experience this affect largely through culture-specific experiences. We learn that certain behaviors are praised and others are condemned in our particular social environment. We learn, to a great extent, how to fulfill this emotional need for praise, how to gain respect (Gilbert, 1997; G. E. Weisfeld, 1980). But how is that different from the hunger motive, which we also learn to fulfill in culture-specific ways? One does not acquire a capacity for a basic affect; one only learns when to experience it (e.g., to fear hot stoves) and how to respond to it.

What evidence is there for regarding pride and shame as a basic emotion? Darwin (1872/1965) introduced and utilized a methodology for identifying behaviors with an evolved basis, including human emotional expressions (analyzed in G. E. Weisfeld, 1982). These methods are now applied to the case of the emotion of pride and shame (for details see G. E. Weisfeld, 1997a; G. E. Weisfeld & Linkey, 1985).

One research tactic is to test for **species-wide prevalence**. Applying this approach to pride and shame, we find general acknowledgment of the universality of *prestige striving*, as Barkow (1975) called it, and its emotional expressions. Although status may not be formalized in all cultures, people everywhere seek the approval of others. Moreover, as Darwin documented, people evidently cringe and blush with shame in all cultures, and stand erect if proud.

Another research tactic is to look for the behavior in **related species**. Human social hierarchies resemble those established by many other animals, including most terrestrial primates. In human and animal hierarchies, individuals compete for high rank and its attendant prerogatives, which include mating opportunities. Dominance encounters usually take the form of conventional (or regulated) competition, ranks tend to stabilize, and violations of the conventions of competition are often resisted vehemently (by the "rage reaction," or "moralistic anger"). For example, an animal whose rank prerogatives are usurped typically retaliates vigorously. Another parallel between human pride/shame and dominance behavior is that people and simians express high rank through similar and doubtless homologous dominance displays, namely erect, expansive posture; relaxed movement; direct gaze; and drawing attention (Hold, 1977). Subordinates exhibit antithetical displays, as Darwin observed. These emotional expressions serve as *aides mémoires* to the principals in a confrontation, reminding them of their respective competitive abilities. In sum, human competitiveness, or prestige striving, is homologous to dominance hierarchization in other primates. The basics of this system (motive to compete, affects, expressions, regulation of competition) reflect a common evolutionary heritage. It is true that humans compete for rank in multifarious ways, often by being of service to others (see Price, chap. 7, this volume, and Gilbert, Price, & Allan, 1995, on "social attention holding power"). Significantly, however, young children in various cultures atavistically compete by fighting, and high-ranking monkeys attract attention (Omark, Strayer, & Freedman, 1980).

The **stereotypy** of certain emotional expressions in humans was cited by Darwin as further evidence for their evolved basis. The stereotypic emotional expressions associated with pride/shame, which include blushing, have been mentioned previously. Another form of stereotypy is a characteristic developmental onset. Pride/shame emerges in children at 2 to 3 years of age, whether it is identified as dominance behavior, rivalry, competitiveness, self-esteem, achievement motivation, gaze aversion when embarrassed, blushing, boasting, praising, reporting feelings of pride, or responding to approval and disapproval (see Keltner & Buswell, 1997; Stipek, 1995). Interestingly, sensitivity to social evaluation emerges at about 2 years, when children respond to approval and disapproval. Not until about age 3, however, are they able to compare their attributes with those of another person, and therefore to compete (Heckhausen, 1984; Stipek, 1995). Not until about age 6 can they place all the children in their social group accurately in a dominance hierarchy (Omark, Omark, & Edelman, 1975). Thus the affective capacity for pride/shame emerges first, but the cognitive ability to make comparisons develops only gradually (cf. the grammatical constructions of positive, comparative, and superlative). The emergence of the affect of pride and shame does not seem to depend on a cognitive capacity for self-awareness. Research revealed no relation between toddlers' touching a red spot on their nose (a test of self-recognition) and their experiencing shame, measured as averted gaze after failure (Schneider-Rosen & Cicchetti, 1991).

Another research approach, one not available to Darwin, is to demonstrate a **specific neural basis** for the behavior. Patients with orbitofrontal cortical damage show distinctive personality changes (e.g., Levin, Eisenberg, & Benton, 1991). Using modern neuroimaging techniques, Damasio, Grabowski, Frank, Galaburda, and Damasio (1994) examined the skull of the famous Phineas Gage, victim of a frontal lobe injury. The areas of extensive bilateral damage included the orbitofrontal cortex. These authors characterized Gage's behavioral changes as "a defect in rational decision making and the processing of emotion" (p. 1102). Others have described patients with orbitofrontal cortical damage as unruly and coarse in speech, manner, and appearance. Patients are less concerned with their occupations or performing other obligations, less responsive to approval and disapproval.

Yet Gage and similar patients tend to retain their previous memory and intelligence, as long as other prefrontal areas are intact. The deficit may lie not in rational decision making, or even in rational decision making about social situations: These patients can readily solve abstract, hypothetical problems about proper behavior (Saver & Damasio, 1991). The deficit seems to be emotional, consistent with this tissue being limbic (Fuster, 1980; Schore, 1994) and affectively sensitive (Passingham, 1993; Schore, 1994).

What seems missing is an affective capacity for pride and shame, a desire for social standing; other emotions are processed appropriately. Homologous lesions in the posteromedial orbital cortex of rhesus monkeys reduce aggression and consequently cause loss of "standing in the community" (Fuster, 1980, p. 69). These effects are not demonstrable until age 24 months; dominance behavior does not appear in intact monkeys until about this time. In some studies, monkeys exhibit inappropriate dominance behavior, such as failure to challenge weaker animals or to submit to stronger ones (reviewed in G. E. Weisfeld, 1997a; G. E. Weisfeld & Linkey, 1985). Other studies, in which a lesioned animal is more aggressive postoperatively but still falls in rank (Mass, 1972), show that something besides aggressiveness has changed. The crucial impairment seems to lie in the animal's inclination and ability to raise its status by responding appropriately to the displays and behavior of others—its capacity for dominance behavior.

This wealth of evidence has persuaded many ethologists that pride and shame is a basic human emotion (see Barkow, 1975; Hold, 1977; Mazur, 1985; McDougall, 1923; Omark et al., 1980; Pugh, 1977; Rajecki & Flannery, 1981; Zivin, 1977). In general, a basic human emotion is a qualitatively distinct affect, pleasant or unpleasant, that occurs universally and cannot be resolved into other emotional modalities.

Some investigators (e.g., Gilbert, 1992, 1997) have distinguished among shame, guilt, embarrassment, humiliation, feelings of failure, and so on. However, as Lewis (1993) stated, "Many events are capable of eliciting any one of them" (p. 566). He reported that some authors distinguish among them merely on the basis of intensity (see Miller & Tangney, 1994). Psychologists and subjects alike tend to blur these terms, although semantic distinctions do sometimes emerge between, say, shame and guilt scenarios; for example, subjects use "shame" more to refer to serious public faux pas, and "guilt" for misdemeanors contemplated privately (Tangney, 1995).

Nevertheless, an ethological appreciation for the similarities in developmental onset, expressions, affect, overt behavior, hormonal changes, and neural bases of shame, guilt, and so on suggests that they have a common biological basis, rather than having evolved separately (for an alternative view, see Gilbert,

1992). For example, in shame, guilt, failure, and embarrassment there is an impulse to exhibit submission displays, such as gaze aversion, and to relinquish resources (G. E. Weisfeld, 1997a). Some of these terms may refer to blends of emotions. For example, "embarrassment" may mean minor awkwardness that evokes an admixture of smiling humorously (Keltner & Buswell, 1997). Similarly, Gilbert (1992) referred to shame and humiliation as having a component of anger. Gilbert (1997) showed the utility of analyzing blends of emotions as they occur in contemporary situations. However, it may be more useful initially to distinguish between emotions with distinct biological bases, such as shame and anger, than between varieties of shame, which probably reflect a common phylogenetic basis. In this way, the unique adaptive utility and affect of each emotion can be identified.

ADAPTIVE VALUE OF DOMINANCE HIERARCHIZATION

We now describe the functioning of dominance behavior, with parallels to human competition highlighted. Obviously, an animal that lacked a motive for social competition would passively drop to the bottom of the hierarchy and would fail to gain vital prerogatives and resources contributing to reproductive success. Thus, one should recognize that an animal's dominance rank is a central determinant of its behavior, that such a rank would be heavily defended, and that a higher rank would be coveted.

Recently there has been some work on the criteria of dominance in humans. Most scholars would probably agree that physical traits are salient for pride and shame, and that this likely reflects the relevance of fighting ability, vigor, and so on for dominance struggles in animals. Similarly, the physical condition of females seems to be used by males to assess reproductive value and hence, to some extent, dominance status. In general, dominance competition seems to be conducted on the basis of traits relevant to reproductive success (G. E. Weisfeld, 1999). That is, the outcomes of dominance competition among same-sex peers have relevance for relations with the opposite sex (see Price, chap. 7, this volume). Dominant males are attractive to females, and dominant females tend to reproduce successfully. This would explain why human adolescents tend to receive similar status rankings from their male and female peers (G. E. Weisfeld, Omark, & Cronin, 1980).

In humans, the salience of physical traits for dominance rank may be universal, but this does not preclude the importance of other traits. Although socially successful individuals tend to be physically attractive regardless of age, sex, and culture (Jackson, 1992), various traits imposed by culture can also act as criteria for dominance. For example, intelligence was also found to be salient for dominance among peers for Chinese adolescents but not Americans, with English boys intermediate (Dong, Weisfeld, Boardway, & Shen, 1996). Physical traits were important in all three societies, however. Some authors (e.g., Sloman, chap. 2, this volume) have justifiably emphasized the importance of physical attractiveness for pride and shame. Others, such as Barkow (1975) and Gilbert (1997, 1998; Gilbert & McGuire, 1998), have pointed out that various additional criteria are germane to social status in humans. Perhaps these positions can be reconciled by saying that physical traits may have universal and primordial salience to human dominance competition, but that other traits that raise a person's social status vary across cultures. To put this in terms of individual selection, people who chose their mates on the basis of criteria appropriate for their particular environment enjoyed high reproductive success, and so those criteria were selected for on both cultural and natural bases.

Given the importance of dominance rank for reproductive success, animals seem to have evolved to seek higher rank, but to do so judiciously. Each animal in a hierarchy tends to challenge its immediate superior, which it is most likely to displace. Likewise, social comparison and achievement motivation research reveals that people tend to set goals that are just above their previous level of accomplishment (reviewed in G. E. Weisfeld, 1980; also see Swallow, chap. 8, this volume). This slight overrating of self may reflect the self-confidence necessary to try to raise one's status.

However, this does not mean that competition for ranks is constant and intense. To the contrary, in many species fighting for rank takes the form of rather safe, ritualistic contests. Moreover, the outcomes of fights tend to be remembered, with the aid of dominance displays, so that once two animals have resolved their dominance relationship, fighting between them is infrequent. Prerogatives are distributed peacefully according to rank. In children (Hartup, 1974) and adolescents (Savin-Williams, 1977), fighting likewise declines as ranks stabilize and become linear (Strayer & Strayer, 1976). As in animals, nonverbal submission displays actually cut off aggression by an attacking child (Ginsburg, 1980) and, in various other studies, induce forgiveness (Keltner & Buswell, 1997). Thus, hierarchical fighting is often mild and infrequent—a boon to each participant. In fact, if one distinguishes between aggression to secure resources and dominance hierarchization, the specific adaptive value of the latter lies in minimizing the amount of this aggression while still maximizing one's rank and prerogatives (Gilbert, 1992).

In humans as in other species, dominance relations provide for the orderly, cooperative allocation of resources according to accomplishments. Likewise, the leader of a small group of people generally performs most of the difficult labor and is rewarded with special privileges (Homans, 1974). In exchange relationships, stability and fairness generally obtain, such that rewards are proportional to services. This homeostatic system can be deranged by any disturbance in equity—by someone usurping excessive prerogatives, by shirking obligations, by offending another, by receiving undue praise, or by being overly generous. Each such disturbance is emotionally unsettling because the ratio of rewards per accomplishments between the individuals involved has been upset, and appropriate readjustments have not yet occurred. According to Trivers's (1971) reciprocal altruism model, homeostasis in dyadic relationships is restored via the affects of guilt and gratitude (perhaps affectly indistinguishable from each other; G. E. Weisfeld, 1997a), anger, and possibly pride (G. E. Weisfeld, 1980). These emotions lead to a readjustment of rewards to performance, to the reestablishment of equity. This system for enforcing reciprocal altruism may be viewed as a special case of the dominance hierarchy model, under which offensive behavior is punished and accomplishments are rewarded. Although Trivers had in mind a reciprocal altruistic relationship between equals, equity tends to be maintained even between individuals of different overall rank. As in an animal dominance hierarchy, each person receives in proportion to his or her contributions, but this equity can be temporarily deranged. Thus, even a king may be embarrassed by having his life saved by a serf, until the king compensates his benefactor.

These acute disequilibria may be seen as superimposed on our chronic set point of self-esteem (or pride / shame). It appears that everyone occupies a more or less permanent social rank with its attendant self-esteem beginning in childhood (Bronson, 1966; Kagan & Moss, 1962). For example, longitudinal research showed that for U.S. boys, social ranks remained quite stable over a 9-year period starting at age 6 to 7, and were reflected by erectness of posture (G. E. Weisfeld & Beresford, 1982). On the other hand, posture was temporarily altered by success or failure on a university examination. When all goes well, we maintain stable relationships of mutual respect with our peers, subordinates, superiors, and the society at large. We can be subordinate without being abjectly humiliated, and we can be superior and still suffer embarrassment. Social competition is regulated (i.e., conventional) or cooperative (see Gilbert, chap. 1, this volume); inequities usually are corrected with a minimum of discord. A similar idea was suggested by Gilbert (1997), who noted that shame results from loss of status, not from a stable low social rank. This idea is reminiscent of relative deprivation theory (Tyler & Smith, 1998). We become accustomed to a particular level of satisfaction, which serves as a baseline for comparison (see Price, chap. 7, this volume). For example, if we are used to eating steak, a hamburger is unappealing, but if we are starving, a hamburger tastes wonderful. Pugh (1977) suggested that these shifts in our baseline level of satisfaction help maintain our effort at improving our situation; that is, they help us to set realistic goals.

PRIDE/SHAME AND SOCIAL WITHDRAWAL

The idea behind the IDS is that depression can be understood in terms of the dominance hierarchy model and the emotion of pride and shame. One such example can be seen in work by Gilbert, Pehl, and Allan (1994) that demonstrated that shame was related to submissive behavior, which was in turn associated with depression. The link forged by serotonin between dominance relations in vervet monkeys and depression in humans is another case in point (see McGuire, Raleigh, Spar, & Troisi, chap. 3, this volume). It seems appropriate, therefore, to try to explain various behavioral manifestations of depression in terms of the normal reactions of animals and humans engaged in dominance competition. Why, for example, do depressed individuals often withdraw socially?

Instead of viewing social withdrawal and avoidance of competition as pathological and cognitive, as Seligman (1974; critiqued by Klinger, 1975) did in regarding them as "learned helplessness," perhaps they can be understood as manifestations of generally adaptive motivational tendencies. Animals that have lost dominance encounters withdraw socially (e.g., Crook, 1970) and exhibit little persistence at problem solving (Richards, 1972). Similarly, laboratory mice, crickets, and sunfish that have been exposed to a series of strong opponents and have been defeated tend then to submit even to weak opponents (e.g., Warren & Maroney, 1958 on monkeys). Likewise, a child can be "conditioned" to succeed or fail at competitive tasks by varying the order of difficulty (Dweck & Reppucci, 1973; Sears, 1937).

How can social withdrawal and avoidance of competition after defeat—the IDS—be explained functionally? Ginsburg and Allee (1942) referred to "the effect of conditioning on dominance–subordination patterns of behavior" in mice (p. 502). After repeated successes (or failures), the individual simply anticipates the same outcome on the next trial and responds accordingly. Thus, an animal that has experienced an unbroken series of defeats may cower before even a much smaller and weaker opponent, because of stimulus generalization—"learned helplessness," if you will. This explanation is not specific to dominance encounters, but would include conditioning to avoid some site where one has been frightened, or to seek out a place where food has been found. The animal avoids situations similar to those that have been aversive in the past, and seeks out situations that have been rewarding—Thorndike's (1927) law of effect. It is not necessary to deal specifically with competitive situations in trying to explain withdrawal from aversive conditions.

However, there may be some specific advantages of withdrawal from competitive situations. In fact, this tendency to withdraw when defeated, although originally simply a consequence of the law of effect, may have been accentuated by natural selection. Defeated animals that quickly withdrew may have been spared further injury, fatigue, and—most saliently—psychologically debilitating defeat (Price, 1967; G. E. Weisfeld, 1980). That is, they may have minimized conditioning to failure by precluding repeated failures. These defeated animals, little the worse for wear, could then wait until some time had passed and then try again. By the same token, a victorious animal might benefit from enhanced assertiveness so as to follow up its current advantage.

To identify this tendency of withdrawal or approach with respect to future competitions, the lay term *self-confidence* may be employed. Research reveals that success enhances self-esteem and self-confidence, and raises goals in most people; analogously, animals that win dominance fights tend to set their sights progressively higher. Unsuccessful animals and people show the opposite reactions (cf. relative deprivation theory). It is presumably adaptive to adjust one's goals in light of previous outcomes. Extremely low self-confidence often results in avoidance of competition, that is, social withdrawal (G. E. Weisfeld, 1980). Low self-confidence (high "fear of failure") frequently leads subjects to set an extremely easy or extremely difficult goal, thus effectively avoiding meaningful challenges. As mentioned earlier, most subjects set moderately difficult goals. Similarly, research by Gilbert, Allan, Ball, and Bradshaw (1996) showed that an individual's level of overconfidence (or "positive information-processing biases," p. 59) was inversely related to shame and submissive behavior.

The possibility that there is a specific physiological mechanism for self-confidence is suggested by the fact that testosterone level falls in defeated monkeys (Rose, Holiday, & Bernstein, 1971), and testosterone increases aggressiveness and competitiveness (Mazur & Booth, 1998). In victorious male monkeys testosterone levels increase, perhaps to enhance their aggressiveness under favorable conditions. Serotonin may play a role here, too.

PRIDE/SHAME AND PHYSIOLOGICAL ADJUSTMENTS

In an early publication on what has become known as the IDS, Price (1967) noted that bodily demobilization after defeat, like that of hibernation, may be adaptive. Under various other conditions bodily mobilization occurs and seems to be adaptive. Cannon (1932) described the mobilization of the body for fight or flight—the "emergency reaction"—via the sympathetic division of the autonomic nervous system. Subsequently, Selye (1952) documented a "general adaptation syndrome," mediated by the anterior pituitary and adrenal cortex, to a wide range of "stressors": elicitors of heat, cold, pain, defeat, and other aversive emotions.

What are the physiological adjustments to victory and defeat, or pride and shame? Gartlan and Brain (1968) and Price (1972) noted parallels between adjustments to defeat in monkeys and those of depression in humans, so the hormonal changes of dominance relations may help to explain some of the manifestations of depression.

The hormonal adjustments to dominance encounters in mammals are now starting to make functional sense. When two unfamiliar animals are placed together, they seek to dominate each other. As they mobilize to fight, their epinephrine and glucocorticoid levels rise. Thus, both the sympathetic division and the adrenal cortex are involved. It is the prospect of social competition that seems responsible, not crowding, environmental novelty, fighting, or even wounding (Gray, 1987). The rise in glucocorticoids occurs for future winners as well as losers (Sapolsky, 1992). Once the dominance relationship has stabilized after a fight, levels of glucocorticoids and catecholamines tend to fall—especially in winners (Sapolsky, 1992). Dominant animals can afford to relax, whereas subordinates must remain vigilant for attacks. Similarly, a female rhesus monkey that established a protective consortship with a male experienced lowered levels of glucocorticoids (Sassenrath, 1970). Because chronically elevated levels of glucocorticoids can compromise growth, reproduction, wound healing, and disease resistance, low rank has an adaptive cost beyond loss of resources. Another hormonal adjustment of victorious male monkeys, mentioned earlier, is a rise in testosterone, which promotes spermatogenesis, anabolism, and competitiveness (Sapolsky, 1992).

Homologous adjustments occur in humans. Competitive situations such as interviewing someone, being interviewed, or taking an examination raise the level of glucocorticoids (Hill et al., 1956; Klopper, 1964; Tepperman, 1973). Once the outcome is decided, physiological demobilization usually follows. But demobilization is generally greater for successful subjects than for those who fail. Criticism elicited a greater decrease in peripheral blood flow (Newton, Paul, & Bovard, 1957) and greater speech muscle tension (Kaplan, Burch, & Bloom, 1965)—both sympathetic responses—than did praise. Similarly, subjects who have failed tend to have higher cortisol levels (Berkeley, 1952; Kemper, 1990). Children (Coopersmith, 1967) and adults (Rosenberg, 1965) with low self-esteem reported more psychosomatic disease, and medical students with better grades had lower cholesterol levels (Bloch & Brackenridge, 1972); these results can be interpreted in terms of chronic physiological mobilization. Dominant people, like monkeys, tend to sleep more deeply than subordinates (Franken, 1998; Levitan, Hasey, & Sloman, chap. 4, this volume). Like male monkeys, men who win competitions (or merely root for the winning team) have elevated testosterone levels (Mazur & Lamb, 1980), whereas testosterone tends to be low in depressed patients (Kemper, 1990).

However, if failure is either unexpected or not accepted, arousal tends to persist. Patients who resist status loss or lose close wrestling matches typically do not undergo a fall in testosterone (Kemper, 1990). Subjects low in achievement motivation—those accustomed to failure—experienced a fall in galvanic skin response (GSR) on failure, but those with high achievement motivation (self-confidence) showed a rise (Raphelson & Moulton, 1958). Similarly, sympathetic arousal was pronounced if the subject found the criticism unjustified and was angered by it (Murray, 1963). This exaggerated and sustained physiological mobilization when failure is not accepted also occurs in clinical depression, thus supporting the IDS model. People suffering from major depression often overproduce glucocorticoids (Levitan et al., chap. 4, this volume; Sapolsky, 1992) and epinephrine (Sachar, Schalch, Reichlin, & Platman, 1972). Apparently they remain mobilized inordinately, leaving them vulnerable to disease. Indeed, depression is associated with less natural killer cell activity and additional psychological problems and disease (Davidson, 1994), often undiagnosed (Kalat, 1995). Even if the individual is intimidated and withdraws socially, he or she may continue to be physiologically agitated by the defeat. The fatigue resulting from sustained mobilization may interfere with attempts to reenter the competitive arena. Incidentally, repeated exposure to high glucocorticoids seems to "wear down" the hippocampus, resulting in inability to reduce glucocortocoid secretion once the stressor has disappeared (LeDoux, 1996).

What about reactions to success—are they always characterized by sharp demobilization? If success is extraordinary or unexpected, perhaps the individual should try to follow up his or her temporary advantage by vigorous self-assertion. In some cases, successful subjects do experience a rise in heart rate and GSR (Shapiro & Leiderman, 1965, 1967). Similarly, exhilaration may cause a rise in glucocorticoids (Persky, Maroc, Conrad, & Breeijen, 1959)—although mania itself is typified by low levels (Schore, 1994). Perhaps mania may be viewed as opportunistic arousal under perceived favorable conditions; manic patients often have high levels of epinephrine (Tepperman, 1973).

In summary, the individual is physiologically mobilized when challenged and demobilizes to an appropriate extent after the outcome is decided. Successful individuals usually enjoy the luxury of sharp demobilization. However, if their success is extraordinary, they may remain mobilized opportunistically. In mania, mobilization under favorable conditions may be exaggerated. Unsuccessful individuals must remain somewhat energized to detect and defend against further challenges, but they demobilize somewhat when the outcome is determined—the normal IDS.

ANGER AND DOMINANCE HIERARCHIES

Another area in which functional analysis of the human emotions may help is in the relation of anger to social status and the dominance hierarchy model. Specifically, an unexpected or undeserved defeat may prompt an intense, even angry, reaction to prevent further erosion of status or to restore the status quo ante. Anger, of course, results in physiological arousal, and so resembles subordination in this regard. Anger tends to raise glucocorticoids as well as catecholamines in animals (Gellhorn & Loofbourrow, 1963) and humans (Nelson, 1972). Kemper (1990) found that patients who were angry, like those who resisted status loss, did not typically undergo a fall in testosterone. Furthermore, recall that Murray (1963) found that the combination of unjustified criticism and anger was associated with sympathetic arousal.

However, the affects and emotional expressions of anger and shame are distinct, and the angry person is inclined to retaliate, not to defer to and concede prerogatives to others. Animals whose territories, dominance prerogatives, mating rights, and so on are violated tend to react with rage (reviewed by G. E. Weisfeld, 1980). Anger, or rage, prompts escalated fighting that punishes violators of social expectations, thereby protecting the individual against exploitation (cf. Trivers, 1971). Anger gives rise to a distinct type of aggression, according to Moyer (1976). Having reviewed a wealth of comparative evidence, he identified several types of aggression, including angry, dominance (or intermale), predatory, maternal, and fear-induced. He argued that these types of aggression are neuroanatomically, affectively, behaviorally, and functionally distinct, and arise under different stimulus and hormonal conditions.

So, then, this question arises: Are there not some cases of justifiable, even desirable, anger? Usually, anger in humans results from perceptions of violations of social norms (Pastore, 1952; G. E. Weisfeld, 1972). In the context of social hierarchies, unfair competition is one example of a violation of social norms. Thus, defeat and its concomitant affect of shame may be complicated by anger at the way in which the competition was conducted. In other words, anger may result if a person feels the competition was unfair and defeat unjust. Gilbert (1997) referred to this situation as *humiliation.*

The importance of social norm violation and inequity to the emotion of anger is underscored by research by Hokanson (1970) and others. Subjects were angered by being insulted, and then their various behavioral reactions were assessed for effectiveness in returning their anger (measured as systolic blood pressure) rapidly to baseline. Aggressing against an inanimate object or innocent bystander did not alleviate anger, nor did doing nothing. Aggressing against the tormentor did work, but so did observing a third party intervene and aggress against the tormentor (Bramel, Taub, & Blum, 1968). Plausible excuses for the insult also reduced anger (Mallick & McCandless, 1966). Thus, only manipulations in which equity was restored were effective, even if the subject did not himself retaliate. Anger arises from perceived violations of social expectations, and is resolved by restoration of propriety or equity.

Another complication is added if anger accompanies depression (a situation sometimes referred to as humiliation, or an ineffective IDS). Anger may prolong and exaggerate the bodily mobilization of depression. Sloman referred to this as resulting from failure to accept defeat (for discussion see Gilbert, 1992, 1997; Sloman, Price, Gilbert, & Gardner, 1994). If the anger is justified, continued arousal may be appropriate, and guidance toward a resolution of the dispute may be desirable. If the anger is unrealistic, withdrawal from the dispute may be in order.

PATHOLOGICAL REACTIONS TO COMPETITIVE OUTCOMES

Given what is known about the role of emotions in social competition, the dominance hierarchy model may help elucidate pathological forms of competitive behavior. That is, certain behaviors may best be understood by considering them under the rubric of the dominance hierarchy model. Here are three examples:

1. Research has revealed that unpopular preadolescent boys are prone to interpret others' actions toward them as hostile (Dodge & Frame, 1982). These low-ranked boys then are prone to become aggressive themselves, thereby further undermining their social standing. Dodge and Frame construed this developmental course as reflecting a cognitive deficit: unpopular boys misperceive how others treat them.

But perhaps these boys' perceptions are veridical. Other data suggest that these boys are unpopular because they are unattractive. Less attractive, less popular boys tend to receive less attention, consideration, and other prerogatives than others throughout the life span (G. E. Weisfeld, 1999). If so, they accurately perceive the treatment they incur, and their anger is in a sense appropriate. Analogously, low-ranking animals tend to fight frequently because they are often picked on (e.g., Masters & McGuire, 1994, on vervet monkeys). High-ranking humans and animals are confidently assertive, seldom initiating a fight but usually accepting a challenge (G. E. Weisfeld, 1994).

2. Pathological mobilization can occur in unhappy marriages. Gottman (1991) showed that divorce is typically preceded by a sustained period of mutual physiological mobilization. In most cases, the husband then withdraws from the wife, and divorce follows. Gottman explained this by noting that mobilization is more profound and taxing for men, which makes adaptive sense given that males are the more competitive and aggressive sex worldwide. This sustained mobilization in unhappy couples may sometimes reflect prolonged dominance competition between them. Observational research has revealed that marriages in which the couple exhibit frequent mutual dominance displays, especially a high ratio of looking while speaking to looking while listening, tend to be unhappy (Noller, 1984). Marriages in which the wife exhibits dominance displays and the husband submits tend to be the most troubled combination.

Perhaps as an evolved precaution against sustained marital competition against the husband, reproductive-age women exhibit a cross-cultural tendency to compete less intensely against mates and potential mates than against other women (C. C. Weisfeld, Weisfeld, & Callaghan, 1982). Women in couples' therapy sessions exhibited more submissive behavior toward their husbands than toward other men (McCarrick, Manderscheid, & Silbergeld, 1981). This "female inhibition in mixed-sex competition" has been shown to occur only in competition against men. Although women are often unaware of this tendency, it is not a generalized "fear of success" (C. C. Weisfeld, 1986). Nor is it due to physical intimidation, because it even occurs in spelling contests (Cronin, 1980). Also, it is more pronounced in women who are better performers: women who are more likely to defeat men and to be less intimidated by them (C. C. Weisfeld et al., 1982).

In theory, competition between mates would also be reduced if men deferred to women. However, men seem to have evolved to be the more competitive sex, consistent with Trivers's (1972) theory. In most mammalian species, males gain mates by being competitive and aggressive, and men are more aggressive and competitive than women (e.g., Schlegel, 1995). Female mammals, in fact, seem to prefer socially dominant, competitive males. In our own species, many correlates of social dominance in men attract women—height, greater age, physical prowess, self-confidence, wealth, dominance displays, and dominant facial features (Buss, 1989; G. E. Weisfeld, 1999). A husband who is outranked by his wife may fail to meet her standards as to what constitutes a socially competent, dominant, competitive man.

Marriages in which the wife dominates decision making or occupies higher socioeconomic status than the husband are relatively unstable and unsatisfying; either moderate husband dominance or equality seems best (G. E. Weisfeld, Russell, Weisfeld, & Wells, 1992). Moreover, it is wives who are more unhappy in wife-dominant marriages than husbands (also see Corrales, 1975; Kotlar, 1965). This is not to say that the relative dominance of husband and wife is the only important factor in marital satisfaction. Many other attributes make a person appealing as a spouse, especially kindness (Buss, 1989). Nevertheless, if a wife has little respect for her husband (i.e., perceives his social rank as low), the marriage is often at risk.

3. Lastly, we cite some recent research at Wayne State University on depression itself. Ziegenhorn (1997) highlighted a sex difference in depression in adolescents. Boys' low social status (roughly, dominance rank) was significantly more closely related to suicidal ideation than was girls' (see Figs. 5.1 and 5.2). Males of low status in the dominance hierarchy may be especially prone to depression and suicide, because low rank is so devastating to a male's reproductive success. Accordingly, sexually active boys were less depressed than sexually inactive boys, whereas the reverse was true for girls (Fig. 5.3). This sex difference was statistically significant. There was also a negative trend between serious suicidal ideation and number of sex partners for boys ($p < .10$), and a positive trend between serious suicidal ideation and being sexually active for girls ($p < .10$).

Consistent with this sociobiological interpretation, one would expect males to be more competitive and to have higher self-esteem than females; to compete, one must have the self-esteem and self-confidence to anticipate success. It is indeed true that males tend to have greater self-esteem and self-confidence than females cross-culturally (C. C. Weisfeld, 1986). At the same time, males' greater need to compete may translate into a wider range of affective outcomes—pride / shame, or euphoria / depression—than for females, resulting in a higher male suicide rate. Nevertheless, more women than men may experience the fairly common condition of depression, possibly because they have a lower average level of self-esteem. The notion that depression often accompanies a loss of biological fitness would also explain its association with loss or

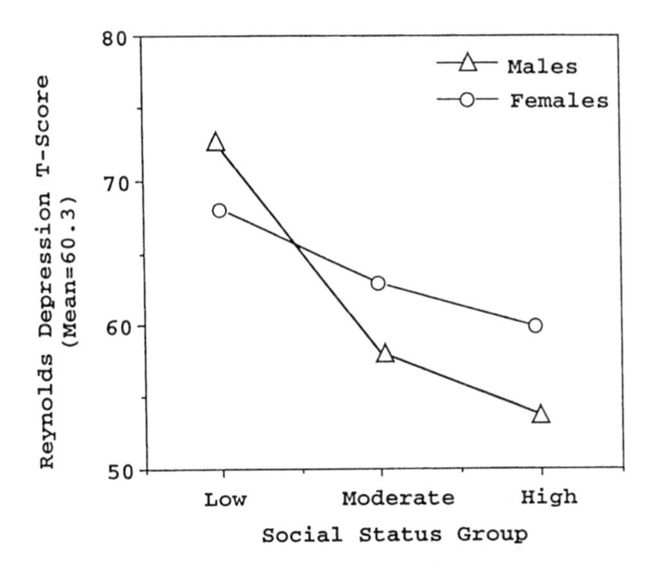

FIG. 5.1. Relation between social status and depression by sex. Main effect for socal status on depression, $F(2,163) = 4.73$, $p = .01$. Scheffe post hoc tests: $p < .05$ for low vs. high status males and for low vs. moderate status males.

serious disease of an offspring or other relative (Suarez & Gallup, 1985), as well as with personal disgrace, marital failure, and isolation from or burdensomeness to kin (deCatanzaro, 1998).

ONE TYPE OF DEPRESSION OR TWO?

Klinger (1975) maintained that animals and humans possess an adaptive tendency to intensify effort in the face of initial frustration and then to relent if unsuccessful. Thus, several common manifestations of depression can be understood as reflections of the anticipation of continued social failure and its accompanying fear: pessimism, self-blame, lack of persistence, poor concentration (a reflection of anxiety), insomnia, reduced interest and exploration (i.e., avoidance of social encounters), conformity (perhaps reflecting low self-confidence), and reduced sexual activity (Gilbert, 1992). The IDS also explains why depressed individuals typically exhibit subordinate displays that may be of diagnostic value: slumped posture, avoidance of eye contact, signs of anxiety, and slow and monotonous speech.

Following Klinger (1975), the notion of the IDS might be extended to any cause of adaptive demobilization (or depression) that results from frustration or difficulty. But should the term be so used? For example, is withdrawal after

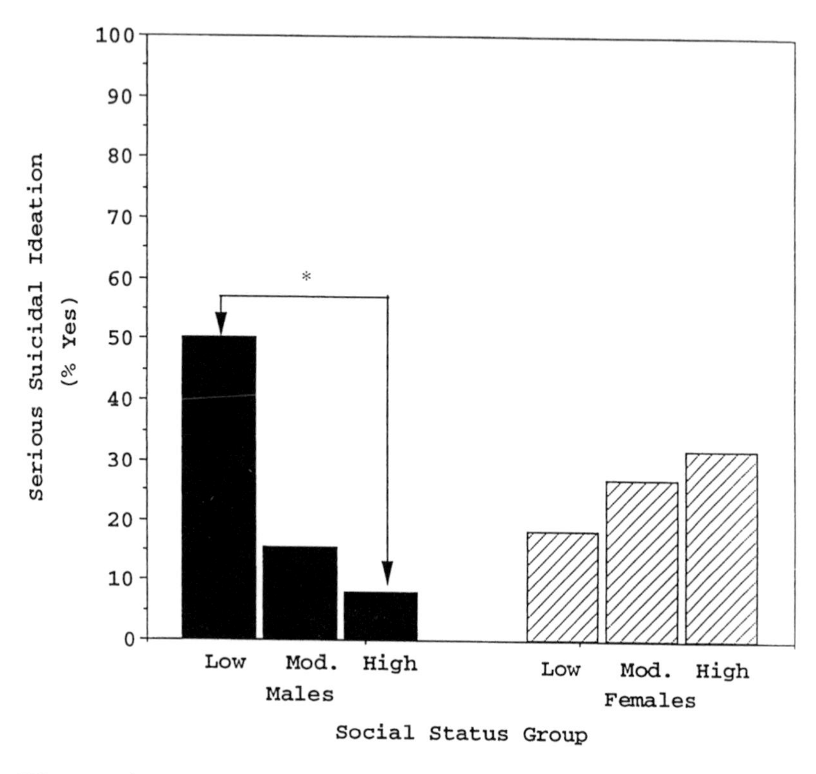

FIG. 5.2. Relation between social status and serious suicidal ideation by sex. *Significant status group difference for low versus high status males, chi square = 5.37, $p < .05$, Fisher's exact test, $p < .10$. (Note: Significant sex difference at high status level, with males reporting less suicidal ideation than females, chi square = 4.60, $p < .05$, Fisher's exact test, $p < .05$.)

defeat essentially the same as withdrawal in bereavement? Are the demobilization of defeat and that of grief similar? Like reactions to failure (or shame), the behavioral and physiological responses to loss of a loved one seem to unfold in adaptive ways. Initially, an infant monkey that is isolated from its mother is highly agitated and tries to find her (McKinney, Suomi, & Harlow, 1971). If the mother is visible, the infant typically calls to her (Coe, Wiener, Rosenberg, & Levine, 1985). The pituitary–adrenal axis is activated, presumably to mobilize the infant, although much more markedly in squirrel monkeys than rhesus monkeys. If the infant fails to rejoin its mother, it eventually becomes sedentary. Similarly, children who are separated from their mothers are often agitated behaviorally and physiologically (Spangler & Grossmann, 1993), and then become withdrawn and depressed physiologically (Bowlby, 1973). A similar pattern of initial invigoration (often followed by anger) and then demobilization and inertia is observed in adults losing a loved one (Parkes, 1972), becoming blind

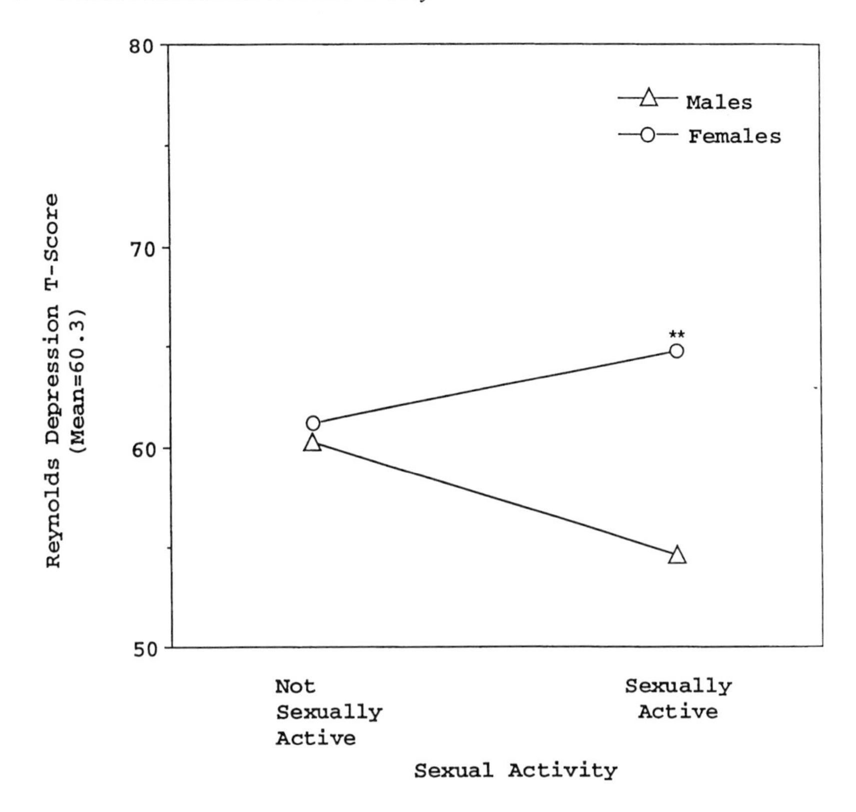

FIG. 5.3. Relation between sexual activity and depression by sex. Significant sex by sexual activity interaction, $F(1,164) = 4.8$, $p < .05$, partial eta squared = .03. **Among sexually active participants, females are significantly more depressed than males, $t = 3.09$, $df = 81$, $p < .01$.

(Fitzgerald, 1970), developing cancer (Orbach & Sutherland, 1954), or suffering a loss of reputation (Averill, 1968). Similarly, inertia is evoked by various other unfavorable conditions, such as cold, heat, food scarcity, disease, and deep body pain (Bolles & Fanselow, 1980).

Despite these similarities in the adaptive processes or reactions involved in the loss of status and in the loss of a loved one, we would argue for regarding emotions and their pathological variants as distinct evolved entities. Indeed, depression seems to assume two forms: grief- and shame-derived. Such a distinction is not new: Beck (1983) noted that the dimensions of sociotropy and autonomy may be useful in distinguishing between these types of depression. In particular, sociotropy is related to the importance of attachment relationships, whereas autonomy is related to the importance of social rank (Robins, Block, & Peselow, 1989). For an excellent review of similar dimensions posed by other researchers, as well as their direct relevance to the IDS, see Gilbert, Allan, and Trent (1995).

Most important, the mediation and development of these two forms of depression are different. Oxytocin reduces separation distress, but not low rank, in various species (Panksepp, 1993). Moreover, different events with different functional consequences—loss of a loved one and defeat in competition—give rise to these two emotions. Their affects and emotional expressions are distinguishable too, despite the fact that sadness is said to occur in both. Their developmental onsets are different: Separation anxiety arises in the first year of life, and pride/shame in the third. Grief and separation distress involve the cingulate gyrus (Panksepp, 1994), whereas pride and shame seem to be localized in the orbitofrontal cortex (see earlier).[1]

A recent review of research on depression secondary to other brain pathology further implicates the cingulate gyrus and orbitofrontal cortex (Dougherty & Rauch, 1997). Three patients experienced depression secondary to a subcortical stroke. All three had decreased anterior cingulate metabolism, which was not true of those patients without secondary depression. Another study, of patients with Huntington's or Parkinson's, found that secondary orbitofrontal hypometabolism was correlated with depressive symptoms. The prefrontal cortex (which includes the orbitofrontal cortex) is also implicated in depression in that two studies have shown decreased uptake of 5-hydroxytryptophan, a serotonin precursor, in this brain region. Depression sometimes also involves the basal ganglia and, possibly in cases complicated by anxiety, the amygdala.

Thus, complicating the issue of the types of depression, various affects besides grief or shame can be involved, especially anxiety and anger, and these affects often interact (Sloman, chap. 2, this volume). Fear of additional failures is virtually unavoidable once a person has suffered a competitive reverse (Gilbert, 1992). Yet in most cases it should be possible to distinguish between the two main emotional forms of depression. Even if pharmacologic treatment were similar for most forms of depression, surely a more specific diagnosis would enhance behavioral intervention. For example, Klinger's (1975) advice that patients be made aware of the essential normality and typical time course of depression seems more suitable for grief than for chronic failure.

Concerning depression arising from shame, Klinger (1975) suggested that patients be advised against persisting in the face of insuperable adversity; one may find better fortune elsewhere. Similarly, Gray (1987) noted that defeated animals often transfer to another group in which their prospects may be brighter. On the other hand, sometimes persistence brings rewards, especially if the failure is an aberration. Analogously, an animal that sustains an unexpected defeat or challenge from a generally weaker opponent may react with vigor, even rage, so as to rectify the situation promptly before a new relationship is stabilized by

[1] Endogenous depression is associated with left frontal lesions and low left frontal activation even in remission (Davidson, 1994). Mania has been linked to right frontal lobe damage, perhaps specifically in the orbitofrontal cortex (Schore, 1994).

the IDS (reviewed by G. E. Weisfeld, 1980). Price, Sloman, Gardner, Gilbert, and Rohde (1994) offered a systematic list of possible therapeutic goals in depression arising from failure: negotiating a peaceful resolution of the competition or conflict, withdrawing from the competition, persisting in the competition in the hope of success, acceptance of defeat, and modifying or redirecting one's goals (see also Sloman and Atkinson, chap. 9, this volume).

If depression indeed takes these two basic forms, perhaps the term Involuntary Subordination (Defeat) Strategy should be reserved for situations involving failure or defeat. Grief does not entail subordination. Moreover, Gilbert, Allan, and Trent (1995) argued that the separation of attachment-related symptomotology and dominance-related symptomotology can further elucidate the various manifestations of depression. The term *depression* itself might eventually be replaced, as it refers both to nonspecific sadness and to physiological demobilization—when in fact the person is usually excessively mobilized.

CONCLUSION

The potential of the IDS concept for organizing our understanding of depression and other clinical conditions seems great indeed. The model suggests that the basic difficulty is emotional, not cognitive. A literature review revealed that most studies show that depressed people actually exhibit less cognitive distortion than normals (Layne, 1983). For these reasons, ethological analyses of psychopathological entities are probably at least as promising as cognitively based ones such as Seligman's and Dodge's. The basic characteristics of human competitive behavior are shared with other primates, thus favoring the use of comparative models over those that assume human "specialness." Viewed in this way, depression then becomes not an incapacity but a distortion of a set of normal emotional responses with evolved, adaptive bases. In theory, each emotional modality that may be involved in a case of depression (e.g., shame, anger, anxiety, loneliness) can be identified by analysis of physiological indicators, emotional expressions, other observable behaviors, and self-reported affects and perceptions. Assessment of any abnormalities can be made, and specific medical and psychotherapeutic interventions initiated.

REFERENCES

Averill, J. R. (1968). Grief: Its nature and significance. *Psychological Bulletin, 70,* 721–748.

Barkow, J. H. (1975). Social prestige and culture: A biosocial interpretation. *Current Anthropology, 16,* 553–572.

Beck, A. T. (1983). Cognitive therapy of depression: New perspectives. In P. J. Clayton & J. E. Barrett (Eds.), *Treatment of depression: Old controversies and new approaches* (pp. 265–290). New York: Raven.

Berkeley, A. W. (1952). Level of aspiration in relation to adrenal cortical activity and the concept of stress. *Journal of Comparative & Physiological Psychology, 45,* 443–449.

Bloch, S., & Brackenridge, C. J. (1972). Psychological performance and biochemical factors in medical students under examination stress. *Journal of Psychosomatic Research, 16*(1), 25–33.

Bolles, R. C., & Fanselow, M. S. (1980). A perceptual-defensive model of fear and pain. *Behavioral & Brain Sciences, 3,* 291–323.

Bowlby, J. (1973). *Attachment and loss: Vol. 2. Separation: Anxiety and danger.* New York: Basic Books.

Bramel, D., Taub, B., & Blum, B. (1968). An observer's reaction to the suffering of his enemy. *Journal of Personality and Social Psychology, 8,* 384–392.

Bronson, W. C. (1966). Central orientations: A study of behavioral organization from childhood to adolescence. *Child Development, 37,* 125–155.

Buss, D. M. (1989). Sex differences in human mate preferences: Evolutionary hypotheses tested in 37 cultures. *Behavioral & Brain Sciences, 12,* 1–49.

Cannon, W. B. (1932). *The wisdom of the body.* New York: Norton.

Coe, C. L., Wiener, S. G., Rosenberg, L. T., & Levine, S. (1985). Endocrine and immune responses to separation and maternal loss in nonhuman primates. In M. Reite & T. Field (Eds.), *The psychobiology of attachment and separation* (pp. 163–199). New York: Academic.

Coopersmith, S. (1967). *The antecedents of self-esteem.* San Francisco: Freeman.

Corrales, R. G. (1975). Power and satisfaction in early marriage. In R. E. Cromwell & D. H. Olson (Eds.), *Power in families* (pp. 197–216). New York: Wiley.

Cronin, C. L. (1980). Dominance relations and females. In D. R. Omark, F. F. Strayer, & D. G. Freedman (Eds.), *Dominance relations: An ethological view of human conflict and social interaction.* New York: Garland.

Crook, J. H. (1970). Social organization and the environment: Aspects of contemporary social ecology. *Animal Behaviour, 18,* 197–209.

Damasio, H., Grabowski, T., Frank, R., Galaburda, A. M., & Damasio, A. R. (1994). The return of Phineas Gage: The skull of a famous patient yields clues about the brain. *Science, 264,* 1102–1105.

Darwin, C. (1965). *The expression of the emotions in man and animals.* Chicago: University of Chicago Press. (Original work published 1872)

Davidson, R. J. (1994). Honoring biology in the study of affective style. In P. Ekman & R. J. Davidson (Eds.), *The nature of emotion: Fundamental questions* (pp. 321–326). Oxford, UK: Oxford University Press.

deCatanzaro, D. A. (1998). *Motivation and emotion: Evolutionary, physiological, developmental, and social perspectives.* Upper Saddle River, NJ: Prentice Hall.

Dodge, K. A., & Frame, C. L. (1982). Social cognitive biases and deficits in aggressive boys. *Child Development, 54,* 1386–1399.

Dong, Q., Weisfeld, G., Boardway, R. H., & Shen, J. (1996). Correlates of social status among Chinese adolescents. *Journal of Cross-Cultural Psychology, 27,* 476–493.

Dougherty, D., & Rauch, S. L. (1997). Neuroimaging and neurobiological models of depression. *Harvard Review of Psychiatry, 5,* 138–159.

Dweck, C. S., & Reppucci, N. D. (1973). Learned helplessness and reinforcement responsibility in children. *Journal of Personality & Social Psychology, 25,* 109–116.

Fitzgerald, R. C. (1970). Reactions to blindness: An exploratory study of adults with recent loss of sight. *Archives of General Psychiatry, 22,* 370–379.

Franken, R. E. (1998). *Human motivation* (4th ed.). Pacific Grove, CA: Brooks/Cole.

Fuster, J. M. (1980). *The prefrontal cortex: Anatomy, physiology, and neuropsychology of the frontal lobe.* New York: Raven.

Gartlan, J. S., & Brain, C. K. (1968). Ecology and social variability in *Cercopithecus aethiops* and *C. mitis.* In P. Jay (Ed.), *Primates: Studies in adaptation and variability* (pp. 253–292). New York: Holt, Rinehart & Winston.

Gellhorn, E., & Loofbourrow, G. N. (1963). *Emotions and emotional disorders.* New York: Hoeber.

Gilbert, P. (1992). *Depression: The evolution of powerlessness.* New York: Guilford.

Gilbert, P. (1997). The evolution of social attractiveness and its role in shame, humiliation, guilt and therapy. *British Journal of Medical Psychology, 70,* 113–147.

Gilbert, P. (1998). What is shame? Some core issues and controversies. In P. Gilbert & B. Andrews (Eds.), *Shame: Interpersonal behavior, psychopathology, and culture* (pp. 3–38). New York: Oxford University Press.

Gilbert, P., Allan, S., Ball, L., & Bradshaw, Z. (1996). Overconfidence and personal evaluations of social rank. *British Journal of Medical Psychology, 69,* 59–68.

Gilbert, P., Allan, S., & Trent, D. R. (1995). Involuntary subordination or dependency as key dimensions of depressive vulnerability? *Journal of Clinical Psychology, 51,* 740–752.

Gilbert, P., & McGuire, M. T. (1998). Shame, status, and social roles: Psychobiology and evolution. In P. Gilbert & B. Andrews (Eds.), *Shame: Interpersonal behavior, psychopathology, and culture* (pp. 99–121). New York: Oxford University Press.

Gilbert, P., Pehl, J., & Allan, S. (1994). The phenomenology of shame and guilt: An empirical investigation. *British Journal of Medical Psychology, 67,* 23–36.

Gilbert, P., Price, J., & Allan, S. (1995). Social comparison, social attractiveness and evolution: How might they be related? *New Ideas in Psychology, 13,* 149–165.

Ginsburg, B. E., & Allee, W. C. (1942). Some effects of conditioning on social dominance and coordination in inbred strains of mice. *Physiological Zoology, 15,* 485–506.

Ginsburg, H. J. (1980). Playground as laboratory: Naturalistic studies of appeasement, altruism, and the omega child. In D. R. Omark, F. F. Strayer, & D. G. Freedman (Eds.), *Dominance relations: An ethological view of human conflict and social interaction* (pp. 341–357). New York: Garland.

Gottman, J. M. (1991). Predicting the longitudinal course of marriages. *Journal of Marital & Family Therapy, 17,* 3–7.

Gray, J. A. (1987). *The psychology of fear and stress.* Cambridge, UK: Cambridge University Press.

Hartup, W. W. (1974). Aggression in childhood: Developmental perspectives. *American Psychologist, 29,* 336–341.

Heckhausen, H. (1984). Emergent achievement behavior: Some early developments. In J. Nicholls (Eds.), *Advances in motivation and achievement: The development of achievement motivation* (Vol. 3, pp. 1–32). Greenwich, CT: JAI.

Hill, S. R., Goetz, F. C., Fox, H. M., Murowski, P. N., Krakauer, L. J., Reifenstein, R. W., Gray, S. J., Reddy, W. J., Hedberg, S. E., St. Marc, J. R., & Thorn, G. W. (1956). Studies on adrenocortical and psychological response to stress in man. *Archives of Internal Medicine, 97,* 269–298.

Hokanson, J. E. (1970). Psychophysiological evaluations of the catharsis hypothesis. In E. I. Megargee & J. E. Hokanson (Eds.), *The dynamics of aggression* (pp. 74–86). New York: Harper & Row.

Hold, B. (1977). Rank and behaviour: An ethological study of pre-school children. *Homo, 28,* 158–188.

Homans, G. C. (1974). *Social behavior: Its elementary forms.* New York: Harcourt Brace Jovanovich.

Jackson, L. A. (1992). *Physical appearance and gender: Sociobiological and sociocultural perspectives.* Albany: State University of New York Press.

Kagan, J., & Moss, H. A. (1962). *Birth to maturity: A study in psychological development.* New York: Wiley.

Kalat, J. W. (1995). *Biological psychology* (5th ed.). Belmont, CA: Wadsworth.

Kaplan, H. B., Burch, N. R., & Bloom, S. W. (1965). Physiological covariation and sociometric relationships in small peer groups. In P. H. Leiderman & D. Shapiro (Eds.), *Psychobiological approaches to social behavior* (pp. 92–109). London: Tavistock.

Keltner, D., & Buswell, B. N. (1997). Embarrassment: Its distinct form and appeasement functions. *Psychological Bulletin, 122,* 250–270.

Kemper, T. D. (1990). *Social structure and testosterone.* New Brunswick, NJ: Rutgers University Press.

Klinger, E. (1975). Consequences of commitment to and disengagement from incentives. *Psychological Review, 82,* 1–25.

Klopper, A. (1964). Physiological background to aggression. In J. D. Carthy & F. J. Ebling (Eds.), *The natural history of aggression* (pp. 65–72). New York: Academic.

Kotlar, S. L. (1965). Middle-class marital role perceptions and marital adjustment. *Sociology & Social Research, 49,* 283–294.

Layne, C. (1983). Painful truths about depressives' cognitions. *Journal of Clinical Psychology, 39,* 848–853.

LeDoux, J. (1996). *The emotional brain.* New York: Simon & Schuster.

Levin, H. S., Eisenberg, H. M., & Benton, A. L. (1991). *Frontal lobe function and dysfunction.* New York: Oxford University Press.

Lewis, M. (1993). Self-conscious emotions: Embarrassment, pride, shame, and guilt. In M. Lewis & J. M. Haviland (Eds.), *Handbook of emotions* (pp. 563–573). New York: Guilford.

Mallick, S. K., & McCandless, B. R. (1966). A study of catharsis of aggression. *Journal of Personality and Social Psychology, 4,* 591–596.

Mass, R. (1972). *The effects of dorsolateral frontal ablations on the social behavior of a caged group of eleven stumptail macaques.* Unpublished doctoral dissertation, Rutgers University, New Brunswick, NJ.

Masters, R. D., & McGuire, M. T. (1994). *The neurotransmitter revolution.* Carbondale: Southern Illinois University Press.

Mazur, A. (1985). A biosocial model of status in face-to-face primate groups. *Social Forces, 64,* 377–402.

Mazur, A., & Booth, A. (1998). Testosterone and dominance in men. *Behavioral & Brain Sciences, 21,* 353–397.

Mazur, A., & Lamb, T. A. (1980). Testosterone, status, and mood in human males. *Hormones & Behavior, 14,* 236–246.

McCarrick, A. K., Manderscheid, R. W., & Silbergeld, S. (1981). Gender differences in competition and dominance during married-couples therapy. *Social Psychology Quarterly, 44,* 164–177.

McDougall, W. (1923). *Outline of psychology.* New York: Scribner's.

McKinney, W. T., Jr., Suomi, S. J., & Harlow, H. F. (1971). Depression in primates. *American Journal of Psychiatry, 127,* 1313–1330.

Miller, R. S., & Tangney, J. P. (1994). Differentiating embarrassment and shame. *Journal of Social and Clinical Psychology, 13,* 273–287.

Moyer, K. E. (1976). *The psychobiology of aggression.* New York: Harper & Row.

Murray, H. A. (1963). Studies of stressful interpersonal disputations. *American Psychologist, 18,* 28.

Nelson, D. H. (1972). Regulation of glucocorticoid release. *American Journal of Medicine, 53,* 590–594.

Newton, G., Paul, J., & Bovard, E. W. (1957). Effect of emotional stress on finger temperature. *Psychological Reports, 3,* 341–343.

Noller, P. (1984). *Nonverbal communication and marital interaction.* Oxford, UK: Pergamon.

Omark, D. R., Omark, M., & Edelman, M. S. (1975). Formation of dominance hierarchies in young children: Action and perception. In T. Williams (Ed.), *Psychological anthropology* (Vol. 14, pp. 87–107). The Hague, Netherlands: Mouton.

Omark, D. R., Strayer, F. F., & Freedman, D. G. (Eds.). (1980). *Dominance relations: An ethological view of human conflict and social interaction.* New York: Garland.

Orbach, C. E., & Sutherland, A. M. (1954). Acute depressive reactions to surgical treatment for cancer. In P. H. Hoch & J. Zubin (Eds.), *Depression* (pp. 237–252). New York: Grune & Stratton.

Panksepp, J. (1993). Neurochemical control of moods and emotion: Amino acids to neuropeptides. In M. Lewis & J. M. Haviland (Eds.), *Handbook of emotions* (pp. 87–107). New York: Guilford.

Panksepp, J. (1994). Evolution constructed the potential for subjective experience within the neurodynamics of the mammalian brain. In P. Ekman & R. J. Davidson (Eds.), *The nature of emotion: Fundamental questions* (pp. 329–399). Oxford, UK: Oxford University Press.

Parkes, C. M. (1972). *Studies of grief in adult life.* New York: International Universities Press.

Passingham, R. (1993). *The frontal lobes and voluntary action.* Oxford, UK: Oxford University Press.

Pastore, N. (1952). The role of arbitrariness in the frustration-aggression hypothesis. *Journal of Abnormal & Social Psychology, 47,* 728–731.

Persky, H., Maroc, J., Conrad, E., & Breeijen, A. (1959). Blood corticotropin and adrenal weight maintenance factor levels of anxious patients and normal subjects. *Psychosomatic Medicine, 21*, 379–386.
Price, J. S. (1967). Hypothesis: The dominance hierarchy and the evolution of mental illness. *Lancet, ii*, 243–246.
Price, J. S. (1972). Genetic and phylogenetic aspects of mood variation. *International Journal of Mental Health, 1*, 124–144.
Price, J. S., Sloman, L., Gardner, R., Jr., Gilbert, P., & Rohde, P. (1994). The social competition hypothesis of depression. *British Journal of Psychiatry, 164*, 309–315.
Pugh, G. E. (1977). *The biological origin of human values.* New York: Basic Books.
Rajecki, D. W., & Flannery, R. C. (1981). Social conflict and dominance in children: A case for a primate homology. In M. E. Lamb & A. Brown (Eds.), *Advances in developmental psychology* (Vol. 1, pp. 87–129). Hillsdale, NJ: Lawrence Erlbaum Associates.
Raphelson, A. C., & Moulton, R. W. (1958). The relationship between imaginative and direct verbal measures of test anxiety under two conditions of uncertainty. *Journal of Personality, 26*, 556–567.
Richards, S. M. (1972). *Tests for biobehavioral characteristics in rhesus monkeys.* Unpublished doctoral dissertation, Cambridge University, Cambridge, UK.
Robins, C. J., Block, P., & Peselow, E. D. (1989). Relations of sociotropic and autonomous personality characteristics to specific symptoms in depressed patients. *Journal of Abnormal Psychology, 98*, 86–88.
Rose, R. M., Holiday, J. W., & Bernstein, I. S. (1971). Plasma testosterone, dominance rank, and aggressive behavior in male rhesus monkeys. *Nature, 231*, 366–368.
Rosenberg, M. (1965). *Society and the adolescent self-image.* Princeton, NJ: Princeton University Press.
Sachar, E. J., Schalch, D. S., Reichlin, S., & Platman, S. S. (1972). Endocrinology of depression: Plasma gonadotrophins in depressive illness: A preliminary report. In T. A. Williams, M. M. Katz, & J. A. Shield, Jr. (Eds.), *Recent advances in the psychobiology of the depressive illnessess* (pp. 229–233). Washington, DC: Department of Health, Education and Welfare.
Sapolsky, R. M. (1992). Neuroendocrinology of the stress-response. In J. B. Becker, S. M. Breedlove & D. Crews (Eds.), *Behavioral endocrinology* (pp. 289–324). Cambridge, MA: MIT Press.
Sassenrath, E. N. (1970). Increased adrenal responsiveness related to social stress in rhesus monkeys. *Hormones & Behavior, 1*, 283–290.
Saver, J. L., & Damasio, A. R. (1991). Preserved access and processing of social knowledge in a patient with acquired sociopathy due to ventromedial frontal damage. *Neuropsychologia, 29*, 1241–1249.
Savin-Williams, R. C. (1977). Dominance in a human adolescent group. *Animal Behaviour, 25*, 400–406.
Schlegel, A. (1995). A cross-cultural approach to adolescence. *Ethos, 23*, 15–32.
Schneider-Rosen, K., & Cicchetti, D. (1991). Early self-knowledge and emotional development: Visual self-recognition and affective reactions to mirror self-images in maltreated and non-maltreated toddlers. *Developmental Psychology, 27*, 471–478.
Schore, A. N. (1994). *Affect regulation and the origin of the self: The neurobiology of emotional development.* Hillsdale, NJ: Lawrence Erlbaum Associates.
Sears, R. R. (1937). Initiation of the repression sequence by experienced failure. *Journal of Experimental Psychology, 20*, 570–580.
Seligman, M. E. P. (1974). Depression and learned helplessness. In R. J. Friedman & M. M. Katz (Eds.), *The psychology of depression: Contemporary theory and research* (pp. 83–125). New York: Wiley.
Selye, H. (1952). *The story of the adaptation syndrome.* Montreal: Acta.
Shapiro, D., & Leiderman, P. H. (1965). Acts and activation: A psychophysiological study of social interaction. In P. H. Leiderman & D. Shapiro (Eds.), *Psychobiological approaches to social behavior* (pp. 110–126). London: Tavistock.
Shapiro, D., & Leiderman, P. H. (1967). Arousal correlates of task role and group setting. *Journal of Personality & Social Psychology, 5*, 103–107.

Sloman, L., Price, J., Gilbert, P., & Gardner, R. (1994). Adaptive function of depression: psychotherapeutic implications. *American Journal of Psychotherapy, 48*, 1–16.
Spangler, G., & Grossmann, K. E. (1993). Biobehavioral organization in securely and insecurely attached infants. *Child Development, 64*, 1439–1450.
Stipek, D. (1995). The development of pride and shame in toddlers. In J. P. Tangney & K. W. Fischer (Eds.), *Self-conscious emotions: The psychology of shame, guilt, embarrassment, and pride* (pp. 237–252). New York: Guilford.
Strayer, F. F., & Strayer, J. (1976). An ethological analysis of social agonism and dominance relations among preschool children. *Child Development, 47*, 980–989.
Suarez, S. D., & Gallup, G. G. (1985). Depression as a response to reproductive failure. *Journal of Social and Biological Structures, 8*, 279–287.
Tangney, J. P. (1995). Shame and guilt in interpersonal relationships. In J. P. Tangney & K. W. Fischer (Eds.), *Self-conscious emotions: The psychology of shame, guilt, embarrassment, and pride* (pp. 114–139). New York: Guilford.
Tepperman, J. (1973). *Metabolic and endocrine physiology.* Chicago: Yearbook Medical.
Thorndike, E. L. (1927). The law of effect. *American Journal of Psychology, 29*, 212–222.
Trivers, R. L. (1971). The evolution of reciprocal altruism. *Quarterly Review of Biology, 46*, 35–57.
Trivers, R. L. (1972). Parental investment and sexual selection. In B. Campbell (Ed.), *Sexual selection and the descent of man 1871–1971* (pp. 136–179). Chicago: Aldine.
Tyler, T. M., & Smith, H. J. (1998). Social justice and social movements. In D. T. Gilbert, S. T. Fiske, & G. Lindzey (Eds.), *Handbook of social psychology* (4th ed., Vol. 2, pp. 595–629). Boston: McGraw-Hill.
Warren, J. M., & Maroney, R. J. (1958). Competitive social interaction between monkeys. *Journal of Social Psychology, 48*, 223–233.
Weisfeld, C. C. (1986). Female behavior in mixed-sex competition: A review of the literature. *Developmental Review, 6*, 278–299.
Weisfeld, C. C., Weisfeld, G. E., & Callaghan, J. W. (1982). Female inhibition in mixed-sex competition among young adolescents. *Ethology & Sociobiology, 3*, 29–42.
Weisfeld, G. E. (1972). Violations of social norms as inducers of aggression. *International Journal of Group Tensions, 2*, 53–70.
Weisfeld, G. E. (1980). Social dominance and human motivation. In D. R. Omark, F. F. Strayer, & D. G. Freedman (Eds.), *Dominance relations: An ethological view of human conflict and social interaction* (pp. 273–286). New York: Garland.
Weisfeld, G. E. (1982). The nature–nurture issue and the integrating concept of function. In B. B. Wolman & G. Stricker (Eds.), *Handbook of developmental psychology* (pp. 208–229). Englewood Cliffs, NJ: Prentice-Hall.
Weisfeld, G. E. (1994). Aggression and dominance in the social world of boys. In J. Archer (Ed.), *Male violence* (pp. 42–69). London: Routledge.
Weisfeld, G. E. (1997a). Discrete emotions theory with specific reference to pride and shame. In N. L. Segal, G. E. Weisfeld, & C. C. Weisfeld (Eds.), *Uniting psychology and biology: Integrative perspectives on human development* (pp. 419–443). Washington, DC: American Psychological Association.
Weisfeld, G. E. (1997b). Research on emotions and future developments in human ethology. In A. Schmitt et al. (Eds.), *New aspects of human ethology* (pp. 25–46). New York: Plenum.
Weisfeld, G. E. (1999). *Evolutionary principles of human adolescence.* New York: Basic Books.
Weisfeld, G. E., & Beresford, J. M. (1982). Erectness of posture as an indicator of dominance or success in humans. *Motivation & Emotion, 6*, 113–131.
Weisfeld, G. E., & Linkey, H. E. (1985). Dominance displays as indicators of a social success motive. In S. Ellyson & J. Dovidio (Eds.), *Power, dominance, and nonverbal behavior* (pp. 109–128). New York: Springer-Verlag.

Weisfeld, G. E., Omark, D. R., & Cronin, C. L. (1980). A longitudinal and cross-sectional study of dominance in boys. In D. R. Omark, F. F. Strayer, & D. G. Freedman (Eds.), *Dominance relations: An ethological view of human conflict and social interaction* (pp. 205–216). New York: Garland.

Weisfeld, G. E., Russell, R. J. H., Weisfeld, C. C., & Wells, P. A. (1992). Correlates of satisfaction in British marriages. *Ethology & Sociobiology, 13,* 125–145.

Ziegenhorn, L. A. (1997). *Social status, affect, and sex in adolescence: An evolutionary psychological perspective.* Unpublished doctoral dissertation, Department of Psychology, Wayne State University, Detroit, MI.

Zivin, G. (1977). Facial gestures predict preschoolers' encounter outcomes. *Social Science Information, 16,* 715–730.

CHAPTER SIX

Social Comparison Processes Among Depressed Individuals: Evidence for the Evolutionary Perspective on Involuntary Subordinate Strategies?

Bram P. Buunk
Veerle Brenninkmeyer
University of Groningen

Social psychologists have long recognized the importance of social comparison for human adaptation and survival. In his theory of social comparison processes, Festinger (1954) argued that individuals prefer to evaluate themselves employing objective and nonsocial standards, but when such objective information is unavailable, individuals will compare themselves with others to evaluate their own characteristics. As pointed out by Mettee and Smith (1977), social comparison theory is a general theory about "our quest to know ourselves, about the search for self-relevant information and how people gain self-knowledge and discover reality about themselves" (pp. 69–70). Festinger (1954) not only discussed this process of self-evaluation, but also emphasized the interpersonal consequences of social comparison by suggesting, for example, that people will seek out the company of others similar to themselves and will try to persuade others to become more like themselves. Although it was Festinger (1954) who used the term *social comparison* for the first time, social comparison processes were already highlighted earlier in the classic work of Hyman (1942), who argued that the assessment of one's own status on such dimensions as financial position, intellectual capabilities, and physical attractiveness is dependent on the group with whom one compares oneself.

In the past decades, social comparison theory has undergone numerous transitions and reformulations. It has developed from being a singular, well-articulated theory to an area of research encompassing many different paradigms and approaches (e.g., Buunk & Gibbons, 1997; Suls & Wills, 1991). In a recent development, it has been linked to evolutionary theory by Gilbert and his colleagues (Gilbert, 1990; Gilbert, Price, & Allan, 1995). According to these authors, social comparison is phylogenetically very old, biologically very powerful, and recognizable in many species. As many other social animals, humans compete with each other for status and prestige in groups. To be socially successful, it is important for most social animals to be able to make a cost–benefit analysis and to assess their resources in comparison to those of others. Individuals should not continually compete and challenge those who will always defeat them, as that would bring substantial costs and waste energy. At the same time, those who can be beaten should be challenged so as not to miss out on opportunities that could be available. In general, social comparison assists individuals in determining their rank in the group, in assessing what others find attractive in them, and, importantly, in providing information on how one should change one's behavior to obtain favorable outcomes. The theory of involuntary subordinate strategies (ISS), based on a wealth of animal data, links this evolutionary perspective on social comparison to depression (Price, Sloman, Gardner, Gilbert, & Rohde, 1994; Sloman, Price, Gilbert, & Gardner, 1994). According to this theory, whereas winners appear to experience a surge in confidence and energy associated with various physiological changes, animals who lose or believe that they will lose a fight or conflict, and thus face a lower rank, usually engage in submissive strategies, limiting their challenging and exploratory behavior and signaling to those higher in rank that one is no longer a threat. By doing so, they prevent aggression from those more powerful and higher in rank and help to restore the relationship with these higher status others (Allan & Gilbert, 1995). From the perspective of ISS theory, depression results when individuals are facing a state of involuntary subordination from which escape through flight or acceptance is blocked. Indeed, Gilbert and Allan (1998) found that a scale for defeat, measuring things such as "I feel that I have not made it in life," and "I feel I have lost important battles in life" correlated highly with depression. According to ISS theory, because depressed individuals are frustrated about what they perceive as a defeat and a loss in rank, they experience feelings of worthlessness, helplessness, envy, and fear. ISS prevent the individual from attempting to make a comeback by inhibiting aggressive behavior to rivals and superiors (but not to dependents), and by putting the individual into a "giving up" state of mind that encourages acceptance of his or her defeat.

In the remainder of this chapter, we review the research literature on social comparison processes among depressed individuals and, when that seems possible and relevant, we relate findings from this literature to ISS theory. For a number of reasons however, the literature in this area is not easy to interpret and synthesize. First, little research has explicitly examined social comparison from the perspective of ISS theory and many social comparison studies are difficult to integrate in this perspective. Second, there have been nearly as many different research paradigms as there have been independent studies on social comparison and depression, making it difficult to compare results across studies. Third, as noted by Ahrens and Alloy (1995) most of the research in this area has involved cross-sectional designs. This implies that differences in social comparison strategies between depressed and nondepressed individuals may reflect causes of depression (e.g., some persons become depressed because they always compare themselves with higher ranking others), concomitants of depression (e.g., depressed individuals are very sensitive to how others are doing because of their mood state), and coping strategies to recover from depression (e.g., depressed individuals try to alleviate their negative mood by comparing themselves with others lower in rank). Fourth, it is often not possible to differentiate between depression as a temporary state and depression as a more stable personality trait, in part because there is no agreement as to which measures tap either type of depression (Weary & Edwards, 1994). Moreover, operationalizations of depression have varied from dysphoria to clinical depression, and although there is increasing evidence that mild depressive symptoms may predict major depressive periods (Hammen, 1997), one could question to what extent social comparison processes among individuals experiencing mild forms of negative affect are similar to those among individuals clinically diagnosed as depressed. Finally, given the degree of comorbidity in depression, research findings about social comparison and depression might actually be about comorbid disorders such as anxiety disorders, eating disorders, and personality disorders (Hammen, 1997). In this context it must also be noted that there is considerable evidence that associations between depression and various measures of social comparison activity may actually reflect the influence of neuroticism (Van der Zee, Buunk, & Sanderman, 1998; Van der Zee, Oldersma, Buunk, & Bos, 1998). Given these limitations, we can only offer a preliminary integration and interpretation of the literature on social comparison and depression. We emphasize that much more focused research in this area seems necessary, including, but not limited to, research directly examining social comparison processes as related to ISS theory. We discuss in this chapter the following issues: (a) perceptions of oneself in comparison with others, (b) the selective processing of social comparison information, (c) the desire for social comparison information and the frequency of social comparison, and (d) the seeking of information about others that may alleviate one's own unfortunate state.

PERCEPTIONS OF ONESELF IN COMPARISON WITH OTHERS

According to some authors, not only the tendency to compare oneself with others is rooted in our evolutionary past, but so is the tendency to perceive oneself as favorable in comparison to others. Among others, Barkow (1989) and Buunk and Ybema (1997) argued that because humans have developed the potential for self-deception and cognitive distortion, they have the possibility to symbolically assign themselves prestige and status in their reference group. Such a reference group need not even be actually present but may be cognitively construed (Barkow, 1989). From an evolutionary perspective, this search for symbolic superiority over others is the translation of the physical struggle among primates for status in a group. In their now-classic paper, Taylor and Brown (1988) cited a number of studies documenting that there is a widespread *superiority bias:* Individuals have a strong tendency to see the self as better than most others or the average other for a wide range of traits and abilities (see also Hoorens, 1993). For example, at least 40% of workers in different jobs think that they are among the best 10% of people in the same profession (Meyer, 1980). Such perceptions of superiority appear to be quite robust and very difficult to change (Alicke, Klotz, Breitenbecher, & Yurak, 1995). More important, such perceptions are closely related to mental health. Headey and Wearing (1988) suggested that to feel above average is the normal state characteristic of a high level of well-being.

ISS theory suggests that depressed individuals experience less superiority than nondepressed individuals as they feel that they have lost the struggle for high status in their reference group. From this perspective, depression creates a self-view in which one is incapable of competing with others. Learned helplessness, which has been suggested as a characteristic of depressed individuals (cf. Hammen, 1997), may be interpreted as indicating an inability to compete succesfully for status in one's reference group. In accordance with ISS theory, it is a well-established finding that depression is characterized by thoughts that are deprecatory and pessimistic with regard to the self (Weary & Edwards, 1994), and that depressed individuals perceive themselves in general as incompetent, worthless, and critical of their own characteristics (Hammen, 1997). Particularly relevant in this context, depressed individuals seem to have less pronounced perceptions of superiority than nondepressed individuals. In a study by Allan and Gilbert (1995), depression was related to relatively less favorable ratings of oneself in comparison to others in terms of rank (e.g., talented, competent) and attractiveness (e.g., likable, attractive). Kuiper and MacDonald (1982) showed that moderately depressed individuals (higher than 8 on the BDI—Beck Depression Inventory; Beck, Ward, Mendelson, Mock, & Erlbaugh, 1961) recalled less negative information about others than nondepressed individuals, suggesting that depressed individuals enhanced themselves less by derogating other people's personality attributes than nondepressed individuals. A study by Furnham and Brewin (1988) showed that depressed individuals felt that negative events were more likely and positive events were less likely to happen to them than to most other people. In a study among elderly women, Heidrich and Ryff (1993, Study 1) showed that the higher the level of depression (assessed with the CES–D; Radloff, 1977), the less well-off one considered oneself in comparison with others (assessed by a measure assessing how well one felt one fared in comparison to others for various domains, e.g., physical health, physical appearance, family relationships, friendships). Even more so, this comparison measure predicted depression in a regression analysis, but did not predict indexes of health, such as the number of health problems. A study by Buunk and Janssen (1992) showed that, particularly among men in midcareer, relative deprivation was related to depression. These perceptions of relative deprivation were, to an important extent, based on the feeling that one had attained less in one's career than similar others.

The fact that depressed individuals perceive themselves as less superior in various ways than nondepressed individuals do, does not necessarily imply that they perceive themselves as inferior to similar others. From a certain perspective, one could even argue that, in line with the theory of *depressive realism,* depressed individuals perceive themselves in a more realistic way than nondepressed individuals do; that is, they perceive themselves as similar to the average other (see Hammen, 1997). In a study by Tabachnik, Crocker, and Alloy (1983), depressed students rated both depression-relevant characteristics (e.g., "I feel alienated" and "I am a boring person") and nondepression-relevant characteristics (e.g., "I am motivated" and "I am creative") to the same extent as applicable to themselves as to the average college student. Nondepressed individuals, however, rated depression-relevant characteristics as less applicable and nondepression-relevant characteristics as more applicable to themselves than to the average college student. A study by Alloy and Ahrens (1987) showed similar results. They examined the predictions for their own success and that of others among depressed individuals (scores higher than 8 on the BDI) and nondepressed individuals (scores lower than 5 on the BDI). Whereas nondepressed individuals showed a self-enhancement bias by overestimating their chances of future success and underestimating their future failure compared to their estimates for others, depressed individuals made similar estimates for themselves and for others. An interpretation of these data in the context of ISS theory would suggest that whereas depressed individuals have given up competing with others higher in rank, the positively biased perspective characterizing nondepressed individuals is precisely the type of optimism necessary to compete succesfully with others.

Remarkably, when the comparison group is specified as other depressed individuals, depressed individuals do appear to show a superiority bias. Albright, Alloy, Barch, and Dykman (1993, Study 1) assessed the level of depression using two measurements with an interval of between 1 and 2 weeks. Depressed individuals were defined as those who both times had a score higher than 9 on the BDI. Nondepressed individuals were defined as those who both times had a score lower than 5. Although depressed participants rated themselves (as in other studies) on depression-relevant and depression-irrelevant characteristics as similar to the average college student, they judged themselves less favorably than the average nondepressed student for both types of characteristics, but more favorably than the average depressed college student. This suggests that the mental state of "giving up" characteristic of ISS is directed only toward nondepressed or higher ranking persons, and that depressed persons may challenge other depressed individuals and compete with such individuals. The findings presented here are in line with the assumption that depressed persons exhibit aggression only downward; that is, toward lower ranking persons. Price et al. (1994) even hypothesized that this form of aggression increases among depressed persons, perhaps as a way of venting one's emotions.

The previous discussion has a number of implications. First, in line with ISS theory, depressed individuals do not perceive themselves as superior to others in general as nondepressed individuals do. They seem to lack the subjective feeling of high status characteristic of nondepressed individuals, and they also lack the optimism about one's chances that seems important to compete successfully with others. Second, although it is sometimes suggested that depressed people view the world as a whole in negative terms, such people do not apparently tend to perceive others more negatively than nondepressed individuals do. In fact, from the perspective of ISS theory, one would not expect someone low in rank to view others particularly negatively, and even more so, given the feelings of inferiority, one might expect those low in rank to view others less negatively than oneself. Third, although depressed individuals feel inferior to nondepressed ones, they still cherish a sense of perceived superiority, at least when their reference group consists of other depressed individuals. This corresponds to the assumption that ISS does not inhibit competition with similarly ranking others and aggression toward lower ranking persons.

A NEGATIVE BIAS IN INTERPRETING SOCIAL COMPARISON INFORMATION

As would be expected on the basis of the notion that humans use cognitive mechanisms to assign themselves a subjectively high status, there is evidence that, in general, individuals interpret social comparison information in self-serving ways. As Goethals, Messick, and Allison (1991) noted, "people wish to perceive themselves as superior to others, and they will in fact construct perceptions of themselves and social reality that support this wish to the maximum degree that physical and social reality permit" (p. 163). In these constructions, cognitive processes such as selective memory, differential availability of information, and biased information processing may play an important role. According to Beck (1967, 1976), depressed individuals are characterized by faulty information processing. Depressive thinking is distorted in that they "selectively attend to the negative events when alternative positive events and interpretations are plausible, and greatly overgeneralize and magnify adversity while minimizing and misinterpreting positive information" (Hammen, 1997, p. 80). They seem to have a negative bias in the interpretation of stimuli that have implications for themselves, such as their performance, and a systematic bias against the self in which their inferences about events have predominantly negative implications for themselves (cf. Furnham & Brewin, 1988).

According to ISS theory, depressed individuals would not show all negative biases to a similar degree, but would in particular exhibit biases that are typical of a feeling of giving up and a de-escalating state of mind that would eventually foster acceptance of their defeat and loss in rank. There is indeed considerable evidence that depressed individuals interpret social comparison information in a less self-serving way than nondepressed individuals do, and especially that they tend to focus on the fact that others are better off than they are, thus confirming their loss in rank and low status. For example, Albright and Henderson (1995) gave depressed (≥ 9 on the BDI) and nondepressed (≤ 8 on the BDI) individuals information about how a target dealt with a negative life event. Each participant received an upward, lateral, or downward target that was constructed on the basis of the participant's own score. Self-ratings in comparison with the target were more unfavorable for depressed as compared with nondepressed individuals. Unlike the nondepressed, the depressed perceived the other as more positive than was objectively true. In a similar vein, Swallow and Kuiper (1993) expected that, after negative feedback, nondepressed individuals would, for reasons of self-protection, avoid upward comparison information, whereas such a self-protective mechanism would not operate as well among depressed individuals. To test this assumption, individuals did a task described as measuring a component of intelligence, after which they could choose from which of four performance categories (e.g., from the lowest 25%) they wanted to see a score. As predicted, after failure feedback, nondepressed individuals (scoring 1 *SD* below average on the CES–D) asked for downward comparison information, which would confirm a feeling of superiority, but depressed individuals (scoring 1 *SD* above average on the CES–D) asked for lateral comparison information.

Other studies employing various research paradigms have also provided support for the assumption that depressed individuals are particularly inclined to focus on the fact that others are better off. For example, McFarland and Miller (1994) found that when confronted with feedback about one's position in a performance distribution, individuals with a negative orientation (a combination of depression [BDI] and pessimism [LOT; Scheier & Carver, 1985]) focused on the number of persons who were better than they are, whereas individuals with a positive orientation focused on the proportion of others who were performing worse than one does. In a related vein, Ahrens (1991) gave participants feedback about the performance of one or two other bogus participants before they performed a spatial abilities task. Participants were told that either one person had a high score, that one person had a low score, or that one had a high score and the other had a low score. In this last condition, the judgments of dysphoric individuals (higher than 9 on the BDI) were similar to those given in the condition in which the other had performed better. However, nondepressed individuals (lower than 5 on the BDI) made judgments in the mixed condition as if they had received the information that the other had performed worse. Finally, a number of survey studies point in the same direction. In a sample of older adults, Heidrich and Ryff (1993, Study 2) found that, in addition to the number of health problems, only the frequency of upward comparisons, and not the frequency of downward comparisons, predicted depression, suggesting that depressed individuals compare more upward. Using an event-recording method, Wheeler and Miyake (1992) found that whereas respondents engaged in downward comparison when they felt happy, they engaged in upward comparison when they felt depressed, suggesting that feeling depressed seems to be accompanied by emphasizing one's inferiority compared to others.

To conclude, a variety of different types of studies suggest that depressed individuals interpret and recall information about their own standing in comparison to that of others in a less self-serving way than nondepressed individuals do. In particular, in line with ISS theory, depressed individuals appear more likely to interpret the same information as indicating that others are doing better than they are. They also seem, in general, to focus on the fact that others are doing better. Although there is little evidence that ineffective cognitive strategies in general predispose someone to depression (Hammen, 1997), from the perspective of ISS theory the evidence discussed so far seems to underline that particular forms of faulty information processing may be characteristic of individuals in a depressed state. That is, information processing that confirms one's defeat and low rank may be part of the ISS and may assist one in accepting one's low status compared to others and in preventing conflict with higher ranking others. Focusing on the fact that others have higher status may sustain feelings of hopelessness and helplessness, thereby blocking the intention to initiate competition with higher ranking persons.

NEED FOR SOCIAL COMPARISON INFORMATION

Findings concerning feelings of superiority in comparison to others and the interpretation of social comparison information, do not indicate how frequently individuals compare themselves in general with others in real life, or how strongly they are inclined to compare their own characteristics with those of others. Although such issues have occupied a central place in social comparison research, ISS theory does not make explicit assumptions about the relation between ISS and the need for comparison. Although animals suffering from ISS are generally vigilant (i.e., they watch out for possible attacks from other animals for reasons of self-defense), this does not automatically mean that they continuously compare their rank with other animals (Price et al., 1994; Sloman et al., 1994). One of the paradigms that seems quite relevant for depression was started by Schachter (1959), who based his research directly on Festinger's (1954) early formulation of social comparison theory. In his well-known studies

Schachter showed that fear due to the prospect of having to undergo an electric shock evoked in most individuals a desire to wait with someone else, preferably someone waiting for the same event, rather than someone in a different situation or someone who had already undergone the shock. As Schachter (1959) concluded, "Misery doesn't love just any kind of company, it loves only miserable company" (p. 24). Schachter tried to show that social comparison was a main motive behind this affiliative desire under threat. However, the findings from these studies have not gone unchallenged. Kulik and Mahler (1997) suggested that the evidence for a number of widely cited conclusions from Schachter's research is scarce. This is particularly true for Schachter's conclusion that there exists a predominant preference for affiliation with similar others under stress, and that the desire for cognitive clarity is a relatively unimportant motive for such preferences. In fact, unlike what Schachter (1959) would have predicted, various studies discussed by Kulik and Mahler suggest that individuals tend to prefer to affiliate with others who are likely to have the greatest information about the threat they face, such as those who have already experienced the stressor.

More support has been found for Schachter's (1959) prediction that, as social comparison theory predicts, especially individuals who are uncertain about their emotional state will engage in social comparison. Several experiments following Schachter's paradigm have shown that social comparison needs are aroused when individuals feel uncertain about how to feel and react (e.g., Gerard, 1963; Gerard & Rabbie, 1961) or when the source of their arousal is unknown (Mills & Mintz, 1972). Correlational studies have indicated that a variety of negative emotions, including frustration and anxiety among disabled individuals (Buunk, 1995) and emotional exhaustion among nurses (Buunk, Schaufeli, & Ybema, 1994), are related to the desire for social comparison information (i.e., the desire to learn more about how similar others feel and respond). More important, in these studies, uncertainty about these emotions seemed to enhance social comparison needs (cf. Buunk, 1994).

Various authors have suggested that depressed individuals are characterized not only by negative and deprecatory thoughts about the self, but also by a high degree of uncertainty regarding themselves and a tendency to focus attention on the self (e.g., Warren & Eachren, 1983; Weary, Elbin, & Hill, 1987). For instance, according to Ahrens and Alloy (1997) and Pyszczynski and Greenberg (1987), whereas nondepressed individuals cope with a negative event by distracting themselves, depressed individuals are more likely to cope with negative events by ruminating and thinking about their situation. Because of their uncertainty and concern about what others think about them, depressed individuals would, according to social comparison theory, be characterized by a heightened tendency to seek out social comparison information. There is indeed some, although not very strong, evidence from correlational studies that depressed individuals show a relatively higher frequency of social comparison. For example, Heidrich and Ryff (1993, Study 1) asked elderly women to indicate how often they engaged in comparisons with others. The higher the level of depression as assessed with the CES–D, the higher the frequency of comparisons was ($r = .35$). Gibbons and Buunk (1999) developed a scale to measure individual differences in social comparison orientation. The scale, validated in about 30 studies, correlated significantly, but rather low with depression: The correlations ranged from .13 for the BDI to .25 for the CES–D, although the correlations of social comparison orientation with self-esteem and particularly with neuroticism were stronger (cf. Van der Zee, Buunk, & Sanderman, 1998; Van der Zee, Oldersma, et al., 1998).

The results from experimental studies examining the desire of social comparison among depressed individuals are mixed. In line with the correlational studies, some studies suggest that, under certain conditions, depressed individuals have a higher tendency to compare themselves with others (see also Weary, Marsh, & McCormick, 1994). For example, Swallow and Kuiper (1992) gave participants feedback on a task that allegedly measured a component of intelligence. For high scorers on the task, information-seeking behavior was not related to depression. Among low scorers however, depressed individuals looked for information about others more than nondepressed individuals (see also Swallow & Kuiper, 1993). There is also more indirect evidence for a heightened interest in social comparison information among depressed individuals. Hildebrand-Saints and Weary (1989) found that more so than nondepressed individuals, depressed individuals who had to interview another individual asked more diagnostic questions even when these questions were of low direct utility (i.e., one would not have to answer questions about the interview, and thus would not need to learn more about the other). This might indicate that depressed individuals look for information about others primarily for self-evaluative reasons. In contrast, a number of experiments suggest that depression is associated by a relatively lower interest in social comparison information. Flett, Vredenburg, Pliner, and Krames (1987) based their expectation that the frequency of comparison would be lower among depressed persons on self-regulation theory (e.g., Carver & Scheier, 1981) that proposes that persons with negative outcome expectancies are inclined to avoid self-evaluative information, probably to avoid embarrassment or discomfort. Flett et al. gave female students an opportunity after an examination to look at the results of other students. Depressed participants (higher than 8 on the BDI) viewed fewer folders and spent less time looking at the folders than nondepressed participants (lower than 6 on the BDI). In the second study, depressed participants (male and female, higher than 15 on the depression subscale of the MAACL; Zuckerman & Lubin, 1965) also viewed fewer folders than nondepressed participants (lower than 16 on the MAACL), although this effect was only marginally significant. As in the first study, they spent less time looking at social comparison information.

How is it possible that depression is sometimes related to a higher and sometimes to a lower interest in social comparison? How can this be interpreted from in the context of ISS theory? First, the introversion and the often characteristic discomfort with social situations may make depressed individuals relatively uninterested in the responses of others (Hammen, 1997). More important, ISS theory would suggest that, unlike what is usually assumed in the literature on depression, depressed individuals are not necessarily characterized by uncertainty: They may know for sure that they face defeat and that they are low in status, making it relatively irrelevant to seek out social comparison information (which does not exclude that they will, when confronted with such information, look for signs confirming their low status). As social comparison theory would suggest, it may be that only when depression is accompanied by uncertainty is the interest in social comparison enhanced (cf. Buunk, 1994). Kuiper and MacDonald (1982) suggested that especially mild-depressive persons might experience heightened uncertainty in comparison with severely and nondepressed persons, and it is possible that mild depressives have a high interest, whereas nondepressives and severely depressives may have a low interest in social comparison information. Clinicians have found that depressed patients tend to exhibit two conflicting tendencies. One is a strong tendency to compare themselves too negatively with others, and the other is a compensatory tendency to compare themselves too favorably, which is unrealistic and leads to further failure. This finding could reconcile many seemingly contradictory findings in the literature.

Particularly relevant in the context here, in their self-worth contingency model, Kuiper and his colleagues (Kuiper, Olinger, MacDonald & Shaw, 1985; Swallow & Kuiper, 1990) argued that particularly depressives characterized by dysfunctional cognitions experience heightened uncertainty (e.g., MacDonald, Kuiper, & Olinger, 1985). Examples of such cognitions, originating from the Dysfunctional Attitude Scale (DAS; Oliver & Baumgart, 1985), are "If I fail partly, it is as bad as being a complete failure," and "My life is meaningless unless I am loved by everyone." According to Swallow (chap. 8, this volume), such beliefs may make individuals construe their social interactions in agonistic terms. If these contingencies are not met, self-worth is threatened and uncertainty about one's self-attributes increases, which may result in a concern about having, in terms of ISS theory, a low rank and status. Individuals high on the DAS have a particularly high degree of uncertainty about the self, as apparent from, for example, a longer rating time when they have to make adjective judgments about themselves. In line with this reasoning, in a scenario study in which participants were asked to imagine failure, average performance, or success, mildly depressed individuals high in dysfunctional cognitions were more interested in obtaining social comparison information (i.e., looking up the scores of other students) than mildly depressed persons low in dysfunctional cognitions and nondepressives high in dysfunctional cognitions (Swallow & Kuiper, 1990). In sum, research on the need for comparison among depressed persons suggests that ISS are not necessarily accompanied by a high need for comparison information. Depressed individuals who are certain about their low status will not feel a need to compare themselves constantly. As social comparison theory would suggest, the need for comparison may increase only when one experiences uncertainty about one's rank.

SOCIAL COMPARISON AS SEEKING OF INFORMATION ABOUT OTHERS THAT MAY ALLEVIATE ONE'S OWN UNFORTUNATE STATE

In the original Schachter (1959) studies, it was assumed that individuals facing a threat would prefer to be in the company of similar others to evaluate their own emotional state. However, Hakmiller (1966) was one of the first authors to emphasize that individuals engage in social comparison not only for reasons of self-evaluation, but also for reasons of self-enhancement; that is, with the purpose of feeling better about themselves. Hakmiller found that when individuals are threatened in a particular dimension they prefer to compare themselves with others who are thought to be worse off than themselves in that dimension, and thus try to assign themselves at least some symbolic status. The potential role of comparisons with others in a bad situation for individuals under threat was given a major impetus by Wills's (1981) integrative paper on downward social comparison theory. Wills argued that in situations that produce a decrease in well-being, individuals will often compare themselves with others who are thought to be worse off. Such comparisons, Wills assumed, assist individuals in improving their negative mood when problem-focused coping is not feasible. From an ISS theoretical point of view, given the low rank and status, and the hopelessness and helplessness that depressed individuals experience, they may look for evidence that others are still worse off.

As noted by Gibbons and Gerrard (1991), downward comparisons might not only enhance one's mood and well-being, but might also reduce a personal sense of deviance. Depressed persons often experience a profound sense of uniqueness or deviance (Coates & Peterson, 1982; Swallow & Kuiper, 1987), and social comparison with others who are experiencing some of the same difficulties may allow them to feel less abnormal or deviant. Realizing that there are others with similar or worse problems might, through a "shared stress" mechanism, help depressed individuals cope with their situation ("I'm not the only one with such problems"). This type of identification was already suggested by Schachter (1959), and it implies a feeling of relief that others are facing the same problems. Although Wills's (1981) theory is generally known as *downward comparison theory*, it emphasizes in fact that the knowledge that others are worse off than oneself, as well as the realization that others are in a similar bad situation as oneself, may alleviate one's lot. Individuals suffering from ISS may benefit from knowing that they are not the only ones who have low status. Low status is perhaps less aversive if one realizes that others are also low in status. In addition, low-status individuals might cooperate and offer each other support to cope with threats from high-ranking individuals. That is, low-status individuals may form alliances with each other (Buunk, 1995).

Although as we noted previously, depressed individuals seem to interpret social comparison information as confirming their low rank and status, there is also some evidence that depressed individuals at the same time appreciate information that others are at least as bad off as they are. In the first place, some research suggests that, unlike nondepressed individuals, depressed individuals feel better after interacting with other depressed individuals, and that the best friends of depressed individuals have higher levels of depression than best friends of nondepressed individuals (Rosenblatt & Greenberg, 1991). In the second place, DeVellis, Holt, Renner, and Blalock (1990) found in a study of arthritis patients that the higher the degree of negative affect, the more patients felt that information about other patients worse off, rather than better off, would be valuable and interesting to arthritis patients like themselves. Third, there is evidence that when confronted with an upward comparison (i.e., a happy person), depressed individuals tend to prefer to solicit negative information about that person (Wenzlaff & Beevers, 1998). Put differently, they try to find information that may indicate that the other person is not so happy after all.

More direct evidence among depressed individuals for the beneficial role of comparisons with others who are also experiencing distress comes from two studies by Gibbons (1986), who examined social comparison processes among depressed (higher than 10 on the BDI) and nondepressed (lower than 4 on the BDI) college students. In the first study, a negative mood was induced in participants by having them write a self-disclosure statement about either a positive or a negative event that had happened during the last year. Next, they were asked for their preferences for information from others. They would have to judge one statement of others who had participated previously in the experiment, grouped from 1 (*very negative*) to 7 (*very positive*). Depressed participants (but not nondepressed) indicated a preference for information from people who were experiencing negative affect, but only when they themselves were also experiencing relatively negative affect, not when their moods had been temporarily improved. In the second study, participants were first asked to describe some event that had had an impact on them. The confrontation with a negative event that had happened to another person (supposedly the story written by the other person in the experiment) improved the mood states of the depressed participants, but not of the nondepressed participants. Thus, depressed individuals seem indeed to derive some solace from the knowledge that others are at least as bad off as they are. This is in line with the evidence described earlier, that, as ISS theory would predict, depressed individuals show aggression toward lower ranking persons.

CONCLUSIONS

This chapter has reviewed the literature on social comparison processes among depressed individuals and has related this literature—as far as possible—to theorizing on ISS. As suggested in other chapters in this volume, social comparison has a long phylogeny, implying that individuals have wired-in mechanisms not only to assess their own rank in the group, but also to process information in such a way that a subjective sense of high status is maintained. According to ISS theory, depression can be viewed as a state of involuntary subordination, characterized by a sense of defeat, frustration, and hopelessness; a lack of challenging and exploratory behavior; and strategies signaling the acknowledgment of one's low status. Although few studies have been directly guided by this perspective, and despite all the problems concerning interpretation of the current literature, our preliminary review suggests that among depressed individuals social comparison mechanisms function in such a way that they reflect and confirm their relatively low status. Although depressed individuals do not perceive themselves on average as inferior to most others, they feel less superior to others than nondepressed individuals do, and they feel inferior to nondepressed individuals. Related to this, there is clear evidence that depressed individuals tend to interpret social comparison information in a less self-serving way than nondepressed individuals. That is, they are inclined to focus more on features of the information that confirm their sense of inferiority, their feeling of defeat, and their low status in the group. Nevertheless, individuals who are depressed are still characterized by a sense of perceived superiority toward other depressives and seem to derive support from the notion that others are worse off, which is in line with the assumption that ISS do not inhibit challenging behavior toward low-ranking individuals. Although there is little unequivocal evidence that depressed individuals are more or less inclined to engage in social comparison than nondepressed individuals, there is some evidence that, in line with social comparison theory, depressed individuals, particularly those who are uncertain about themselves, are open to social comparison information. Thus, depressed individuals seem inclined to seek out information about their rank only as long as it is not clear what their rank is. The fact that ISS alone do not enhance the need for comparison information is easy to understand, as ISS imply a defeat that does not have be assessed again. In general then, the findings reviewed in this chapter are compatible with the notion that depressed individuals are characterized by a subjective low status in their group and that they interpret information about others to confirm their low status. At the same time, adaptive mechanisms are still present among depressed individuals, as they seem to assume that they are better than other depressed individuals and seem to look for evidence that other individuals experience similar or even worse problems. Although research on social comparison and depression has become far removed from what Festinger (1954) was originally interested in, and although the literature on social comparison and depression is by no means consistent, this chapter hopefully contributes to stimulating research on the role of social comparison among depressed individuals from the perspective of ISS theory. Relating ISS to social comparison might not only help in understanding how depressed individuals interpret their social world, but also in expanding and elaborating current work on social comparison and well-being.

ACKNOWLEDGMENTS

The authors thank Pieternel Dijkstra and Diederik A. Stapel for their helpful comments on an earlier version of this chapter.

REFERENCES

Ahrens, A. H. (1991). Dysphoria and social comparison: Combining information regarding others' performances. *Journal of Social and Clinical Psychology, 10*(2), 190–205.

Ahrens, A. H., & Alloy, L. B. (1997). Social comparison processes in depression. In B. P. Buunk & F. X. Gibbons (Eds.), *Health, coping, and well-being: Perspectives from social comparison theory* (pp. 389–410). Mahwah, NJ: Lawrence Erlbaum Associates.

Albright, J. S., Alloy, L. B., Barch, D., & Dykman, B. M. (1993). Social comparison by dysphoric and nondysphoric college students: The grass isn't always greener on the other side. *Cognitive Therapy and Research, 17*(6), 485–509.

Albright, J. S., & Henderson, M. C. (1995). How real is depressive realism? A question of scales and standards. *Cognitive Therapy and Research, 19*(5), 589–609

Alicke, M. D., Klotz, M. L., Breitenbecher, D. L., & Yurak, T. J. (1995). Personal contact, individuation, and the better-than-average effect. *Journal of Personality and Social Psychology, 68*(5), 804–825.

Allan, S., & Gilbert, P. (1995). A social comparison scale: Psychometric properties and relationship to psychopathology. *Personality and Individual Differences, 19*(3), 293–299.

Alloy, L. B., & Ahrens, A. H. (1987). Depression and pessimism for the future: Biased use of statistically relevant information in predictions for self versus others. *Journal of Personality and Social Psychology, 52*(2), 366–378.

Barkow, J. H. (1989). *Darwin, sex, and status: Biological approaches to mind and culture.* Toronto: University of Toronto Press.

Beck, A. T. (1967). A study of problem solving by Gibbons. *Behaviour, 28*(1–2), 95–109.

Beck, A. T. (1976). *Depression: Clinical, experimental, and theoretical aspects.* New York: International Universities Press.

Beck, A. T., Ward, C. H., Mendelson, M., Mock, J., & Erlbaugh, J. (1961). An inventory for measuring depression. *Archives of General Psychiatry, 4,* 561–571.

Buunk, B. P. (1994). Social comparison processes under stress: Towards an integration of classic and recent perspectives. In M. Hewstone & W. Stroebe (Eds.), *European review of social psychology* (Vol. 5, pp. 211–241). Chichester, UK: Wiley.

Buunk, B. P. (1995). Comparison direction and comparison dimension among disabled individuals: Towards a refined conceptualization of social comparison under stress. *Personality and Social Psychology Bulletin, 21*(4), 316–330.

Buunk, B. P. (1998). Social comparison and optimism about one's relational future: Order effects in social judgment. *European Journal of Social Psychology, 28*(5), 777–786.

Buunk, B. P., & Gibbons, F. X. (Eds.). (1997). *Health, coping, and well-being: Perspectives from social comparison theory.* Mahwah, NJ: Lawrence Erlbaum Associates.

Buunk, B. P., & Janssen, P. P. M. (1992). Relative deprivation, and mental health among men in midlife. *Journal of Vocational Behavior, 40*(3), 338–350.

Buunk, B. P., Schaufeli, W. B., & Ybema, J. F. (1994). Burnout, uncertainty, and the desire for social comparison among nurses. *Journal of Applied Social Psychology, 24*(19), 1701–1718.

Buunk, B. P., & Ybema, J. F. (1997). Social comparisons and occupational stress: The identification-contrast model. In B. P. Buunk & F. X. Gibbons (Eds.), *Health, coping, and well-being: Perspectives from social comparison theory* (pp. 359–388). Hillsdale, NJ: Lawrence Erlbaum Associates.

Carver, C. S., & Scheier, M. F. (1981). *Attention and self-regulation: A control-theory approach to human behaviour.* New York: Springer-Verlag.

Coates, D., & Peterson, B. A. (1982). Depression and deviance. In G. Weary & H. L. Mirels (Eds.), *Integrations of clinical and social psychology* (pp. 154–170). New York: Oxford University Press.

DeVellis, R. F., Holt, K., Renner, B. R., & Blalock, S. J. (1990). The relationship of social comparison to rheumatoid arthritis symptoms and affect. *Basic and Applied Social Psychology, 11*(1), 1–18.

Festinger, L. (1954). A theory of social comparison processes. *Human Relations, 7,* 117–140.

Flett, G. L., Vredenburg, K., Pliner, P., & Krames, L. (1987). Depression and social comparison information-seeking. *Journal of Social Behaviour and Personality, 2*(4), 473–484.

Furnham, A., & Brewin, C. R. (1988). Social comparison and depression. *Journal of Genetic Psychology, 149*(2), 191–198.

Gerard, H. B. (1963). Emotional uncertainty and social comparison. *Journal of Abnormal and Social Psychology, 66*(6), 568–573.

Gerard, H. B., & Rabbie, J. M. (1961). Fear and social comparison. *Journal of Abnormal and Social Psychology, 62,* 586–592.

Gibbons, F. X. (1986). Social comparison and depression: Company's effect on misery. *Journal of Personality and Social Psychology, 51*(1), 140–148.

Gibbons, F. X., & Buunk, B. P. (1999). Individual differences in social comparison: The development of a scale of social comparison orientation. *Journal of Personality and Social Psychology, 76,* 129–142.

Gibbons, F. X., & Gerrard, M. (1991). Downward comparison and coping with threat. In J. Suls & T. A. Wills (Eds.), *Social comparison: Contemporary theory and research* (pp. 317–345). Hillsdale, NJ: Lawrence Erlbaum Associates.

Gilbert, P. (1990). Changes: Rank, status and mood. In S. Fisher & C. L. Cooper (Eds.), *On the move: The psychology of change and transition* (pp. 33–52). Chichester, UK: Wiley.

Gilbert, P., & Allan, S. (1998). The role of defeat and entrapment (arrested flight) in depression: An exploration of an evolutionary view. *Psychological Medicine, 28,* 584–597.

Gilbert, P., Price, J., & Allan, S. (1995). Social comparison, social attractiveness and evolution: How might they be related? *New Ideas in Psychology, 13*(2), 149–165.

Goethals, G. R., Messick, D. M., & Allison, S. T. (1991). The uniqueness bias: Studies of constructive social comparison. In J. Suls & T. A. Wills (Eds.), *Social comparison research: Contemporary theory and research* (pp. 149–176). Hillsdale, NJ: Lawrence Erlbaum Associates.

Hakmiller, K. L. (1966). Threat as a determinant of downward comparison. *Journal of Experimental Social Psychology, 2*(Suppl. 1), 32–39.

Hammen, C. (1997). *Depression.* Hove, UK: Psychology Press.

Headey, B., & Wearing, A. (1988). The sense of relative superiority—Central to well-being. *Social Indicators Research, 20*(5), 497–516.

Heidrich, S. M., & Ryff, C. D. (1993). The role of social comparisons processes in the psychological adaptation of elderly adults. *Journals of Gerontology, 48*(3), 127–136.

Hildebrand-Saints, L., & Weary, G. (1989). Depression and social information gathering. *Personality and Social Psychology Bulletin, 15*(2), 150–160.

Hoorens, V. (1993). Self-enhancement and superiority biases in social comparison. In W. Stroebe & M. Hewstone (Eds.), *European review of social psychology* (Vol. 4, pp. 113–139). Chichester, UK: Wiley.

Hyman, H. (1942). The psychology of status. *Archives of Psychology,* No. 269, 94.

Kuiper, N. A., & MacDonald, M. R. (1982). Self and other perception in mild depressives. *Social Cognition, 1*(3), 223–239.

Kuiper, N. A., Olinger, L. J., MacDonald, M. R., & Shaw, B. F. (1985). Self-schema processing of depressed and nondepressed content: The effects of vulnerability to depression. *Social Cognition, 3*(1), 77–93.

Kulik, J. A., & Mahler, H. I. M. (1997). Social comparison, affiliation, and coping with acute medical threats. In B. P. Buunk & F. X. Gibbons (Eds.), *Health, coping, and well-being: Perspectives from social comparison theory* (pp. 227–261). Mahwah, NJ: Lawrence Erlbaum Associates.

MacDonald, M. R., Kuiper, N. A., & Olinger, L. J. (1985). Vulnerability to depression, mild depression, and degree of self-schema consolidation. *Motivation and Emotion, 9*(4), 369–379.

McFarland, C., & Miller, D. T. (1994). The framing of relative performance feedback: Seeing the glass as half empty or half full. *Journal of Personality and Social Psychology, 66*(6), 1061–1073.

Mettee, D. R., & Smith, G. (1977). Social comparison and interpersonal attraction: The case for dissimilarity. In J. M. Suls & R. L. Miller (Eds.), *Social comparison processes: Theoretical and empirical perspectives* (pp. 69–102). Washington, DC: Hemisphere.

Meyer, H. H. (1980). Self-appraisal of job performance. *Personnel Psychology, 33*(2), 291–295.

Mills, J., & Mintz, P. M. (1972). Effect of unexplained arousal on affiliation. *Journal of Personality and Social Psychology, 24*(1), 11–13.

Oliver, J. M., & Baumgart, E. P. (1985). The Dysfunctional Attitude Scale: Psychometric properties and relation to depression in an unselected adult population. *Cognitive Therapy and Research, 9*(2), 161–167.

Price, J., Sloman, L., Gardner, R., Gilbert, P., & Rohde, P. (1994). The social competition model of depression. *British Journal of Psychiatry, 164,* 309–315.

Pyszczynski, T., & Greenberg, J. (1987). Depression, self-focused attention, and self-regulatory perseveration. In C. R. Snyder & C. E. Ford (Eds.), *Coping with negative life events: Clinical and social psychological perspectives* (pp. 105–129). New York: Plenum.

Radloff, L. S. (1977). The CES–D Scale: A self-report depression scale for research in the general population. *Applied Psychological Measurement, 1*(3), 385–401.

Rosenblatt, A., & Greenberg, J. (1991). Examining the world of the depressed: Do depressed people prefer others who are depressed? *Journal of Personality and Social Psychology, 60*(4), 620–629.

Schachter, S. (1959). *The psychology of affiliation.* Palo Alto, CA: Stanford University Press.

Scheier, M. F., & Carver, C. S. (1985). Optimism, coping, and health: Assessment and implications of generalized outcome expectancies. *Health Psychology, 4,* 219–247.

Sloman, L., Price, J., Gilbert, P., & Gardner, R. (1994). Adaptive function of depression: Psychotherapeutic implications. *American Journal of Psychotherapy, 48*(3), 401–416.

Suls, J. M., & Wills, T. A. (Eds.) (1991). *Social comparison: Contemporary theory and research.* Hillsdale, NJ: Lawrence Erlbaum Associates.

Swallow, S. R., & Kuiper, N. A. (1987). The effects of depression and cognitive vulnerability to depression on judgments of similarity between self and other. *Motivation and Emotion, 11*(2), 157–167.

Swallow, S. R., & Kuiper, N. A. (1990). Mild depression, dysfunctional cognitions, and interest in social comparison information. *Journal of Social and Clinical Psychology, 9*(3), 289–302.

Swallow, S. R., & Kuiper, N. A. (1992). Mild depression and frequency of social comparison behaviour. *Journal of Social and Clinical Psychology, 11*(2), 167–180.

Swallow, S. R., & Kuiper, N. A. (1993). Social comparison in dysphoria and nondysphoria: Differences in target similarity and specificity. *Cognitive Therapy and Research, 17*(2), 103–122.

Tabachnik, N., Crocker, J., & Alloy, L. B. (1983). Depression, social comparison, and the false consensus effect. *Journal of Personality and Social Psychology, 45*(3), 688–699.

Taylor, S. E., & Brown, J. D. (1988). Illusion and well-being: Social psychological perspective on mental health. *Psychological Bulletin, 103*(2), 193–210.

Van der Zee, K., Buunk, B. P., & Sanderman, R. (1998). Neuroticism and reactions to social comparison information among cancer patients. *Journal of Personality, 66*(2), 175–194.

Van der Zee, K., Oldersma, F., Buunk, B. P., & Bos, D. (1998). Social comparison preferences among cancer patients as related to neuroticism and social comparison orientation. *Journal of Personality and Social Psychology, 75*(3), 801–810.

Warren, L. W., & McEachren, L. (1983). Psychological correlates of depressive symptomatology in adult women. *Journal of Abnormal Psychology, 92*(2), 151–160.

Weary, G., & Edwards, J. A. (1994). Social cognition and clinical psychology: Anxiety, depression, and the processing of social information. In R. S. Wyer, Jr., & T. K. Srull (Eds.), *Handbook of social cognition, Vol. 1: Basic processes; Vol. 2: Applications (2nd ed.)* (Vol. 2, pp. 289–338). Hillsdale, NJ: Lawrence Erlbaum Associates.

Weary, G., Elbin, S., & Hill, M. G. (1987). Attributional and social comparison processes in depression. *Journal of Personality and Social Psychology, 52*(3), 605–610.

Weary, G., Marsh, K. L., & McCormick, L. (1994). Depression and social comparison motives. *European Journal of Social Psychology, 24*(1), 117–129.

Wenzlaff, R. M., & Beevers, C. G. (1998). Depression and interpersonal responses to others' moods: The solicitation of negative information about happy people. *Personality and Social Psychology Bulletin, 24*(4), 386–398.

Wheeler, L., & Miyake, K., (1992). Social comparison in everyday life. *Journal of Personality and Social Psychology, 62*(5), 760–773.

Wills, T. A. (1981). Downward comparison principles in social psychology. *Psychological Bulletin, 90*(2), 245–271.

Zuckerman, M., & Lubin, B. (1965). *Manual for the Multiple Affect Adjective Checklist.* San Diego, CA: Educational and Industrial Testing Service.

CHAPTER SEVEN

Subordination, Self-Esteem, and Depression

JOHN PRICE

Self-esteem is a complex subject with an enormous literature (Andrews, 1998; Wells & Marwell, 1976), but one surprising and important fact stands out clearly: People tend to give themselves a global rating on a self-concept scale that expresses self-worth and value. Ever since Maslow (1940/1973) first revealed the enormous variation of different people's self-rating, investigators have confirmed again and again that people make overall ratings of themselves and these tend to remain fairly constant during adult life.

In this chapter I do not review the details of self-esteem such as the difference between "core" self-esteem and other self-concepts, or the fragility (or otherwise) of self-esteem (see Andrews, 1998). Nor do I offer a review of the social psychological literature on the relation of social comparison and self-esteem (see Suls & Wills, 1991). Rather, I develop an evolutionary model that emphasizes the importance of adaptive strategies and their evolutionary change during the course of human phylogeny. In particular, I argue that self-esteem derives from a phylogenetically ancient agonistic strategy set that contains the alternative strategies of escalation (fight) and de-escalation (flight and submission; Archer & Huntingford, 1994; Price, 1998).

Human self-esteem is of pivotal relevance to workers in the mental health field, because people with low self-esteem appear to be predisposed to most psychiatric disorders, particularly to depressive disorders and anxiety states (Robson, 1988). Four questions emerge about the role of self-esteem in phylogenetic adaptation:

- Why do people have an urge to compare themselves with others and form an opinion of their relative worth?

- Why is there such wide individual variation in self-esteem, so that some have the sense of being lords of creation whereas others feel apologetic for their very existence?
- Why do we make a global rating of ourselves and others, rather than respecting different qualities in different people?
- Why is there such a close linkage between self-esteem and moods of elation and depression?

It is argued that these questions can be answered by postulating that human self-esteem evolved out of a reptilian precursor, whose organization in the reptilian brain was laid down at a time when the only interaction between members of the same sex was agonistic behavior.

THE SELF AS A GLADIATOR

To account for the evolution of agonistic behavior strategies, behavioral ecologists introduced the term *resource-holding potential* (RHP), a measure of fighting capacity that predicts the outcome or potential outcome of an agonistic encounter (Hack, 1997; Krebs & Davies, 1993; Parker, 1974, 1984). RHP has the scientific status of an intervening variable or hypothetical construct; that is, it is like a black box, the contents of which cannot be measured directly. It is defined by its input and output. On the input side go all those influences that contribute to fighting capacity (or lack of it) like previous successes or failures in combat, size, strength, skill, weaponry, and the availability of allies. On the output side, there is the probability of attack (rather than withdrawal) in an agonistic encounter; and there is a display of RHP that is directed to the world in general and consists of such things as confident or diffident bearing, upright or slouched posture, and measured or furtive gait.

When entering an agonistic encounter, contestants want to win, but, on the other hand, they do not want to risk injury by fighting a more powerful adversary. They have therefore evolved the capacity for comparing their own RHP with that of a rival (Dixon, 1998; Price, 1988). This is not an easy comparison, because they cannot just put the two RHPs next to each other as they might do when comparing the colors of two fabrics. They have to compare their own estimate of their own RHP, derived from a number of sources, with what they can see of the display of RHP of the rival, discounting any possible bluff the rival may be putting on. This is a complex calculation, and it is not surprising that we have developed the concept of *global RHP* so that we can compare our own global RHP with that of a rival. If two rivals both estimate that their global RHP is as good or better than the rival's, they fight and enter on an increasingly intense escalation of fighting methods until one of the combatants is driven to accept that his or her RHP is less than that of the rival, and then he or she submits. In doing so, they could be said to adopt a yielding subroutine or involuntary subordinate strategy (Price, Sloman, Gardner, Gilbert, & Rohde, 1994/1997) in which their RHP is reduced further, so that the disparity between the former rivals is increased and the chance of further fighting is reduced.

In calculating relative RHP, it is likely that a verdict of *favorable* or *unfavorable* is made—favorable meaning that one's own RHP seems higher, unfavorable meaning that the other person's RHP seems higher. If one decides on favorable relative RHP, one attacks; if one decides on unfavorable relative RHP, one backs off. It clearly benefits both parties if an agreed decision about relative RHP can be made as soon as possible. Then time is not wasted fighting. Therefore we can expect adult animals to be very good at assessing relative RHP, so that the proportion of encounters in which both parties make an initial assessment of favorable relative RHP is reduced to a minimum. This is the same as saying that there should be a wide range of variation in RHP in any population. Ethological studies indicate that in social animals RHP is determined in adolescence, for instance during the rough-and-tumble play and mock fighting of adolescent baboons, which ensures that by the time their lethal canine teeth have erupted, few doubtful cases of relative RHP between members of the same group remain to be determined. This fits with clinical observations on humans that the adolescent peer group is the last major formative influence on self-esteem.

THE PHYLOGENY OF SELF-ESTEEM

RHP

It is likely that the RHP system is deeply embedded in our brains, having been with us since the time of the common human and reptilian ancestor some 250 million years ago (MacLean, 1990). That is why we compare ourselves with each other, having an innate need to make an estimation of relative RHP in all social encounters and to refine our own RHP discriminating capacity. Because the need to calculate relative RHP rapidly has been with us so long, we now have a tendency to use the global rating of self-esteem, even though, in present times, the advantage of doing so is minimal.

The reason for the evolution of variation in RHP has been revealed by the analysis of fighting strategies by evolutionary game theory (Parker, 1984). The payoff for a "hawk" or escalating strategy is high, if the rest of the population are "doves" and de-escalate (give in) when confronted, but the hawk strategy becomes increasingly less advantageous, and the dove strategy correspondingly more advantageous, as the proportion of hawks in the population rises (the hawks all escalate their fights and kill each other off). This is called *negative frequency-dependent selection* (a phenotype becomes less fit as its frequency rises) and, along with balanced polymorphism, it is an important means of maintaining genetic variation in populations. Moreover, the choice of hawk or dove strategy may be phenotype dependent in what is called the assessor strategy and then a comparison of relative RHP may settle the issue without the need for fighting (Parker, 1974). Also, it seems likely that human groups function more efficiently if there is a wide variation of RHP between members, allowing an uncontested distribution of leader and follower roles, and because humans cannot exist except in groups, a human completely lacking the capacity for developing both high and low RHP would have impaired fitness.

These rules concerning RHP management may be relics of our reptilian past, but they are still with us. However, there have been a lot of changes during subsequent evolution. One is the change from agonistic to prestige competition (Barkow, 1975, 1991) and the effect this has had on our self-concept, partly replacing the self-concept of RHP with that of *social attention-holding potential* (SAHP; Gilbert, Price, & Allan, 1995; Stevens & Price, 1996). Another is the development of signals that raise and lower the RHP and SAHP of the recipient (Price, 1998)—a type of signal that has been enormously facilitated by the development of language, and that therefore has become a particularly human type of signal. In the rest of this chapter I hope to show how these changes have influenced the transition from reptilian RHP to human self-esteem. Following that, I explore how self-esteem develops in the human being.

SAHP

During the course of mammalian evolution, with the development of parental behavior, pair bonding, and alliances, the RHP mechanisms of the human brain became modified by the new structures subserving affiliation so that self-esteem came to have a much wider base than fighting capacity.

An important change was the switch, albeit incomplete, from agonistic competition to prestige competition. Instead of intimidating rivals, individuals began to compete for the approbation of significant others and even the group as a whole. The old self-concern about how powerful I am, who can I beat in combat, and so on, changed to worries about how attractive I am, who will listen to me if I stand up and speak, who will vote for me if I stand for office, and, in general, concerns about how much others are prepared to invest in that individual. Gilbert (1989) named the self-concept that arises from these concerns SAHP. Like RHP it is a black box, defined by its input and output. The input to SAHP is the perception of approbation or disapprobation by fellow group members, especially high-ranking and prestigious members. The output, as with RHP, is partly in a general bearing of confidence as opposed to diffidence, and partly in decisions between self-assertion and self-effacement on social occasions.

However, this new self-concept of SAHP is still connected to the underlying reptilian complex and is subject to the mechanisms that generate variation and ensure globality. In fact one needs a global SAHP just as much as one needs a global RHP. If you have to decide suddenly whether to intervene in a debate, you have to make a snap decision, and there is no time for a careful weighing of your good and bad qualities. Likewise, variation is needed, so that social occasions are dominated by a few leaders who have high prestige (the systemic correlate of SAHP) and are not swamped by attempts to speak by every member of the group.

Mate Value

In many animals, the attractiveness of a male to a female depends on his social rank or the quality of his territory, so there is no need for a self-concept defining sexual attractiveness apart from the sexual implications of RHP. Likewise, the attraction of a female for a male depends on her stage in the sexual cycle, and this is a state variable and not a trait variable.

In humans, however, there is no doubt that the concept of mate value is important in determining both sexual and nonsexual behavior (Buss & Schmitt, 1993) and that there is assortative mating for mate value (Sloman & Sloman, 1988). Males attribute mate value to females, and if their own mate value is high, they tend to court a female of high mate value, and vice versa. A female with high mate value is more likely to reject male suitors with low mate value. Females go to great lengths to emphasize, and even falsify, their mate value. It has been suggested that the pursuit of high mate value underlies the behavior of patients with anorexia nervosa (Abed, 1998). Possibly the same applies to extremes of body-building behavior in men.

We do not know how the variables of RHP, SAHP, and mate value combine in the brain and join with other self-concepts to form human self-esteem. However, we do know that in human depressive states all forms of self-rating are lowered, and this reflects the pervasiveness of depressed mood.

SOURCES OF SELF-ESTEEM (ONTOGENY)

Direct Comparison

We still compare ourselves directly with others (Swallow & Kuiper, 1988) in the way that animals compare RHP. We look to see whether we are bigger, more beautiful, more elegant, better connected, or whatever, and if we find we are, our esteem is boosted. If we find the comparison is unfavorable to us, our self-esteem is lowered. Of course, we can control this process to some extent, by deciding with whom we will compare ourselves—much work has been done on the causes of upward comparison and downward comparison (Buunk & Brenninkmeyer, chap. 6, this volume; Tennen & Affleck, 1993).

Another motive for direct comparison with others is to determine whether we are the same—are we wearing the same uniform, speaking with the same accent, justifying the same opinions? This type of comparison is concerned with group membership, and differs from competitive comparison that is concerned with relative rank within the group (Gilbert et al., 1995).

Achievement of Success

In some people the comparison is mainly an internal one, between their actual selves and their ideal selves—the selves they know they could or should be, derived from parental expectations; instructions received on how to behave; and the values of heroic figures from real life, biography, and fiction. This concept resembles the idea that low self-esteem is a function of the gap between level of aspiration and performance, as expressed over a century ago by James's (1890) formula:

$$\text{self-esteem} = \frac{\text{successes}}{\text{pretensions}}$$

The result of success or failure has been shown to be affected by attributional style, so that people who attribute success to their own efforts and failure to bad luck or other external causes are likely to gain more in self-esteem than those who make the reverse attributions (Tennen & Affleck, 1993). And, as James pointed out, it is success and failure in areas that are important to that individual that really count; James would be unaffected by failure in a test of Greek language, but he would be very sensitive to any question of his competence in psychology.

People who base their self-esteem on their mastery of their environment, whether physical or social, were called *autonomous* types by Beck (1987). To the extent that depression is due to a loss of self-esteem, they are vulnerable to depression in any situation in which they fail in their own eyes.

Mirroring by Others

Self-esteem may be conferred on the individual by others, with signals of submission, attention, respect, approval, praise, affection, and love (or the reverse). Each person sees his or her value mirrored in the eyes of society. This source of self-esteem was emphasized by Cooley (1902) and Mead (1934/1961), leading figures of the Chicago pragmatists at the turn of the century, at the same time that James was emphasizing the importance of individual achievement.

Mirroring starts in early childhood. Freud was not exaggerating when he wrote, "A man who has been the indisputable favourite of his mother keeps for life the feeling of a conqueror" (Whybrow, Akiskal, & McKinney, 1984, p. 82). Everyone is familiar with the sight of parents and other adults surrounding a small child and cheering, clapping, and screaming with delight when the child surmounts some little obstacle in his or her path. Parents are highly motivated to make their children feel good about themselves. As Kohut put it, they are mirroring the child's "grandiose self" (Siegel, 1996). Other children, however, are made by their parents to feel that they are worthless and bad, and even that their very existence has been a terrible mistake. Reports like this are common from patients seen in a psychiatric clinic. From the beginning of life, therefore, there is likely to be a wide variation in self-esteem, depending on the message given to the child. It is difficult not to conclude that parents are deliberately (but not consciously) inculcating either a high self-esteem strategy or a low self-esteem strategy in their children, and sometimes hedging their bets by treating their children differently (Price et al., 1994/1997).

Another sensitive period for the formation of self-esteem is adolescence. In this case it is not the parents but the peers who mirror the individual. In fact, by adolescence, parents seem to have largely lost the capacity to boost their children or put them down. In the clinic we see many patients with lifelong low self-esteem who have had a bad experience in adolescence. Some are rejected by their peers because they are fat or ugly or clumsy; others have bad luck because they have moved into a strange peer group at the wrong time. By the end of adolescence, self-esteem seems to solidify and become very much less open to influence, for good or ill. Adult changes in self-esteem (other than those due to mood change) are usually accompanied by major changes in work or marital situation.

The majority of patients seen in the psychiatric clinic suffer from low self-esteem, and the majority of these answer "no" to one of the following two questions:

1. Did you feel loved and valued by your parents in early childhood?
2. Did you feel accepted and valued by your adolescent peer group?

Some patients answer *no* to both questions, and, indeed, it seems likely that those who enter adolescence with low self-esteem induced by their parents are likely to find it more difficult to be accepted by the peer group.

Psychotherapy often sets out to give the patient a corrective emotional experience, aimed at supplying something the patient missed out on during development (Knobloch & Knobloch, 1979).

It seems likely that individual psychodynamic psychotherapy can compensate for a lack of positive mirroring from the parent during early childhood and that group therapy can compensate for the lack of acceptance by the peer group during adolescence.

Self-Esteem Based on Group Membership

In some cultures self-esteem is based largely on membership of family, social group, tribe, or nation. Initiation rites are designed to break down individual self-esteem and replace it with self-esteem based on group membership. Families vary enormously in the self-esteem they offer to members; many psychiatric patients have a negative view of their family of origin, whereas for others the family is a source of great, even excessive pride.

At the highest level, self-esteem depends on meaning, on whether the individual can see himself or herself in a comprehensible and satisfactory relationship with the rest of the universe.

Signals That Affect Self-Esteem

We have seen, I hope, that the idea of animal RHP can throw light on human self-esteem. Working in the other direction, the mechanisms of human self-esteem may throw some light on animal RHP. I have already noted that one of the sources of self-esteem is mirroring by other people. This involves the use of signals, which do not alter fighting capacity, except to the extent that a more confident individual fights better. If someone keeps receiving the message, "You are a horrible person," he or she is likely to feel bad and "put down." Likewise, if he or she keeps getting the message, "You are a wonderful person," he or she is likely to feel boosted and good. This means that we can classify signals (or messages, or communications) into those that raise the self-esteem of the recipient (boosting signals), those that lower it (putting-down signals), and those that do not affect the self-esteem of the recipient (Price, 1992).

If we go back to animals, we can now classify as putting-down signals all those elements of agonistic behavior associated with threat, attack, and escalation. After all, the purpose of fighting is to prove that your RHP is higher than your rival's. But here we are forced to make a condition. Fighting, or mutual RHP management, is all about the breaking of symmetry (Kortmulder, 1998), and if there is no breaking of symmetry, then there is no change in the RHP of either contestant. Therefore, we must restrict our definition of putting-down signals: They are those that lower RHP if they are not returned in full measure—that is, those that result in asymmetry. What is lowering to RHP is not to be able to return the blows or insults of the other person. If a blow is returned, the emotion felt is that of anger; if a blow is not returned, the emotion felt is that of being chastened, and this subjective feeling of being chastened is the emotional correlate of a drop in RHP.

Animals that are defeated make submissive signals to the winner. It seems likely that these are the earliest, most primitive form of boosting signals, the receipt of which raises the RHP of the winner. The message of a submissive signal is, "You are more powerful than me," which is probably as near to "You are wonderful" as an animal without language can get. Perhaps RHP is also raised by the experience of delivering a blow to the rival that is not returned.

McGuire and his colleagues showed that the receipt of submissive signals is associated with a rise in blood serotonin (McGuire & Troisi, 1998). It is likely, therefore, that all boosting signals have this effect. The receipt of putting down signals seems to be associated with rises in catecholamines or corticosteroids, depending on the circumstances.

Boosting and Putting-Down Signals in the Hedonic Mode

The evolution of prestige competition has seen the evolution of new types of boosting and putting-down signals. Approbation, praise, adulation, and all signals of both individual and group approval serve to raise self-esteem, and probably they evolved out of animal submissive signals. Now, however, they no longer express a difference in RHP and SAHP between sender and receiver: They are no longer comparisons; they are evaluations of the receiver, sometimes as an individual in an absolute sense (as in a book review), sometimes of the individual compared to another individual (as in voting at elections). However, they are not comparisons of the evaluator and the person evaluated. Likewise, putting-down signals probably evolved out of animal threat signals, but now they take the form of group disapprobation and they do not imply an agonistic relation between the sender and receiver. Along with these signals has evolved the role of evaluator, so that each group member is an evaluator of every other group member.

Self-Esteem and Depression. There is a two-way recursive interaction between self-esteem and depression. Part of the depressive response consists of a lowering of self-esteem. Yet lowering of self-esteem can trigger an episode of depression. Moreover, people with low (and labile) self-esteem are more vulnerable to depression (Brown, Andrews, Harris, Adler, & Bridge, 1986). Mood change can be seen as a self-esteem management mechanism, moderating self-esteem to fit with current social circumstances.

If times are adverse, depression lowers self-esteem, and the individual takes a less prominent role in social interaction; but if things are going well, elation helps the individual to cope with the increased social demands of high rank. In fact mood change is the only rapid method of changing self-esteem after adolescence is completed. Self-esteem can be changed by prolonged intensive therapy or by life experience, but often one sees patients who lead very successful lives but are still encumbered with low self-esteem consolidated in childhood and adolescence. Change by life experience is like going up the stairs of a skyscraper, whereas mood change is like using the elevator.

Self-Esteem and Subordination. In egalitarian societies like that of the Kalahari Bushmen, the value of global self-esteem and wide variation in self-esteem is less than in hierarchical societies. As James pointed out, self-esteem depends on successes, but this only applies in societies in which success is admired. When conspicuous success is treated with disapprobation, as with the Bushmen, there are likely to be less people who think themselves better than everyone else. A culture of counterdominance prevails, and anyone who rises too high is brought down a peg by group response (Boehm, 1993). The atmosphere of counterdominance is vividly portrayed in the first act of Shakespeare's *Julius Caesar.*

It is in hierarchical societies that low self-esteem and depression come into their own. Some people are doomed to eternal subordination, and they can adapt to this at more than one level of the triune mind and brain (MacLean, 1990). They can become humble, and have genuine admiration for those fortunate enough to be at the top of the pecking order, or they can become depressed, dysthymic personalities, whose depression takes away their power to alter their situation. In dysthymic personality it is assertive (competitive) and sexual initiative that is inhibited, whereas the ability to carry out instructions is relatively unimpaired (Akiskal, 1990).

Regardless of the lifelong strategy of high or low self-esteem, social circumstances may change, and there may be a need for a formerly high-ranking individual to adapt to low rank. This is where an episode of major depression is adaptive. Depression lowers self-esteem so that the individual falling in rank is accommodated to his or her reduced circumstances. Depression also lowers resource value or the importance one attaches to things, so that the loss of the trappings of former high rank will give less incentive to regain them. Depression lowers the sense of ownership, so that the loss of resources and territory will not arouse indignation. In particular, severe depression alters thinking about former status in such a way that high former wealth or position is denied, even to a delusional degree, so that the motivation to regain former rank is reduced. All these changes help to alter and readjust the individual who is accustomed to command, and to accommodate him or her to a subordinate role in which he or she has to obey orders (Gardner & Price, 1999). Thus, the individual avoids group ostracism and helps to ensure group cohesion (Leary & Downs, 1995). The homeostasis of the group is achieved at the expense of mood change in the individual.

In the case of the individual who rises in rank, these changes occur in the reverse direction. If his or her rise in rank is not sanctioned by the social group, he or she is likely to be regarded as suffering from hypomania (Gardner & Price, 1999). In the case of the subordinate individual who gets even more depressed, we can usually detect an element of failed rebellion. Sometimes extra demands for subordination are made, and for a time the victims rebel until their additional depression (called *double depression*) reconciles them to these even harsher indignities. We see this in a wife who is married to a cruel tyrant, and in the employee who is bullied by a boss he or she does not respect. These cases are difficult to treat because the depression is serving the function of inhibiting rebellion, and to cure the depression without altering the overall social situation is likely to lead to yet another failed rebellion and a recurrence of depression.

Why Have a Self-Concept at All? A quantified self-concept is necessary for what has been called a phenotype-dependent strategy set (Parker, 1982). This is a choice, between two or more possible strategies, that depends on some quality of the individual making the decision. For instance, a male monkey trying to decide whether or not to attack a harem owner, with a view to taking over his females, has to have some idea of whether he is a good fighter. Likewise, a young adult male chimpanzee may wish to proposition an estrus female of the group; in so doing, he risks being attacked by a more dominant male, and so he needs to know whether the female is likely to accept his proposition; that is, he should know his own mate value.

Phenotype-Independent Strategy Sets

Apart from competing and mating, individual properties are not important in decision making. Take foraging, for example. In deciding whether to hunt or to gather, or where to go to find fruits, the relevant information concerns the condition of the environment and not the condition of the foragers themselves. If the only decisions humans had to make were concerned with foraging, we might not have a self-concept at all, and there would be no such thing as high and low self-esteem. There are a number of foraging strategies open to mankind, but the choice depends on environmental factors rather than on the individual's phenotype (this may not be true in extreme cases; e.g., a very nearsighted man might choose to gather rather than to hunt).

Apart from the phylogenetically recent trait of mate value, it is with social competition that the self-concept comes into its own. Man needs a self-concept to make the calculation of relative RHP, and it seems likely that this has been going on for at least 250 million years. Even with the newly evolved prestige competition, he needs an idea of his SAHP to regulate his balance between self-assertion and self-effacement on social occasions. It is a sobering thought that if there were no social competition, or if we just engaged in scramble rather than contest competition, we might have no self-concept at all. Our faculty for self-awareness, introspection, and even for consciousness may in the long run be a spin-off from the adaptations that subserved competitive behavior. The self, indeed, may be a consequence of sexual selection.

SUMMARY

The likely phylogeny of human self-esteem is outlined. It started in our early vertebrate years, when it was necessary to assess one's own fighting capacity (RHP) and compare it with a rival's to decide between alternative strategies of escalation and de-escalation in agonistic encounters. Then a self-concept of mate value was added so that knowledge of one's sexual attractiveness to the opposite sex could be used to decide between alternative courtship strategies. In the past 10 million years or so, prestige competition has been supplanting agonistic competition, so that it became important to be attractive to an audience rather than intimidating to a rival, and the variable of SAHP has evolved to decide between self-assertion and self-effacement on social occasions. These three sources of self-esteem tend to move together, especially during mood change, so that in depression all three are lowered, and a lowering of any one of the three still has the power to induce depressed mood.

REFERENCES

Abed, R. T. (1998). The sexual competition hypothesis of eating disorders. *British Journal of Medical Psychology, 71*, 525–547.

Akiskal, H. S. (1990). Towards a definition of dysthymia: Boundaries with personality and mood disorders. In S. W. Burton & H. S. Akiskal (Eds.), *Dysthymic disorder* (pp. 1–12). London: Gaskell.

Andrews, B. (1998). Self-esteem. *The Psychologist, 11*, 339–342.

Archer, J., & Huntingford, F. (1994). Game theory models and escalation of animal fights. In M. Potegal & J. F. Knutson (Eds.), *Dynamics of aggression: Biological and social processes in dyads and groups* (pp. 3–32). Hillsdale, NJ: Lawrence Erlbaum Associates.

Barkow, J. H. (1975). Prestige and culture: A biosocial interpretation. *Current Anthropology, 16*, 553–572.

Barkow, J. H. (1991). Precis of Darwin, sex and status: Biological approaches to mind and culture. *Behavioral and Brain Sciences, 14*, 295–334.

Beck, A. T. (1987). Cognitive models of depression. *Journal of Cognitive Psychotherapy, 1*, 5–37.

Boehm, C. (1993). Egalitarian behaviour and reverse dominance hierarchy. *Current Anthropology, 34*, 227–254.

Brown, G. W., Andrews, B., Harris, T., Adler, Z., & Bridge, L. (1986). Social support, self-esteem and depression. *Psychological Medicine, 16*, 813–831.

Buss, D. M., & Schmitt, D. P. (1993). Sexual strategies theory: An evolutionary perspective on human mating. *Psychological Review, 100*, 204–232.

Cooley, C. H. (1902). *Human nature and the social order.* New York: Scribner's.

Dixon, A. K. (1998). Ethological strategies for defence in animals and humans: Their role in some psychiatric disorders. *British Journal of Medical Psychology, 71*, 417–446.

Gardner, R., Jr., & Price, J. S. (1999). Sociophysiology and depression. In T. Joiner & J. C. Coyne (Eds.), *The interactional nature of depression: Advances in interpersonal approaches* (pp. 247–268). Washington, DC: APA Books.

Gilbert, P. (1989). *Human nature and suffering.* Hove, UK: Lawrence Erlbaum Associates.

Gilbert, P., Price, J., & Allan, S. (1995). Social comparison, social attractiveness and evolution: How might they be related? *New Ideas in Psychology: An International Journal of Innovative Theory in Psychology, 13*, 149–165.

Hack, M. A. (1997). Assessment strategies in the contests of male crickets, Acheta domesticus. *Animal Behaviour, 53*, 733–747.

James W. (1890). *Principles of psychology* (Vol. 1). New York: Holt.

Knobloch, F., & Knobloch, J. (1979). *Integrated psychotherapy.* New York: Aronson.

Kortmulder, K. (1998). *Play and evolution: Second thoughts on the behaviour of animals.* Leiden, The Netherlands: International Books.

Krebs, J. R., & Davies, N. B. (1993). *An introduction to behavioural ecology* (3rd ed.). Oxford, UK: Blackwell Scientific.

Leary, M. R., & Downs, D. L. (1995). Interpersonal functions of the self-esteem motive: The self-esteem system as a sociometer. In M. H. Kernis (Ed.), *Efficacy, agency and self-esteem* (pp. 123–144). New York: Plenum.

MacLean, P. D. (1990). *The triune brain in evolution.* New York: Plenum.

Maslow, A. (1973). *Dominance, self-esteem and self-actualization* (R. Lawry, Ed.). Monterey, CA: Brooks-Cole. (Original work published 1940)

McGuire, M. T., & Troisi, A. (1998). *Darwinian psychiatry.* New York: Oxford University Press.

Mead, G. H. (1961). Taking the role of the other. In T. Parsons, E. Shild, K. D. Naegele, & J. R. Pitts (Eds.), *Theories of society: Foundations of modern sociological theory* (Vol. 1, pp. 739–740). New York: The Free Press. (Original work published 1934)

Parker, G. A. (1974). Assessment strategy and the evolution of fighting behaviour. *Journal of Theoretical Biology, 47,* 223–243.

Parker, G. A. (1982). Phenotype-limited evolutionarily stable strategies. In King's College Sociobiology Group, Cambridge (Eds.), *Current problems in sociobiology* (pp. 173–201). Cambridge, UK: Cambridge University Press.

Parker, G. A. (1984). Evolutionarily stable strategies. In J. R. Krebs & N. B. Davies (Eds.), *Behavioural ecology: An evolutionary approach* (2nd ed., pp. 30–61). Oxford, UK: Blackwell.

Price, J. S. (1988). Alternative channels for negotiating asymmetry in social relationships. In M. R. A. Chance (Ed.), *Social fabrics of the mind* (pp. 157–195). Hove, UK: Lawrence Erlbaum Associates.

Price, J. S. (1992). Accentuate the positive, eliminate the negative: The role of boosting and putting-down signals in mental health. In D. R. Trent (Ed.), *Promotion of mental health* (Vol. 1, pp. 89–102). Aldershot, UK: Avebury.

Price, J. S. (1998). The adaptive function of mood change. *British Journal of Medical Psychology, 71,* 465–477.

Price, J. S., Sloman, L., Gardner, R., Gilbert, P., & Rohde, P. (1997). The social competition hypothesis of depression. In S. Baron-Cohen (Ed.), *The maladapted mind: Classic readings in evolutionary psychopathology* (pp. 241–253). Hove, UK: Psychology Press. (Original work published 1994)

Robson, P. J. (1988). Self-esteem—A psychiatric view. *British Journal of Psychiatry, 153,* 6–15.

Siegel, A. M. (1996). *Heinz Kohut and the psychology of the self.* London: Routledge.

Sloman, S., & Sloman, L. (1988). Mate selection in the service of human evolution. *Journal of Social and Biological Structures, 11,* 457–468.

Stevens, A., & Price, J. (1996). *Evolutionary psychiatry: A new beginning.* London: Routledge.

Suls, J., & Wills, T. A. (1991). *Social comparison: Contemporary theory and research.* Hillsdale, NJ: Lawrence Erlbaum Associates.

Swallow, S. R., & Kuiper, N. A. (1988). Social comparison and negative self-evaluations: An application to depression. *Clinical Psychology Review, 8,* 55–76.

Tennen, H., & Affleck, G. (1993). The puzzles of self-esteem: A clinical perspective. In R. F. Baumeister (Ed.), *Self-esteem: The puzzle of low regard* (pp. 241–260). New York: Plenum.

Wells, E. L., & Marwell, G. (1976). *Self-esteem: Its conceptualization and measurement.* Beverly Hills: Sage.

Whybrow, P. C., Akiskal, S. H., & McKinney, W. T. (1984). *Mood disorders: Toward a new psychobiology.* New York: Plenum.

PART IV

Psychotherapeutic Approaches

CHAPTER EIGHT

A Cognitive Behavioral Perspective on the Involuntary Defeat Strategy

STEPHEN R. SWALLOW
Private Practice, Oakville, Ontario

Theoretical accounts of depression have focused on a range of mechanisms putatively mediating the development and maintenance of this ubiquitous phenomenon. Biologically oriented researchers, for example, have made important advances in explicating the role of particular neurophysiological processes in mediating depressive symptomatology. At the same time, psychologically oriented researchers have made significant progress in describing the role of various psychosocial factors in the onset and maintenance of depression. To date, however, biological and psychological accounts seem to have evolved along relatively independent lines. This has led to a certain degree of fragmentation—and sometimes even partisanship—in the conceptualization and clinical management of depression.

Some writers have argued that the dualism evident in the present corpus of depression research belies the absence of a unifying theoretical framework capable of integrating both neurophysiological and psychosocial data (cf. Cacioppo & Berntson, 1992; Gilbert, 1995; Sperry, 1993). Evolutionary theory is increasingly gaining currency as one such integrative theoretical framework. More specifically, the involuntary defeat strategy (IDS) model of depression, with its emphasis on dominant and submissive subroutines, represents one attempt to formulate depression within the larger integrative framework of evolutionary biology. The particular issue explored in this chapter is how the IDS model may interface with one prominent psychologically based approach to depression, namely the cognitive approach. I attempt to demonstrate that an integration of evolutionary and cognitive perspectives may address the lacunae in each respective approach and, as such, contribute to a more satisfactory and ultimately more useful formulation of the phenomenon of depression. Toward this end, I present a brief overview of both the cognitive and the IDS formulations of depression. In following sections, I consider how the IDS perspective may address certain gaps in the cognitive model, and, in turn, how an understanding of the role of cognitive factors in depression may enhance the theoretical rigor and the clinical utility of the IDS approach. The chapter concludes with case material illustrating this point.

THE COGNITIVE MODEL OF DEPRESSION

Overview

Cognitive conceptualizations of depression spring from a simple premise: Human emotions are based on ideas. This notion was articulated as early as the 1st century B.C. by the Stoic philosopher Epictetus who stated, "Men are disturbed not by things but by the views which they take of them." Beck's (1976) cognitive formulation of depression represents the most influential clinical application of this perspective. According to Beck, depression arises and is maintained by systematic distortions in thinking that occur at a number of levels in the information processing system (see Fig. 8.1).

Negative automatic thoughts are the distressing ideas or images that occur in a seemingly involuntary fashion as part of the individual's ongoing stream of consciousness. In depression, these thoughts hold an almost unquestioned plausibility, although they typically reflect a negatively flavored construction of real-

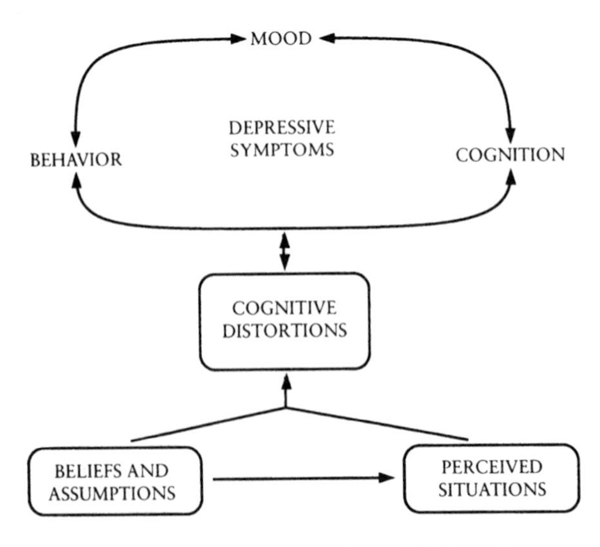

FIG. 8.1. A cognitive behavioral model of depression.

ity. Beck noted that negative automatic thoughts typically involve unflattering views of the self (e.g., "I am a loser"), as well as negative views of the world (e.g., "No one likes me") and the future (e.g., "I'll never amount to anything"). These three themes constitute what Beck labeled the *cognitive triad*.

Negative automatic thoughts, in turn, are hypothesized to reflect the outworking of habitual errors in logic and reasoning. Examples of such errors include overgeneralization, black-and-white thinking, jumping to conclusions, and selective attention to negative information (i.e., the negative filter). In addition, depressed persons tend to exhibit biases in the way they assign causes to negative outcomes. More specifically, depression has been linked to a pattern of internal (i.e., self-directed), global (i.e., overgeneralized), and temporally stable attributions for untoward events (Alloy, Abramson, Metalsky, & Hartlage, 1988).

At the root of depressive thinking, according to Beck's (1976) formulation, are rigid and enduring *core beliefs* or *schemas* that direct subsequent cognitive processes and, as such, regulate individuals' responses to life events. According to the cognitive model, these schemas are acquired via personal experience and may take the form of absolutistic rules or contingencies (e.g., "If I make a mistake then I am a complete failure"), or attitudes (e.g., "My value depends on what others think of me"). Within this model, the depressive pattern of information processing is activated when depressogenic belief structures are impinged on by thematically related life events. The ultimate goal of cognitive therapy—the therapeutic application of Beck's cognitive model—is to help patients identify, evaluate, and revise these core beliefs and attitudes.

Comment

As a descriptive account of how depressed individuals think, the cognitive model has served an important heuristic function, spawning a large and continually evolving literature. Moreover, the therapeutic application of this model is recognized as one of the most effective treatments for depression. Recent outcome studies suggest that it rivals the efficacy of the major antidepressants in acute treatment (Elkin et al., 1989; Murphy, Simons, Wetzel, & Lustman, 1984), and may actually reduce the risk of posttreatment relapse relative to acute treatment with antidepressant medications (Blackburn, Eunson, & Bishop, 1986; Evans et al., 1992; Simons, Murphy, Levine, & Wetzel, 1986). Nevertheless, the model is vulnerable to a number of important criticisms that highlight the potential value of a broader integrative framework.

One criticism of the cognitive model relates to its failure to address adequately the question of why individuals who are depressed or vulnerable to depression think as they do (Gilbert, 1992). Many cognitive theorists invoke Piagetian learning concepts to explain the development and the nature of depressive thinking patterns. According to this view, individuals generate idiosyncratic templates or schemas as they encounter and assimilate new information in their interactions with the environment. This view has been criticized, however, as neglecting the inherently purposive nature of most if not all human activity—including cognitive activity—and as portraying the individual as an aimless processor of information, "a collector of plans or maps, with little said about how images or trips become attractive to the person and how selections are made among alternative desired outcomes" (Pervin, 1989, p. 6).

A second major problem with the cognitive model—at least in its more orthodox expression—is the empirical fact that the dysfunctional core beliefs thought to underlie depressive cognition are mood state dependent. In Beck's (1976) formulation, depressogenic cognitive schemas (i.e., underlying beliefs, assumptions, etc.) represent relatively enduring diatheses to depression. However, there is now evidence that these negative schemas obtain only in the presence of depressed affect (Haaga, Dyck, & Ernst, 1991; Hollon, DeRubeis, & Evans, 1987; Miranda & Persons, 1988; Miranda, Persons, & Byers, 1990; Segal & Ingram, 1994; Teasdale, 1983). These findings have seriously challenged rigid notions of cognitive primacy in depression. Instead, they suggest that depressive cognition is one component in a more complex system involving synchronous and reciprocal relations among affect, behavior, and cognition.

A third and related problem with the cognitive model is its tendency to localize depression within the individual, paying relatively less attention to the role played by environmental factors such as life events, social and economic context, and culturally defined structures of power. In fairness, the cognitive model does specify an important role for life events in precipitating depression, but holds that life events are only significant from an etiological perspective to the extent that they impinge on thematically related core beliefs (i.e., the congruency hypothesis). Theorists from feminist and interpersonal schools of thought (e.g., Coyne, 1976) have taken the lead in criticizing this position as underrepresenting the inherently depressogenic nature of circumstances and systems involving the maintenance of power imbalances, subjugation, and oppression.

A fourth problem with the cognitive model has been its difficulty in conceptually articulating with approaches emphasizing the biological substrate of depression. To be sure, recently published research has demonstrated that cognitive therapy is able to effect significant change in the neurochemical processes involved in depression (Joffe, Segal, & Singer, 1996). However, the model is largely silent on the mechanisms by which cognitive change translates into neurochemical change and, conversely, on the processes by which alterations in neurochemistry may engender change at the cognitive level.

THE IDS APPROACH

Price and colleagues (e.g., Price, 1972; Price & Sloman, 1987; Price, Sloman, Gardner, Gilbert, & Rhode, 1994; Sloman, chap. 2, this volume) have articulated a model in which depression is conceptualized as the outworking of a biological, genetically preprogrammed response pattern evolved to inhibit aggression and promote reconciliation in the wake of hierarchical or competitive defeat. They labeled this pattern the IDS. According to this viewpoint, the IDS is triggered when one senses that one is losing (or will lose) an agonistic encounter and cannot win. In such cases, continued display of anger may be maladaptive in as much as it could prolong a hopeless conflict and result in undue loss or even death at the hand of a more powerful other (see Gilbert, chap. 1, this volume; Sloman, chap. 2, this volume). The IDS inhibits anger by generating painful feelings of inferiority, shame, worthlessness, sadness, anergia, and so on, from which individuals are motivated to escape. Escape subroutines may include flight or acceptance (i.e., of defeat or subordinate status), both of which may terminate the IDS. Where escape is blocked, however, the IDS may intensify, culminating in an intense and prolonged depressive response (Gilbert, chap. 1, this volume; Gilbert & Allan, 1998). It is therefore important to distinguish between the IDS, which is assumed to have adaptive significance, and depression, which is typically regarded as maladaptive much as we would distinguish between a transient fight or flight response on the one hand and a more protracted anxiety disorder on the other.

Comment

One of the chief difficulties with the IDS formulation of depression is the paucity of explicit empirical tests of its major tenets (but see Brown, Harris, & Hepworth, 1995; Gilbert, chap. 1, this volume). A second concern relates to its imprecision with respect to individual differences in depressive vulnerability. What factors determine, for example, whether or not a particular interaction is construed as agonistic? Why are some individuals able to escape the IDS through acceptance whereas others are blocked in this regard? Clearly these questions demonstrate the importance of applying an individual differences perspective within the IDS framework.

COGNITIVE THEORY FROM AN IDS PERSPECTIVE

To reiterate, the IDS model maintains that the complex psychobiological pattern previosly described (i.e., inferiority, shame, anhedonia, anergia, etc.) originally evolved as a self-protective response to situations involving perceived defeat, subordination, or loss. More specifically, according to the IDS perspective, dysphoric phenomenology may be functional in animals (without the capacity for complex elaboration) as it serves to terminate overt expressions of aggression or anger in the wake of a struggle one cannot win, to signal "no threat" to potentially dangerous conspecifics, to appease or to facilitate reconciliation with more powerful adversaries, and to promote escape or acceptance (Gilbert, chap. 1, this volume). In cases in which the IDS fails to produce these outcomes, however (e.g., in cases where escape is blocked, reconciliation is rejected, acceptance is inhibited, etc.), a clinical depression may ensue, conceptualized as a chronically activated IDS. This account implies (a) that self-denigrating cognition may be part of a submissive defensive response to terminate the motive to keep trying in no-win situations, and (b) that the overarching goal of this system is self-protection. If this is true, then it would make sense for cognitive theorists to conceptualize depressive thinking patterns in terms of their previously evolved functional significance as well as in terms of their content or structure.

In turn, such a conceptualization may have important implications for the way cognitive therapists address negative thinking in depression. To illustrate, consider the case of a woman who insists that she is "no good." Traditional cognitive approaches would ask the woman to consider evidence for and against the proposition that she is no good, focus on the cognitive errors of emotional reasoning or labelling, employ logical analysis to dispute this notion, and perhaps even explore the childhood origins of this negative self-schema. The IDS perspective would suggest, however, that the woman may be motivated to view herself as no good to avoid some putative threat to self (e.g., being "cut down to size" by another person) and as such, may be quite resistant to give up this self-denigrating belief, despite its logical or empirical vacuity. Therapeutically, this motivation can be clarified by asking patients to consider what the belief that they are no good may be protecting them from, or conversely, what concerns would be raised for them if they did not think that way about themselves.

COGNITIVE MEDIATION OF THE IDS

As noted in the previous section, an integration of cognitive and evolutionary approaches to depression suggests some intriguing solutions to a number of conceptual and practical difficulties with the cognitive model. In this section, I look at the interface of these two approaches from a slightly different perspective. Clearly, the postulated IDS represents an evolved strategy. At the same time, the IDS response is activated via the mediation of processes involving perception and appraisal. In this respect, the IDS is closely analogous to the stress response (interested readers may wish to consult Lazarus & Folkman, 1984, for a more detailed discussion of the role of appraisal processes in the anxiety response). Consequently, it may be useful to identify the critical junctures in the activation of the IDS response at which cognitive factors are operative. Such an analysis may help shed light on certain individual difference variables that may predispose individuals to an IDS response. This, in turn, may suggest important targets for cognitively oriented intervention strategies.

Figure 8.2 presents a schematic representation of the processes involved in the activation of the IDS response. This figure highlights a number of important

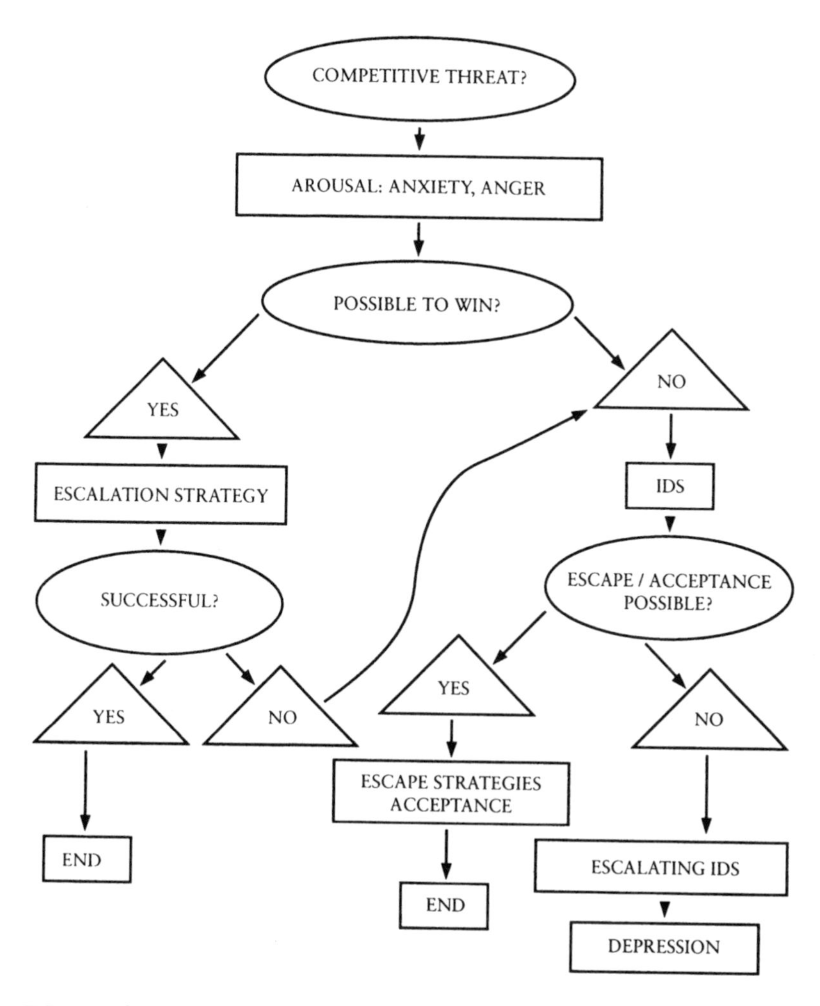

FIG. 8.2. Flow diagram of processes putatively involved in the activation, escalation, and termination of the IDS response.

junctures at which cognitive factors may operate to mediate the IDS response. I examine each of these in turn.

Cognitive Appraisals of Agonistic Threat

According to the IDS model, this complex psychobiological response pattern is activated in the context of a losing competitive encounter. As such, the IDS response is more likely to be activated in individuals with the tendency to construe interpersonal situations in agonistic or highly competitive terms. Interestingly enough, there is convergent evidence that certain groups of individuals prone to becoming depressed (i.e., individuals with a self-critical or autonomous personality diathesis) exhibit a tendency to perceive others as hostile and rejecting, to perceive their interactions with others as unpleasant or threatening (Zuroff, Stotland, Sweetman, Craig, & Koestner, 1995), and to elicit hostility from others (Coyne, 1976).

How might we account for the tendency to construe personal interactions as agonistic encounters? From a cognitive point of view, I would argue that many of the core beliefs hypothesized to predispose individuals to depression actually do so, as they lead individuals to construe interpersonal encounters in competitive, hostile, or hierarchical terms. These rules or beliefs may focus on putative attributes or motives of others (e.g., "Don't trust others—they'll stab you in the back if you give them a chance") or on the nature of the world (e.g., "It's a dog-eat-dog world," or "Life's a zero-sum game—happiness always comes at someone else's expense"). Alternatively, beliefs in which a sense of personal value or worth is viewed as contingent on personal superiority (e.g., "It is a terrible thing to be average," or "I must do better than others to be recognized or loved") might lead individuals to construe many social interactions as agonistic encounters (Gilbert, 1992). Individuals with such beliefs tend to view others as competitors for scarce resources and, as such, feel threatened by them.[1]

To summarize, the IDS perspective would predict that, all else being equal, individuals with the tendency to construe social interactions in agonistic terms may be more likely to experience the IDS response, and as such, would be more vulnerable to depression. From a more applied standpoint, this analysis suggests that cognitive therapists may profitably target for change clients' interpersonal construals where those construals are predominantly agonistic or hierarchical in nature.

Cognitive Appraisals of Defeat

Although the tendency to construe social interactions in hierarchical terms may be a prerequisite to the activation of the IDS, it is far from a sufficient condition. According to the IDS model, individuals must also construe their social interactions to be losing competitive encounters. Appraising an agonistic situation as a defeat may involve a number of cognitive processes. Here I discuss two important factors: self-efficacy judgments and social comparison processes.

Self-Efficacy Appraisals. People's expectations about their ability to deal with particular situations and their beliefs regarding the ultimate outcomes of their

[1]By contrast, individuals with the dependent or sociotropic personality diathesis tend to see others as potential rejectors, are vulnerable to seeing themselves as less attractive or desirable than are nonsociotropic individuals, and are subject to submissive behavior and unfavorable social comparisons (Gilbert, Allan, & Trent, 1995).

actions constitute what Bandura (1977) has labeled *self-efficacy.* Within an agonistic context, self-efficacy judgments concern the individual's expectations regarding his or her capacity to handle the opponent and ultimately, to win. Consequently, from the IDS point of view, self-efficacy judgments may play an important role in determining (a) whether one will choose to engage at all in a particular hierarchical struggle, (b) whether one will mobilize escalation strategies in the wake of an initial defeat, and (c) how long one will sustain a losing struggle before coming to the conclusion that he or she cannot win.

Individuals with low self-efficacy expectations may tend to avoid hierarchical struggles altogether, because, from their point of view, their best efforts are likely to result in defeat at best, and in humiliation and retribution at worst. Consequently, for such individuals, the IDS response may be triggered in a seemingly automatic fashion by the mere threat of personal antagonism. Interestingly enough, this pattern of conflict avoidance is characteristic of individuals high in dependency—a personality subtype associated with heightened vulnerability to depression (Zuroff & Mongrain, 1987). The need for constant reassurance of others' approval that characterizes dependent individuals might, in fact, reflect heightened vigilance for any sign of interpersonal agonism that, because of their low self-efficacy expectations, might automatically signify defeat and hence elicit the IDS.

The therapeutic application of this formulation is relatively straightforward. From a cognitive perspective, low self-efficacy expectations may be operationalized in terms of propositional beliefs such as "I can't stand conflict," "It's disastrous if someone I know doesn't like me," "People who rock the boat get into big trouble," or "There's no point in standing up for myself; I'll just get knocked down in the end anyway." Consistent with cognitive behavioral methodologies, these kinds of beliefs may be challenged via evidence-gathering exercises that incorporate the use of appropriate strategies for self-assertion and imaginal or in vivo exposure techniques.

Social Comparison Processes. Comparing oneself to others (i.e., engaging in social comparison) provides individuals with important information concerning, among other things, the likelihood of winning in some competitive or agonistic encounter. Where individuals perceive themselves to fall short on personal dimensions relevant to the outcome of a potentially agonistic interaction, they may feel defeated and, as such, experience a preemptive IDS response. Consequently, individuals with a chronic tendency to make unfavorable self–other comparisons would be particularly vulnerable to chronic IDS activation and, hence, be at risk for depression.

Social comparison judgments involve a complex set of social cognitive variables, each of which, in turn, may influence the degree to which a particular comparison outcome is construed as being favorable or unfavorable. The frequency with which individuals engage in social comparison, the nature of the target others with whom individuals tend to make comparisons, the types of dimensions on which individuals engage in self–other comparisons, and the personal interpretation of these comparisons are all examples of variables that could directly affect the subjective valence of social comparison outcomes (see Buunk & Brenninkmeyer, chap. 6, this volume). In turn, individual differences on these variables may constitute a predisposition to making unfavorable social comparisons and, by extension, to experiencing a chronically activated IDS response, low self-esteem, and ultimately depression (Swallow & Kuiper, 1988).

Indeed, a number of recent studies have identified several ways in which the social comparison patterns of individuals with the tendency to experience depression may differ from those of their nondepressed counterparts. As one example, mildly depressed individuals have been shown to engage in social comparison much more frequently than nondepressives in the wake of negative personal outcomes (e.g., failure). As a result, mildly depressed individuals tend to make a disproportionate number of unfavorable social comparisons (Swallow & Kuiper, 1992). In another study, mildly depressed participants displayed a greater preference for comparisons with higher ranking others than did nondepressives, particularly following negative personal outcomes, thereby increasing the likelihood of receiving unflattering feedback (Swallow & Kuiper, 1993). This finding is particularly striking in light of other studies indicating that depressed individuals fail to discount unfavorable comparisons when their targets have been unfairly "advantaged" in some way (Sharp & Tennen, 1983).

Taken together, these studies suggest that individuals prone to depression might engage in social comparison in ways that tend to increase the likelihood of unfavorable comparisons. Consequently, they might be more prone to concluding preemptively that they cannot win in an agonistic encounter, and as such, they might be particularly likely to enter the IDS stream. From a therapeutic standpoint, dysfunctional social comparison patterns may be targeted directly (e.g., by encouraging more evenhandedness in comparison choices, reducing comparison frequency, teaching discounting, etc.) or indirectly (e.g., by addressing beliefs that may underlie these patterns, such as "I am nothing if I am not better than everyone else"). (See Swallow, 1995, for a more detailed discussion of the therapeutic implications of the literature on social comparison and depression.)

Cognitive Mediators of Acceptance and Reconciliation

As shown in Fig. 8.2, the IDS is conceptualized as an inevitable response to the perception that one cannot win in an agonistic struggle. The IDS response itself represents a noxious affective state that individuals are typically motivated to terminate. Physical escape from the territory of the winner (i.e., flight) represents the most obvious means of terminating the IDS. According to the model outlined in earlier chapters, individuals for whom physical escape is not possible may avoid becoming ensnared in a more protracted IDS response through the processes of acceptance and reconciliation. *Acceptance* refers to the process by which individuals let go of their struggle to win, concede defeat, and move on. *Reconciliation* refers to the process by which a nonagonistic relationship is (re)established between the winner and the loser in the wake of an agonistic encounter. In this section, I explore a number of cognitively oriented individual difference variables that may mediate the processes of acceptance and reconciliation following agonistic defeat.

Self-Complexity. Individuals differ with respect to the degree to which various personal attributes, abilities, and social roles are represented in memory as either discrete or, alternately, as interrelated aspects of self. This variable has been labeled *self-complexity.* Individuals high in self-complexity possess a flexible view of self that incorporates a wide range of relatively independent attributes, abilities, and social roles. When such people experience a threat to or a loss of one aspect of self (e.g., they lose the role of spouse following the death of a partner), they may compensate by shifting their focus onto other aspects of self (e.g., they may begin to place greater emphasis on their role as parent or on their athletic abilities). By contrast, individuals low in self-complexity have self-views that contain fewer elements or in which the elements are highly interrelated. As such, a threat to any one aspect of self may seriously undermine the foundation of the individual's sense of self. Linville (1985) aptly characterized such individuals as having placed "all their eggs in one cognitive basket" (p. 94).

As already noted, acceptance involves the ability to concede defeat, to let go of a competitive struggle, and to move on with life. Individuals find this easier to do when their self-conceptions do not rest entirely on the ability, attribute, or social role that has just been challenged. For individuals high in self-complexity, the importance of any given loss may be discounted (e.g., "I may have lost at tennis, but I am a very competent chess player") and as such, acceptance may be facilitated. However, this route may be unavailable for those individuals whose self-concept is less complex. Consequently, these individuals may find acceptance more difficult, and as such, may be more prone to a protracted IDS response. Indeed, Linville (1987) demonstrated a clear relation between low self-complexity and depression.

Attributional Style. When untoward events occur (e.g., a competitive loss), people typically formulate private explanations or attributions for these events, presumably in an effort to make the world more predictable or less uncertain. The way in which individuals make sense of agonistic losses may have a bearing on their ability to escape from the IDS response. To illustrate, faced with a loss, many individuals would tend to attribute this outcome to factors that have little or nothing to do with themselves. In short, such individuals would make excuses for their losses (cf. Snyder & Higgins, 1988). Attributing one's losses to external factors, by definition, reduces the personal significance of the loss and, as such, may make it easier to accept. By contrast, other individuals would tend to attribute untoward outcomes to global weaknesses or deficiencies in themselves that are stable over time. This tendency to make internal, global, and stable attributions for failure or loss would, in theory, make it much more difficult to achieve acceptance because, by definition, the personal implications of the outcome would be greatly magnified. In line with this notion, the tendency to make internal, global, and stable attributions for untoward outcomes has been identified as a vulnerability marker for depression (Barnett & Gotlib, 1988; Peterson & Seligman, 1984).

Dysfunctional Core Beliefs. Finally, the ability to terminate an IDS response in the wake of agonistic loss may be mediated by certain types of beliefs or rules that make it difficult for the individual to achieve acceptance. To illustrate, some individuals may maintain personal rules or maxims such as, "Never give up," "Don't be a quitter," or "Only weaklings back down." Others may harbor catastrophic beliefs about the implications of failure (e.g., "To fail at one thing is to be a complete failure," "To lose now is to lose everything," or "I will never recover from this defeat"). Rules or beliefs such as these may heighten the personal significance of one's losses and reduce the likelihood of acceptance, thereby increasing the probability of a protracted IDS response.

Summary

Up to this point, I have attempted to illustrate how the IDS model of depression may articulate with a cognitive perspective on this disorder. I have argued that the cognitive approach can be both more satisfying theoretically and more useful clinically when viewed from the perspective of evolutionary biology. In turn, I have attempted to show that cognitive factors play a crucial role in mediating the genetically preprogrammed biological and psychological response patterns that constitute the IDS.

This analysis reinforces the important point that the phenomena comprising what has been labeled the IDS should not—indeed cannot—be conceptualized in reductionistic, all-or-nothing terms. On the contrary, depression is a highly complex response system, incorporating both phylogenetically and ontogenetically relevant processes.

Case Examples

The following cases illustrate some of the potential benefits of incorporating evolutionary and cognitive constructs into psychotherapeutic work.

Case 1. The patient was a 55-year-old executive working for a large corporation. He presented with stress and depression in relation to a problematic relationship with his boss, by whom he felt demeaned and undervalued. The patient described several humiliating instances in which his boss—a woman several years his junior—had publicly criticized his work. His referral for psychological help was precipitated in the wake of an unflattering performance review that he found demeaning and inaccurate. The department in which he worked had been subject to a number of cutbacks, and the patient felt that his position might be in jeopardy. He expressed a sense of hopelessness about his situation and a sense of outrage at what he perceived as the unconscionable treatment that he had received.

This patient's case clearly exemplifies several features of the IDS. He perceived himself to be in a one-down, defeated position vis-à-vis his boss. He also felt that he could not rectify this situation due to the power imbalances inherent in the hierarchical structure of the corporate organization. He was angry at what he saw as his mistreatment, but afraid to express his anger for fear that he would be fired at a time in his life when he felt particularly vulnerable from a financial perspective. Consequently, although he found himself angry and defeated, he also felt unable to escape the situation in any meaningful fashion. Thus he was stuck with a chronically engaged IDS. As such, the therapeutic task was to disengage the IDS in some manner.

The disengagement of the IDS was accomplished by addressing a number of the cognitive factors responsible for blocking acceptance and escape. First, we attempted to challenge the patients belief that he could not leave his position or that being fired would be a disaster. Considerable attention was devoted to decatastrophizing these previously unthinkable outcomes. The patient acknowledged that, although losing his job would be inconvenient and could result in the necessity to adjust his lifestyle in certain ways, it would not be the end of the world. In fact, he noted that he had been able to make a reasonably good living in the past as a private consultant in his field. The goal of this intervention was to provide the patient with some sense that escape was possible—if not necessarily desirable—at that point in time, and that if he stayed in the unpleasant situation, it was by choice, not necessity that he did so.

Second, the patient's tendency to overinvest himself in his career was explored as a means of loosening the hold of the IDS. In particular, the patient was encouraged to review the many roles that he occupied (i.e., father, husband, son, friend, etc.) and to prioritize them with respect to their importance. In doing this, we discovered that his family was actually of primary importance to him, and his career was a distant second or third priority. This exercise was designed to enhance his perceived self-complexity on the assumption that doing so might facilitate his acceptance of defeat in one role, thereby terminating the IDS.

Third, attributional work focusing on the patients perceptions of the motivations of his boss was undertaken to modulate his appraisal of having been defeated by her and thereby modulate his anger toward her. To illustrate, a variety of possible motivations were discussed, including several that had not occurred to him. The patient had assumed that his boss was hungry for power and interested only in using him as a rung on the way to the top of the corporate ladder. The possibility that his boss's reactions were motivated by her own professional insecurity or by her sense of being threatened by the patient's superior credentials and experience had not occurred to him. A consideration of these alternate possibilities enabled the patient to become somewhat more accepting of his boss's behavior, which, in turn, modulated his anger toward her to some extent, thereby undermining the necessity of the IDS.

Fourth, some of the patient's core beliefs were examined and challenged—particularly those that set the stage for a continuation of the IDS. As one example, the patient expressed his belief that his career "should always be on an upward trajectory—continually improving." His current situation involved a clear violation of this "should" and as such, was engendering a great deal of anger and resentment. Cognitive work focusing on more flexible, reasonable alternatives to this rather demanding belief were considered (e.g., "I would prefer my career to be advancing, but if it is not, it is not the end of the world"). This more flexible approach tended to promote greater acceptance of his situation, thereby reducing the intensity of his IDS.

Several behavioral strategies were introduced to complement the cognitive work just outlined. For example, the patient was encouraged to develop a detailed, concrete contingency plan for losing his job. This was done to complement the work of decatastrophizing described earlier and to provide the patient with a more credible sense that escape was possible—if not necessarily desirable—at that point in time. As another example, the patient was encouraged to fortify his other roles by, say, scheduling more time with his family, planning outings with his wife or with his friends, or making some time for other valued activities.

As it turned out, the patient did eventually lose his job. However, due in part to the work just described, he was able to accept this loss and implement his contingency plans. As part of this transition, he found himself relying more heavily on the support and affirmation of family and friends, which he found to be very helpful.

Case 2. The patient was a 35-year-old high school teacher with a history of very severe depression initially activated in the wake of the birth of her first child 6 years earlier. There had been frequent suicidal rumination culminating in one extended hospitalization 2 years earlier. The patient was a bright, articulate woman who had enjoyed a successful career both before and after the birth of her children. At the time of her seeking cognitive therapy she was not working.

As part of our assessment, the patient completed a daily thought record on which she described situations in which she noticed her mood dropping, and then attempted to record the automatic thoughts that were "running through her head" in that situation. This procedure revealed that in the wake of even very minor mistakes or interpersonal conflicts, the patient's thinking became dominated by disturbing nihilistic thoughts focusing on the meaninglessness and pointlessness of life in general, as well as on the futility and vacuity of her own life in particular. These thoughts quite naturally activated marked feelings of hopelessness, along with an overwhelming desire "not to be here" (i.e., not to live). During such episodes, she completely discounted the value of the various roles she occupied (e.g., mother, wife, friend, volunteer) and wrote off as insignificant all of her many accomplishments and achievements. Despite initial efforts to challenge the accuracy of the patient's rather bleak perspective via standard cognitive therapy techniques (e.g., evidence gathering, identifying cognitive distortions, alternative questioning), these views were tenaciously maintained.

One of the insights yielded by an integration of the cognitive and IDS approaches is that cognitions, like other forms of behavior, are purposive or goal directed. Consequently, in my formulation of the case described here, I hypothesized that the patient's tendency to think in depressogenic, nihilistic terms was subserving important biosocial goals for her; that is, that her negative patterns of thought were instrumental or functional in some way. Thus, rather than dismissing the patient as resistant or continuing to hammer away at the obvious distortions in her thinking, therapeutic attention was turned to the function that this pattern of thought was serving for her. Variants of the following questions were posed: What if you believed that your life actually mattered, and that what you do is actually meaningful and significant in some way? Would that raise any concerns for you? Is there any way in which your nihilistic thinking may help you, or is there something that it gets you, or is there something it protects you from in some way? Very quickly we determined that indeed, the thought that "nothing matters" served to buffer the patient's anxiety about failure, to which she had been sensitized by a family background in which high standards were set, and in which—according to the patient's perception—failure would not be tolerated. In IDS terms, the patient's anxiety was activated in situations in which she anticipated a losing agonistic encounter (e.g., criticism, humiliation, etc.). The IDS—in the form of nihilistic, self-derogating cognition—was therefore preemptively activated to obviate such an encounter, turn off the anxiety she was experiencing, and buffer any anger she might experience should such an encounter materialize.

This insight set the stage for several important therapeutic steps. First, it enabled the patient to *decenter.* Safran and Segal (1990) defined this process and its importance as follows:

> Decentering is a process through which one is able to step outside of one's immediate experience, thereby changing the very nature of that experience. This process allows for the introduction of a gap between the event and one's reaction to that event. By developing the capacity to observe oneself and one's own reactions,

> one begins to distinguish between reality and reality as one construes it. Stepping outside of one's current experience fosters a recognition that the reality of the moment is not absolute, immutable, or unalterable, but rather something that is being constructed. In addition to the process of reflexive self-observation, there is a second component that is involved in the process. This is one of seeing oneself as an agent in the construction process. There is thus also a process of accepting responsibility by seeing one's own role in the construction process. (p. 117)

Second, this insight allowed us to begin to examine the cognitive elements of the anxiety for which her nihilistic thinking was assumed to constitute a defensive coping response. So, for example, the patient was able to identify thoughts such as "If I make a mistake someone will criticize and humiliate me" or "Conflict with others is dangerous, and leads to being hurt and rejected." The developmental roots of such beliefs could be probed (another decentering technique) and the beliefs themselves could be evaluated and subjected to empirical appraisal.

A third therapeutic strategy involved building behavioral skills related to handling conflict and criticism, to provide the patient with alternative means of dealing with the anxiety engendered by such situations, hence obviating the activation of the IDS.

The formulation just outlined appeared to resonate quite strongly with the patient's own sense of her depressive experience, and she responded very favorably to the corresponding interventions. At termination she was evidencing markedly diminished levels of depression.

REFERENCES

Alloy, L. B., Abramson, L. Y., Metalsky, G. I., & Hartlage, S. (1988). The hopelessness theory of depression: Attributional aspects. *British Journal of Clinical Psychology, 27,* 5–12.

Bandura, A. (1977). Self-efficacy: Toward a unifying theory of behavioral change. *Psychological Review, 84,* 191–215.

Barnett, P. A., & Gotlib, I. H. (1988). Psychosocial functioning in depression: Distinguishing among antecedents, concomitants, and consequences. *Psychological Bulletin, 104,* 97–126.

Beck, A. T. (1976). *Cognitive therapy and the emotional disorders.* New York: International Universities Press.

Blackburn, I. M., Eunson, K. M., & Bishop, S. (1986). A two-year naturalistic follow-up of depressed patients treated with cognitive therapy, pharmacotherapy and a combination of both. *Journal of Affective Disorders, 10,* 67–75.

Brown, G. W., Harris, T. O., & Hepworth, C. (1995). Loss, humiliation and entrapment among women developing depression: A patient and nonpatient comparison. *Psychological Medicine, 25,* 7–21.

Cacioppo, J. T., & Berntson, G. G. (1992). Social psychological contributions to the decade of the brain: Doctrine of multilevel analysis. *American Psychologist, 47,* 1019–1028.

Coyne, J. C. (1976). Towards an interactional description of depression. *Psychiatry, 39,* 28–40.

Elkin, I., Shea, T. M., Watkins, J. T., Imner, S. T., Sotsky, S. M., Collins, J. F., Fiester, S. J., & Parloff, M. B. (1989). National Institute of Mental Health treatment of depression collaborative research program. *Archives of General Psychiatry, 46,* 971–982.

Evans, M. D., Hollon, S. D., DeRubeis, R. J., Piasecki, J. M., Grove, W. M., Garvey, M. J., & Tuason, V. B. (1992). Differential relapse following cognitive therapy and pharmacotherapy for depression. *Archives of General Psychiatry, 49*, 802–808.
Gilbert, P. (1992). *Depression: The evolution of powerlessness.* New York: Guilford.
Gilbert, P. (1995). Biopsychosocial approaches and evolutionary theory as aids to integration in clinical psychology and psychotherapy. *Clinical Psychology and Psychotherapy, 2*, 135–156.
Gilbert, P., & Allan, S. (1998). The role of defeat and entrapment (arrested flight) in depression: An exploration of an evolutionary view. *Psychological Medicine, 28*, 585–598.
Gilbert, P., Allan, S., & Trent, D. (1995). Involuntary subordination or dependency as key dimensions of depressive vulnerability. *Journal of Clinical Psychology, 51*, 740–752.
Haaga, D. A. F., Dyck, M. J., & Ernst, D. (1991). Empirical status of cognitive theory of depression. *Psychological Bulletin, 110*, 215–236.
Hollon, S. D., DeRubeis, R. J., & Evans, M. D. (1987). Causal mediation of change in treatment for depression: Discriminating between nonspecificity and noncausality. *Psychological Bulletin, 102*, 139–149.
Joffe, R., Segal, Z. V., & Singer, W. (1996). Change in thyroid hormone levels following response to cognitive therapy for major depression. *American Journal of Psychiatry, 153*, 411–413.
Lazarus, R. A., & Folkman, S. (1984). *Stress, appraisal, and coping.* New York: Springer.
Linville, P. W. (1985). Self-complexity and affective extremity: Don't put all your eggs into one cognitive basket. *Social Cognition, 3*, 94–120.
Miranda, J., & Persons, J. B. (1988). Dysfunctional attitudes are mood-state dependent. *Journal of Abnormal Psychology, 97*, 76–79.
Miranda, J., Persons, J. B., & Byers, C. N. (1990). Endorsement of dysfunctional beliefs depends on current mood state. *Journal of Abnormal Psychology, 99*, 237–241.
Murphy, G. E., Simons, A. D., Wetzel, R. D., & Lustman, P. J. (1984). Cognitive therapy and pharmacotherapy. *Archives of General Psychiatry, 41*, 33–41.
Pervin, L. A. (1989). *Goal concepts in personality and social psychology.* Hillsdale, NJ: Lawrence Erlbaum Associates.
Peterson, C., & Seligman, M. E. (1984). Causal explanations as risk factors for depression: Theory and evidence. *Psychological Review, 91*, 347–374.
Price, J. (1972). Genetic and phylogenetic aspects of mood variations. *International Journal of Mental Health, 1*, 124–144.
Price, J., & Sloman, L. (1987). Depression as yielding behavior: An animal model based on Schjelderup-Ebb's pecking order. *Ethology and Sociobiology, 8*(Suppl.), 85–98.
Price, J., Sloman, L., Gardner, R., Gilbert, P., & Rhode, P. (1994). The social competition hypothesis of depression. *British Journal of Psychiatry, 164*, 309–315.
Safran, J. D., & Segal, Z. V. (1990). *Interpersonal process in cognitive therapy.* New York: Basic Books.
Segal, Z. V., & Ingram, R. E. (1994). Mood priming and construct activation in tests of cognitive vulnerability to unipolar depression. *Clinical Psychology Review, 14*, 663–695.
Sharp, J., & Tennen, H. (1983). Attributional bias in depression: The role of cue perception. *Cognitive Therapy and Research, 7*, 325–332.
Simons, A. D., Murphy, G. E., Levine, J. L., & Wetzel, R. D. (1986). Cognitive therapy and pharmacotherapy for depression: Sustained improvement over one year. *Archives of General Psychiatry, 43*, 43–48.
Snyder, C. R., & Higgins, R. L. (1988). Excuses: Their role in the negotiation of reality. *Psychological Bulletin, 104*, 23–35.
Sperry, R. W. (1993). The impact and promise of the cognitive revolution. *American Psychologist, 48*, 878–885.
Swallow, S. R. (1995). Social comparison behavior and low self-regard: Empirical developments and therapeutic implications. *The Behavior Therapist, 18*, 72–73.

Swallow, S. R., & Kuiper, N. A. (1988). Social comparison and negative self-evaluations: An application to depression. *Clinical Psychology Review, 8,* 55–67.

Swallow, S. R., & Kuiper, N. A. (1992). Mild depression and frequency of social comparison behavior. *Journal of Social and Clinical Psychology, 11,* 167–180.

Swallow, S. R., & Kuiper, N. A. (1993). Social comparison in dysphoria and nondysphoria: Differences in target similarity and specificity. *Cognitive Therapy and Research, 17,* 103–122.

Teasdale, J. D. (1983). Negative thinking in depression: Cause, effect, or reciprocal relationship? *Advances in Behavior Research and Therapy, 5,* 3–25.

Zuroff, D. C., & Mongrain, M. (1987). Dependency and self-criticism: Vulnerability factors for depressive affective states. *Journal of Abnormal Psychology, 96,* 14–22.

Zuroff, D. C., Stotland, S., Sweetman, E., Craig, J. A., & Koestner, R. (1995). Dependency, self-criticism, and social interaction. *British Journal of Clinical Psychology, 34,* 543–553.

CHAPTER NINE

Social Competition and Attachment

LEON SLOMAN
LESLIE ATKINSON
Centre for Addiction and Mental Health, Toronto, Ontario

Attachment theory, like the social competition model, is founded within a biological-evolutionary framework. The tendency of the infant and young child (and adult in times of danger) to maintain proximity with a protective other has been genetically determined during the evolutionary history of the human species. The maintenance of proximity increased the probability of survival and procreation in the environment within which the human species evolved. Statistics on traffic fatalities indicate that this evolutionary mechanism continues to operate, with a disproportionate number of deaths occurring among young, unaccompanied children (see Bowlby, 1973). The biological-evolutionary underpinnings of attachment theory render its study particularly germane in the context of social competition theory. Furthermore, the mother–child relationship is the child's first experience in a hierarchical system, with the mother clearly serving as the dominant partner.

This chapter surveys the attachment literature pertinent to social competition and explores the interrelation between attachment and social competition theories. Some of the ideas about the interrelation emanate from discussions with Hilburn-Cobb (for more information about social competition theory, see Sloman, chap. 2, this volume). We commence with a few observations from the primate literature illustrating the close association between attachment and social competition systems. We then survey some of the developmental and personality literature pertinent to both attachment and social competition. Finally, the clinical utility of jointly considering both attachment and social competition is instantiated with a case study.

ATTACHMENT AND COMPETITION AMONG PRIMATES

Because the attachment and social competition models are evolution-based theories, the nonhuman primate data are informative with respect to relations between these behavioral systems. In this section, we use primate data to show the connection between these two systems, their mutually augmentative nature, and their shared neurobiology.

Within the Macaque species, the mother lies at the base of both attachment and social status systems. Macaques have a powerful matrilineal order of rank inheritance whereby offspring come to outrank all troupe members subordinate to their mother, excepting mature males. These genealogically dominant infants are often younger and weaker than their subordinates. However, experimental removal of the mother precipitates a rapid decline in status among these infants, with potential for physical victimization (see Perusse, 1992). This state of affairs demonstrates the matrilineal basis of both the attachment and social competition systems, at least within the macaque troupe.

The primate data also illustrate how one theory might inform or augment the other. With specific reference to rhesus monkeys but presumably generalizable beyond them, Boccia (1992) pointed out that an important role of the mother is to provide situations of conflict and frustration: "The mother engages in weaning behavior, restriction of activity, blocking of goals, and other such behaviors. These require active coping, problem solving, and negotiation on the part of the infant" (p. 512).

The adaptive function of the mother's role as frustrator is immediately evident within the social competition model. However, it has been neglected by attachment theorists, who have focused on infancy and emphasized the importance of maternal sensitivity in fostering these very skills (i.e., coping, problem solving, negotiation; Ainsworth, Blehar, Waters, & Wall, 1978). In all probability, both perspectives are valid and it is by bringing both to bear that we might best explain certain aspects of human behavior.

Kraemer (1992) reviewed the evidence on neurotransmitters and the first attachment of the primate infant to its caregiver from a neurobiological perspective. He noted the lifelong dysregulation within and between the norepinephrine, dopamine, and serotonin systems when monkeys experience an early and long separation from their mothers. Of interest, all these systems have been implicated in aggression (Rogeness & McClure, 1996) and the fight or flight response, both behavioral systems that are central to social competition (see Levitan, Hasey, & Sloman, chap. 4, this volume).

ATTACHMENT AND SOCIAL COMPETITION, DEVELOPMENT AND PERSONALITY

As mentioned, the attachment system serves a protective function, as it preserves caregiver–dependent proximity in times of potential threat. From a phenomenological perspective, the child maintains proximity because closeness to the caregiver is associated with felt security (Sroufe & Waters, 1977). In responding sensitively to the distressed infant, the caregiver helps the infant regulate his or her affect. Furthermore, when caregivers respond to the child's emotional distress with empathy and labeling, the young child learns that emotional expression will not overwhelm the parent or the child and that these affects are shareable and tolerable experiences. This enables the child to develop a secure style of attachment, defined by confidence in the availability of attachment figures in times of need, the ability to obtain comfort with closeness, and the reliance on both self and others in the regulation of emotional arousal (Cassidy, 1994).

When a parent consistently rejects the overtures of a distressed child, that child perceives the parent as unresponsive. The child comes to downplay the recognition, importance, and behavioral manifestation of those emotions. This child learns to self-regulate, in less than optimal manner, without the support of a protective caregiver. This anxious-avoidant style is characterized by insecurity in others' intentions and a preference for physical and emotional distance.

Should the parent respond to emotional bids inconsistently, then the child might express more distress than circumstances warrant and thereby increase the probability of response on the part of the parent. This child comes to depend on others for the regulation of emotion and shows little reliance on self-regulation. The anxious-ambivalent style is characterized by insecurity concerning others' responses together with desire for physical proximity and emotional intimacy and a high fear of rejection.

When the caregiver is frightened (as when he or she has experienced an unresolved trauma, such as loss) or frightening (as when he or she is abusive), the infant displays contradictory tendencies to approach and avoid his or her mother in disorganized fashion (Main & Solomon, 1986, 1990). Disorganization is not a behavioral category as are secure, avoidant, and ambivalent classifications; it is a dimension of behavior that may be assigned in addition to a primary classification. The impact of disorganization on emotion regulation has not been explored because disorganization only exists within the context of the classifications outlined earlier (Cassidy, 1994).

Of particular import here, avoidant and ambivalent children show deficits in emotion regulation in comparison to secure youngsters. Indeed, style of regulating emotion is a defining feature of attachment classification (Cassidy, 1994). Emotion regulation is also central to social competition; success in this arena is tied to the appropriately modulated expression of submissive and dominance behaviors.

Children need to learn when it is appropriate to challenge, how to challenge, and when to submit. Parents who are rigid or easily threatened may respond to normal developmental behavior by labeling it as bad or unacceptable with the result that the child becomes overly submissive, passive aggressive, or very aggressive. In general, factors that contribute to the development of secure attachment will enable the child to handle conflict and challenge well. Studies indicate that avoidant and disorganized attachments are associated with externalizing (aggressive, disruptive) behaviors, especially for boys (Egeland, Kalkoska, Gottesman, & Erickson, 1990; Greenberg, DeKlyen, Speltz, & Endriga, 1997; Speltz, Greenberg, & DeKlyen, 1990; Sroufe, Egeland, & Kreutzer, 1990). Troy and Sroufe (1987) found that insecure attachment leads to problems handling competitive encounters. They showed that insecurely attached infants are likely to behave as victims or bullies in later childhood, whereas children who are securely attached are unlikely to become either.

Greenberg et al. (1997) hypothesized that problem behaviors may be "necessary strategies to engage the attachment/caretaking behaviors of some parents—strategies that may have some functional value for the child in such relationships, although maladaptive in the social world at large" (p. 201). Taking a different perspective, Hilburn-Cobb (1998) proposed that the child who relates to his or her caregivers through aggressive or challenging behavior may have forsaken the attachment system altogether, attempting instead to self-regulate by attaining functional goods (e.g., cash, use of the family car) through the use of the dominance system. Both hypotheses, although radically different, show the interrelated development of attachment and social competition systems.

Main, Kaplan, and Cassidy (1985) and Hazan and Shaver (1987) applied infant attachment models to adults. The securely attached adult is described as autonomous. The anxious-avoidant child corresponds to the dismissing adult and the anxious-ambivalent child corresponds to the preoccupied adult. Autonomous adults deal with distress by adopting constructive instrumental coping strategies and seeking support from significant others (Mikulincer, 1998). Secure persons' confidence in their own skills allows them to open their schemas to threatening information, to revise erroneous beliefs, and to tolerate distress-related cues (Mikulincer, 1997). Secure persons are in a good position to decide whether to take a hawk or dove approach in a competitive encounter.

Mikulincer (1998; Mikulincer & Florian, 1998) postulated that avoidant adults tend to deal with insecurity and distress by detaching themselves from distress-related cues. Their habitual way of regulating affect consists of defensive attempts to deactivate the attachment system (Kobak, Cole, Ferenz-Gillies, & Fleming, 1993). It also includes compulsive attempts to attain self-reliance as a way of compensating for reluctance to depend on others (Mikulincer, 1998). This enhancement of their sense of self-reliance may result in self-inflation.

Mikulincer (1998) proposed that the "positive self-view exhibited by avoidant people might imply that their self-esteem is so low and fragile that they cannot tolerate discovery of the slightest flaw. This idealisation of the self seems to be a defense against the experience of rejection by others upon the recognition of personal deficiencies" (p. 432). Mikulincer's hypothesis was that attachment-related regulatory mechanisms are manifested in a person's self-view. Mikulincer quoted Tesser (1988), who surveyed evidence that a person's attempt to compensate for his or her deficiencies in one domain is manifested in a tendency to make known to others self-aspects that are positive. Mikulincer went on to argue that an avoidant person's habitual way of managing distress involves inflation of positive self-views. When avoidant persons deal with distress by deactivating their attachment system and enhancing their sense of self-reliance, they are trying to show they can cope. One way of demonstrating this is by competitive success, which entails an activation of their dominance system (Hilburn-Cobb, 1998). Instead of seeking affiliation, they try to achieve consolation by presenting themselves as strong and capable of rising to challenge. This type of dominance behavior needs to be differentiated from dominance behavior associated with secure attachment. The securely attached individual who succeeds and rises in the hierarchy feels pride (Weisfeld & Wendorf, chap. 5, this volume). This is reflected, for example, in the joyous exhibitionism of the football player who scores a touchdown. When the dominance behavior is specifically intended to regulate distress, competitive success may temporarily reduce distress, but there is only limited pride in the accomplishment—the need to succeed has a compulsive quality.

Mikulincer (1998) found that "both avoidant persons' positive self-view and anxious-ambivalent persons' negative self-view were strengthened by failure, which might have activated regulatory strategies" (p. 425). This might be interpreted to mean that avoidant persons, to prove they can succeed on their own, respond to failure by relying on their own resources and one way of achieving this is by an activation of the dominant system. Conversely, anxious-ambivalent persons respond to failure by an activation of the subordinate system. Both the avoidant and anxious-ambivalent individuals are at a disadvantage in relation to the securely attached in that they are less able to revise erroneous beliefs and obtain or benefit from affiliative support. Mikulincer (1998) found that, when the avoidant person was informed that a positive self-view was not a sign of self-reliance, the positive self-view was not strengthened by failure. That is, when individuals realized the dominant strategy would be ineffective, they did not use it.

Anxious-ambivalent persons deal with distress by minimizing the distance between themselves and their attachment figures. That is, they hyperactivate the attachment system and attempt to win others' love by clinging and hypervigilant controlling behaviors (Mikulincer, 1998; Shaver & Hazan, 1993) that emphasize negative self-aspects. Mikulincer (1998) believed that anxious-ambivalent persons' negative self-view might partly be derived from the internalization of negative attachment experiences and partly from the activation of regulatory strategies. However, he concluded, this activation may "further exacerbate this negative self-view" (p. 432). Mikulincer said, "Specifically, anxious-ambivalent persons' regulatory attempts to hyperactivate personal weaknesses and their sense of helplessness to convince an audience that they need external help to deal with life's problems and to elicit each others' compassion may favor the formation of a negative self-view" (p. 421).

When one cannot meet a challenge, one may adopt a subordinate position and admit one's shortcomings. This enables one to avoid the pain and frustration of further defeat. The anxious-ambivalent person's adoption of the subordinate stance has another important goal, namely to elicit support from an attachment figure to soothe distress. This is achieved by activation of both attachment and subordinate systems (Hilburn-Cobb, 1998). Gilbert (chap. 1, this volume) refers to these as affiliative submissive behaviors. Because of their habitual style of relating to others, anxious-ambivalent persons are more prone to develop rejection sensitivity, characterized by a premature triggering of the involuntary defeat strategy (IDS) so that these individuals exhibit an ineffective functioning of both their attachment and their dominant and subordinate systems. The IDS is discussed by Sloman (chap. 2, this volume) and the dominant and subordinate system is discussed by Gilbert (chap. 1, this volume) and by Weisfeld and Wendorf (chap. 8, this volume).

Mikulincer (1998) found that "avoidant persons' positive self-view and anxious-ambivalent persons' negative self-view were strengthened by distress related words and weakened by the presence of a friend" (p. 428). Mikulincer found it hard to explain the effect of having a friend present. However, the presence of a friend may alleviate distress. Therefore, a friend would reduce the avoidant person's need to activate the dominance system and reduce the need for the anxious-ambivalent person to activate the subordinate system in coping with distress. Consequently, the avoidant person has less need for an inflated self-view and the anxious-ambivalent person has less need for a devalued self-view. Importantly, individuals' attachment experiences relate to the different psychological impact of friendship and, presumably, the alliances these entail. This is an important consideration from the perspective of social competition.

Persons who are securely attached cope with distress without hyperactivating or deactivating the attachment system (Kobak et al., 1993). Therefore, secure persons' strategies for affect regulation produce little variation in self-view. They are able to self-regulate without resorting to either dominant or submissive strategies. It should be noted that the secure individual may make conscious use of a submissive strategy, for example, by highlighting his or her own inadequacies to make the other individual feel at ease. Having scanned the literature on attachment and social competence theories (linking the two via emotion regulation and self-concept), we illustrate the clinical utility of jointly considering attachment and social competence with a case study.

THE CASE OF CINDY

After we outline Cindy's history and her relationship with her parents, we describe the family system and the implications for the individual members. After we analyze the family system in terms of the social competition model and attachment theory, we demonstrate the therapeutic relevance of these two models. We argue that the use of these models greatly enriches our understanding of Cindy and her family and that an integration of social competition and attachment theory models provides a more comprehensive perspective than either model alone.

Cindy was a 16-year-old girl living with her parents. She was recovering from a major depressive episode, for which there was no clear-cut precipitant or robust family history. She was being treated with medication and family therapy, because it was believed that her depression was tied to her family dynamics. Cindy and her father felt that they had communicated freely when she was a preteen, and that this was no longer the case. Cindy's increased demands for independence escalated at the time of her reaching adolescence and, just prior to her depressive illness, major conflicts developed between Cindy and her father over how much freedom she should enjoy

Cindy reacted with frustration to her failure to get more support from her parents and claimed it was a "waste of time" to challenge her parents over anything, because they "were always right." She complained that her parents failed to acknowledge that some of her decisions were "the product of careful thought." Her father, on the other hand, complained that Cindy failed to appreciate the fact that his decisions were made with her "best interests at heart."

As therapy progressed, Cindy's mother came to feel more at ease, more assertive with Cindy's father, and she showed more warmth. She also showed a real talent for making productive use of therapeutic insights. Cindy continued to challenge her father, even though she felt these efforts were futile. Her father expressed much frustration over his inability to assert any authority over Cindy and blamed his wife for undermining his effort to do so. The father complained that, when he tried to be strong and firm with Cindy, his wife would become angry and frustrated with him. He said, "I feel that I am worrying about it on my own and that frustrates me even more. It has me in a quandary. It is making me sick." These comments were interpreted as his reaction to the mother's increased assertiveness. Cindy's father was convinced that his firmness and punishments of his daughter were in her best interests. Furthermore, he felt these were the times that he most needed her mother's support but, instead of providing this support, his wife turned on him and undermined what he was trying to achieve. As one explored the source of the mother's anger at the father, it became apparent that the father's treatment of Cindy reminded the mother of her own feelings of victimization as a child by her authoritarian father.

As Cindy began to feel more comfortable in the sessions, she revealed an ability to express herself in a humorous, satirical fashion. When her parents were asked whether they felt proud of Cindy's newfound ability to be so articulate and entertaining, her mother said she did, but her father reacted with apparent confusion. In response to a query about his reaction, Cindy's father said that he had struggled to understand her quick mind, but found it hard to follow what she was saying.

Family Dynamics

Whereas Cindy's father argued that he was acting in Cindy's best interests by setting limits on her behavior, her mother attacked him for being excessively rigid and punitive. Her father felt discouraged and undermined by his wife's attacks and his frustration and discouragement were compounded by Cindy's refusal to accept his authority. The mother felt comfortable expressing her anger with Cindy, but her father felt guilty about expressing his and, when he tried to set limits on her behavior, he was uncompromising. One could say that the father's effort to get Cindy to accept his authority reflected his need to bolster his self-esteem and assuage his guilt by proving what he was doing was in Cindy's best interests.

Cindy interpreted her father's discipline as a put-down and denial of the freedom to which she was entitled. She interpreted her mother's covert support as evidence that her father was being unreasonable. It therefore became a matter of principle for her to oppose her father. However, because her mother sent a covert message that she did not support the father's discipline, her failure to give Cindy more overt support resulted in Cindy feeling let down by both her parents.

When the sessions began, Cindy's mother appeared intimidated by Cindy's father and she was unable to confront him directly. There was an open struggle between Cindy and her father and a covert struggle between the parents. There was also a struggle between Cindy and her mother with her mother in the unenviable position of feeling that she had to oppose Cindy, although she sympathized with Cindy's position. As a result, all three family members felt engaged in struggles they could not win and all three seemed to feel hopeless and discouraged.

Dominance and Subordinate Systems

When the mother felt angry with the father for being so severe with Cindy, she tended to keep these feelings to herself until they became too powerful to control. When Cindy's mother revealed how she felt, during a session, the father claimed to have no idea how his wife felt, which came as a surprise to her. The fact that Cindy and her parents felt their mutual struggles were futile led to a triggering of their IDS, which left them all feeling inadequate, helpless, and hopeless. Cindy's father compensated for his feelings of inadequacy by becoming more rigid and controlling of Cindy. Her mother compensated by covertly supporting Cindy against her father and Cindy compensated by her determination not to give in. Cindy said to father "you can punish me as long as you want, but you will never convince me you are right."

Interaction Between Attachment and Dominance and Subordinate Systems

Because Cindy's parents were absorbed in their own unresolved conflict and unsatisfied attachment needs, they were not psychologically available to Cindy or to each other. Cindy and her father were seeking each other's affection, but each felt abandoned by the other. Cindy appears to have adopted what Crittenden (1992, 1997), in the context of preschool attachment, described in terms of a Type A (avoidant) defended strategy with a compulsive caregiving subpattern. From the perspective of survival (remembering that attachment theory is founded within an evolutionary context), the avoidant strategy enables the individual to maintain optimal distance from the attachment figure, not so close as to invite rebuff (and potential loss of protection), not so far away as to be vulnerable in times of threat. From the perspective of emotion regulation (and consonant with the demands of physical distance) the avoidant individual attempts to modulate his or her own emotional arousal without interpersonal support (again, "unreasonable" demands on the caregiver might entail rebuff and loss of protection). Typically, avoidant individuals rely heavily on the cognitive processing of emotional informaton (Crittenden, 1992, 1997). This is exemplified in quotes provided earlier, wherein Cindy focused on the validity of her and her father's ideas, overlooking how the father–daughter relationship made each of them feel. This strategy is defended because it protects Cindy from the full experience of negative emotion.

Although the avoidant individual attempts to maintain an optimal distance from the caregiver, he or she must also find ways to engage the caregiver and maintain accessibility. Therefore, Cindy attempted to entertain her father, as described earlier, in an overly bright fashion that contrasted with her usual depressed and angry presentation. This strategy, with its false affect, muted demands, and alluring quality, reflects an attempt to blunt further psychological retreat on the part of the father. Furthermore, this attempt represents a form of role reversal (Crittenden, 1992, 1997); in trying to help her father modulate his emotions (while falsifying her own), Cindy has taken on the role of caregiver.

As Thompson (1994) pointed out, an important feature of emotions is that they can be regulated to attain goals within a given context. Within the context of attachment, one would expect children to regulate their emotions to achieve proximity to an attachment figure (Cassidy, 1994). With reference to Cindy, we see how this process can go awry. Her father's distress at Cindy's quest for independence may have elicited and intensified her attempts to maintain optimal distance. Yet her solicitous behavior, with its implications of role reversal, also represented a threat to her father's dominance. Here we see an example of attachment needs and hierarchical imperatives working at cross-purposes.

Another reason that Cindy's attempts to regulate the caregiving relationship may have failed lies in the fact that they were mismatched with her father's attachment strategy. In contrast to Cindy's avoidant or dismissing state of mind and her reliance on cognitive coping, her father appeared to have adopted what Crittenden (1992, 1997) described as Type C (ambivalent/resistant) and the coercive strategy. Ambivalent individuals emphasize affect and feeling states in their interpersonal relationships, at the expense of cognition. This was substantiated by quotes from the father offered earlier. Given their different orientations, it is not surprising that her father acknowledged that he could not understand Cindy, and Cindy, for her part, protested that her father would never convince her that her ideas were wrong. Of interest, Crittenden described the intense display of feelings among ambivalent/resistant preschoolers as a means of coercing the caregiver. Certainly Cindy's father's affective displays in this case were predominantly and overtly coercive. Moreover, Crittenden suggested that the coercive strategy functions only in the presence of the attachment figure and that coercive children are extremely clingy. These considerations provide further evidence of role reversal; her father's coercion (itself a direct manifestation of both attachment style and social competition) might be seen as the complementary response to Cindy's attempt to both provide caregiving and assert her independence. Her father is trying to recapture control and, at the same time, retain his daughter as caregiver. Again, however, the mismatch in attachment orientations, the one cognitive and defended, the other emotional and coercive, may have precluded effective communication between Cindy and her father. Fonagy et al. (1997) noted the role of attachment asymmetry between parents and child in the context of externalizing behaviors.

In this discussion, we see the conflation of attachment and social competition issues. Thus far, we have discussed social competition in the context of attachment, but the reverse is also possible. Cindy's parents also tried to resolve attachment issues through dominance and subordination strategies. For example, her father's activation of his dominance system in asserting his authority was, literally, his way of reestablishing a closer tie with Cindy; that is, her father was asserting his authority in the service of thwarting Cindy's independence. Furthermore, by expecting Cindy and her mother to acknowledge he had Cindy's interests at heart, he was trying to ease the discomfort he felt in taking a strong stand; that is, he was not comfortable assuming the dominant role. Similarly, Cindy's mother's attacks on Cindy's father were her way of being supportive of Cindy, although they simultaneously undermined her father's dominance.

Cindy's mother's receptivity to the therapist's observations enabled her to make positive changes in her own behavior, and she was also able to objectively examine the current family interactions. She was also able to acknowledge how some of her anger at her husband, when he was punishing Cindy, was derived from her anger with her own father for being so authoritarian. We categorized her as having a secure type of attachment.

Although Cindy's subordinate system was activated during her depression, she tried to utilize it to obtain soothing from others. For example, when the therapist said that being depressed could have an adaptive value in certain situations, Cindy responded "by making the person who is bullying you feel guilty." She went on to say, "but I don't want to ask anyone for their pity."

Cassidy (1994) claimed:

> Given that the ultimate goal of the insecure/avoidant infant is to maintain proximity to an attachment figure who is known to reject attachment behaviors, the expression of emotions that can be construed as an attempt to elicit care may have dangerous consequences for the child. . . . If she increases her demands and becomes more clingy, she risks being rebuffed further. Avoidance and the masking of negative emotion reduce the infant's arousal level and thereby prevent the direct, possibly dangerous expression of anger toward the attachment figure. (p. 235)

Applying this to Cindy, when she became more needy as a result of becoming depressed, her parents' inability to respond supportively would have exacerbated her depression. However, as Cindy's depression responded to medication, she tried to alleviate her distress by reverting to the avoidant strategy. Cindy now continues to make good progress and medication has been almost discontinued.

It should be noted that our formulations of Cindy and her parents' attachment styles were made for heuristic reasons only. These formulations were based on some salient characteristics rather than formal assessments.

Therapeutic Implications

During the course of therapy, Cindy became more in touch with her own needs, more informed about the family interactional patterns, and more assertive. It was suggested that her verbal performance was her way of trying to reestablish the close relationship she had enjoyed with her father prior to her teenage years. The therapist suggested to Cindy and her father that, although the apparent basis of their conflicts was Cindy's desire to have more freedom, the more important underlying issue for both of them was their wish to reestablish the closeness that had once existed between them. Cindy agreed, and the therapist, trying to support Cindy without undermining her father, said that it was often difficult for parents in their stage of life (his and the therapist's), to understand and appreciate their children's sense of humor. The therapist was using his dominant position in the family hierarchy (by virtue of his role as "doctor" or "expert") to support one family member without undermining the other.

The therapist tried to be balanced in his support of all family members, but Cindy was the strongest advocate for the continuation of the family sessions and she gradually became more trusting of the therapist. Cindy's behavior could be interpreted both in terms of social competition theory and attachment theory. From a social competition perspective, Cindy was seen as having accepted the therapist's implicit offer of alliance so that she could be more overt in asserting her partnership and challenging her father within the family. In attachment terms, Cindy came to see the therapist as a secure base, someone who would support her interpersonal explorations and help regulate the increased affectivity this would entail.

At another stage, it was suggested that the family's struggles represented a form of overcompensation for their feelings of inadequacy, because they all felt they could not win. It was proposed that their next challenge would be to learn how to argue without triggering their IDS.

When the therapist initially raised the concept of the IDS, it was described as a biological response that evolved because it played an important role in preventing conflict, or ensuring that conflicts did not get out of hand. If, for some reason, the IDS was prematurely triggered or overly persistent, this could manifest as emotional disturbance. An analogy was drawn (Price, 1988) between the IDS and "shivering." Shivering is automatically triggered by cold, but can be prevented by warm clothing. The IDS is also automatically triggered and can be prevented by avoiding engaging in conflicts one cannot win, and by being forceful and assertive when one can win. In the case of Cindy, the automatic thoughts (see Swallow, chap. 8, this volume) responsible for triggering her IDS were explored. After challenging the basis for her negative self-evaluation, small experiments in self-assertion were prescribed. They were called experiments so that Cindy would not think in terms of success or failure. Although the ostensible purpose was to gather information, any successful self-assertion was considered progress. Cindy was able, with help, to acknowledge other occasions when she had been assertive, which served to build up her confidence. After a while, she became more assertive with her family, but still had difficulty with people she did not know. She said what helped her most at those times was thinking about her close friends. This illustrates the close interrelation between the competitive and the affiliative systems, which is to be expected, as support from friends or allies can make a crucial difference when competing for power or status.

When Cindy's mother was informed that her way of handling the discomfort triggered by the memory of her father's abuse was to make her husband the "bad guy," she responded that she had just become aware that her husband was doing this in Cindy's best interest. The father's anger with Cindy for challenging him was compounded by his wife's attacks on him. He dealt with his discomfort at having so much anger by justifying his hard-line stance and claiming that what he was doing was "in Cindy's best interest." He was informed that his discomfort over his anger and his wife's attacks on him was getting in the way of his efforts to discipline Cindy. He responded by expressing an interest in learning how to deal with his anger and frustration in a more productive fashion.

Cindy's depression is now much improved. The two main and interrelated goals in working with this family were to establish more secure attachments between the family members and to develop a more flexible, functional hierarchy. One way of realizing the first objective was having the therapist provide a secure base for all family members, enabling them to explore new ways of relating to each other and removing the barrier of mistrust compounded by misunderstanding each other's intentions. The therapist's interpretation of the family dynamics provided the family with a coherent narrative. To achieve the second aim, an effort was made to promote a more flexible and efficient operation of the dominance and subordination behavioral system (see chapter Levitan et al., chap. 4, this volume). As the parents developed a better mutual understanding, their negotiating skills improved, resulting in better teamwork between them. As a result, when her father did take a hard line with Cindy, he knew he had his wife's support, which enabled him to feel more self-confident. This enabled him to avoid triggering his IDS, thereby helping him to become more flexible and to avoid becoming involved in unproductive power struggles. As the atmosphere improved, the parents became more responsive to Cindy and more accepting of her need for independence. This helped Cindy feel more supported by both her parents. She was able to resolve issues around her own sense of identity and engage in conflicts without triggering her IDS and becoming depressed.

GENERAL CONSIDERATIONS

When the therapist is perceived by the client to be reliably available (physically and psychologically) within explicitly stated contractual limits and in the context of stress and adversity, the therapist comes to serve as a secure base for the client. This tends to permit the IDS to be more flexible and more effective, which often manifests as increased self-assertiveness and fewer depressive symptoms. The implications of attachment theory for family systems have only recently been the subject of more intensive study. Byng-Hall (1995) presented the concept of a secure family base as a way of providing the systemic framework necessary for family therapists. Byng-Hall stressed the need for children to sense that the relationships between adults are sufficiently collaborative to ensure that care is available at all time. He says, "The shared working model of the secure family base is of family members supporting each other to care for their members" (p. 46). By way of contrast, the social competition model fits in very well with a family systems model and in particular the school of structural family therapy (Minuchin & Fishman, 1981). Structural family therapists view problems as an indication of an imbalance in the family's organization, particularly a malfunctioning hierarchical arrangement with unclear parent and child subsystem boundaries. The therapeutic approach centers on strengthening the structural foundation for family functioning; in particular a generationally appropriate hierarchy, with parents maintaining a strong leadership unit and with boundaries that are neither too diffuse or too rigid. In terms of social competition theory, the therapist aims to achieve these goals by promoting a more efficient functioning of the dominance and subordinate systems.

The interaction between Cindy and her father illustrates how Cindy's insecure attachment led to ineffective functioning of her dominance and subordinate system. The premature triggering of her mother's IDS caused her to become angry with her husband when he tried to set firm limits on Cindy and this, together with Cindy's constant challenging of her father's authority, contributed to the triggering of his IDS and the ineffective functioning of his dominance system. As Cindy's mother learned to avoid triggering her own IDS and became more assertive with her husband, she revealed herself as being securely attached, enabling her to become more supportive of other family members. Because both Cindy and her father were insecurely attached, they endeavored to relieve their distress through the activation of their dominance system, but this failed to ease their tension. The therapist initially became the base of a more secure attachment. He later enabled the family members to develop more secure attachments with each other and facilitated the more effective functioning of their dominance and subordinate systems.

REFERENCES

Ainsworth, M. D., Blehar, M. C., Waters, E., & Wall, S. (1978). *Patterns of attachment: A psychological study of the Strange Situation.* Hillsdale, NJ: Lawrence Erlbaum Associates.

Boccia, M. L. (1992). Refining the attachment model. *Brain and Behavior, 15,* 511–512.

Bowlby, J. (1973). *Attachment and loss: Vol. 2. Separation, anxiety, and anger* (pp. 174–175. London: Penguin.

Byng-Hall, J. (1995). Creating a secure family base: Some implications of attachment theory for family therapy. *Family Process, 34,* 45–58

Cassidy, J. (1994) Emotion regulation: Influences of attachment relationships. In N. A. Fox (Ed.), The development of emotion regulation. *Monographs of the Society for Research in Child Development, 59*(2–3, Serial No. 240), 228–283.

Crittenden, P. M. (1992). Quality of attachment in the preschool years. *Development and Psychopathology, 4,* 209–241.

Crittenden, P. M. (1997). Patterns of attachment and sexual behavior: Risk of dysfunction versus opportunity for creative integration. In L. Atkinson & K. J. Zucker (Eds.), *Attachment and psychopathology* (pp. 47–96). New York: Guilford.

Egeland, B., Kalkoska, M., Gottesman, N., & Erickson, M. (1990). Preschool behavior problems: Stability and factors accounting for change. *Journal of Child Psychology and Psychiatry, 31,* 891–909.

Fonagy, P., Target, M., Steele, M., Steele, H., Leigh, T., Levinson, A., & Kennedy, R. (1997). Morality, disruptive behavior, borderline personality disorder, crime and their relationship to security of attachment. In L. Atkinson & K. J. Zucker (Eds.), *Attachment and psychopathology* (pp. 223–274). New York: Guilford Press.

Greenberg, M. T., DeKlyen, M., Speltz, M. L., & Endriga, M. C. (1997). The role of attachment processes in externalizing psychopathology in young children. In L. Atkinson & K. J. Zucker (Eds.), *Attachment and psychopathology* (pp. 196–222) New York: Guilford.

Hazan, C., & Shaver, P. (1987). Romantic love conceptualised as an attachment process. *Journal of Personality and Social Psychology, 52,* 511–524.

Hilburn-Cobb, C. (1998). *Adolescent disorganization of attachment and its relation to psychopathology.* Paper presented at Attachment and Psychopathology; Second International Conference. Toronto, Canada.

Kobak, R. R., Cole, H. E., Ferenz-Gillies, R., & Fleming, W. S. (1993). Attachment and emotion regulation during mother–teen problem solving: A control theory analysis. *Child Development, 64,* 231–245.

Kraemer, G. W. (1992). A psychobiological theory of attachment. *Behavioral and Brain Sciences, 15,* 493–541.

Main, M., Kaplan, N., & Cassidy, J. (1985). Security in infancy, childhood, and adulthood: A move to the level of representation. In I. Bretherton & E. Waters (Eds.), Growing points in attachment theory and research. *Monographs of the Society for Research in Child Development, 50*(1–2, Serial No. 209), 66–104.

Main, M., & Solomon, J. (1986). Discovery of a new, insecure-disorganized/disoriented attachment pattern. In M. Yogman & T. B. Brazelton (Eds.), *Affective development in infancy* (pp. 95–124). Norwood, NJ: Ablex.

Main, M., & Solomon, J. (1990). Procedures for identifying infants as disorganized/disoriented during the Ainsworth Strange Situation. In M. T. Greenberg, D. Ciccetti, & E. M. Cummings (Eds.), *Attachment in the preschool years: Theory, research, and intervention* (pp. 121–160). Chicago: University of Chicago Press.

Mikulincer, M. (1997). Adult attachment style and information processing: Individual differences in curiosity and cognitive closure. *Journal of Personality and Social Psychology, 72,* 1217–1230.

Mikulincer, M. (1998). Adult attachment style and affect regulation: Strategic variations in self-appraisals. *Journal of Personality and Social Psychology, 75,* 420–435.

Mikulincer, M., & Florian, V. (1998) Appraisal of and coping with a real life stressful situation: The contribution of attachment styles. *Personality and Social Psychology Bulletin, 21,* 406–414.

Minuchin, S., & Fishman, H. C. (1981). *Family therapy techniques.* Cambridge, MA: Harvard University Press.

Perusse, D. (1992). Attachment: A view from evolutionary biology and behavior genetics. *Behavioral and Brain Sciences, 15,* 521–522.

Price, J. S. (1988). The adaptive function of mood change. *British Journal of Medical Psychology, 71,* 465–477.

Rogeness, G. A., & McClure, E. B. (1996). Development and neurotransmitter: Environmental interactions. *Development and Psychopathology, 8,* 183–199.

Shaver, P. R., & Hazan, C. (1993). Adult romantic attachment: Theory and evidence. In D. Perlman & W. Jones (Eds.), *Advances in personal relationships* (Vol. 4, pp. 29–70). London: Jessica Kingsley.

Speltz, M. L., Greenberg, M. T., & DeKlyen, M. (1990). Attachment in preschoolers with disruptive behavior: A comparison of clinic-referred and nonproblem children. *Development and Psychopathology, 2,* 31–46.

Sroufe, L. A., Egeland, B., & Kreutzer, T. (1990). The fate of early experience following developmental change: Longitudinal approaches to individual adaptation in childhood. *Child Development, 61,* 1363–1373.

Sroufe, L. A., & Waters, E. (1977). Attachment as an organizational construct. *Child Development, 48,* 1184–1199.

Tesser, A. (1988). Toward a self-evaluation maintenance model of social behavior. In L. Berkowitz (Ed.), *Advances in experimental social psychology: Vol 21. Social psychological studies of the self* (pp. 181–227). New York: Academic.

Thompson, R. A. (1994). Emotion regulation: A theme in search of definition. In N. A. Fox (Ed.), The development of emotion regulation. *Monographs of the Society for Research in Child Development, 59,* (2–3, Serial No. 240), 25–52.

Troy, M., & Sroufe, L. A. (1987). Victimization among preschoolers: Role of attachment relationship history. *Journal of American Academy of Child and Adolescent Psychiatry, 26,* 166–172.

CHAPTER TEN

Concluding Comments

LEON SLOMAN
Centre for Addiction and Mental Health, Toronto, Ontario

PAUL GILBERT
Kingsway Hospital, Derby, UK

This volume has presented a model of depression that purports to account for the evolutionary function of the mechanisms that contribute to a number of forms of depression. We call this the *social rank model,* although in fact much of what is outlined here is how moods, emotions, and social behaviors that evolved in hierarchical social relationships over millions of years have to be seen as integrated with those that evolved later to serve attachment needs. We have used case examples to illustrate how this model enables us to help our clients learn more health-promoting ways of managing thwarted goals, anger, and conflict. However, the relevance of other models in helping us to achieve these aims has also been outlined. For example, attachment theory highlights the value of promoting secure attachments in our clients and it was suggested that the presence of secure attachments will promote the effective functioning of mechanisms like the involuntary defeat strategy (IDS), acceptance, and submission, which are designed to bring conflict to an end. Depression has been conceptualized as a fail-safe strategy and the therapist can present alternatives at a higher level of organization. Therapy based on evolutionary principles aims to replace unconscious behavioral strategies with conscious ones.

IS DEPRESSION ADAPTIVE?

It is often asked how depression could be adaptive when it causes such misery and may end in suicide. The authors in this volume have made clear that no evolutionist argues that serious forms of depression are adaptive. Rather it is the effort to understand adaptive mechanisms that have become maladaptive that is at issue. Just as panic disorder may not be adaptive in the modern environment, our understanding of it increases when we understand the nature of a threat detection and flight system. Depression is similar. Before we can understand its pathological forms we need to understand its normal functions. In this we have argued that depression is adaptive when it turns off defensive fight–flight behavior and leads to acceptance of limitations or defeats. It becomes maladaptive when the smooth function of the IDS breaks down. This is possible in situations in which a person wishes to continue fighting but continues losing or when an individual cannot escape from aversive situations or when he or she cannot come to terms with losing (e.g., due to problems in the attachment system).

Such a view does not however argue that all depressions are only related to life histories and life events. There is good evidence that some depressions are genetically influenced. For example, for disorders such as bipolar affective illness, evidence suggests that genes for excessive mood variation may have been positively selected and offer advantages provided their rates do not exceed certain frequencies in populations (Wilson, 1998). But as Wilson pointed out, such genetic effects may be operating through mechanisms that control agonistic and competitive behavior. We are a long way from understanding the genetic linkages to depression, but we believe that such research can be advanced when we are better able to understand the normal adaptive functions of mood variation, rather than just seeing depression as a disease that is not underpinned by systems that have adaptive functions.

INTERACTIONS

Attachment theory and the IDS model are evolutionary—biological in nature so that the integration of the IDS model with a pharmacotherapeutic model that focuses on brain neurotransmitters would seem quite natural. Cognitive behavioral therapy can also be seen as a means of raising resource-holding power and other components of self-esteem and of rendering the basis for these self-appraisals realistic. The social rank model of depression is the linchpin of an integrative approach to diverse phenomena like submissive behaviors, conceptions of self-esteem, social comparison theory, brain neurotransmitter parameters of subordination, and mood disorders. Psychomotor retardation is one feature of the IDS that can play an important role in terminating competitive conflict. Rising status is generally associated with feelings of pride, erect carriage, and firm, brisk steps. Falling status is associated with shame, bowed head and shoulders, and slow, dragging footsteps. A reciprocal relation exists between postural patterns and self-esteem. It has been proposed that physical attractiveness and probably other indications of attractiveness associated with high or rising status act as signs to expedite mate selection and are thus fundamental to mate selection among humans (Sloman & Sloman, 1988).

However, a fuller exploration of various ramifications of the social rank model will have to await future research and therapeutic studies. We believe that human depression is a complex, multidetermined state, and the IDS model provides a valuable added perspective. The adaptive function of the IDS is to assist individuals in giving up attachments, be they to things, persons, or status. The individual suffering from the IDS type of depression must give up the unattainable goal or incentive before recovery can take place.

The incorporation of ethological concepts also provides a broad, comprehensive model of family functioning because it encompasses genetic and biosocial factors within which certain types of individual psychopathology and family dysfunction can be more readily understood. We stress that the presence of secure attachments and the smooth functioning of ritual competitive behavior play a pivotal role in the prevention of individual disturbance and family dysfunction, reducing dysfunction if this develops. It also permits family members to be supportive of each other's growth and development.

REFERENCES

Sloman, S., & Sloman, L. (1988). Mate selection in the service of human evolution. *Journal of Social and Biological Structures, 11,* 457–468.

Wilson, D. (1998). Evolutionary epidemiology and manic depression. *British Journal of Medical Psychology, 71,* 375–396.

Author Index

A

Abed, R. T., 169, *176*
Abramson, L. Y., 23, *44,* 183, *196*
Adams, M., 106, *112*
Adams, N., 15, *38*
Adler, N. E., 34, *38*
Adler, W. Z., 25, *39*
Adler, Z., 173, *176*
Affleck, G., 169, 170, *177*
Aghajanian, G. K., 100, *110*
Agren, H., 78, *90,* 99, *109*
Ahrens, A. H., 149, 151, 153, 155, *161*
Ainsworth, M. D., 200, *212*
Akil, H., 97, *114*
Akiskal, H. S., 174, *176*
Akiskal, S. H., 170, *177*
Albanese, M., 99, *113*
Alberts, S. C., 97, *113*
Albright, J. S., 151, 153, *161*
Alicke, M. D., 150, *161*
Allan, J. S., 101, *110*
Allan, S., 6, 11, 13, 17, 22, 25, 29, 31, 32, 33, 34, 35, 36, *38, 41,* 50, 51, 52, *66,* 88, *91,* 123, 127, 129, 137, 139, *141,* 148, 150, *161, 162,* 168, 170, *176,* 185, 188, *197*
Allee, W. C., 128, *141*
Allison, S. T., 152, *162*
Alloy, L. B., 149, 151, 155, *161, 163,* 183, *196*
Altmann, J., 97, *113*
American Psychiatric Association, 21, *38,* 47, *66,* 71, 80, 81, *90*
Amsterdam, J. D., 97, *109*
Anand, A., 100, *109*
Anderson, J. L., 101, *110*
Anderson, K., 33, *40*
Andrews, B., 29, *38,* 165, 173, *176*
Andrews, M. W., 29, *44,* 73, *93*
Anisman, H., 14, *38*
Anton, R. F., 76, *93*
Arato, M., 97, *109*
Archer, J., 4, 5, 6, 32, *38,* 165, *176*
Arger, P., 97, *109*
Arrindell, W. A., 3, 17, 33, *38*
Asberg, M., 99, 100, *109, 114*
Asnis, G. M., 100, *111*
Astill, J. L., 99, *110*
Atkinson, L., 66, *66*
Attar-Levy, D., 78, *92*
Atzwanger, K., 116, *118*
Aurora, R. C., 100, *112*
Averill, J. R., 137, *139*

B

Baber, R., 100, *112*
Bailey, A., 89, *90, 92*
Bailey, K., 4, 36, *39*

Bailey, W. H., 14, *45*
Ball, L., 29, *41*, 129, *141*
Ballenger, J. C., 99, *110*
Bandura, A., 180, *196*
Banki, C. M., 97, *109*
Barch, D., 151, *161*
Barden, N., 98, 108, *109*
Barkow, J. H., 5, 22, *39*, 122, 124, 126, *139*, 149, 150, *161*, 168, *176*
Barlow, D., 14, 15, 24, 25, 36, 37, *40*
Barnett, P. A., 192, *196*
Barthelms, H., 101, *114*
Barton, S., 11, *39*
Bassoff, T., 29, *44*, 73, *93*
Bateson, G., 56, *66*
Baumeister, R. E., 5, 22, 34, 36, *39*
Baumgart, E. P., 157, *163*
Baxter, L. R., 77, *90*
Beach, S. R. H., 27, *39*
Beahrs, J. O., 23, *39*
Beam, C., 97, *113*
Beasley, C. M., 89, *90*
Beck, A. T., 29, 31, 36, *39*, 137, *139*, 150, 152, *161*, 170, *176*, 182, 183, 184, *196*
Beersma, D. G. M., 101, 106, *109*
Beevers, C. G., 159, *164*
Belsher, G., 36, *39*
Bench, C. J., 78, *90*
Benkelfat, C., 77, *92*, 100, *109*
Benton, A. L., 123, *142*
Beresford, J. M., 127, *144*
Berger, M., 88, *90*
Berkeley, A. W., 130, *140*
Berkestijn, H. W. B. M., 101, 106, *109*
Bernstein, I. S., 7, *39*, 129, *143*
Berntson, G. G., 181, *196*
Berrettini, W. H., 107, *109*
Berridge, M., 116, *118*
Bertilisson, L., 99, *109*
Bethea, C. L., 105, *111*
Bifulco, A., 25, 29, *39*
Birchwood, M., 26, 34, *44*
Birtchnell, J., 3, 22, *39*
Bishop, S., 183, *196*
Bissette, G., 97, *109*, *113*
Biver, E., 77, *91*
Blackburn, I. M., 183, *196*
Blalock, S. J., 159, *162*
Blatt, S. J., 30, *39*
Blehar, M. C., 200, *212*
Bless, E., 99, *110*
Blessed, G., 100, *113*
Blier, P., 77, *92*
Bloch, S., 130, *140*
Block, P., 137, *143*
Bloom, S. W., 130, *141*
Blum, B., 132, *140*
Boardway, R. H., 125, *140*
Boccia, M. L., 200, *212*
Boehm, C., 173, *176*
Boice, R., 15, *38*
Bolles, R. C., 137, *140*
Bond, A. J., 99, *110*
Booth, A., 105, *112*, 129, *142*
Bornstein, R. F., 21, *39*
Bos, D., 149, 156, *164*
Bossert, S., 88, *90*
Botchin, M. B., 76, *91*
Bovard, E. W., 130, *142*
Bowlby J., 5, *25*, *39*, 48, *66*, 72, *91*, 136, *140*, 199, *212*
Boyce, T., 34, *38*
Boyko, O. B., 97, *112*
Brackenridge, C. J., 130, *140*
Bradshaw, Z., 29, *41*, 129, *141*
Brain, C. K., 129, *140*
Bramel, D., 132, *140*
Brammer, G. L., 22, *44*, 73, 74, *92*, *93*, 99, 108, *113*
Breeijen, A., 131, *143*
Breitenbecher, D. L., 150, *161*
Bremner, J. D., 100, 104, 108, *109*
Brewerton, T. D., 107, *109*
Brewin, C. R., 150, 153, *162*
Bridge, L., 173, *176*
Brinder, R. B., 25, *43*
Broman, C. L., 32, *39*
Bronen, R. A., 100, 104, 108, *109*
Bronson, W. C., 127, *140*
Brooke, S., 97, *109*
Brough, S., 36, *41*

Brown, G. L., 99, 100, *110*
Brown, G. M., 99, 107, *112*
Brown, G. W., 25, 26, 32, 34, *39,* 173, *176,* 185, *196*
Brown, J. D., 150, *163*
Brown, R. G., 78, *90*
Buchner, D. M., 116, *117, 118*
Buck, R., 10, *39*
Bunney, W. E., 100, *110*
Bunnk, B. P., 149, 150, 155, 156, 157, 159, *161, 162, 164*
Burch, N. R., 130, *141*
Burggraf, S. A., 30, *44*
Bushnell, W., 108, *114*
Buss, D. M., 3, 4, 5, 21, *39,* 134, *140,* 169, *176*
Buswell, B. N., 123, 125, 126, *141*
Byers, C. N., 184, *197*
Bymaster, F. P., 89, *93*
Byng-Hall, J., 211, *212*

C

Cacioppo, J. T., 181, *196*
Calabrese, J. R., 97, 106, *111*
Callaghan, J. W., 133, *144*
Campbell, A. J., 116, *117*
Cannon, W. B., 129, *140*
Carroll, B. J., 98, *110*
Carver, C. S., 153, 156, *162, 163*
Caryl, R.G., 4, 5, 6, *40*
Cassidy, J., 201, 202, 207, 209, *212, 213*
Caudle, J. M., 97, *113*
Chalmers, D. T., 87, *92,* 98, *112*
Champion, L. A., 26, *40*
Champoux, M., 98, 108, *111*
Chan, T., 90, *91,* 99, 108, *112*
Chance, M. R. A., 8, 16, 17, 19, 20, *40*
Chapais, B., 21, *40*
Charig, E. M., 100, *110*
Charney, D. S., 100, 104, 107, 108, *109, 110, 112, 113*
Chen, J., 77, *92*
Chenery D., 18, *40*
Cherek, D. R., 99, *112*
Chesney, M. A., 34, *38*
Chevron, E. S., 30, *39*
Chollet, E., 79, *93*
Chorpita, B. E., 14, 15, 24, 25, 36, 37, *40*
Christensen, A. V., 108, *111*
Chrousos, G. R., 106, *110*
Cicchetti, D., 29, *42,* 123, *143*
Clark, C., 3, *40*
Clarke, A. S., 76, 87, 72, *91*
Clarke, I. J., 105, *112*
Cleare, A. J., 99, *110*
Cloninger, C. R., 77, *91*
Coates, D., 158, *162*
Coccaro, E. E., 99, *110, 111*
Cochrane, N., 33, *40*
Coe, C. L., 136, *140*
Cohen, L., 99, *111*
Cohen, R. M., 107, *110*
Cohen, S., 34, *38*
Cole, H. E., 202, 204, *213*
Cole, J. C., 101, *114*
Cole, S. W., 90, *91,* 99, 108, *112*
Collins, D., 99, *112*
Collins, J. F., 183, *196*
Conrad, E., 131, *143*
Cooley, C. H., 170, *176*
Coopersmith, S., 130, *140*
Coplan, J. D., 29, *44,* 73, *93*
Corrales, R. G., 134, *140*
Coryell, W. A., 77, *91*
Costello, C. G., 36, *39*
Coulter, M. E., 101, 106, *110*
Cowen, P. J., 100, *110*
Coyer, P. F., 100, *110*
Coyne, J. C., 23, *40,* 184, 188, *196*
Craig, J. A., 188, *198*
Craik, K. H., 3, 21, *39*
Crane, J. B., 77, *91*
Cress, M. E., 116, *117, 118*
Crittenden, P. M., 207, 208, *212*
Crocker, J., 151, *163*
Cronin, C. L., 125, 133, *140, 145*
Cronin, H., 5, *40*
Crook, J. H., 128, *140*
Cummings, J. L., 116, *118*

Cutler, D., 25, *41*
Czeisler, C. A., 101, *110*

D

Daan, S., 15, *43*
Daly, M., 5, *40, 45*
Damasio, A. R., 123, 124, *140, 143*
Damasio, H., 123, *140*
Dantzer, R., 15, *43*
Darwin, C., 115, *118,* 122, *140*
David, M. M., 101, 106, *110*
Davidson, R. J., 131, 138, *140*
Davies, N. B., 5, 7, *42,* 165, *176*
Davis, C. M., 99, *112*
Davis, K. L., 101, *114*
de Boer, S. E., 15, *43*
de Haas-Johnson, A., 97, *109*
De Kloet, E. R., 105, *110, 111*
de la Vega, E., 100, *114*
de Montigny, C., 77, *92*
de Waal, F. M. B., 4, 5, 6, 18, 19, 20, 21, *40*
Dean, P., 100, *109*
Decaria, C. M., 99, *111*
deCatanzaro, D. A., 135, *140*
DeKlyen, M., 202, *213*
Delgado, P. L., 100, *109, 110, 112, 113*
Delvenne, V., 77, *91*
DeMaertelaer, V., 77, *91*
DeMeo, M., 77, *92*
DeMyer, M. K., 100, *110*
DeRubeis, R. J., 183, 184, *197*
DeVellis, R. F., 159, *162*
Dey, H., 100, 104, 108, *109*
Diksic, M., 77, *92*
Dinan, T. G., 100, *113*
Dirlich, G., 88, *90,* 101, *114*
Dittrich, A., 73, *93*
Dixon, A. K., 10, 11, 12, 15, 18, 19, 30, 34, 36, 37, *40,* 166, *176*
Dixon, N. F., 23, *40*
Dodge, K. A., 133, *140*
Doerr, P., 101, *114*
Dolan, R. J., 78, *90*
Dong, Q., 125, *140*
Doraiswamy, P. M., 97, *112*
Dougherty, D., 138, *140*
Dougherty, D. M., 99, *112*
Downey, G., 58, *66*
Downs, D. L., 174, *176*
Drevets, W. C., 100, 108, *110*
Driscoll, R., 30, *40*
Duck, T., 116, *118*
Dunbar, R. I. M., 7, 8, 23, *40*
Duncan, J., 100, 104, 108, *109*
Duncan, W. C., 101, *114*
Dunnick, N. R., 97, *113*
Dweck, C. S., 128, *140*
Dyck, M. J., 184, *197*
Dykman, B. M., 151, *161*

E

Ebert, M. H., 99, 100, *110, 111*
Eccard, M. B., 97, *113*
Edelman, M. S., 123, *142*
Edwards, J. A., 149, 150, *164*
Egeland, B., 202, *212, 213*
Ehlers, C. L., 101, *110*
Eibl-Eibesfeldt, I., 20, 21, *40*
Eisenberg, H. M., 123, *142*
Eklund, K., 97, *113*
Ekman, P., 18, *40*
Elbin, S., 155, *164*
Elkin, I., 183, *196*
Ellenbogen, M. A., 100, *109*
Ellinwood, E. H., 97, *112*
Elliott, R., 31, *42*
Elliott, R. K, 31, *41*
Emery, G., 29, 31, 36, *39*
Emrich, H. M., 101, *114*
Endriga, M. C., 202, *213*
Engleman, E. A., 89, *93*
Erickson, M., 202, *212*
Erlbaugh, J., 150, *161*
Ernst, D., 184, *197*
Ervin, F. R., 100, *114*
Esler, M., 105, *112*
Esselman, P. C., 116, *117*
Essock-Vitale, S. M., 80, 81, 86, 89, *91, 92*
Ettmeier, W., 88, *90*

Eunson, K. M., 183, *196*
Evans, M. D., 183, 184, *197*

F

Fanselow, M. S., 137, *140*
Faucher, I., 76, 87, *92,* 98, 99, *112*
Fava, G. A., 33, *40*
Fava, M., 33, *40,* 99, *110*
Feldman, S. I., 58, *66*
Feline, A., 78, *92*
Ferenz-Gillies, R., 202, 204, *213*
Festinger, L., 147, 154, 161, *162*
Fiatarone, M. A., 116, *118*
Fiester, S. J., 183, *196*
Figiel, G. S., 97, *112*
Fisch, H. U., 10, 12, 18, 34, 37, *40*
Fishman, H. C., 211, *213*
Fitzgerald, R. C., 137, *140*
Flannery, R. C., 124, *143*
Fleming, W. S., 202, 204, *213*
Flett, G. L., 156, *162*
Florian, V., 202, *213*
Flory, J. D., 87, *91*
Flowers, J., 116, *118*
Fluoxetine Bulimia Nervosa Collaborative (FBNC) Study Group, 99, *110*
Foerster, R. S., 31, *41*
Folkman, S., 34, *38,* 186, *197*
Fonagy, P., 208, *212*
Fox, H. M., 130, *141*
Fox, P. T., 78, *92, 93*
Frackowiak, R. S. J., 78, 79, *90, 93*
Frame, C. L., 133, *140*
Frank, E., 101, *110*
Frank, R., 123, *140*
Franken, R. E., 130, *140*
Freedman, D. G., 123, 124, *142*
Fremald, B., 6, *42*
Friedman, S., 29, *44,* 73, *93*
Frischknecht, H. R., 15, *41, 42*
Friston, K., 79, *93*
Friston, K. J., 78, *90*
Fuller, R. W., 99, *110*
Fullerton, M. J., 105, *112*
Funder, J. W., 105, *112*
Furnham, A., 150, 153, *162*
Fusselman, M. J., 78, *93*
Fuster, J. M., 124, *140*

G

Gaebel, W., 80, *91*
Galaburda, A. M., 123, *140*
Gallucci, W., 97, 106, *111*
Gallup, G. G., 135, *144*
Ganzini, L., 25, *41*
Garcia-Borreguero, D., 107, *114*
Gardner, R., 4, 8, 21, *41, 43,* 49, 50, *67,* 89, *92,* 107, *111,* 132, 139, *143, 144,* 148, 152, 154, *163,* 167, 171, 174, *176, 177,* 184, *197*
Gartlan, J. S., 129, *140*
Garvey, M. J., 183, *197*
Geller, E., 99, *113*
Gellhorn, E., 131, *140*
Gemar, M. A., 56, *67*
Geoffroy, M., 108, *111*
George, K. P., 76, 87, *91*
George, M. S., 78, *91,* 100, *111*
Gerard, H. B., 155, *162*
Gerety, M. B., 116, *118*
Gergel, I., 108, *114*
Gerken, A., 97, *111*
Gerner, R. H., 77, *90*
Gerrard, M., 158, *162*
Gibbons, F. X., 156, 158, 159, *162*
Gilbert, P., 1, 3, 4, 5, 6, 7, 8, 10, 11, 13, 15, 17, 18, 20, 22, 24, 25, 26, 29, 30, 31, 32, 33, 34, 35, 36, *38, 40, 41,* 49, 50, 51, 52, 53, 57, *66, 67,* 88, 89, *91, 92,* 122, 123, 124, 125, 126, 127, 129, 132, 135, 137, 138, 139, *141, 144,* 148, 150, 152, 154, *161, 162, 163,* 167, 168, 170, 171, *176, 177,* 181, 183, 184, 185, 188, *197*
Gillin, J. C., 101, *114*
Ginsburg, B. E., 128, *141*

Ginsburg, H. J., 126, *141*
Glazer, H. I., 14, *45*
Goering, P. N., 106, *112*
Goethals, G. R., 152, *162*
Goetz, R. C., 130, *141*
Gold, P. W., 97, 106, *110, 111*
Goldman, D., 100, *113*
Goldman, S., 77, *91*
Goodall, J., 19, 20, *41*
Goode, S., 89, *92*
Goodwin, D. W., 77, *91*
Goodwin, F. K., 99, 100, 101, *110, 112, 114*
Gorman, J. M., 29, *44,* 73, *93*
Gotlib, I. H., 192, *196*
Gottesman, I., 89, *92*
Gottesman, N., 202, *212*
Gottman, J. M., 133, *141*
Grabowski, T., 123, *140*
Grant, E. C., 89, *91*
Gray, J. A., 9, 10, 27, *41*, 130, 138, *141*
Gray, S. J., 130, *141*
Greenberg, J., 155, 159, *163*
Greenberg, J. R., 30, *41*
Greenberg, L. S., 30, 31, *41, 42*
Greenberg, M. T., 202, *213*
Greenberg, R. L., 29, 31, *39*
Grewal, A., 107, *112*
Gross, M., 107, *110*
Grossmann, K. E., 136, *144*
Grove, W. M., 183, *197*
Grunhaus, L., 97, *114*
Gundlah, C., 105, *111*
Gunnar, M., 29, *42*
Gut, E., 88, *91*
Guze, S. B., 77, *91*
Gwirtsman, H. E., 99, *111*

H

Haaga, D. A. F., 184, *197*
Hack, M. A., 166, *176*
Hadar, U., 79, *93*
Hageman, W. J. J. M., 3, 17, 33, *38*
Hakmiller, K. L., 158, *162*
Halberg, F., 101, *111*
Haley, J., 56, *66*
Hammen, C., 34, *42,* 149, 150, 151, 152, 154, 157, *162*
Hardy, P., 78, *92*
Harker, L. A., 6, 14, 20, 30, *42*
Harlow, H. F., 72, *91,* 136, *142*
Harlow, M. K., 72, *91*
Harper, D. G., 101, 106, *111*
Harper, R. C., 18, *42*
Harris, T. O., 25, 26, 32, 34, *39,* 173, *176,* 185, *196*
Hart, J., 29, *42*
Hartlage, S., 183, *196*
Hartung, J., 23, *42*
Hartup, W. W., 21, *42,* 126, *141*
Hasert, M. R., 98, 108, *111*
Hasey, G., 116, *118*
Haskett, R. F., 97, *114*
Hazan, C., 202, 203, *213*
Headey, B., 150, *162*
Healy, D., 101, *111*
Heckhausen, H., 123, *141*
Hedberg, S. E., 130, *141*
Hegadoren, K. M., 106, *112*
Heidrich, S. M., 150, 154, 155, *162*
Henderson, M. C., 153, *161*
Hendrie, H. C., 100, *110*
Heninger, G. R., 100, *109, 110, 111, 113*
Henke, R., 99, *113*
Henry, J. P., 15, 16, *42*
Hepworth, C., 25, 26, 32, 34, *39,* 185, *196*
Herbert, J. L., 99, *110*
Herscovitch, P., 78, *91*
Hesen, W., 105, *111*
Higgins, R. L., 191, *197*
Higley J. D., 6, *42,* 76, 87, *91*, *92*, 98, 99, 108, *111, 112*
Higley, S., 6, *42*
Hilburn-Cobb, C., 61, *66,* 202, 203, 204, *213*
Hildebrand-Saints, L., 156, *162*
Hill, M. G., 155, *164*
Hill, S. R., 130, *141*
Hinde, R. A., 10, 11, 18, *42*

Hobfoll, S. E., 27, *42*
Hofer, M. A., 72, *91*
Hoffner, E., 79, *93*
Hokanson, J. E., 132, *141*
Hold, B., 123, 124, *141*
Holiday, J. W., 129, *143*
Hollander, E., 99, *111*
Hollon, S. D., 183, 184, *197*
Holsboer, F., 97, 98, 108, *109, 111*
Holt, K., 159, *162*
Homans, G. C., 126, *141*
Homatidis, S., 116, *118*
Honore, P., 100, *112*
Hoofdakker, R. H., 101, 106, *109*
Hooley, J. M., 25, 26, *42*
Hoorens, V., 150, *162*
Horowitz, L. M., 3, *42*
Horrobin, D., 87, *92*
Horwitz, B., 78, *91*
Hubain, P., 77, *91*
Huber, C., 12, 18, 34, *40*
Huber, L., 30, *40*
Hunter, D., 116, *118*
Huntingford, F., 165, *176*
Huret, J.-D., 78, *92*
Husain, M. M., 97, *112*
Hyman, H., 147, *163*

I

Imner, S. T., 183, *196*
Ingram, R. E., 184, *197*
Innis, R. B., 100, 104, 108, *109*

J

Jackson, D. D., 56, *66*
Jackson, L. A., 125, *141*
James, O., 27, *42*
James, W., 170, *176*
Janssen, P. P. M., 150, *161*
Jauhar, P., 101, *111*
Jenkins, J. H., 26, *42*
Jewart, R. D., 97, *113*
Jimerson, P. C., 100, *110*
Joels, M., 105, *111*
Joffe, R. T., 99, 107, *112,* 184, *197*
Johnson, C., 73, *92*
Johnson, E. H., 32, *39*
Johnson, R. C., 90, *91,* 99, 108, *112*
Jolly, C., 8, 16, 17, 20, *40*

K

Kagan, J., 127, *141*
Kahn, R. L., 34, *38*
Kahn, R. S., 100, *111*
Kalat, J. W., 131, *141*
Kalin, N. H., 97, *113*
Kalkoska, M., 202, *212*
Kalma, A., *42*
Kammerer, C. M., 76, 87, *91*
Kaplan, A. S., 99, 107, *112*
Kaplan, H. B., 130, *141*
Kaplan, J. R., 76, *91,* 97, *109*
Kaplan, N., 202, *213*
Karlsson, J., 97, *113*
Karmacsi, L., 97, *109*
Karno, M., 26, *42*
Kaufman, G., 29, *42*
Kaufman, I. C., 48, *66*
Kavoussi, R. J., 99, *110, 111*
Kaye, W. H., 99, *111*
Kellman, D., 99, *111*
Kellner, C. H., 97, 106, *111*
Kellner, R., 33, *40*
Keltner, D., 6, 14, 20, 30, *42,* 123, 125, 126, *141*
Kemper, T. D., 3, *42,* 130, 131, *141*
Kennedy, R., 208, *212*
Kennedy, S. H., 106, 107, *112*
Kessler, 88, *91*
Ketter, R. A., 78, *91*
Ketter, T. A., 78, *91,* 100, *111*
Kevles, B., 21, *42*
Kiesler, D. J., 3, 22, *42, 45*
Kilts, C. D., 97, *113*
King, S. T., 98, 108, *111*
Kirk, L., 100, *112*
Klein, D. F., 58, *66*
Klein, W. J., 100, *110*
Klerman, G. L., 33, *45*
Kling, M. A., 97, 100, 106, *111*

Klinger, E., 25, *42,* 48, 50, *66,* 128, 135, 138, *141*
Klopper, A., 130, *142*
Klotz, M. L., 150, *161*
Knobloch, F., 171, *176*
Knobloch, J., 171, *176*
Knowles, J. B., 101, 106, *110*
Knutson, B., 90, *91,* 99, 108, *112*
Kobak, R. R., 202, 204, *213*
Koestner, R., 188, *198*
Kohut, H., 57, *66*
Komesaroff, P. A., 105, *112*
Koolhaas, J. M., 15, *43*
Kortmulder, K., 172, *176*
Kotlar, S. L., 134, *142*
Kotun, J., 97, *114*
Kowalski, R. M., 18, *43*
Kraemer, G. W., 76, 87, 72, *91,* 200, *213*
Krakauer, L. J., 130, *141*
Krames, L., 156, *162*
Kravitz, E. A., 73, *92*
Krebs, J. R., 5, 7, *42,* 165, *176*
Kreutzer, T., 202, *213*
Krieg, J.-C., 88, *90*
Krishnan, K. R. R., 97, *112, 113*
Kronauer, R. E., 101, *110*
Krystal, J. H., 100, 104, 107, 108, *109, 112*
Kuiper, N. A., 29, *44,* 150, 153, 156, 157, 158, *163,* 169, *177,* 190, *198*
Kulik, J. A., 155, *163*
Kulling, R., 15, *42*
Kupfer, D. J., 76, 87, *91,* 101, *110*
Kwee, M. G. T., 3, 17, 33, *38*

L

Laber-Laird, K., 76, *93*
Lagerspetz, K. M. J., 15, *43*
Lam, R. W., 107, *112*
Lamb, T. A., 130, *142*
Landis, H., 100, *110*
Lateur, B. J., 116, *117*
Layne, C., 139, *142*
Lazarus, R. A., 186, *197*
Leary, M. R., 5, 18, 22, *39, 43,* 174, *176*
Leary, T., 22, *43*
LeCouteur, A., 89, *92*
Leder, R., 97, *113*
LeDoux, J., 131, *142*
Leiderman, P. H., 131, *143*
Leigh, T., 208, *212*
LeMoal, M., 15, *43*
Lesage, A. D., 106, *112*
Leshner, A. I., 15, *43*
Levin, H. S., 123, *142*
Levine, J. L., 183, *197*
Levine, S., 136, *140*
Levinson, A., 208, *212*
Levitan, R. D., 99, 106, 107, *112*
Levitt, A. J., 99, 107, *112*
Lewine, R. J., 97, *113*
Lewis, D. A., 104, *112*
Lewis, H. B., 30, *43*
Lewis, M., 124, *142*
Leyton, M., 77, *92*
Liebowitz, M. R., 108, *114*
Lierle, D. M., 14, 15, *45*
Lilienfeld, S. O., 36, *43*
Lilly, A. A., 76, 87, *92,* 98, 99, *112*
Lindell, S. G., 6, *42*
Lindern, L. V., 101, *114*
Lingsma, M. M., 3, 17, 33, *38*
Linkey, H. E., 122, 124, *144*
Linnoila, M., 6, *42,* 76, 87, *91, 92,* 98, 99, 100, 107, 108, *109, 111, 112, 113, 114*
Linville, P. W., 191, *197*
Lipositis, Z., 104, *112*
Lipper, S., 100, *114*
Lisansky, J., 33, *40*
Little, K. Y., 87, *92,* 98, *112*
Liu, J., 99, *111*
Loofbourrow, G. N., 131, *140*
Looper, J., 99, *113*
Loosen, P. T., 97, *113*
Lopez, J. E., 87, *92,* 98, *112*
Loriaux, D. L., 97, 106, *111*
Lotstra, F., 77, *91*
Lubin, B., 156, *164*

Lund, R., 101, *114*
Lurie, S. N., 97, *112*
Lustman, P. J., 183, *197*
Luxen, A., 77, *91*
Lydiard, R. B., 108, *114*

M

MacDonald, M. R., 150, 157, *163*
MacLean, A. W., 101, 106, *110*
MacLean, P. D., 3, 4, 11, 12, 36, 37, *43*, 167, 174, *176*
Madsen, D., 76, 77, *92*
Mahler, H. I. M., 155, *163*
Maier, S. F., 13, 14, 25, 37, *43*, 52, *66*
Main, M., 201, 202, *213*
Malamuth, N. M., 5, *39*
Malison, R., 100, 104, 108, *109*
Malle, B., 24, *43*
Mallick, S. K., 132, *142*
Mancewicz, A., 116, *118*
Manderscheid, R. W., 133, *142*
Mann, J. J., 76, 77, 84, 87, *92*, *93*
Manuck, S. B., 76, 87, *91*, 97, *109*
Margherita, A. J., 116, *117*
Marinelli, D. L., 97, *109*
Marino, L., 36, *43*
Markowitz, P. I., 99, *112*
Marks, I. M., 8,9, *43*
Maroc, J., 131, *143*
Maroney, R. J., 128, *144*
Marsh, G., 81, *92*
Marsh, J., 81, *92*
Marsh, K. L., 156, *164*
Marshall, E. F., 100, *113*
Martenssen, B., 99, *109*
Martinot, J.-L., 78, *92*
Marwell, G., 165, *177*
Masica, D. N., 89, *90*
Maslow, A., 165, *176*
Mass, R., 124, *142*
Masters, R. D., 133, *142*
Maynard Smith, J., 5, *43*, 51, *66*
Mazoyer, B., 78, *92*
Mazur, A., 105, *112*, 124, 129, 130, *142*
Mazziotta, J. C., 77, *90*
McAllister, K. H., 10, 37, *40*
McBride, P. A., 77, *92*
McCandless, B. R., 132, *142*
McCarrick, A. K., 133, *142*
McCarthy, M., 99, *110*
McClure, E. B., 200, *213*
McCormick, L., 156, *164*
McDonald, C., 30, *39*
McDougall, W., 124, *142*
McDougle, C. J., 100, *109*
McEachren, L., 155, *164*
McFarland, B. H., 25, *41*
McFarland, C., 153, *163*
McGuire, M. T., 5, 18, 22, 23, 25, 30, 36, *41*, *43*, 44, 53, 57, *66*, 72, 73, 74, 76, 80, 81, 86, 89, *91*, *92*, *93*, 98, 99, 108, *113*, 126, 133, *141*, *142*, 172, *177*
McKinney, W. T., 76, 87, *91*, 136, *142*, 170, *177*
Mead, G. H., 170, *177*
Meerlo, P., 15, *43*
Mehlman, P. T., 6, *42*, 76, 87, *91*, *92*, 98, 99, *112*
Meltzer, H. Y., 100, *112*
Mendelson, M., 150, *161*
Mendlewicz, J., 77, *91*
Messick, D. M., 152, *162*
Metalsky, G. I, 183, *196*
Mettee, D. R., 147, *163*
Meyer, H. H., 150, *163*
Michaud, B., 15, *43*
Miczek, K. A., 101, 106, *111*, *114*
Mikulincer, M., 202, 203, 204, *213*
Miller, D. T., 153, *163*
Miller, H. M., 100, 104, 108, *109*
Miller, R. S., 124, *142*
Mills, J., 155, *163*
Minchiello, M. D., 99, *110*
Mintz, P. M., 155, *163*
Minuchin, S., 211, *213*
Miranda, J., 184, *197*
Mitchell, S. A., 30, *41*
Miyake, K., 154, *164*
Miyawaki, E., 99, *113*

Mock, J., 150, *161*
Moeller, F. G., 99, *112*
Moller, S. E., 100, *112*
Mongrain, M., 30, *45,* 189, *198*
Mooney J. J., 101, *110*
Moore, E. A., 90, *91,* 99, 108, *112*
Moore-Ede, M. C., 101, *112*
Moran, P., 29, *39*
Mormede, R., 15, *43*
Moss, H. A., 127, *141*
Moul, D. E., 107, *114*
Moulton, R. W., 130, *143*
Moyer, K. E., 132, *142*
Muldoon, M. E., 87, *91*
Muller, O. A., 97, *111*
Mulrow, C. D., 116, *118*
Murowski, P. N., 130, *141*
Murphy, B., 87, *92*
Murphy, D. L., 100, 107, *114*
Murphy, G. E., 183, *197*
Murphy-Weinberg, V., 97, *114*
Murray, H. A., 130, 131, *142*
Mzengeza, S., 77, *92*

N

Neilson, M., 33, *40*
Nelson, D. H., 131, *142*
Nemeroff, C. B., 97, *109, 112, 113*
Nesse, R., 4, *43,* 27, 35, *43,* 49, *66*
Newton, G., 130, *142*
Ng, X. C. K., 100, 104, 108, *109*
Nielsen, D. A., 100, *113*
Nieman, L. K., 97, 106, *111*
Nishizawa, S., 77, *92*
Noller, P., 133, *142*
Nordahl, T. E., 107, *110*
Nordstrom, P., 100, *114*
Nurnberger, J. I., Jr., 107, *109*
Nuutila, A., 99, *112, 114*

O

Ohman, A., 18, *43*
Oikkacjm, D. B., 73, *93*
O'Keane, V., 100, *113*
Oldersma, F., 149, 156, *164*
Oldham, J. M., 99, *111*
O'Leary, K. D., 27, *39*
Olinger, L. J., 157, *163*
Oliver, J. M., 157, *163*
Omark, D. R., 123, 124, 125, *142, 145*
Omark, M., 123, *142*
Orbach, C. E., 137, *142*
Oren, D. A., 107, *110, 114*
Ozaki, N., 107, *114*

P

Palmour, R. M., 100, *109*
Panksepp, J., 138, *142*
Pappata, S., 78, *92*
Pardo, J. V., 78, *92*
Pardo, R. J., 78, *92*
Parekh, P. I., 78, *91*
Parikh, S. V., 106, *112*
Park, S., 33, *40*
Parker, G. A., 6, 22, *43,* 166, 167, 168, 174, *177*
Parkes, C. M., 136, *142*
Parkinson, B., 25, *43*
Parloff, M. B., 183, *196*
Pasi, A., 15, *42*
Passingham, R., 124, *142*
Pastore, N., 132, *142*
Paul, J., 130, *142*
Pauley, J. D., 72, 73, *93*
Paull, W. K., 104, *112*
Pava, J., 99, *110*
Paykel, E. S., 33, *45*
Pecins-Thompson, M., 105, *111*
Peet, M., 87, *92*
Pehl, J., 29, *41,* 127, *141*
Perini, G. I., 33, *40*
Perry, E. K., 100, *113*
Perry, R. H., 100, *113*
Persky, H., 131, *143*
Persons, J. B., 184, *197*
Perusse, D., 200, *213*
Pervin, L. A., 184, *197*
Peselow, E. D., 137, *143*

Peterson, B. A., 158, *162*
Peterson, C., 13, 14, 25, 37, *43,* 52, *66,* 192, *197*
Phelix, C., 104, *112*
Phelps, M. E., 77, *90*
Phillips, W., 89, *90*
Piasecki, J. M., 183, *197*
Pickar, D., 97, 106, *111*
Pickersgill, M. J., 3, 17, 33, *38*
Pickles, A., 89, *92*
Pierrynowski, M., 116, *118*
Pihl, R. O., 100, *114*
Pilowsky, I., 33, *43*
Pirke, K. M., 101, *114*
Pitts, C. D., 108, *114*
Pizzino, A., 14, *38*
Platman, S. S., 130, *143*
Pliner, P., 156, *162*
Pohorecky L. A., 14, *45*
Poland, R. E., 76, *91*
Pollack, D. B., 22, *44,* 72, 73, *92,* 99, 108, *113*
Pollard, W. E., 97, *113*
Post, R. M., 56, *66,* 78, *91,* 97, 100, 106, 107, *111, 113, 116, 118*
Potvin, J. H., 89, *90*
Power, M. J., 26, *40*
Pratto, F., 24, *43*
Price, J. S., 4, 6, 11, 12, 14, 21, 22, *41, 43,* 49, 50, 60, *67,* 89, *92,* 123, 128, 129, 132, 139, *141, 143, 144,* 148, 152, 154, *162, 163,* 165, 166, 167, 168, 170, 171, 172, 174, *176, 177,* 184, *197,* 210, *213*
Price, L. H., 100, 104, 108, *109, 110, 113*
Przybeck, T. R., 77, *91*
Pugh, G. E., 124, 127, *143*
Putnam, F., 116, *118*
Pyszczynski, T., 155, *163*

Q

Quinlan, D. M., 30, *39*

R

Raab, A., 15, *43*
Rabbie, J. M., 155, *162*
Radloff, L. S., 150, *163*
Radtke, H. L., 3, *44*
Raichle, M. E., 78, *92,* 100, 108, *110*
Rajecki, D. W., 124, *143*
Raleigh, M. J., 22, *44,* 72, 73, 74, *92, 93,* 98, 99, 108, *113*
Raphelson, A. C., 130, *143*
Rauch, S. L., 138, *140*
Rawlings, R., 100, *113*
Ray, J. C., 32, *44, 97, 113*
Reddy, W. J., 130, *141*
Reed, D., 97, *113*
Rehm, L. P., 30, *44*
Reibring, L., 78, *90*
Reichlin, S., 130, *143*
Reifenstein, R. W., 130, *141*
Reiman, E. M., 78, *93*
Reite, M., 72, 73, *93*
Renner, B. R., 159, *162*
Reppucci, N. D., 128, *140*
Reul, J. M. H. M., 98, 105, 108, *109, 110*
Reus, V. I., 90, *91,* 99, 108, *112*
Reynolds, S., 25, *43*
Rhode, P., *see* Rohde, P.
Rice, L. N., 31, *42*
Rich, D., 100, 104, 108, *109*
Richards, S. M., 128, *143*
Riley, W. T., 32, 33, *44*
Rimon, R., 99, *112*
Risby, E. D., 97, *113*
Risch, S. C., 97, *113*
Ritvo, E. R., 99, *113*
Rivier, J., 97, *114*
Robertson, S., 89, *92*
Robins, C. J., 137, *143*
Robson, P. J., 165, *177*
Roca, C. A., 105, *113*
Rogeness, G. A., 200, *213*
Rohde, P., 49, 50, *67,* 89, *92,* 139, *143,* 148, 152, 154, *163,* 167, 171, *177,* 184, *197*
Rooke, O., 26, 34, *44*

Rose, R. M., 129, *143*
Rosenbaum, J. F., 33, *40, 99, 110*
Rosenberg, L. T., 136, *140*
Rosenberg, M., 130, *143*
Rosenblatt, A., 159, *163*
Rosenblum, L. A., 29, *44,* 73, *93*
Rosenthal, N. E., 107, *110, 114*
Rosnick, L., 99, *111*
Rothenfluh, T., 73, *93*
Roy, A., 97, 106, *111*
Rubinow, D. R., 105, *113*
Rush, A.J., 36, *39*
Russell, R. J. H., 134, *145*
Rutter, M., 89, *90, 92*
Ryff, C. D., 150, 154, 155, *162*

S

Sachar, E. J., 130, *143*
Safran, J. D., 195, *197*
Salomon, R. M., 100, 104, 108, *109*
Salzman, C., 99, *113*
Sandeen, E. E., 27, *39*
Sanderman, R., 3, 17, 33, *38,* 149, 156, *164*
Sandnabba, K., 15, *43*
Saoud, J. B., 99, *111*
Sapolsky, R. M., 15, 17, 27, 32, *44,* 52, *67,* 73, *93,* 97, *109, 113,* 130, *143*
Sarnoff, I., 30, *44*
Sassenrath, E. N., 130, *143*
Saver, J. L., 124, *143*
Savin-Williams, R. C., 126, *143*
Scalia-Tomba, G. P., 99, *109*
Schachter, S., 154, 155, 158, *163*
Schalch, D. S., 130, *143*
Schatzberg, A., 99, *113*
Schaufeli, W. B., 155, *162*
Schechtman, K. B., 116, *118*
Scheff, T. J., 24, *44*
Scheier, M. F., 153, 156, *162, 163*
Scheinin, M., 99, *112*
Scheld, J. T. M., 35, *44*
Schjelderup-Ebbe, T., 50, 52, *67*
Schlegel, A., 134, *143*
Schmale, A., 48, *67*
Schmidt, J. A., 3, 22, *45*
Schmidt, P. J., 105, *113*
Schmitt, A., 116, *118*
Schmitt, D. P., 169, *176*
Schneider, L. H., 14, *45*
Schneider-Rosen, K., 123, *143*
Schore, A. N., 29, *44,* 124, 131, 138, *143*
Schou, J. S., 108, *111*
Schreiber, W., 88, *90*
Schultz, D. P., 73, *93*
Schulz, H., 101, *114*
Schut, A. G., 99, *110*
Schwartz, J., 99, *113*
Schutzer, W. E., 105, *111*
Schwartz, J., 99, *113*
Schwartz, J. M., 77, *90*
Schwartz, P. J., 107, *114*
Scott, J. C., 3, 24, 29, *44*
Scott, L. C., 78, *90*
Sears, R. R., 128, *143*
Segal, Z. V., 56, *67,* 184, 195, *197*
Segrin, C., 23, *44*
Seiler, C., 72, 73, *93*
Seligman, M. E. P., 13, 14, 25, 37, *43, 44,* 52, *66,* 128, *143,* 192, *197*
Selin, C. E., 77, *90*
Selye, H., 129, *143*
Semple, W. E., 107, *110*
Seyfarth, R., 18, *40*
Shapiro, D., 131, *143*
Sharp, J., 190, *197*
Shaver, P. R., 203, *213*
Shaw, B. F., 36, *39,* 157, *163*
Shay J., 87, *92*
Shea, P. A., 100, *110*
Shea, T. M., 183, *196*
Shen, J., 125, *140*
Sherman, B. M., 104, *112*
Shively, C. A., 76, *93*
Short, R., 72, 73, *93*
Sidanius, J., 24, *43*
Siegel, A. M., 171, *177*
Siegfried, B., 15, *41, 42*
Siever, L. J., 99, 100, 101, *114*
Silbergeld, S., 133, *142*

Simon, H., 15, *43*
Simons, A. D., 183, *197*
Simson, P. G., 14, *45*
Singer, W., 184, *197*
Sklar, L. S., 14, *38*
Skodol, A. E., 99, *111*
Slater, S., 100, *114*
Sloman, L., 4, 11, 12, 14, *43*, 49, 50, 56, 58, 60, *67*, *89*, *92*, 116, *118*, 132, 139, *144*, 148, 152, 154, *163*, 167, 169, 171, *177*, 184, *197*, 217, *217*
Sloman, S., 169, *177*, 217, *217*
Smeets, J., 15, *44*
Smith, G., 147, *163*
Smith, H. J., 127, *144*
Smith, S. E., 100, *114*
Smuts, B., 18, *40*
Snelbaker, A. J., 107, *114*
Snyder, C. R., 191, *197*
Solomon, J., 201, *213*
Sotsky, S. M., 183, *196*
Soubrie, P., 99, *114*
Soufer, R., 100, 104, 108, *109*
Spangler, G., 136, *144*
Speltz, M. L., 202, *213*
Spence, M. A., 76, 87, *91*
Spence, N. D., 33, *43*
Sperry, R. W., 181, *197*
Spitz, R., 72, *93*
Sroufe, L. A., 201, 202, *213*, *214*
St. Marc, J. R., 130, *141*
Staib, L. H., 100, 104, 108, *109*
Stalla, G. K., 97, *111*
Stallworth, L. M., 24, *43*
Stam, H. J., 3, *44*
Stanley, M., 100, *114*
Steele, M., 208, *212*
Stein, D. J., 99, *111*
Stein, M. B., 108, *114*
Steingard, R., 99, *110*
Sternberg, D. E., 100, *111*
Stevens, A., 168, *177*
Stipek, D., 123, *144*
Stipetic, M., 97, *113*
Stojwas, M. H., 84, *93*
Stotland, S., 188, *198*
Strayer, F. F., 123, 124, 126, *142*, *144*
Strayer, J., 126, *144*
Suarez, S. D., 135, *144*
Suckow, R. F., 100, *111*
Suls, J., 165, *177*
Suls, J. M., 148, *163*
Sumida, R. M., 77, *90*
Suomi, S. J., 6, *42*, 76, 87, *91*, *92*, 98, 99, 108, *111*, *112*, 136, *142*
Sutherland, A. M., 137, *142*
Svrakic, D. M., 77, *91*
Swallow, S. R., 29, *44*, 153, 156, 157, 158, *163*, 169, *177*, 190, *197*, *198*
Swann, A. C., 99, *112*
Sweeney, J. A., 84, *93*
Sweetman, E., 188, *198*
Sybesma, H., 105, *110*
Syme, S. L., 34, *38*
Syrota, A., 78, *92*

T

Tabachnik, N., 151, *163*
Taghzouti, K., 15, *43*
Tangney, J. P., 30, *44*, 124, *142*, *144*
Target, M., 208, *212*
Taub, B., 132, *140*
Taub, D. M., 6, *42*, 76, 87, *91*, *92*, 98, 99, *112*
Taylor, S. E., 150, *163*
Teasdale, J. D., 25, 26, *42*, 56, *67*, 184, *198*
Tennen, H., 169, 170, *177*, 190, *197*
Tepperman, J., 130, 131, *144*
Terpstra, J., 90, *91*, 99, 108, *112*
Tesser, A., 203, *213*
Thase, M. E., 84, *93*
Thompson, R. A., 207, *214*
Thoren, P., 99, *109*
Thorn, G. W., 130, *141*
Thorndike, E. L., 128, *144*

Tierney, H., 77, *92*
Toates, F., 14, 15, 16, 32, 37, *44*
Tokola, R., 100, *113*
Tomlinson, B. E., 100, *113*
Tornatzky W., 101, 106, *111, 114*
Totterdell, P., 25, *43*
Traskman, L., 99, *109*
Traskman-Bendz, L., 99, 100, *114, 109*
Treiber, F. A., 32, 33, *44*
Trent, D., 188, *197*
Trent, D. R., 137, 139, *141*
Trestman, R. I., 99, *114*
Tricou, B. J., 100, *112*
Trivers, R., 4, 5, 7, 8, *44*
Trivers, R. L., 127, 132, 134, *144*
Troisi, A., 23, 25, 36, *43*, 72, 74, 80, *92*, 172, *177*
Troy, M., 202, *214*
Tuason, V. B., 183, *197*
Tupling, S., 116, *118*
Turner, J., 97, *113*
Turner, R. A., 90, *91*, 99, 108, *112*
Tvede, K., 108, *111*
Tyler, T. M., 127, *144*

V

Vaccarino, F. J., 107, *112*
Vale, W., 97, *114, 114*
van de Poll, N. E., 15, *44*
van de Zwan, S. M., 15, *44*
Van den Hoofdakker, R. H., 15, *43*
van der Dennen, J. M. G., 5, 23, *45*
Van der Molen, H. T., 3, 17, 33, *38*
Van der Zee, K., 149, 156, *164*
van Hoek, G., 30, *40*
van Oyen, H. G., 15, *44*
van Praag, H. M., 100, *111*
van Ryn, M., 26, *45*
Vickers, J., 6, *42*, 76, 87, *91, 92*, 98, 99, *112*
Vinokur, A. D., 26, *45*
Virkkunen, M., 99, 100, *112, 113, 114*
Vitkus, J., 3, *42*
Volkart, R., 73, *93*
Von Bardeleben, U., 97, *111*
Von Holst, D., 11, 16, *45*
von Zerssen, D., 88, *90*, 101, *114*
Vredenburg, K., 156, *162*

W

Wagner, C. C., 3, 22, *45*
Wagner, E. H., 116, *117*
Wagner, P. E., 30, *44*
Wall, S., 200, *212*
Walleus, H., 97, *113*
Walser, A., 12, 18, 34, *40*
Ward, C. H., 150, *161*
Warren, J. M., 128, *144*
Warren, L. W., 155, *164*
Waser, P. G., 15, *41, 42*
Waterhouse, B., 76, 80, *93*
Waterhouse, J. M., 101, *111*
Waters, E., 200, 201, *212, 213*
Watkins, J. T., 183, *196*
Watson, S. J., 87, *92*, 97, 98, *112, 114*
Weakland, J., 56, *66*
Wearing, A., 150, *162*
Weary, G., 149, 150, 155, 156, *162 164*
Wehr, T. A., 101, 107, *114*
Weisfeld, C. C., 133, 134, *144, 145*
Weisfeld, G. E., 122, 124, 125, 126, 127, 128, 129, 132, 133, 134, 139, *140, 144, 145*
Weiss, J. M., 14, *45*
Weiss, S. R., 99, *111*
Weiss, S. R. B., 56, *66*
Weissman, M. M., 33, *45*
Weller, M. P. L., 101, *111*
Wells, E. L., 165, *177*
Wells, P. A., 134, *145*
Wenzlaff, R. M., 159, *164*
Werner, P., 73, *93*

Wetzel, R. D., 183, *197*
Wetzler, S., 100, *111*
Wheeler, L., 154, *164*
Whybrow, P. C., 170, *177*
Widerlov, E., 97, *113*

Widlocher, D. J., 115, *118*
Wiener, S. G., 136, *140*
Wiesel, F.-A., 78, *93*
Wilkinson, R. G., 17, 34, *45*
Williams, J. L., 14, 15, *45*
Williams, J. M., 56, *67*
Willner, R., 14, 16, *45*
Wills, T. A., 148, 158, *163, 164,* 165, *177*
Wilson, D., 216, *217*
Wilson, M., *5, 40, 45*
Winokur, A., 97, *109*
Wirz-Justice, A., 101, *114*
Wise, R., 79, *93*
Wolfe, E., 57, *66*
Wolff, E., 116, *118*
Wolfson, A. N., 99, *113*
Wolkowitz, O. M., 90, *91,* 99, 108, *112*
Wolpe, J., 86, *93*
Wolwer, W., 80, *91*
Wong, D. T., 89, *93*
Woods, M. G., 32, 33, *44*

Y

Ybema, J. F., 149, 155, *162*
Yoshimura, N. N., 100, *110*
Young, E. A., 97, *114*
Young, S. N., 77, *92,* 100, *109, 114*
Yurak, T. J., 150, *161*
Yuwiler, A., 22, *44,* 73, 74, *92, 93,* 99, 108, *113*

Z

Ziegenhorn, L. A., 134, *145*
Zielenzny, K., 33, *40*
Zimbardo, P. G., 30, *44*
Zis, A. R., 107, *112*
Zivin, G., 124, *145*
Zucker, K. J., 66, *66*
Zuckerman, M., 156, *164*
Zuckerman, S., 49, *67*
Zuroff, D. C., 30, *39, 45,* 188, 189, *198*

Subject Index

A

Abuse, 61–62, 81, 106
Acceptance, 54, 60, 190–192
Achievement, 130
Activation, IDS, 187
Adaptive cycles, 55, 56
Adolescence, 171, *see also* Self-esteem
Adrenal gland, 97
Affiliative behavior, 21–22, 97
Aggression
  cerebrospinal fluid responsivity to 5-hydroxyindoleacetic acid, 76
  conspecific and submissive behaviors, 4–5
  depression, 33, 151–152, 159
  encounters and biological rhythm, 101
  love-dove strategies, 22
  minimization and adaptive value of dominance hierarchy, 126
  nonexpressed and arrested fight behavior, 13
Agonistic encounters, 49, 166, 185, 188
Agonistic threat, *see* Threat, agonistic
Alliance formation, 10
Ambivalent defensive strategies, 10–11
Ambivalent escape, 35–36
(-Aminobutyric acid (GABA), 14
Amygdala, 138
Anger
  arousal and competitive strategy set, 55
  dominance hierarchies, 131–132
  suppression and depression, 32–33, 64–65, 185
Anhedonia, 36
Antidepressants, 98, 108
Anxiety, 31
  -ambivalence, 203–204
  -avoidance, 201
Arousal control, 12
Arrested fight/flight, *see also* Fight behavior; Flight behavior
  depression link, 27, 28,32–36
  submissive strategies, 10–13
Attachment
  dominance/subordinate systems, 207–209
  social competition, development, and personality, 201–204
  theory
    biological-evolutionary framework, 199
    infant response to separation, 48
    involuntary defeat strategy model interactions, 216
Attack behavior, 30
  -flight, 11
Attribution, 191–192

Atypical depression, 106, *see also* Depression
Autism, 89
Aversive, 14
Avoidance, 201–202, 207
  learning, 14

B

Baboons, 15, 97
Basal ganglia, 138
BDI, *see* Beck Depression Inventory
Beck Depression Inventory (BDI), 117
  need for social comparison information, 156
  negative bias in interpreting social comparison information, 153
  perceptions of oneself in comparison with others, 150, 151
  social comparison information and alleviation of one's own state, 159
Behavior, rules, 82
Bereavement, 135–136
Bias, 152–154, 183
Biological rhythms, 101–102, 106
Biological treatment, IDS, 108
Biology, involuntary defeat strategy
  maladaptive, 104–106
  normal, 102–104
Bipolar disorder, 107–108
Birds, 11
Blocked escape, 11–12, 12
Blood flow, 78–79
Blood pressure, 15
Bonobos, 20
Boosting signals, 172, 173–175
Braced readiness state, 16
Brain, pathology, 138
Bulimia nervosa, 99
Buspirone, 100

C

Care-eliciting signals, *see* Signals, care-eliciting
Caregiver-dependent interactions, 201–201
Catecholamines, 130
Causal modeling, 82
Central nervous system (CNS), 71, 73–76
Cerebrospinal fluid (CSF), 76, 98
Chimpanzees, 18, 19–20
Chronobiological disturbances, 101–102, 106
Circadian rhythms, 101
CNS, *see* Central nervous system
Coercive strategy, 207
Cognitive appraisals, defeat, 187–190
Cognitive behavior, *see also* Involuntary defeat strategy
  involuntary defeat strategy, 184–185
    mediation, 186–196
    theory, 185–186
  model of depression, 182–184
Cognitive theory, 185–186
Cognitive therapy, 183
Cognitive triad, 182–183
Competition
  attachment in primates, 200
  depression, 24, 49
  evolution and boosting/putting-down signals, 173
  involuntary defeat strategy, 54, 58, 59, 101–105
  pathological reactions of outcomes, 132–135
  phylogeny of self-esteem, 168
  social withdrawal advantages, 128
  trigger of submissive behavior, 7
Competition by attraction, 53
Competitive strategy set, 54–55
COMT, 14
Conflicts, 5, 11, 58
  interpersonal, 17
Conscious wishes, 8
Conservation-withdrawal theory, 48
Contest-competitive strategies, 7
Coping, 202
Core beliefs, 183, 184, 188, 192
Corticotropin releasing hormone (CRH), 108

Corticotropin-releasing factor (CRF), 97
Cortisol
competitive encounter and levels, 102
dominance encounters in humans, 130
maladaptive involuntary defeat strategy, 105
primate social behavior and depression, 97
social defeat strategies, 16
Corticosterone, 16
Cost–benefit analysis, 148
CRF, *see* Corticotropin-releasing factor
CRH, *see* Corticotropin-releasing hormone
Criticism, 18, 130, 183–184
CSF, Cerebrospinal fluid
Cut-off posture, 12
Cyproheptadine, 22

D

DAS, *see* Dysfunctional Attitude Scale
DD, *see* Dysthymic disorder
Decentering technique, 195–196
De-escalation strategy, 4–6, *see also* Escalating strategy
Defeat
blocked escape behavior, 11
depression correlation, 148
biological changes associated with, 52
-entrapment role, 52–53
social competition model, 50
group support and acceptance, 57
involuntary defeat strategy trigger, 55
involuntary submissive strategies, 25–27
learned helplessness and experience, 128
Defensive behavior, 8, 73, 88, 125
Demobilization, 14, 52, 130
Depression
adaptiveness, 215–216
anger correlation, 132
arrested fight correlation, 32–33, 113
biological rhythm correlation, 101
cognitive model, 182–184
cognitive appraisals of defeat, 190
defeat and entrapment role, 52–53
dominance hierarchy model, 127–128
etiology, 47
glucocorticoid and epinephrine levels, 130
glucose metabolism abnormalities, 78, 79
hypothalamic–pituitary–adrenal axis and primate social behavior, 97–98
involuntary defeat strategy
correlation, 55–56, 62, 64
maladaptive and subtypes, 106–108
model, 24–32
natural killer cell activity, 131
one type or two, 135–139
pathological reactions to competitive outcomes, 134, 135
reassurance *see*
king behavior, 23
recovery and social distancing, 35
self as gladiator, 166–167
self-esteem
correlation, 169–175
phylogeny, 167–169
self-ratings lowering, 169
serotonergic mechanisms, 77, 98–101
social comparison information
alleviation of one's own state, 158–159
negative bias in interpretation, 152–154
need for, 154–158
perceptions of oneself in comparison with others, 149–152
social competition model, 49–50
submissive behavior problem, 3
subordinate status perception, 24

Depressive realism, 151
Design, IDS, 58, 59
Development, 29, 81, 202
Developmental onset, pride/shame, 123, 138
Dexamethsone, 97, 98
Diagnostic and Statistical Manual of Mental Disorders (DSM-IV), 47, 71, 80–81
Dihydroxyphenylalanine (L-DOPA), 78
Direct comparison, self-esteem sources, 169–170
Discrete emotions theory
  adaptive value of dominance hierarchization, 125–127
  anger and dominance hierarchies, 131–132
  one type of depression or two, 135–139
  pathological reactions to competitive outcomes, 132–135
  pride/shame
    single basic emotion, 121–125
    physiological adjustments, 129–131
    social withdrawal, 127–129
Distance, maintenance, 16
Distortion, 152, *see also* Depression
Distress, 82–83, 204
Divorce, 57
Dominance
  Attachment correlation, 204, 206–211
  maladaptive involuntary defeat strategy, 105–106
  pride/shame parallel, 122
  serotonin levels in nonhuman primates, 73–75
  subordinate interactions and reverted escape strategy, 19
Dominance hierarchy
  adaptive value, 125–127
  anger, 131–132
  model
    pathological reactions to competitive outcomes, 133–135
    social competition understanding, 121, 123
    serotonergic mechanisms, 98, 99
    threat and arrested flight strategy, 12
  triggers of submissive behavior, 7–8
L-DOPA, *see* Dihydroxyphenylalanine
Double depression, 174, *see also* Depression
Dove strategies, 5, *see also* Hawk-dove strategy; Love-dove strategy
Downward comparison theory, 158
DSM-IV, *see* Diagnostic and Statistical Manual of Mental Disorders
Dysfunctional Attitude Scale (DAS), 157
Dysphoric phenomenology, 185
Dysregulated states, 25
Dysregulation, 72, *see also* Regulation/dysregulation theory
Dysthymic disorder (DD)
  clinical examples, 62–64
  implications for psychobiological model of social interactions, 79–80
  interpretation of findings using RDT, PET, and physiological data, 86–88
  PET studies, 77–79
  serotonin measures and social status, 73–77
  symptoms, 80–86

E

Effective involuntary defeat strategy, 54, 56–58
Elderly, 150–151, 155–156
Emotion, regulation, 201–202
Enclosed avoidance strategies, 16–17, 35
Entrapment, 34, 52–53, 57
Environment, low/high-stress, 87–88
Environmental domain, 25–26

Epinephrine, 129, 130
Escalating strategy, 5, 54–55, 187, *see also* De-escalating strategy
Escape behavior, 9–10, 14, 34, 36
Estrogen, 105
Evaluators, 173
Event-recording method, 153
Events, negative, 82, 150, 153, 155
Evolution, 167
Evolutionary game theory, 167
Evolutionary mechanisms, depression, 48–49
Evolutionary theorists, 5
Evolutionary theory, 148
Executive function, 50

F

Facial signals, *see* Signals
Facilitative function, 50
Failed struggle, 25, 26
Family dynamics, 206
Fear, 138
Fear dove strategy, 6
Feedback, 153
Fenfluramine, 22, 100
Fight behavior, 132, 166
Flight behavior, 9–10, 57
Flight from the self, 36
Fluoxetine, 89–90
Foraging, 175
Friendly/hostile submission, 22–23
Friendship, 204

G

GABA, *see* (-Aminobutyric acid
Gait, 116
Galvanic skin response (GSR), 130, 131
Game theory, 5
GC, *see* Hippocampal glucocorticoid
Gender, 134, 135, 136, 137
Gene–neural pathways, 8
Gift giving, 20
Globality, *see also* Resource-holding potential; Social attention-holding potential
  resource-holding potential and rival comparisons, 166–167
  self ratings and expression of self-worth, 165
  social attention-holding potential, 168–169
Glucocorticoids, 129, 130, 131
Glucose, 77–79
Goals, 5, 126, 129
Grief, 11, *see also* Depression
  -derived depression, 136–138
Group
  defense and submissive display behaviors, 23
  interaction variables and involuntary defeat strategy effectiveness, 57
  membership and formation of self-esteem, 171–172
  triggers of submissive behavior, 7
GSR, *see* Galvanic skin response

H

Hawk strategies, 5, *see also* Dove strategies
  –dove strategy, 50–51, 167–168
5-HIAA, *see* 5-Hydroxyindoleacetic acid
Hippocampal glucocorticoid (GC), 97, 98
Hormonal states, 15
Hormones, 129
Hostile mood, 33, 99
5-HT, *see* 5-Hydroxytryptamine
5-HTP, *see* 5-Hydroxytryptophan
Humans
  depression and psychomotor retardation, 116
  dominance encounters and physiological changes, 130
  mate value and phylogeny of self-esteem, 169
  serotonin levels and social status, 76–77
  social comparisons and submissive behavior, 6–7

submissive display strategies, 18, 21
5-Hydroxyindoleacetic acid (5-HIAA), 76, 98, 99–100
5-Hydroxytryptamine (5-HT), 18, 78, 87, *see also* Serotonin
Hypercortisolemia, 98, 105
Hypoarousal/hyperarousal, 105, 106, 107
Hypometabolism, 80, 87
Hypothalamic–pituitary–adrenal (HPA) axis
involuntary defeat strategy, 102, 104, 105, 108
primate social behavior and depression, 97–98

I

IDS, *see* Involuntary defeat strategy
If A do B rule, 8
Illness strategies, 20–21
Immune functions, 16
Impulse control, 99
Impulsivity, 99
Incentive–disengagement cycle, 48–49
Ineffective involuntary defeat strategy, 55–56
Infantile strategies, 20–21
Infants, 97
Inferiority. 29, 62
Injury, 49, 50
Insult, 132
Intelligence, 125
Internal states, 25
Interpersonal conflicts, *see* Conflicts
Involuntary subordinate strategies (ISSs), 153
Involuntary defeat strategy (IDS)
case study, 192–194
cognitive mediation
case examples, 192–196
cognitive appraisals of agonistic threat, 187–188
cognitive appraisals of defeat, 188–190
cognitive mediators of acceptance and reconciliation, 190–192
depression
acceptance, 60
approach, 184–185
biological changes in defeat, 52
clinical examples, 60–65
competitive strategy, 54–55
defeat situations, 135, 139
effective, 54
effectiveness, 56–58
evolutionary explanations, 48–49
functions, 51
hawk–dove strategies, 50–51
ineffective, 55–56
relation between design and function, 58
role of defeat and entrapment, 52–53
shame, 53
social competition model, 49–50
submissive behavior and psychopathology, 51–52
symptoms, 96
timing of submission, 58–60
voluntary submission, 60
insecure attachment and dominance/subordinate systems, 210–211
triggers, 16
Involuntary submissive strategies
defeat, 25–27
development, 29
internalization of put-down signals, 30–31
model, 27–29
powerlessness and involuntary subordination, 31–32
shame, 29–30
social comparisons and social rank, 29
Involuntary subordinate self-perception, 27, 29
Involuntary subordinate strategies (ISSs)

need for social comparison information, 154, 156–158
perceptions of oneself in comparison with others, 150–152
social comparison
depression, 148–149
information and alleviation of one's own state, 158–159
model of depression, 50
ISSs, *see* Involuntary subordinate strategies

K

Kindling, 56

L

Law of effect, 128
Leaden paralysis, 106
Learned helplessness
antidepressants and biological treatment of involuntary defeat strategy, 108
depression link, 52
effects on escape behavior, 13, 14
perceptions of oneself in comparison with others, 150
social withdrawal and pride/shame, 128
Learned motive, 122
Life events, *see* Events
Localization, depression, 184
Locomotor activity, 116–117
Logic, 183
Loss of control strategies, 13–15
Losses, 191–192
Loved one, loss, 136–137
Love–dove strategy, 21–22

M

Macaques, 49, 200
Machiavellians, 77
Major depressive disorder, biological correlates of IDS, *see also* Depression
biological treatment, 108
biology of primate social hierarchical behavior, 97–102
integrative model and social hierarchy, 102–108
Maladaptive cycles, 55, 56
Manic patients, 131
MAO, *see* Monoamine
Marriage, 133–134
Mate value, 169, 175
Mating, 10
Melancholia, 106, 107
Mental health, 150
Mental illness, 30
Metabolism, 71
Metachlorophenylpiperazine, 100
Mice, 128
Mind games, 5–6
Mirroring, 170–171
Mobilization, controlled, 17
Monkeys
affiliative submissive behaviors, 22
attachment and competition, 200
separation distress and depression, 136
serotonin levels and social status, 73–75, 98
testosterone levels and defeat, 129
Monoamine (MAO), 14
Mood disorders, 101
Mood states, 49, 78, 116
Moralists, 77
Mortality rate, 6, 16
Motor activation deficit hypothesis, 14

N

Natural killer cell, 131
Negative automatic thoughts, 182, 183
Negative frequency-dependent selection, 167
Neurophysiology, escape behavior, 9
Neurotransmitter pathways, 16
Neurotransmitters, 200
Nondepressed individuals, 151, 153, *see also* Depression

Nonhuman primates, *see also* Individual entries
affiliative submissive behavior, 21
competitive loss and symptoms of depression, 95–96
dominance encounters and physiological changes, 129–130
reverted escape strategy, 19
serotonin levels and social status, 73–76, 98, 99
triggers of submissive behavior, 6
Nonverbal signs, 115

O

Omega-3 fatty acids, 87
Orbitofrontal hypometabolism, 138
Overconfidence, 29
Oxytocin, 138

P

Parasympathetic nervous system, 15
Parents, self-esteem, 170–171
Parkinson's disease, 116
Pecking order, 11, 50
Pedigree, influences, 81
Perceptions, self, 149–152
Personality, 57–58, 201–204
PET, *see* Positron emission tomography
Phenotype-dependent strategy set, 174, 175
Pituitary gland, 97
Positron emission tomography (PET)
dysthymic disorder study, 71, 86–88
mood states in brain, 77–79
seasonal affective disorder demonstration, 106
tryptophan depletion and depression, 100
Powerlessness, 31–32
Praise, 130
Predators, 7, 10
Prefrontal cortex, 138
Prefrontal–limbic–striatal regions
dysfunction and depression, 100
involuntary defeat strategy
antidepressants and biological treatment, 108
maladaptive, 105
normal biology, 102, 103, 104
Pressure, group, 57
Prestige competition, *see* Competition, prestige
Prestige striving, 122–123
Pride/shame, 121–125, *see also* Shame
Primates, *see also* Individual entries
affiliative submissive behavior, 21
attachment and competition, 200
competitive defeat and depression symptoms, 96
social ranking behavior and signs of psychological distress, 115
submissive display strategies, 18
Problem solving, 71, 128
Prozac, *see* Fluoxetine
Psychobiological activation, 8
Psychobiological model of social interactions, 79–80
Psychomotor retardation, 115–117
Psychopathology, 3
Psychosomatic disease, 130
Putting-down signals, 30–31, 172, 173–175

R

Rats, 15, 101
RDT, *see* Regulation–dysregulation theory
Rearing experiences, 29
Reasoning, 183
Reassurance *see*king, 20, 23
Rebellion, 174
Reciprocal altruism model, 127
Reconciliation, 190–192
Regulation, 72
Regulation–dysregulation theory (RDT), 71–72, 73, 86–88
Rejection, 18
Rejection sensitivity, 58, 106
Relative deprivation,151
theory, 127

Reproduction, 125, 126
Reptiles, 3, 11
Reptilian past, 168
Resource-holding potential (RHP)
calculation, 167
characterization, 166
love–dove strategies, 22
phenotype-dependent strategy set, 175
phylogeny of self-esteem, 167–168
signals that affect self-esteem, 172
Resources
acquisition and social defeat strategies, 16
allocation and adaptive value of dominance hierarchy, 126–127
control of social/nonsocial and psychopathology, 14
pursuit
flight behavior, 10
hawk–dove strategies, 51
regulation of allocation and mood, 49
value and effectiveness of involuntary defeat strategy, 56–57
Respect, 18
Reverted escape strategy, 19–20
Reward, 10
RHP, *see* Resource-holding power
Risk, injury, 49, 50
Risk harm, 5
Rodents, 15, 101, 128
Role strain, 27, *see also* Depression

S

SAD, *see* Seasonal affective disorder
Safety stimuli, 10
Safety-mediated behavior, 88
SAHP, *see* Social attention-holding potential
Schemas, 183
Seasonal affective disorder (SAD), 36, 107
Secondary depression, 138, *see also* Depression
Security/insecurity, 201, 202
Self, as gladiator, 166–167
Self-attacking, 30
Self-complexity, 191
Self-concept, 174–175
Self-confidence, 129
Self-consciousness, 30
Self-criticism, 30
Self-efficacy judgments, 188–189
Self-enhancement, 158
Self-esteem
depression link, 29
dysthymic disorder, 83–84, 86
effectiveness of involuntary defeat strategy, 57–58
phylogeny, 167–169
role in phylogenetic adaptation, 165–166
sources of, 169–175
subordination link, 173–174
successful competition link, 134
Self-evaluations, 31, 33, 156
Self-monitoring, 82, 86
Self–other relationships, 27, 29
Self-punishment, 30
Self-regulation, 201, 202, 207
Self-reliance, 202–203
Self-view, 204
Self-worth contingency model, 157
Separation anxiety, 200
Separation distress, 136
Septo-hippocampal system, 17
Serotonergic mechanisms, 98–101
Serotonin
abnormal activity and link to depression, 104, 105
dominance relations, 128
normal biology of involuntary defeat strategy, 102, 103
seasonal affective disorder, 106
social status
nonhuman primate studies, 73–76
primate studies, 76–77
submissive signals and levels, 172
Serotonin reuptake inhibitor (SSRI), 99
Sex differences, 73, 88, 134

Sex hormones, 105
Sexual activity, 20, 134, 137
Shame, 29–30, 53
-derived depression, 136–139, *see also* Depression
Signaling function, 50
Signals, 18, 21, 172
Sleep, 101, 106
Social animals, 167
Social anxiety, 3
Social attention-holding potential (SAHP), 22, 168–169, 175
Social attractiveness, 22
Social avoidance, 30
Social behavior, 22, 97–101
Social closeness, 20
Social comparison
attachment, 200–204
clinical case, 205–211
cognitive appraisals of defeat, 189–190
depression, 29
need for information, 154–158
negative bias in interpreting information, 152–154
perceptions of self in comparison with others, 149–152
*see*king information about others that may alleviate one's own state, 158–159
general considerations, 211–212
triggers of submissive behavior, 6–7
Social competence, 76
Social competition
attachment, 202, 208
dysthymic disorder, 89
model and involuntary defeat strategy, 49–50
neurotransmitters, 200
Social defeat strategies, 15–16
Social distancing, 34–35
Social dominance orientation, 24
Social environment, 27, 83, 129–130
Social evaluation, 123
Social functioning, 81
Social hierarchies, 7–8
Social interactions, 72, 79–80
Social norm, 132
Social rank, *see* Social status
Social signals, 15, 86
Social status, *see also* Social rank
acquisition and role of affiliative submissive behaviors, 22
adaptive value, 130
criteria and reproductive success, 126
depression link, 29, 134, 135
dominance hierarchies and triggers of submissive behavior, 7
dysthymic disorder, 89
gait speed in humans, 116
group and social comparison, 148
loss, 34, 127, 174
model, 216
serotonin levels in monkeys, 73–75
theory and defeat state, 25
Social support networks, 86, 89
Social undermining, 26–27
Social withdrawal, 106, 127–129
Social/nonsocial resources, *see* Resources
Species differences, 8
Species-wide prevalence, 122
SSRI, *see* Serotonin reuptake inhibitor
Status-attacking behaviors, 27
Stereotypy, 123
Strategies, meaning, 8
Stress, 14–16
Stress hormones, 14, 16, 97
Subdominants, 16
Submissive behavior
anxiety/ambivalence, 204
involuntary defeat strategy
link to depression, 51–52
timing, 58–60
marriage, 133
self-esteem link, 173–174
serotonin levels in nonhuman primates, 73–75
varieties as forms of social defense
arrested fight and flight, 32–37

involuntary submissive strategies: toward a model of depression, 24–27
model, 27–32
social threats and de-escalating behaviors, 4–6
submissive display strategies, 17–24
submissive strategies, 8–17
triggers, 6–8
Submissive display strategies, *see* Submissive behavior, varieties as forms of social defense
Submissive signals, *see* Signals
Success/failure, 55, 56, 131, 170
Suicide, 100, 134, 136
theory, 34
Superiority bias, 150, 151
Symbolic superiority, 150
Sympathetic nervous system, 15
Symptomatology, dysthymic disorder, 81–86

T

Tension, diffusion, 20
Termination, involuntary defeat strategy, 187, 190
Territorial hierarchies, 7–8
Testosterone, 105–106, 129
Threats
agonistic and cognitive appraisals of involuntary defeat strategy, 187–188
escape/flight behavior, 10
preference for affiliation with similar others, 155
external and group defense behavior, 23
social and strategies against aggressive conspecifics, 4–6
Traumatic experiences, 106, *see also* Events, negative
Tree shrews, 16
Tryptophan hydroxylase, 100
Tryptophan, 22, 100
Two-chair therapy technique, 30–31
Tyrosine hydroxylase, 16

U

Ultradian rhythm, 101
Uncertainty, 157

V

Voluntary submission, 60

W

Wolf pups, 20
Word tasks, 78–79